Methodologies in Developmental Sciences

The Methodologies in Developmental Sciences book series seeks to explore different developmental methodologies in the human sciences. The focus of the series is to bring together different theoretical or empirical contributions, through edited volumes or monographs, that allow the elaboration or reassessment of different contributions to the development of innovative methodologies for the study of human development.

The objective of the series is to both open space for new contributions and to revive in the contemporary academic community innovative theories and methodologies that have been forgotten in the history of psychology without clear reasons, such as the Ganzheitpsychologie (Psychology of Wholeness) school, with its emphasis on exploring the processes of psychological development from a multilevel genetic methodology. Ganzheitpsychologie, however, is not the only focus of the series, which is open to all contributions aimed at developing a multidisciplinary, multilevel, and genetic approach to the study of culturally situated developmental processes.

The series invites scholars and researchers from around the world and from different disciplines in the field of developmental sciences – such as developmental psychology, educational psychology, anthropology, evolutionary psychology, social psychology, clinical psychology, and education – to submit their book proposals. Both theoretical or empirical contributions are welcome, which can be developed through a monographic book or an edited volume.

Enno Freiherr von Fircks

Studying Leadership from a Microgenetic Perspective

Towards a Cultural-Psychological Theory of Leadership

Springer

Enno Freiherr von Fircks
Department of Psychology
Sigmund Freud University Vienna
Wien, Austria

ISSN 3004-8532 ISSN 3004-8540 (electronic)
Methodologies in Developmental Sciences
ISBN 978-3-031-90213-0 ISBN 978-3-031-90214-7 (eBook)
https://doi.org/10.1007/978-3-031-90214-7

This Springer imprint is published by the registered company Springer Nature Switzerland AG
The registered company address is: Gewerbestrasse 11, 6330 Cham, Switzerland

Declarations

Conflict of Interest The author declares no conflict of interest.

Funding The author did not receive any funding.

Ethical Approval Ethical approval was confirmed by the Ethics Committee of Sigmund-Freud-University (QCXFQ5QPBWEP4P90500).

Consent to Participate Participants were informed and provided their explicit consent to participate.

Consent for Publication Participants provided their consent for publication of the anonymized data.

Author's Contribution The article is a single contribution of Enno Freiherr von Fircks.

Additional Information In partial requirements for the PhD program 006 at SFU.

Preface: An Actualized Meta-Code for Leadership

Cultural psychology is a young and emerging discipline. It is a holistic psychology that considers both the individual in their goal-directedness and their meaningful cultural embeddedness as starting points (Valsiner, 2014, 2021). At its core lies the interplay—or better, the tension—between the person and the social (cultural) environment, which constitutes the heart of cultural psychology (von Fircks, 2024a). From this holistic approach, various cultural-psychological traditions have emerged, such as Bruner's narrative cultural psychology (Bruner, 1996, 1997), Boesch's symbolic action theory (Boesch, 1991), and Valsiner's semiotic cultural psychology (Valsiner, 2007). Yet, these diverse approaches share a common fate: there is a relative scarcity of applied writings in cultural psychology, which tend to focus on education (Marsico, 2018), development (Eckensberger, 2003), or organizational psychology more broadly (Bendassolli, 2019). However, leadership psychology from a cultural-psychological standpoint remains the exception rather than the rule.

Leadership, nevertheless, is omnipresent and affects individuals on various levels. It impacts us on the macro level, for example, through political gatekeepers, parliaments, and governments. Yet, leadership also impacts us on a micro level, penetrating our everyday lives. Leadership is evident in the classroom when teachers guide students through a subject. It is present in parenting when caregivers teach their children how to eat with a knife and fork (or with hands in other cultures). Leadership occurs when we ask for directions in an unfamiliar city or collaborate in teams at work to prepare a presentation within a short timeframe. These examples clearly demonstrate that leadership is a cross-disciplinary field relevant to developmental psychology, educational psychology, and organizational psychology. Without theories of leadership or naïve assumptions about leadership on the part of key individuals under study, actions within these fields would not take place, and thus, their scientific inquiry would be impossible. This underscores the undeniable relevance of leadership psychology.

From the perspective of cultural psychology, we aim to approach leadership psychology without reductionism. What does this mean? We do not wish to reduce leadership to a single individual who vertically structures a company or a social organization. This very meta-code is fundamentally criticized in the first chapter because it mythically distorts the social understanding of culture and leadership. Instead, we adopt a different premise: *leadership is a dialogical endeavor that always involves or excludes another person.* Even the act of ignoring other perspectives—those of my employees, students, or children—is a dialogical action that becomes oppressively ignorant rather than constructive. This means that the exclusion of other perspectives and needs, the isolation from the social organization to which we are always connected, constitutes a dialogical action, or rather, a dialogical negation.

The negation of dialogical productivity—through the exclusion of others' perspectives and needs—has dramatic consequences not only for the productivity of the social organization but also for its symbolic self-image. Conversely, there are also productive examples: leadership can effectively integrate the perspectives of others and consider their needs (von Fircks, 2023, 2024b). This is not a social utopia or an idealistic vision of leadership; on the contrary, leadership can also adopt a democratic form (Lewin et al., 1939), leveraging the potential for action and motivation of others. In many cases, this allows the diverse life worlds of a company or social organization to be better represented. Leadership, therefore, can foster cooperation on various levels, enabling a shared object, goal, or strategy to be adequately examined and negotiated. This negotiation not only ensures that all individuals feel involved in the social organization (such as a company) but also ensures that the product resulting from this cooperation reflects the diverse perspectives and needs of the team members. This negotiated product—the crystallization of cooperative leadership—is not only essential for the self-identity of team members but also draws on their unique strengths and abilities, rounding out the product holistically (speaking in economic terms as well).

The following book illustrates the consequences of understanding leadership from this holistic and dialogical perspective, as well as what happens when leadership diverges from this negotiated, dialogical, and holistic approach. In other words, we analyze various case studies of leadership—both successful and unsuccessful—and examine the mechanisms through which leadership success or failure arises, along with the social and personal reactions (actions) that follow. One thing can be stated in advance: the consequences can be dramatic and have a profound impact on the entire company or social unit. To examine these case studies methodically, we lay out our cultural-psychological theory of leadership in the first chapters, before rigorously describing, analyzing, and interpreting the case studies. In line with our dialogical meta-code, these interpretations are presented to certain study participants, and the significance of the findings is dialogically negotiated and deepened. When conducted properly, research does not dominate its participants but includes them dialogically and perspectively. Such research not only expands the understanding of its participants but also stimulates future research fields. This underscores the scientific value of involving participants in our scientific work and interpretations. Research, too, is a field that should be more sensitive to leadership.

Ultimately, our alternative theory of leadership revolves around the goal-directedness of individuals, whose actions intersect and require planning for the next steps. This convergence may seem trivial, but the mechanisms that guide the transition from coming together to collaboration are anything but trivial. On the contrary, everyday life—and this book—clearly show that leadership is neither self-evident nor can it be implicitly taken for granted. On the contrary, the implicit acceptance of leadership forms a tension-laden foundation for conflicts which, if unaddressed, develop a momentum of their own that burdens the entire company or social organization. Leadership, however painful it may be, must reconcile the purposes of different individuals—without allowing the leader's own purposes to dominate those of team members. This creates an explosive set of emotions within the organization, leading to unproductive conduct that becomes uncontrollable through their own momentum. The empirical studies presented in this book speak volumes in this regard.

To conclude, we now summarize the meta-codes outlined in this book to assist readers in navigating the various chapters, whether theoretical or empirical in nature:

(A) Leadership is a pre-disciplinary field that concerns various social organizations and is not limited to the workplace. Leadership remains omnipresent, underscoring the need for a deeper approach to the topic.
(B) Leadership and leadership research must not be reduced to the individual. On the contrary, they must understand individuals within their meaningful social units, which are subject to certain dynamics.
(C) Leadership and leadership research should explore the interplay of individual purposes that either hinder or promote cooperation. The tension between the goals of oneself and others is a central factor impacting the course of leadership and its adaptation.
(D) Leadership is inherently a dialogical field. The manner in which dialogue occurs—or is blocked—is crucial for the trajectory of leadership, its adaptation, and, consequently, for leadership research. This dialogical field spans various levels (vertical and horizontal), which can also interact.

These meta-codes of a cultural-psychological theory of leadership will be elaborated in the following chapters. For now, they serve as a dialogical offering from the author to engage with the various themes of an alternative theory and research of leadership. May the readers co-construct that perspective as well.

Vienna, Austria Enno Freiherr von Fircks

References

Bendassolli, P. F. (Ed.). (2019). *Culture, work and psychology: Invitations to Dialogue*. IAP.

Boesch, E. E. (1991). *Symbolic action theory and cultural psychology*. New York, NY: Springer New York.

Bruner, J. (1996). *The culture of education*. Harvard University Press. https://doi.org/10.2307/j.ctv136c601
Bruner, J. (1997). *Sinn, Kultur und Ich-Identität*. Carl Auer.
Eckensberger, L. H. (2003). Wanted: A contextualized psychology based on action theory. In T. S. Saraswathi (Ed.), *Cross-cultural perspectives in human development*. New Delhi: Sage.
von Fircks, E. F. (2023). Cultural resources for leadership: When a Banana is more than a Banana. *Human Arenas*, *6*(3), 444–461. https://doi.org/10.1007/s42087-021-00231-0
Fircks, E. (2024a). *Learning with William Stern: Personology for future*. IAP.
Freiherr von Fircks, E. (2024b). Culture and leadership: A Lewinian perspective of organizational problem solving. *Human Arenas*, *7*(1), 1–14. https://doi.org/10.1007/s42087-021-00256-5
Lewin, K., Lippitt, R., & White, R. K. (1939). Patterns of aggressive behavior in experimentally created "social climates." *Journal of Social Psychology, 10*(2), 269–299. https://doi.org/10.1080/00224545.1939.9713366
Marsico, G. (2018). The challenges of the schooling from cultural psychology of education. *Integrative Psychological and Behavioral Science*, *52*(3), 474–489. https://doi.org/10.1007/s12124-018-9454-6
Valsiner, J. (2007). *Culture in minds and societies*. New Delhi: Sage.
Valsiner, J. (2014). *An invitation to cultural psychology*. Los Angeles: Sage.
Valsiner, J. (2021). *General human psychology*. New York: Springer.

Competing Interests The author has no competing interests to declare that are relevant to the content of this manuscript.

Contents

Chapter 1
Defining Leadership as a Social Function: Beyond the Big-Hero Myth

The Social Imperative of Leadership

Leadership has always been, and continues to be, a fundamentally social function (Bavelas, 1960; von Fircks, 2021, 2023a). Despite this, the social nature of leadership remains a subject of debate, both historically and in contemporary literature (Collinson et al., 2018; Schweiger et al., 2020). This is especially true with the rise of leadership models such as charismatic and authentic leadership (Conger & Kanungo, 1998; Gardner et al., 2011; Novicevic et al., 2006). One of the most widely celebrated models, transformational leadership, often regarded as the gold standard (Hoch et al., 2018), embodies what is known as the *hero myth*. In this model, a leader transforms employees through individualized consideration, idealized influence, intellectual stimulation, and inspirational motivation, all based on the leader's own vision and premises (Bass, 1990, 1999; Bass & Avolio, 1993).

This perspective, however, contradicts dominant traditions in communication psychology, such as Bühler's Organon model (Bühler, 1934), which posits that meaning is co-constructed by both sender and receiver. In this model, communication requires both parties to engage from different perspectives to express, appeal, or transmit a message. How that message is internalized and understood, however, remains a deeply subjective process (Stern, 1935).

Despite the prevalence of popular leadership styles such as transformational, transactional, and situational leadership, the literature on leadership is far from settled. Each year, new models emerge as researchers and scholars attempt to demonstrate the incremental value of their approaches. As a result, leadership studies are crowded with competing models, each striving to prove its effectiveness according to various criteria, such as job satisfaction, performance, and commitment (Dhar & Mishra, 2001; House & Podsakoff, 2013). Most of these models, however, share a common focus: they center on the actions of the leader within an organization or public service setting. This focus on the individual leader gives rise to the *hero myth*

E. Freiherr von Fircks, *Studying Leadership from a Microgenetic Perspective*, Methodologies in Developmental Sciences,
https://doi.org/10.1007/978-3-031-90214-7_1

of leadership—the belief in a strong leader who singularly shapes and transforms their environment, often overshadowing the social aspects that have historically been essential to leadership theory (Lewin et al., 1939) and how people perceive leadership today (von Fircks, 2020).

What many leadership models overlook is the social and organizational function of leadership (Klenke, 2008a, b). Numerous scholars agree that leadership must be understood as a social resource that influences the dynamics within a field of social interaction, affecting how various stakeholders, such as colleagues and employees, position themselves (Baldursson & Schmitt, 2024; Valkiainen & Jakobs, 2023; von Fircks, 2024a, b). It is no surprise that contemporary leadership theories draw from fields such as social psychology, cultural psychology, and psychodynamics (Jancosek, 2024; Tsuchimoto, 2024), highlighting the inherently social aspects of leadership that emerge when two or more individuals come together to negotiate tasks and strategies (von Fircks, 2022).

Therefore, leadership is best understood as a social process, rather than an individual endeavor. *The hero myth* obscures the collaborative efforts of employees and colleagues, who co-construct leadership based on their own needs and perspectives (Lambert, 2009). Leadership, in this view, is not the product of one individual imposing a vision but rather a negotiated process that takes into account the social dynamics of the organization.

Beyond the Hero Myth of Leadership

The *hero myth* of leadership presents a monological view that oversimplifies the dynamics of leadership and fails to capture the complexity of interactions between individuals in the workplace (Bruner, 1997; Lambert, 2002). In reality, leadership is shaped through discussions—whether in informal networks or formal settings such as focus groups—about what leadership is and what it should become (Baldursson & Schmitt, 2024). Just because management deems a particular issue important, it does not mean employees will automatically agree or align with that perspective. In fact, employees often resist certain measures imposed by management, adapting them instead to fit their specific work-related needs.

This points to leadership as a social function of organizing that is continuously restructured and redefined. Its intended meaning can be modified, or even entirely replaced, by previously contradictory or alternative approaches to leadership. It is a truism that neither the leader nor the employees remain static; instead, both evolve in response to ever-changing social, economic, and environmental demands.

This example illustrates that leadership is an evaluative social process that involves making sense of new and existing demands. Both leaders and followers must navigate these demands together in order to achieve a specific goal (Boulanger, 2024; Ghazi & von Fircks, 2024; von Fircks, 2024c). Moreover, this process is not only shaped by external organizational demands but also by the evolving personal goals and needs of individuals, which shift as part of their personal development (von Fircks, 2024d). These personal changes affect how people negotiate and redefine the meaning of leadership—how it is understood in the present and how it should develop in the future.

Consider a concrete example to ground these ideas. In Germany, same-sex marriage was not legalized until 2017, largely due to opposition from the conservative party, which viewed marriage as a union between a man and a woman, in line with the German constitution. In an interview, Chancellor Angela Merkel shared that her perspective on the issue evolved after meeting with a same-sex couple who wanted to adopt children, something that was not possible at the time due to existing legislation (Der Spiegel, 2017). This emotional dialogue with the couple led Merkel to reassess her views, even though she did not personally vote for the new legislation. However, she facilitated a parliamentary vote where deputies could vote according to their conscience, rather than party lines, which ultimately allowed the legislation to pass.

This example highlights the interaction between personal and social factors that are central to the notion of leadership. Merkel's shift in perspective did not occur in isolation but as part of a complex cultural and social experience, in this case by engaging directly with a same-sex couple. While her overall stance did not change drastically—she still believed in allowing deputies to vote based on conscience—her position was refined through dialogue with those affected. This underscores that leadership is a dynamic, evolving process within an organization, in this case, a political party and a government.

The study of leadership, therefore, must focus on the antecedents that lead to changes in leadership and their broader consequences for both the leader and the organization.[1] While acknowledging leadership as a social and dynamic organizational function is not new to the field (despite the dominance of static, monological leadership theories), the key to advancing this research lies in understanding the mechanisms that enable leaders and followers to revise their understanding of leadership and the resulting implications. Leadership research has repeatedly emphasized the social imperative, but this alone is insufficient. The field must go further by exploring the psychological processes that give rise to the broad, hypergeneralized notions of leadership (von Fircks, 2021, 2023a).

This approach is referred to as *microgenetic* (Wagoner, 2009) and focuses on the processes that underlie psychological functions, in contrast to approaches that focus more statically on outcomes (Valsiner, 2017). Applying a microgenetic perspective to leadership studies is relatively new (von Fircks, 2022) and offers a promising way to explore how leadership meanings are formed, negotiated, and transformed over time.

[1] In Chap. 2, we will see that this focus is called action-theoretical microgenesis.

Interiorization of Meaning-Making Patterns for Understanding Leadership

The process of internalizing dialogue is considered a key mechanism for leadership development (Hermans, 1999, 2001; Mead, 1934/2015; von Fircks, 2020). Dialogue serves as the medium through which meaning is negotiated and realized (Jancosek, 2024; Wang & Shuangshuang, 2024). For example, imagine a doctor advising patients to eat healthier and exercise more. One patient may respond by saying he lacks the time and requests an alternative solution, such as diet pills. In this scenario, the patient rejects the doctor's initial guidance and seeks a new course of action, effectively renegotiating the leadership dynamic over his personal health.

Unfortunately, many paradigms in leadership studies fail to incorporate a dialogical approach (Klenke, 2008a, b). Instead, they often resort to simplistic frameworks like the hero myth, using psychological questionnaires that are less resource-intensive. However, more recent research (Boulanger, 2024; von Fircks, 2020) has initiated a cultural-psychological perspective, integrating *Dialogical Self Theory*. These studies focus on meaningful conversations—between leaders and followers, as well as among leaders and among followers—seeking to understand how leadership, as a hyper-generalized meaning field, is co-constructed and operationalized by various agents (Tsuchimoto, 2024). According to Valsiner's (2014) theory, this hyper-generalization process entails defining leadership boundaries (leadership versus non-leadership) and determining the conditions under which these boundaries are activated or renegotiated.

A striking example of this boundary-shifting occurred during the COVID-19 pandemic. During this crisis, people accepted new limits on leadership (especially state guidance) that previously would have been deemed unacceptable, allowing the state to regulate personal privacy in unprecedented ways. The dialogical approach to leadership challenges the notion of introducing new leadership styles that only reinforce the hero myth. Instead, it emphasizes the social and cultural mechanisms that reshape leadership itself (Barge & Schlueter, 1991; von Fircks, 2021, 2023a; Ola, 2017).

Many scholars argue that the continuous proliferation of leadership styles adds little value to the existing literature, as incremental improvements are often marginal. Consequently, there is a growing recognition that leadership research must shift away from leadership styles and instead focus on leadership as a social resource that can manifest both interpersonally and intrapersonally (Klenke, 2004). This perspective considers the internalization of a hyper-generalized meaning-making field as essential to understanding leadership dynamics.

Classic leadership theories, such as transformational and transactional leadership, have shown that the effectiveness of a particular style depends largely on the context—whether public or private sector—as well as individual characteristics (Abbas & Ali, 2023; Judge & Piccolo, 2004). For example, public sector leaders often have fewer opportunities to offer rewards, so they must find other ways to motivate employees. These complexities demonstrate that no single leadership style can be universally labeled as the "gold standard," as previous literature often suggested. Leadership is far more nuanced and context-dependent than such generalizations allow.

The earlier example of Angela Merkel illustrates the dynamic and dialogical nature of leadership. Merkel's perspective on same-sex marriage evolved not in isolation but through her engagement with a same-sex couple, immersing herself in their experiences and holding various conversations with them. Some reports even mentioned her intention to visit the couple's home, though her busy schedule prevented it (Der Spiegel, 2017). This example underscores that leadership goes beyond mere conversation and negotiation; it involves stepping into the lived experience of others, whether as a leader or a follower, and engaging with their cultural and personal realities (von Fircks, 2023a, b).

Such leadership is inherently dialogical, not only through verbal exchange but through interaction with the broader social and personal contexts in which those conversations occur. This is a fundamental aspect of leadership psychology, rooted in Kurt Lewin's *field theory* and his work with Ronald Lippitt (Lewin et al., 1939).

In 1939, Lewin and Lippitt conducted the now-famous *Iowa Leadership Studies*, which explored how different leadership climates—autocratic, democratic, and laissez-faire—affected group dynamics, including productivity, cooperation, and satisfaction. They focused on groups of ten-year-old boys and found that leadership atmospheres significantly impacted the patterns of conduct and interaction of group members. Despite the influence of this research, its field-theoretical methodology gradually declined after Lewin's death (Marrow, 1957, 1969).

It is surprising that contemporary leadership literature has largely sidelined these social beginnings, treating Lewin's contributions merely as a historical footnote, often acknowledging their role in laying the foundation for modern organizational development (Burnes, 2007). However, as this work will demonstrate, Lewin's theoretical and methodological legacy remains highly relevant to contemporary leadership psychology, offering valuable insights for studying leadership as a dynamic, socially embedded process (see Chap. 2).

Axiomata of Leadership Theories

When studying leadership from a social-psychological or cultural-psychological perspective, it is important to be aware of the underlying assumptions, or meta-codes, that shape our research (Valsiner, 2017). These meta-codes often crystallize into specific paradigms, as previously discussed, but they require explicit elaboration. In this context, our meta-code for understanding leadership can be described as social, interpretative, and dialogical. This perspective will influence the theoretical frameworks and methodologies we employ as we seek to define leadership from an alternative viewpoint.

Classic leadership theories have been critiqued for being monological, failing to capture the inherently social nature of leadership. From a contemporary perspective, what is missing in these traditional theories is a critical engagement with their own meta-codes and paradigms. They do not consider how their theoretical foundations could be enriched by incorporating dialogical and social approaches, a point also raised by Klenke (2008c). This raises a fundamental contradiction that has not been thoroughly addressed in the management and leadership literature.

Most research in the fields of industrial and organizational psychology is dominated by discussions of democratic, fair, and equitable leadership. Recent scholarship highlights a shift in the way organizations are conceptualized, moving toward open systems that evolve through the contributions of all members (Fröhlich, 2024). Concepts like holacracy (Valkiainen & Jakobs, 2023), appreciative inquiry (Coghlan et al., 2003), and systems theory (Fröhlich, 2024) reflect this trend toward more democratic models of organization. Yet, it remains puzzling that the hero myth in leadership theory persists in modern research, even as organizations and organizational psychology have embraced ideas of democracy, fairness, and equity.

This reveals a striking contradiction between the way organizations are understood and how leadership is still operationalized. While organizations are increasingly seen as co-constructed, evolving systems, leadership continues to be framed in terms of individual action and control. This tension is not only theoretical; it impacts employees, who are often caught between these conflicting paradigms. On one hand, they are asked to contribute to the collective evolution of the organization, while on the other hand, they are subject to leadership models that emphasize top-down, individualized control.

This theoretical and practical gap can be bridged by applying insights from cultural psychology (Boesch, 1991; Cole, 1998; Straub, 2020; Valsiner, 2014, 2019, 2021). Cultural psychology examines how social environments and personal meaning-making processes intersect, which is precisely what happens in leadership interactions. Leaders propose initiatives that employees must then interpret and relate to, creating a space for negotiation and reinterpretation that is often charged with emotional and cognitive complexity (see Chaps. 5 and 6).

In this sense, leadership is not a static function but an ongoing process of meaning-making, where both leaders and followers contribute to the evolution of roles, expectations, and outcomes. Cultural Psychology helps us understand this dynamic interplay by exploring how the broader social context influences personal and organizational change. As a result, leadership can be redefined as a dialogical process that evolves in response to the contributions and needs of all participants.

By embracing this dialogical and democratic approach, we can reconcile the gap between how organizations are understood and how leadership is practiced. This approach enables us to move beyond the outdated hero myth and toward a more inclusive, co-constructed model of leadership that reflects the evolving nature of modern organizations.

Purposefulness and Effectiveness of Leadership

Leadership is inherently a purposeful activity, aimed at achieving new goals. Traditionally, the effectiveness of leadership styles has been evaluated through their impact on job performance, job satisfaction, commitment, and various health outcomes (Arnold, 2017; Munir et al., 2012). While these criteria are important, particularly the shift toward considering health outcomes and the relationship between leadership and salutogenesis (Kossuth & Cilliers, 2002), it is necessary to broaden the concept of effectiveness. For many employees and leaders, effectiveness may encompass more than job satisfaction or improved performance. People often engage in their work not solely because their leaders make them more efficient, but because of deeply personal purposes that give their work meaning (Bendassolli, 2017, 2022). Leadership, however, has long overlooked the significance of this purpose-driven engagement (Bendassolli, 2024).

To work with purpose means feeling at home in one's environment, or in other words, experiencing a sense of wholeness. The salutogenic model (Blättner, 2007; Lorenz, 2016; Magistretti et al., 2019) demonstrates that people do not merely work to earn a living. While economic necessity is important, it is often peripheral to their personal system of purposes. Employees and leaders are driven by hierarchies of needs that extend beyond financial goals. They seek to create values in the world that benefit the greater social good and foster an environment where individuals can realize their potential within society.

Leadership research rarely investigates whether leadership interactions contribute to the unfolding of these personal systems of purpose. This is partly because leadership interventions have traditionally focused on justifying leadership styles based on economic outcomes, such as increases in revenue and profit margins. If we are to make leadership and management more democratic and dialogical, we must move beyond these conventional criteria for evaluating effectiveness. Leadership, while a social organizational function, must also be person-centered. For employees to internalize leadership, they must be able to link leadership interventions to their personal system of purposes (Plas, 1996).

A sustainable organizational structure is only possible when employees are encouraged not just to adopt external goals, but to negotiate and align these with their own internal purposes. This process leads to the creation of something new and more meaningful within the tension between external and internal goals (von Fircks, 2024f). Leadership that fosters this negotiation can result in an I/World equilibrium (Boesch, 2021), where individuals feel mastery over their work and life, increasing their capacity to handle future challenges both professionally and personally (Ghazi & von Fircks, 2024). While job satisfaction and performance may improve as a result, these are secondary outcomes of the deeper integration of personal and organizational goals.

Consider a real-life example from a participant in one of my previous studies (von Fircks, 2024e). This participant worked in a therapeutic role at a hospital. In some cases, her clients had progressed to a point where they required something beyond the scope of her defined tasks—such as emotional support or small talk. The participant recognized the need to provide this extra-role care, despite not being part of her formal duties. Fortunately, her leader allowed her the autonomy to adapt her role to meet the patient's needs. This example illustrates that leadership needs to be flexible, particularly in understanding how employees derive meaning from their work. In this case, the participant found purpose because she was able to autonomously assess the situation and draw upon her own resources to address the needs of the client.

This example underscores the importance of flexibility in leadership, particularly in allowing employees to engage with their work in meaningful ways. Leadership that allows individuals to align their personal purposes with their professional responsibilities leads to deeper satisfaction and a sense of purpose that transcends traditional measures of effectiveness like job performance or satisfaction. Instead, leadership effectiveness should be evaluated based on whether it enables individuals to integrate external expectations with their internal systems of purpose, fostering a more meaningful and engaged approach to work.

Toward an Alternative Operationalization of Leadership

To summarize how leadership can be alternatively operationalized based on the introductory paragraphs, several key insights emerge.

Leadership can be reconceptualized beyond the traditional hero myth of a singular figure leading an organization (Marrow, 1957, 1969). Instead, it can be viewed as a social function that serves as an inter-personal resource. This resource can be internalized by followers and colleagues, allowing specific leadership interventions to be connected to the unique systems of purpose of individual employees. The goal is to synthesize inner and outer teleology, enabling both leaders and followers to find meaningfulness in their work environments.

For this synthesis to occur, leadership must be negotiated as an adaptive interpersonal and intra-personal resource between leaders and followers. This negotiation requires mutual understanding through dialogue, where both parties discuss their interpretations of leadership and envision an ideal future state. Such a process creates a hyper-generalized meaning field that is subject to change based on personal and contextual demands, necessitating continuous re-negotiation. Leadership research should therefore focus on the antecedents that prompt the re-actualization of this meaning field. This inquiry is inherently microgenetic, aiming to explore the dynamic elements that contribute to a cohesive understanding of leadership, recognizing that as parts of the system evolve, the overall leadership pattern will also transform. For example, if a particular aspect of a leadership pattern—such as the leader's communication style—is rejected, the entire leadership dynamic may be altered as a result.

The power of leadership lies in addressing employees' distinct systems of purpose and facilitating the integration of leadership interventions into their personal objectives. Leaders should identify specific intersections where personal appropriation can occur and actively support this process (von Fircks, 2023c). Recognizing that these systems of purpose are not static, discussions around leadership must embrace the dynamic nature of both personal and organizational goals. This shift in focus encourages a move away from traditional outcome criteria, such as job satisfaction and performance, toward more personalized, purpose-driven criteria that genuinely reflect the impact of leadership interventions.

In this work, we acknowledge various critiques, particularly those stemming from managerial concerns that may perceive our social, dialogical, and interpretative approach to leadership as chaotic or anarchic. To address these concerns, we aim to establish a theory that aligns with our social, dialogical, and semiotic paradigm—a perspective that has been notably absent in contemporary leadership literature, despite recent contributions from cultural psychology scholars (Jancosek, 2024; Tsuchimoto, 2024; von Fircks, 2024a, b; Zeigan, 2024). Our goals include exploring how employees can connect their self-purposes with external purposes to create a higher synthesis within the interplay of social and personal realms. Additionally, we will evaluate how this understanding of leadership can sustainably assist individuals in achieving their self-purposes while demonstrating that such a perspective can remain manageable for organizational leaders.

While we recognize that these goals are ambitious, we assert that courage is essential for meaningful transformation (May, 1994). In the subsequent chapters, we will delve into the theoretical implications of a dialogical, social, and interpretative leadership theory, as well as address methodological questions pertinent to this theory. This groundwork will prepare us for an empirical, autoethnographic (and ethnographic) exploration of dynamic leadership.

References

Abbas, M., & Ali, R. (2023). Transformational versus transactional leadership styles and project success: A meta-analytic review. *European Management Journal, 41*(1), 125–142. https://doi.org/10.1016/j.emj.2021.10.011

Arnold, K. A. (2017). Transformational leadership and employee psychological Well-being: A review and directions for future research. *Journal of Occupational Health Psychology, 22*(3), 381–393. https://doi.org/10.1037/ocp0000062

Baldursson, E., & Schmitt, C. (2024). Beyond hierarchical power in organizations—A perspective from critical cultural psychology [manuscript submitted for publication]. In E. von Fircks (Ed.), *Culture and leadership: From approximation towards Symbiosis*. IAP.

Barge, J. K., & Schlueter, D. W. (1991). Leadership as organizing: A critique of leadership instruments. *Management Communication Quarterly, 4*(4), 541–570. https://doi.org/10.1177/0893318991004004006

Bass, B. M. (1990). From transactional to transformational leadership: Learning to share the vision. *Organizational Dynamics, 18*(3), 19–31. https://doi.org/10.1016/0090-2616(90)90061-S

Bass, B. M. (1999). Two decades of research and development in transformational leadership. *European Journal of Work and Organizational Psychology, 8*(1), 9–32. https://doi.org/10.1080/135943299398410

Bass, B. M., & Avolio, B. J. (1993). Transformational leadership and organizational culture. *Public Administration Quarterly, 17*(1), 112–121.
Bavelas, A. (1960). Leadership: Man and function. *Administrative Science Quarterly, 4*(4), 491–498. https://doi.org/10.2307/2390765
Bendassolli, P. F. (2017). Emptiness and work: A meaning-making perspective. *Integrative Psychological and Behavioral Science, 51*(4), 598–617. https://doi.org/10.1007/s12124-017-9391-4
Bendassolli, P. F. (2022). Work and purpose: A return to Sisyphus and Bartleby. *Culture & Psychology, 28*(3), 327–341. https://doi.org/10.1177/1354067X211065482
Bendassolli, P. F. (2024). Work and depression: A meaning-making perspective. *Culture & Psychology*. Advance online publication. https://doi.org/10.1177/1354067X241226452
Blättner, B. (2007). Das Modell der Salutogenese. *Prävention und Gesundheitsförderung, 2*(2), 67–73. https://doi.org/10.1007/s11553-007-0057-3
Boesch, E. E. (1991). *Symbolic action theory and cultural psychology*. Springer.
Boesch, E. E. (2021). *Musik, Sprache und die Sehnsucht nach dem Paradies*. Psychosozial-Verlag.
Boulanger, D. (2024). The concept of dialogical and developmental movement: Who is leading the dance and how? [manuscript submitted for publication]. In E. von Fircks (Ed.), *Culture and leadership: From approximation towards Symbiosis*. IAP.
Bruner, J. (1997). The culture of education. In *The culture of education*. Harvard University Press.
Bühler, K. (1934). *Sprachtheorie. Die Darstellungsfunktion der Sprache*. G. Fischer.
Burnes, B. (2007). Kurt Lewin and the Harwood studies: The foundations of OD. *The Journal of Applied Behavioral Science, 43*(2), 213–231. https://doi.org/10.1177/0021886306297004
Coghlan, A. T., Preskill, H., & Tzavaras Catsambas, T. (2003). An overview of appreciative inquiry in evaluation. *New Directions for Evaluation, 2003*(100), 5–22. https://doi.org/10.1002/ev.96
Cole, M. (1998). *Cultural psychology: A once and future discipline*. Harvard university press.
Collinson, D., Smolović Jones, O., & Grint, K. (2018). 'No more heroes': Critical perspectives on leadership romanticism. *Organization Studies, 39*(11), 1625–1647. https://doi.org/10.1177/0170840617727784
Conger, J. A., & Kanungo, R. N. (1998). *Charismatic leadership in organizations*. Sage Publications.
Dhar, U., & Mishra, P. (2001). Leadership effectiveness. *Journal of Management Research, 1*(4), 254–266.
Fircks, E. (2021). Culture and leadership: A Lewinian perspective of organizational problem solving. *Human Arenas, 4*, 1–14. https://doi.org/10.1007/s42087-021-00227-w
Fircks, E. F. (2023a). Cultural resources for leadership: When a banana is more than a banana. *Human Arenas, 6*(3), 444–461. https://doi.org/10.1007/s42087-022-00292-8
Fircks, E. (2023b). A new fertile psychology? A practical book review essay. *Human Arenas, 6*(3), 855–868. https://doi.org/10.1007/s42087-021-00254-7
Fircks, E. (2023c). Categorizing personal appropriation processes of cultural givens and investigating their personal and collective functions. *Human Arenas, 6*, 1–14. https://doi.org/10.1007/s42087-022-00293-7
Fircks, E. (2024a). Towards a theoretical understanding of culture and leadership [manuscript submitted for publication]. In E. von Fircks (Ed.), *Culture and leadership: From approximation towards Symbiosis*. IAP.
Fircks, E. (2024b). Between Lewin and Vygotsky: Understanding leader-follower interactions through a cultural psychological lens [Manuscript submitted for publication]. In E. von Fircks (Ed.), *Culture and leadership: From approximation towards Symbiosis*. IAP.
Fircks, E. (2024c). Taoistic insights for a new understanding of cultural leadership [manuscript submitted for publication]. In E. von Fircks (Ed.), *Culture and leadership: From approximation towards Symbiosis*. IAP.
Fircks, E. (2024d). *Learning with William Stern. Personology for future*. IAP.
Fircks, E. (2024e). *Conservativism: A cultural-psychological exploration*. Springer.

Fircks, E. (2024f). Raising questions with Lamiell about future research directions of critical Personalism: A book review essay. *Integrative Psychological and Behavioral Science*, 1–11.
Fröhlich, T. (2024). System's theory and leadership [Manuscript submitted for publication]. In E. von Fircks (Ed.), *Culture and leadership: From approximation towards Symbiosis*. IAP.
Gardner, W. L., Cogliser, C. C., Davis, K. M., & Dickens, M. P. (2011). Authentic leadership: A review of the literature and research agenda. *The Leadership Quarterly, 22*(6), 1120–1145. https://doi.org/10.1016/j.leaqua.2011.09.007
Ghazi, A., & von Fircks, E. (2024). From an emotional autoethnography towards a theory of symbolic action leading (SAL) [manuscript submitted for publication]. In E. von Fircks (Ed.), *Culture and leadership: From approximation towards Symbiosis*. IAP.
Hermans, H. J. M. (1999). Dialogical thinking and self-innovation. *Culture & Psychology, 5*(1), 67–87. https://doi.org/10.1177/1354067X9951004
Hermans, H. J. (2001). The construction of a personal position repertoire: Method and practice. *Culture & Psychology, 7*(3), 323–366. https://doi.org/10.1177/1354067X0173005
Hoch, J. E., Bommer, W. H., Dulebohn, J. H., & Wu, D. (2018). Do ethical, authentic, and servant leadership explain variance above and beyond transformational leadership? A meta-analysis. *Journal of Management, 44*(2), 501–529. https://doi.org/10.1177/0149206317720678
House, R. J., & Podsakoff, P. M. (2013). Leadership effectiveness: Past perspectives and future directions for research. *Organizational Behavior*, 55–92. https://doi.org/10.4324/9780203763209-7
Jancosek, N. (2024). The leaders of figure skating: Mothers of pink skirts [manuscript submitted for publication]. In E. von Fircks (Ed.), *Culture and leadership: From approximation towards Symbiosis*. IAP.
Judge, T. A., & Piccolo, R. F. (2004). Transformational and transactional leadership: A meta-analytic test of their relative validity. *Journal of Applied Psychology, 89*(5), 755–768. https://doi.org/10.1037/0021-9010.89.5.755
Klenke, K. (2004). *Women and leadership: A contextual perspective*. Springer publishing company.
Klenke, K. (2008a). Qualitative research as paradigm. In K. Klenke (Ed.), *Qualitative research in the study of leadership* (pp. 3–29). Emerald.
Klenke, K. (2008b). Qualitative research as paradigm. In K. Klenke (Ed.), *Qualitative research as a method* (pp. 31–55). Emerald.
Klenke, K. (2008c). Case studies in leadership research. In K. Klenke (Ed.), *Qualitative research as a -method* (pp. 57–84). Emerald.
Kossuth, S. P., & Cilliers, F. (2002). The relationship between leadership dimensions, cultural beliefs and salutogenic functioning. *South African Journal of Labour Relations, 26*(1), 65–95.
Lambert, L. (2002). *The constructivist leader*. Teachers College Press.
Lambert, L. (2009). Constructivist leadership. In J. Murphy & K. S. Louis (Eds.), *The essentials of school leadership* (2nd ed., pp. 112–132). Sage Publications.
Lewin, K., Lippitt, R., & White, R. K. (1939). Patterns of aggressive behavior in experimentally created "social climates". *Journal of Social Psychology, 10*(2), 269–299. https://doi.org/10.1080/00224545.1939.9713366
Lorenz, R. F. (2016). *Salutogenese: Grundwissen für Psychologen, Mediziner, Gesundheits-und Pflegewissenschaftler*. Ernst Reinhardt Verlag.
Magistretti, C. M., Lindstrĝm, B., & Eriksson, M. (2019). *Salutogenese kennen und verstehen: Konzept, Stellenwert, Forschung und praktische Anwendung*. Hogrefe AG.
Marrow, A. J. (1957). *Making management human*. McGraw-Hill Book Company.
Marrow, A. J. (1969). *The practical theorist; the life and work of Kurt Lewin*. Basic Books.
May, R. (1994). *The courage to create*. WW Norton & Company.
Mead, G. H. (2015). *Mind, self & society*. The University of Chicago Press. (Original work published 1934).
Munir, F., Nielsen, K., Garde, A. H., Albertsen, K., & Carneiro, I. G. (2012). Mediating the effects of work–life conflict between transformational leadership and health-care workers' job satisfaction and psychological wellbeing. *Journal of Nursing Management, 20*(4), 512–521. https://doi.org/10.1111/j.1365-2834.2012.01420.x

Novicevic, M. M., Harvey, M. G., Ronald, M., & Brown-Radford, J. A. (2006). Authentic leadership: A historical perspective. *Journal of Leadership & Organizational Studies, 13*(1), 64–76.

Ola, B. (2017). A critique of conceptual leadership styles. In P. Godbole, D. Burke, & J. Aylott (Eds.), *Why hospitals fail* (pp. 57–69). Springer. https://doi.org/10.1007/978-3-319-56224-7_5

Plas, J. M. (1996). *Person-centered leadership*. Sage.

Schweiger, S., Müller, B., & Güttel, W. H. (2020). Barriers to leadership development: Why is it so difficult to abandon the hero? *Leadership, 16*(4), 411–433. https://doi.org/10.1177/1742715020927207

Spiegel, D. (2017, June 28). a-26084d54–0001–0001-0000-000001154866. *DER SPIEGEL, Hamburg, Germany*. https://www.spiegel.de/politik/deutschland/ehe-fuer-alle-angela-merkel-traf-lesbisches-paar-schon-2013-a-1154866.html

Stern, W. (1935). *Allgemeine Psychologie auf personalistischer Grundlage*. Martinus Nijhoff.

Straub, J. (2020). *Handlung, interpretation, kritik: grundzüge einer textwissenschaftlichen Handlungs-und Kulturpsychologie* (Vol. 18). Walter de Gruyter GmbH & Co KG.

Tsuchimoto, T. (2024). Transductive leadership: Rupture and transition of a beginning teacher in a Japanese school abroad [Manuscript submitted for publication]. In E. von Fircks (Ed.), *Culture and leadership: From approximation towards Symbiosis*. IAP.

Valkiainen, V., & Jakobs, C. (2023). The impact of radical self-management: The formation of organisational culture that supports the satisfaction of basic human needs in Holacracy [manuscript submitted for publication]. In E. von Fircks (Ed.), *Culture and leadership: From approximation towards Symbiosis*. IAP.

Valsiner, J. (2014). *An invitation to cultural psychology*. Sage.

Valsiner, J. (2017). *From methodology to methods in human psychology*. Springer.

Valsiner, J. (2019). *Ornamented lives. Advances in cultural psychology*. IAP.

Valsiner, J. (2021). *General human psychology*. Springer.

von Fircks, E. F. (2020). Existential humanistic leadership (EHL) as a dialogical process: Equality of the non-equality in organizations. *Integrative Psychological and Behavioral Science, 54*, 719–741. https://doi.org/10.1007/s12124-020-09553-0

von Fircks, E. (2022). Interdependence and cultural resources to mediate change: What was missing in Engeström's third generational activity theory. *Human Arenas*, 1–13. https://doi.org/10.1007/s42087-021-00283-2

Wagoner, B. (2009). The experimental methodology of constructive microgenesis. In J. Valsiner, N. Chaudhary, M. C. D. P. Lyra, & P. C. M. Molenaar (Eds.), *Dynamic process methodology in the social and developmental sciences* (pp. 99–121). Springer.

Wang, J., & Shuangshuang, X. (2024). The dynamics between leaders and Jiti: Using leadership education for developmental intervention in a Chinese charitable vocational training program [Manuscript submitted for publication]. In E. von Fircks (Ed.), *Culture and leadership: From approximation towards Symbiosis*. IAP.

Zeigan, H. (2024). Management by participation in schools [manuscript submitted for publication]. In E. von Fircks (Ed.), *Culture and leadership: From approximation towards Symbiosis*. IAP.

Chapter 2
Toward a Cultural-Psychological Theory of Leadership: Getting Inspiration from Boesch, Lewin, and Vygotsky

The Need for a Social, Dialogical, and Interpretative Theory of Leadership

Leadership must be examined from a dialogical, social, and interpretative perspective. This conclusion stems from our earlier discussions in the preceding chapter, emphasizing the necessity of studying leadership as a dynamic phenomenon. In this context, it is crucial to incorporate both the dynamics of individuals and the dynamics of their environments. This approach is supported by Simon's satisficing model, which posits that individuals make decisions within a bounded context, impacted by their momentary cognitive abilities (personal) and the immediate structure of their field of experience (Simon, 1955).

Further support for this perspective can be found in *William Stern's Critical Personalism*, which asserts that individuals can alter the significance of their need hierarchies and may willfully change their value hierarchies through which they interpret the world (Stern, 1906, 1923, 1924). However, individuals must also adjust their positions toward the world in response to environmental challenges, particularly in the workplace. For example, when management decides to produce and market a new product, initiate fresh projects, or execute promotions, employees must adapt their positions to these evolving environmental demands. Therefore, workers are not merely confronted with fixed structures at work but engage with dynamic processes that crystallize into new structures (a process-oriented perspective).

What is essential to study within the context of leadership is how a fixed entity, such as a current leader-follower interaction pattern (structure), is re-negotiated and subsequently solidified into an updated leader-follower interaction pattern. In other words, the aim of this manuscript is to conduct a genetic study of psychological

E. Freiherr von Fircks, *Studying Leadership from a Microgenetic Perspective*, Methodologies in Developmental Sciences,
https://doi.org/10.1007/978-3-031-90214-7_2

functions that are established dialogically—and which can be called microgenetic (Wagoner, 2009).

Leadership, as presented here, must facilitate personal and social re-adjustment. For instance, an employee may need to shift their focus due to new organizational demands, such as the introduction of a new product. Leadership, therefore, cannot merely assist an employee in re-positioning themselves either personally or socially; it must also consider the interplay between personal and social demands. For example, if management decides to launch a new product, an employee interested in marketing rather than production must navigate this dynamic.

Leontiev (1978) elaborated on the distinction between meaning-making and sense-making, focusing on how individuals relate to shared social meaning constructions personally. For instance, a child may be required to attend school to gain an education, which reflects a shared social meaning within society. However, the individual child may relate to this shared social meaning in unique ways, such as feeling motivated to attend school because they aspire to become a physician. Thus, personal and social meaning constructions interact to create new and higher meanings.

In this light, leadership must remain attuned to the interaction between personal and social domains of meaning-making (Ghazi & von Fircks, 2024). The authors demonstrated that employees promoted to engage with shared social meaning constructions personally experience a powerful I/World balance that fosters a sense of ease and wholeness. Establishing a temporary equilibrium in which individuals—both employees and leaders—feel completely at ease is a necessary component of effective leadership that bridges the social and personal domains of meaning-making.

The Need for a Unifying Cultural-Psychological Theory of Leadership

To achieve this goal, there is a pressing need for a theoretical framework that allows us to understand leadership dynamically, considering both social and personal meaning-making patterns. In the previous chapter, we established that this theoretical orientation resides within the domain of Cultural Psychology. However, Cultural Psychology encompasses a variety of traditions. In this chapter, I aim to illustrate different traditions and theories within Cultural Psychology and their relevance to the study of leadership. I will demonstrate how these orientations can serve as a framework through which leadership can be analyzed both dynamically and holistically. Specifically, I will include discussions of Lewin's *Field Theory*, Boesch's *Symbolic Action Theory*, and Vygotsky's *Cultural-Historical Approach*. By synthesizing insights from Lewin, Boesch, and Vygotsky, I seek to formulate a cultural-psychological approach that can enrich the applied study of leadership, which will be further developed in this chapter and the subsequent ones.

Explaining Field Theory with Kurt Lewin

Let us begin with Kurt Lewin, the founding father of Field Theory in psychology (Marrow, 1969). A German psychologist, Lewin was deeply interested in the holistic study of psychological phenomena. He was associated with the Gestalt movement in Germany, which emphasized the figure-ground relationship in perceptive and receptive phenomena (Koffka, 1922; Schönpflug, 1992; Wertheimer, 1938). One of the central tenets of the Gestalt movement is the notion that the whole is greater than the sum of its parts (Stern, 1906). This concept posits that the parts of a system interact dynamically to create a higher-order structure that transcends the individual components. Gestalt psychologists sought to demonstrate that altering one or two components of a system affects the entire organization, revealing that psychological functions operate at the intersection of dynamic whole-part interactions and reconfigurations (Ash, 1998).

Another important aspect of Gestalt psychology pertains to the figure-ground relationship, which suggests that perception is influenced by the background context. For example, a tree's perception can differ significantly depending on whether it is set against a green meadow or a dense forest.

However, Lewin criticized early Gestalt psychology for its lack of connection to actual human conduct (*Handlung*), which he felt was sidelined in the classic experiments of early Gestalt psychologists (Lewin, 1926)—that were more perceptual in nature. Lewin's theory must be understood within its historical context; he sought to move beyond the confines of associationism (early stimulus-response psychology). He was dissatisfied with the limitations that associationism imposed on understanding the dynamics between individuals and their social environments, which he regarded as critical factors influencing the drive, will, and purpose of actions (Ash, 1992; Lewin, 1926; Marrow, 1969). *Thus, Lewin established an action-oriented Gestalt psychology* (Adelman, 1993).

Having set aside historical considerations, we can now examine the general premises of Lewin's Field Theory and subsequently explore how this theory can enhance our understanding of leadership.

Between Life-Spaces, Needs, and Experiential Units

Lewin's Field Theory is fundamentally centered around the concept of life-space (Lewin, 1982a, b). The life-space of an individual is not merely an objective representation of physical reality (Lewin, 1982c); rather, it encompasses the individual's concrete experiences concerning their material environment (Lewin, 1982d). This experiential perspective is inherently driven by specific personal and social needs (Lewin, 1926). Thus, needs serve as the driving force behind the psychological and personal appropriation of the material environment (Lewin, 1933, 1935).

To illustrate the psychological appropriation of the physical environment, Lewin (1917) employs the prominent example of the dichotomy between war and non-war (peace). A soldier, for instance, perceives objects and events in the environment differently than a civilian, such as a wanderer. The functional qualities (valences) of objects—such as a meadow, a forest, or a house within the forest—vary according to the needs of the respective individual. The soldier may use the house as a hiding place, while the wanderer may view it as a space for relaxation. Therefore, life-space reflects the psychological experience of the physical environment in relation to an individual's underlying need structure (Lewin, 1926).

According to Lewin, there is no universal figure-ground relationship inherent in the perception and experience process; rather, it is contingent upon psychological conditions—specifically, whether needs are pressing or not—that determines the formation of a figure-ground relationship. Lewin's work shifts the focus to the personal and social conditions under which the physical and material environment is experienced, marking the beginning of potential actions.

Moreover, Lewin did not merely emphasize the significance of needs as the organizing factors of human conduct (Lewin, 1936); he sought to challenge the prevailing narrative of associationism (Lewin, 1926). To illustrate his critique of associationism, Lewin utilizes concrete examples and thought experiments. For instance, when a person writes a letter to a friend, they experience a specific need—such as the desire to send the letter to that friend. This need prompts the individual to consult their memory and consider potential mailboxes. As the person walks around the city, they are more likely to pay attention to signs or mailboxes that will help them fulfill their pressing need. Here, the individual's personal need organizes and structures perception and memory, forming the basis for subsequent actions in the present moment.

Once the need is satisfied (i.e., the letter is placed in the mailbox), the individual experiences a transformation in their life-space (Lewin, 1936). The pressing need transitions into a neutral state, resulting in a reorganization of their memory and perception. The individual can then redirect their attention to other pressing needs and utilize their memory for different purposes.

In contrast, associationism posits, according to Lewin (1926), that the more mailboxes an individual perceives, the more likely they are to want to send a letter to a friend. In essence, any sighting of a mailbox prompts the desire to send a letter. For Lewin, this assertion is flawed; once the letter has been sent, the need and drive to send it recedes from the foreground to the background of the individual's life-space (Lewin, 1926). Consequently, when encountering another mailbox, the person will not react because their need has already been fulfilled. The same principle applies to more fundamental needs. Once a person has satisfied their basic hunger, the mere presentation of food stimuli will no longer provoke hunger, thus failing to penetrate their current life-space. This phenomenon occurs because only objects related to pressing needs are included in an individual's life-space; once a need is satisfied, the corresponding object (stimulus) reverts to being merely part of the physical environment rather than remaining within the individual's life-space.

The Wholistic Study of the Field in Time

Thus far, our analysis has centered on the driving force of needs, which are crucial to the notion of life-space and serve as the primary motor for human conduct. However, we must expand our understanding by addressing another critique that Lewin articulated in his various works (Lewin, 1933, 1935, 1936). The German psychologist expressed dissatisfaction with the atomistic behavior of his contemporaries (Lewin, 1926), advocating instead for an analysis of how different functions interrelate within an individual's life-space. For Lewin, life-space is organized into distinct structures (*Gebilde*) that are inherently interconnected. These structures, due to their interdependence, are not fixed in time; rather, they can be altered through an individual's own actions or by the actions of another person who enters one's life-space with the intention of effecting change based on their own needs. Consequently, contrary to Lewin's major critiques (Leeper, 1949), his conception of life-space does not conflict with developmental premises in psychology (von Fircks, 2022a, 2022b).

In this context, life-space encompasses more than merely the expression of a specific need by an individual and the environmental stimuli that possess particular valences for fulfilling that need. The situation is far more complex, as individuals also confront specific resistances and hindrances that necessitate circumvention. For example, an individual desiring to eat chocolate and intending to move toward the chocolate bars may encounter significant social obstacles in doing so. Their partner might comment, "*Chocolate again...this is unhealthy,*" prompting the individual to either refrain from satisfying their need, attempt to neutralize the respective resistance (e.g., "I need chocolate to concentrate"), or make a detour (e.g., "I will get the chocolate when this person isn't looking").

This scenario illustrates the dynamics of Lewinian field theory, where additional structures enter the individual's life-space, complicating the pursuit of goals or fulfillment of needs, and potentially rendering them impossible. Lewin demonstrated in his various works (Lewin, 1936) that individuals either leave the field, thereby refraining from satisfying their need, or seek alternative means to overcome interpersonal barriers and satisfy their underlying needs (Lewin, 1935). Figure 2.1 illustrates the premise of interconnected structures within a life-space.

Lewin employed an intriguing example involving a conflict between a husband and wife (Lewin, 1982e). In Fig. 2.1, the life-space of the husband (time 1) reflects his experiential unit. In this example, the husband wishes for his wife to move closer to him, toward structure A, which aligns with his needs. He is willing to relocate to A as an expression of goodwill. However, he encounters a specific barrier that necessitates reevaluating his approach to reaching structure A. Thus, he must develop a circumvention strategy to neutralize this barrier or create a detour. In this case, his primary interpersonal relationships (i.e., friendships) suggest that agreeing to meet his wife in A would indicate personal weakness, while remaining in B would convey strength. Consequently, he cannot ignore his friends, as they are significant to his needs for belonging and appreciation. Nevertheless, he devises a

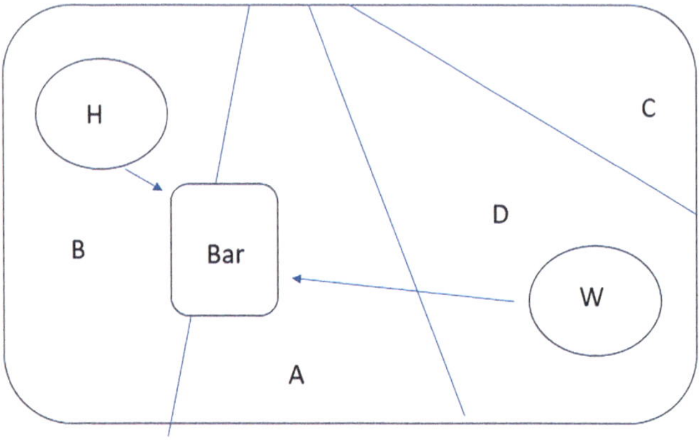

Fig. 2.1 Life-space Husband (Time 1) (H = husband, W = wife, Bar = barrier, a,b,c,d = zones) (taken and adapted from Lewin, 1982e)

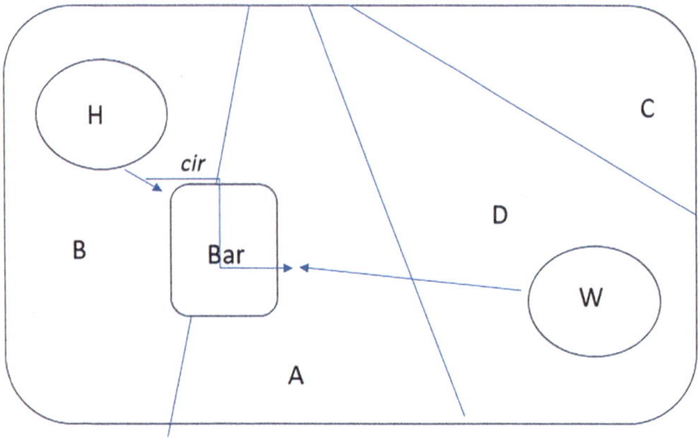

Fig. 2.2 Life-space Husband (Time 2) (cir = circumvention strategy) (taken and adapted from Lewin, 1982e)

circumvention strategy to address the barrier. He explains to his friends that meeting in A represents a compromise, which is not a sign of weakness, but rather a demonstration of strength and intelligence. Therefore, while the husband desires his wife to move to A, he faces challenges in doing so. Ultimately, he overcomes these challenges through a specific circumvention strategy, allowing him to navigate to A and, importantly, to transcend the barrier (see Fig. 2.2).

Now, the life-space of the husband may diverge significantly from that of the wife (see Fig. 2.3). For instance, the wife may wish to move to C because she is not interested in resolving a potential conflict. In fact, she views the conflict as unnecessary and is reluctant to meet her husband in a compromise zone. Additionally, the wife perceives her husband as already situated in A rather than in B, leading her to believe that he does not need to make any effort to come closer to her. This

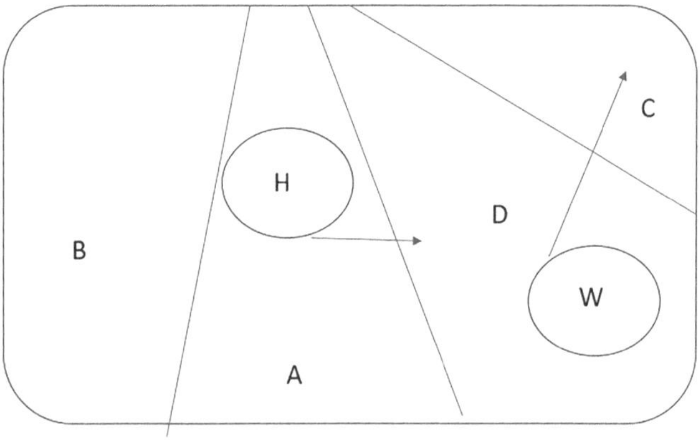

Fig. 2.3 Life-space (experiential unit) of the wife (taken and adapted from Lewin, 1982e)

perception is reinforced by her belief that there are no barriers in her husband's life-space. As a result, the wife intends to move to C, experiencing no obstacles in her path toward that zone. Figure 2.3 illustrates the life-space (experiential unit) of the wife.

Thus, what emerges from the analysis of the different life-spaces of the husband and wife is a complex representation of their experiential units. This complexity highlights how each partner perceives the other, along with fundamental characteristics of their current life-space, including barriers and circumvention strategies. It is important to note that the life-space—particularly the different directional arrows—indicates the intentions of each individual and their expectations regarding how the other will move. Tension arises from discrepancies between one partner's intentions and the expected intentions of the other significant social actor (von Fircks, 2024c). Additionally, we have identified specific relationships as unique units and structures that may obstruct movement toward a specific zone, such as friends who advise that meeting halfway with one's spouse may undermine masculinity.

For illustrative purposes, our analysis simplifies the multitude of forces at play within the life-space of both the husband and wife. In reality, one must consider the presence of multiple barriers and the interconnectedness of these obstacles. Having illuminated the experiential units of each partner individually, Lewin directs attention to a subsequent time point (t3) to examine the actual actions executed by both the husband and wife. He seeks to analyze how their intentions and expectations materialize into concrete actions that alter the field-theoretical situation. This alteration sets the stage for another critical moment in time (again, t3) that is pivotal for the personal experiences of the individuals involved (see Fig. 2.4).

In the current social field, we can observe that the wife has moved from D to C, while the husband has moved from B to A, each navigating barriers in their respective paths. Notably, despite both partners making progress, they are not converging; rather, they are maintaining their distance in addressing the issue. Furthermore, we

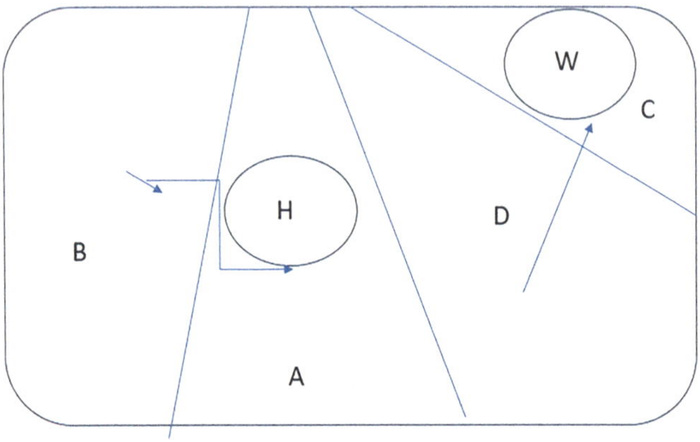

Fig. 2.4 Social field t3 (taken and adapted from Lewin, 1982e)

can discern that while the husband attempted to approach his wife, she moved further away from him. This observation raises important questions regarding the underlying needs that motivate each partner's movement toward or away from the other.

At this point in the analysis, we turn our focus to t4, where both the husband and wife experience the social field in divergent ways relative to their needs and life-spaces. The husband, feeling disappointment and frustration, may wish to distance himself further from A and return to B. His anger stems from his perception that his wife has not demonstrated any willingness to meet him halfway, leading him to feel literally pushed away. In contrast, the wife, sensing that the current distance could jeopardize their relationship, fears that her husband might consider ending the partnership due to the growing gap between them. This fear drives her to contemplate approaching him in hopes of reconciling and settling their conflict.

Here, we witness the emergence of a new need within the social field: the need to preserve their relationship. This new need intertwines with the previously pressing needs of both partners, illustrating the complex interplay of emotions and motivations that characterize their interaction. This dynamic perspective underscores how needs are not static; rather, they evolve and intertwine over time as individuals navigate their relational landscape.

By depicting this evolving conflict between husband and wife, we address the dynamics inherent in their relationship. We account for both their pressing needs and the emergence of new needs that arise in the context of their interaction. This perspective serves to counter the criticisms of Lewinian field theory posited by Leeper (1949), who argued that Lewin's Gestalt psychology failed to consider developmental processes that may unfold during basic interactions. From a microgenetic viewpoint (explained below), however, we can see how Lewin's field theory effectively accommodates the emergence of novel needs and interactions within the relational field.

Nonetheless, it is essential to recognize that Lewin's theory does have limitations, particularly regarding the ontogenetic aspects of development within the field. For instance, it may struggle to adequately represent the complexities involved in the transition from childhood to adolescence and how those developmental stages impact interpersonal dynamics. This gap suggests that while Lewin's framework provides valuable insights into immediate interactions and needs, it may require additional elaboration to fully capture the nuances of longer-term developmental processes within relationships—something that is crucial for leader development, too.

The Forgotten Developmental Imperative of Lewin's Field Theory

The discussion of the marital conflict (Lewin, 1982e) provides a foundation for understanding that Lewin's field theory encompasses a complex Gestalt-theoretical and developmental perspective. Lewin is concerned not only with the influence of needs and their role in organizing an individual's life-space into specific zones but also with the emergence of new needs that arise from personal intentions and the expectations or anticipations regarding the generalized social other's actions, driven by their own needs. This emphasis underscores the interconnectedness of psychological functions (in this case, needs), which are crucial for both the individual's self-conception and the interpretation of the self of the social other within their respective life-spaces.

In essence, Lewin's field theory is inherently social and dialogical, making it a significant meta-theory for the operationalization of leadership interactions. Through his field theory, Lewin illustrates the dynamic interplay between experience and action. Constructive experiences, informed by the hierarchy of needs, shape actions, which subsequently serve as the basis for future experiences, leading to an altered need hierarchy. Consequently, actions transform the material environment, initiating a process through which individuals can experience their circumstances from a renewed perspective.

> Diese Analyse der Geschichte einer Ehe vollzog sich in einer Serie von drei Schritten. Erstens eine getrennte Analyse der psychologischen Situation von Ehemann und Ehefrau zum Zeitpunkt 1 mit dem Zweck, das nächstfolgende Verhalten jedes einzelnen abzuleiten. Zweitens die Darstellung der soziologischen (objektiven) Situation, die sich daraus im Zeitpunkt 2 ergibt. Drittens die Ableitung der daraus entstehenden psychologischen Situation für Mann und Frau im Zeitpunkt 2 mit Hilfe der Gesetze der Wahrnehmung. Das würde die Grundlage für die nächste Folge des Dreischritts abgegeben, der mit der Analyse der psychologischen Situation der beteiligten Personen beginnt, um ihren nächstfolgenden Schritt vorauszusagen. (Lewin, 1982a, p. 247).
>
> The analysis of the history of a marriage underwent three different steps. First, a separate analysis of the psychological situation of wife and husband to a timepoint 1 for the purpose of explaining the actions of both of them. Second, a depiction of the sociological and objective situation that results within timepoint 2. Third, we deduce the psychological

> situation of man and woman within timepoint 2 for timepoint 3 with the help of the laws of perception. This would be the basis for the next triad that will start with the psychological situation of the implied persons in order to predict the next actions. (Lewin, 1982a, p. 247, author's translation)

This triad is essential for Lewin in understanding any form of interaction. In this context, Lewin aims to transcend the subject-object dichotomy in psychology by considering the constructive and interpretative dimensions of the individual—specifically, how one experiences a given situation, which subsequently shapes their actions in distinct ways. Simultaneously, he examines how actions objectively unfold and influence the situation in specific directions. The objective social field of action, which is altered by various interrelated actions stemming from the interactions of multiple individuals, serves as the material for the subsequent personological experiences of those involved.

Field Theory and Its Implications for the Study of Leadership

Having elaborated on some key premises of Lewinian field theory, we now need to explore its implications for the study of leadership. Consider a couple who seeks help from a counseling service to address their issues. In this context, the couple's counselor functions as a leader, guiding them toward resolving their problems independently. The counselor enters the field to investigate the pressing needs of both the husband and the wife, aiming to determine why the wife is distancing herself from her husband while identifying the husband's actual needs to approach her.

In this scenario, the counselor can validate the husband's efforts to overcome barriers (e.g., "You stood up for your relationship despite the resistance from your friends") while also exploring the circumstances under which the wife might be willing to approach her husband. The wife may interpret her husband's actions as an attempt to resolve the conflict simply so that she can resume her household duties, whereas he may actually be motivated by a desire for warmth, appreciation, and intimacy. Thus, the reasons for their movements toward or away from each other are ambivalent. The counselor's role is to illuminate the needs driving these patterns of conduct and to facilitate mutual understanding of each partner's motives and need structures.

The counselor can facilitate this interpretation of each other's life-space, helping the partners become aware of the genuine needs motivating their actions. For instance, a Rogerian technique might be employed, in which the husband and wife summarize each other's positions and underlying needs, ensuring that the other feels the summary is accurate (Rogers, 1995). Following this, the couple, with the counselor's guidance, can discuss concrete actions that can fulfill both partners' needs. This intervention aims to facilitate a reinterpretation of the social other's intentions and needs, thereby restructuring one's life-space—not merely by readjusting one's own position but by experiencing the partner's perspective within one's own life-space.

Additionally, another strategy can be implemented based on Lewinian field theory: the counselor might encourage the couple to change their actions first, which can subsequently alter their interpretation of the material, social, and physical environment. For instance, the counselor could suggest that the couple engage in two or three dates per week to spend quality time together. This approach aims to foster both physical and psychological re-engagement, setting the stage for a reinterpretation of each partner's life-space that reveals the genuine needs of the other. During these dates, the couple not only experiences an altered social field (by being closer together) but may also gain insight into each other's motivations within the relationship. The counselor encourages them to act first, setting aside their interpretations of each other's life-spaces to see what develops through their interactions.

In conclusion, we observe that the counselor, as a leader, possesses two distinct strategies. First, the leader can assist clients in reinterpreting their life-space, which prepares the ground for an altered experience of the social other, essential for subsequent actions. Alternatively, the leader can alter the social field of action initially, changing the dynamics of the field (one's objective positions), which in turn impacts how each individual experiences the field.

Leadership in Innovation and Team Maintenance

The action-interpretative stance of leadership extends beyond the confines of a couple's counseling office and can be applied to various organizational contexts. Consider the following scenario: a leader aims to launch a new product within their enterprise but feels uncertain about its acceptance by customers. To address this, the leader consults employees for insights into the product and suggestions for improvements to enhance its marketability.

This approach can be elucidated through the two strategies proposed by Lewin. First, the leader might invite employees to share their needs and perceptions regarding the product in a brainstorming session. This engagement could yield valuable information about how the product is interpreted and constructed by employees, as well as potential customers, which could subsequently inform the re-conception of the product or the development of a preliminary prototype.

Alternatively, the management team may choose a different approach. They could construct the prototype first and then present it to the employees for feedback. In this scenario, employees are encouraged to reflect on their needs and life-spaces in relation to the tangible product, which could lead to an updated version of the prototype, resulting in a 2.0 iteration of the product. In this case, the first strategy relies on brainstorming and gathering ideas from the employees' experiential units, while the second strategy utilizes an altered social field of action—where the already produced prototype invites employees to reflect on their experiences within the changed material environment.

To illustrate how research fits into the study of leadership, we have delineated these strategies into two distinct categories. However, in practice, organizations often employ a combination of both Lewinian strategies to enhance product development, particularly in up-starts. In such cases, employees may be invited to participate in initial brainstorming sessions while also overseeing the transition from multiple prototypes to a finalized product (Fircks, 2024a, b, c, d, e, forthcoming).

Consequently, leadership not only utilizes both strategies but can also integrate them for various purposes. For example, the leader may recognize the importance of not only addressing the needs of employees (followers) but also anticipating how new needs may emerge as employees confront an altered social field of action. This dynamic interaction may facilitate microgenetic development within the employees' experiential units (von Fircks, 2023a).

Implications for Leadership Derived from Field Theory

Having briefly outlined how leadership can utilize a Lewinian perspective, we can now draw preliminary conclusions regarding the tenets of field theory and its implications for leadership.

A. Individuals exist not only within a material, physical, or biological environment but also within a psychological environment constructed based on their material circumstances. The driving force behind the construction of this psychological environment—referred to by Lewin as life-space—is the emergence of personal or social needs. When a need is pressing, individuals interact with their environment in ways that differ from when that need has already been satisfied. Consequently, future expectations are shaped by whether a need remains unfulfilled; for instance, an unsatisfied need creates psychological tension that can catalyze action. In this context, individuals appropriate their environment to address pressing needs. Moreover, multiple psychological environments can coexist, as different individuals possess varying underlying and pressing needs. The emergence and resolution of needs alter the figure-ground relationship of experience and subsequently frame actions in distinctive ways. The strength of any given action, essentially its motivational basis, derives from the importance of the need within the individual's hierarchy of needs. Thus, field theory challenges the axioms of associationism, positing that once a need is fulfilled, repeated exposure to a stimulus does not lead to a reorganization of life-space and, consequently, of actions.

B. The life-space, as an experiential unit, is organized into distinct structures or zones (Marsico, 2016; Tateo & Marsico, 2021; von Fircks, 2023b). Within these zones, individuals not only encounter barriers and resistances but also project their social others within the field, which is central to fulfilling their needs. Individuals experience their intentions alongside the expected intentions of significant others. Because life-space is a subjective experience shaped by needs, one's life-space may not align with that of a significant social other. As a result, differing pressing needs may lead to drastically divergent possible actions.

C. This Lewinian perspective can be readily applied to contemporary understandings of leadership. For example, a couple's counselor can assist and guide partners in reinterpreting their life-spaces—specifically, how they position themselves and each other—which frames subsequent actions. This can be achieved through person-centered techniques, such as those advocated by Rogers (1995), whereby individuals are invited to articulate their understanding of the other's position. However, this strategy represents just one option; the counselor may also first alter the social (objective) field of action by encouraging clients to spend time together. This adjustment in the social field presents the couple with new material for actualizing their life-spaces.

In our discussion regarding the applicability of these strategies in entrepreneurial contexts, we observed that management—particularly in up-starts—often employs both strategies to develop and continuously improve potential products. Leadership, therefore, should not only facilitate altered states of consciousness (life-spaces) through specific techniques but also engage in modifying the material environment. This approach provides concrete impulses that enable employees to alter their experiences independently. Interestingly, this dynamic perspective of leadership has always been inherent in Kurt Lewin's writings; however, it has not been fully comprehended or optimized for applied psychology. Despite being recognized as one of the founding figures in the scientific study of leadership and group dynamics (Lewin et al., 1939), Lewin was not alone in developing a complex field-theoretical psychology. Other scholars, such as Boesch (1991), also contributed significantly to this domain.

Boesch's Symbolic Action Theory

Ernst E. Boesch (1916–2014) was a Swiss psychologist recognized as one of the founding figures of Cultural Psychology (Lonner & Hayes, 2007; Simão, 2001). Prior to his academic career, Boesch worked as a school psychologist and a developmental worker in Thailand. These diverse experiences informed his understanding of how culture shapes individuals holistically (Boesch, 1991), which he later applied to establish Cultural Psychology at the University of Saarbrücken (Valsiner, 1997). His work was notably influenced by the French analyst Pierre Janet (Janet, 1929), particularly in how specific patterns of meaning-making (termed secondary actions) frame conduct (Boesch, 1975). It is not surprising that this action-theoretical approach aligns closely with Lewin's work, a connection that Boesch explicitly acknowledged (Boesch, 1991, p. 9).

Boesch's conception of Cultural Psychology was significantly shaped by a loose association with psychoanalysis. This connection stemmed not only from his intellectual ties to Pierre Janet but also from his own psychoanalytic training and published works exploring the links between Cultural Psychology and psychoanalysis (Boesch, 1977/2006). Contrary to viewing cultural psychology as a scientific meta-theory detached from individual experiences, Boesch criticized Cross-Cultural Psychology for its treatment of agency, asserting that culture does not grant agency in the same manner (Boesch, 1991, 1996). Instead, he emphasized the dynamic interplay between personal domains (needs, goals, values) and the social imperatives present in any situation (family goals, etc.), situating Cultural Psychology at the intersection of inner and outer tensions (Boesch, 1998, 2005, 2021).

Actions as the Means to Reach an I/World Balance

Boesch's theory commences with the notion of action. An action serves as a personal instrument for effecting change in the outer world in specific ways (von Fircks, 2023c, 2024a, b). Consequently, action is essential for achieving a particular I/World balance (Boesch, 1998, 2005). This relationship is grounded in the idea that actions—except in the context of play—derive their impetus from underlying needs, goals, and values. Individuals strive to align the outer world with their inner selves, seeking to achieve what Boesch terms *Ich-Synthonie.* However, this I/World balance is not static; it must be preserved and actualized over time, which is a critical aspect of Boesch's Symbolic Action Theory. Once an individual attains this balance, they cannot maintain it indefinitely. As external circumstances present new challenges and personal priorities shift, individuals are compelled to seek re-establishment of their I/World balance repeatedly. This dynamic characteristic is fundamental to Boesch's meta-theory.

In this context, action becomes symbolic, as it inherently reflects the individual's underlying needs or motivations to modify their environment in deeply personal ways (Boesch, 1991). Thus, an action is executed in response to a specific need and goal structure unique to the individual. Importantly, within a social system, such as the workplace, an action may fulfill multiple needs and goals simultaneously. For example, a family dining together each evening satisfies not only the physiological need for nourishment but also fosters connections and provides opportunities for communication, thereby addressing the needs for belonging and relational closeness (von Fircks, 2024d). In this light, Boesch (1991, 2021) describes the concept of polyvalence, suggesting that actions are inherently polyvalent, serving multiple, interconnected goals and needs.

> It might be helpful to formulate this polyvalence of goals in a different way, and say that action may be - or most of the time is - composed of several combined or "bundled" intentions. Indeed, in making his pot, the potter may want: to have the finished product, but also at the same time to enjoy the activity of creating the pot; to please his child; to impress others with his skill; to sell it in order to be able to buy food. Thus, the goal of the potter will not just be a pot capable of holding water, but it must submit to criteria of enjoyment, elegance, beauty, status. Profitability, and others, which are as much personal as cultural. An action derives its unity from its material focus, but its intentions may be diverse. The fact that most of the time we are not (or not completely) conscious of this diversity does not mean that it is not real. (Boesch, 1991, p. 46)

When individuals master their personal demands within a given social environment (action field), they not only develop a sense of mastery over both personal and social challenges, but they also cultivate a deep-seated trust in themselves and their identity (Boesch, 1991). This trust is essential for the development of what Boesch refers to as *action potential (Handlungspotential)* (Boesch, 2005). The ability to assert oneself in various situations amidst diverse social and cultural demands is fundamental to defining a robust action potential. In this context, action potential emerges as a critical attribute that enables individuals to anticipate the next moment, fostering the courage to navigate the unknown and confront new challenges (von Fircks, 2023d).

> Since action potential consists not simply in specific skills of mastery, but in a general ability to act, it must imply a readiness to confront changing situations: the reinforcing of one's action potential therefore requires not only a structuring of constancies (without which orientation would be impossible), but also both the experience and anticipation of change. Often, therefore, action goals are chosen for their newness and variation, and the successful encountering of imprevisible action conditions often is experienced as a substantial reinforcement of one's action potential- or self-perception. (Boesch, 1991, p. 14)

Myths and Fantasms as Action Regulators

Having extensively discussed the personal motivations driving individuals to act upon the material world, we must now consider the social dimensions inherently present within any action field. Boesch's Cultural Psychology does not adopt a monistic perspective; rather, it underscores the significance of social contexts in shaping an individual's action potential (Boesch, 1991).

According to Boesch, every situation is framed by specific myths that carry particular normative values to which individuals are expected to conform socially. For instance, consider a young child attending school. The child is not merely expected to attend and pass the time as they see fit; rather, their family and teachers encourage them to listen attentively and strive to become a mature and responsible citizen through diligent work in school. In this context, the child encounters the myth of responsible citizenship, which entails certain action imperatives (Boesch, 2005).

Each myth consists of specific "my-themes," whereby the myth of responsible citizenship encompasses various interconnected themes that collectively form its overarching structure (Boesch, 1991). Boesch (2021) asserts that the meaning of a myth can be understood by unraveling these diverse yet interrelated my-themes. Often, these myths are embedded in particular narratives or texts that permeate individuals' environments. In the case of the child, the myth of responsible citizenship may manifest through various influences, such as a specific type of newspaper provided by their parents, books promoting a strong work ethic, or interactions with family members who share stories emphasizing this theme, among many other possible examples.

> [Myths] exemplify underlying central themes and attitudes toward life, but it is important not to lose sight of the fact that such central themes can be expressed in many different ways. Myths, therefore, are here treated as collectively accepted means of explanation, justification, and exhortation, which might be expressed in the form of myth-stories, but also of my-themes, that is, isolated themes relating to the underlying myth, be they the theme of a story, like little Red Riding Hood, be they in the form of proverbs or other popular exhortations. In other words, a myth is a superordinate pattern of explanation and motivation regulating social action. (1991, p. 124)

Interestingly, a myth encompasses "should-values," which dictate how individuals ought to conduct themselves in specific social situations. These should-values are invariably linked to underlying social needs prevalent within a particular group or community (von Fircks, 2023e). For instance, a child's family may aspire for their child to achieve autonomy as quickly as possible and contribute positively to the advancement of their hometown or neighborhood. Consequently, myths often encode specific social needs, highlighting the concept of polyvalence, which underscores the meaning-making patterns inherent in myths.

In essence, when an individual encounters a particular myth, they are simultaneously confronted with the collective or social needs present within their action field, shaped by the people surrounding them—such as family, peers, teachers, and colleagues. The influence of myths is evident in the subtlety with which my-themes permeate an individual's daily experiences, as exemplified by the child in our scenario. The texts and narratives with which we engage—thereby confronting us with various my-themes—are frequently not immediately conscious to us (Boesch, 1991). They exist as integral parts of our environment, making it challenging to perceive them beyond their taken-for-grantedness. In summary, myths regulate our experiences from a social perspective by compelling us to adhere to certain should-values that are crucial for the meaningful preservation of a given community.

However, myths are not the sole regulators of action within a community; equally significant are personal regulators that interact with the social ones. In this context, Boesch introduces the concept of "fantasms," which encapsulate private or personal needs. What, then, constitutes a fantasm?

> [A] fantasm is here regarded as a kind of overarching goal; it concerns the nature of the anticipated ego-world relationship of the individual, including both hopes and fears. The personal contents the individual gives to a term like "happiness" would constitute a fantasm, as would the subjective meaning given to the term "self-realization" or "order". (Boesch, 1991, p. 124)

Fantasms reveal significant private needs and goals of an individual. However, they often manifest in a masked fashion (Boesch, 1977/2006) and may exist within the individual's unconscious. Consequently, fantasms can present themselves symbolically to both the individual and their audience. Boesch categorizes this symbolism into three types: functional, analogous, and situational. A key task of psychoanalysis, according to Boesch, is to unravel these symbols and raise awareness of one's need hierarchy, ultimately altering this hierarchy and transforming the figure-ground relationship of perception and experience.

To illustrate this concept, consider a student who attends school to become a mature and responsible citizen, a value encoded in the surrounding myth. In this scenario, the student might disregard the expectations of their social environment and instead pursue their own fantasms. For instance, the student may prioritize spending time with friends over adhering to the mythic structure of academic achievement. Similarly, when parents express a desire for their child to study medicine, the child might focus on their passion for acting instead of conforming to their parents' aspirations.

These fantasms are also encoded in the individual's environment. An examination of the student's room may provide insights into the fantasmatic structure of their consciousness and unconsciousness. For instance, the room might be adorned with posters of movie stars or a collection of DVDs that reflect a strong interest in acting. Through psychoanalytic techniques, such as free association, the individual can uncover the motivations behind their desire to become an actor.

Observing the student while they watch a film can reveal their reactions, which can be thematized in follow-up interviews to explore the symbolism underlying their actions. This exploration might uncover that the student is drawn to acting because it allows them to feel free, creative, and spontaneous, as well as to receive public appreciation—an affirmation they may have lacked in past relationships (analogous symbolism).

The arrangement and decoration of one's personal space, particularly one's room, vividly reflect their prevailing fantasms. Fantasms wield significant power over the individual, as they relate to the person's psychological depth, ideals, future goals, and essential needs. Children often react negatively when their personal belongings are threatened, as these items represent the core of their private world, showcasing the interrelatedness of their fantasms.

Incorporating the notion of fantasms is vital across various domains of psychology (Stern, 1935; von Fircks, 2024e) since this process enables the revelation of the driving forces behind one's actions—specifically, important personal needs.

The Interaction of Fantasms and Myths

In Boesch's Cultural Psychology, it's essential to recognize that the relationship between myths and fantasms is not simply dualistic; rather, they exist in a complex interplay that warrants exploration. Neither a myth nor a fantasm stands alone; when we discuss one, we must also consider its counterpart.

For instance, a person confronted with specific Christian mythemes—such as caring for others, the poor, or the elderly—has the freedom to respond to this mythic structure in various ways. Consider an individual raised by parents who are pastors, who instill the belief that giving is better than receiving. Despite this upbringing, the individual is not pre-determined to follow a similar path; they may choose a different vocation altogether.

Imagine this person accepts the underlying myth structure of their environment but is disenchanted with the dogma of organized religion. They may opt to become a physician, driven by a fantasm that embodies the desire to care for people regardless of their faith. In this case, the myth of caring for the social other aligns with their personal aspiration to help others, thus allowing the individual to appropriate and transform the myth to fit their identity.

This example illustrates that while a person may accept the ethical implications of a myth, they do not simply internalize it. Instead, they integrate it into their personal system of values (von Fircks, 2024e). Moreover, when individuals embrace certain myths within their action fields, they don't merely absorb these myths; they actively consolidate their importance alongside their personal needs. For instance, a person who may not subscribe to the religious beliefs of their parents might still participate in church activities, like volunteering at a soup kitchen. This engagement allows them to fulfill significant private needs while also connecting with the broader mythemes of the myth.

The church exemplifies a polyvalent space (von Fircks, 2024d) where individuals can relate to a variety of myths, thus granting them the freedom to interpret their beliefs according to personal needs.

Crucially, the interaction between myths and fantasms involves ongoing, overt, and tacit negotiations between personal and social dimensions of existence. A compelling illustration of this negotiation can be found in the Netflix series *Sex Education*, where Erik, an English African Christian, grapples with his community's acceptance of his sexuality. He asserts that he will only consider baptism if he is accepted as a homosexual; otherwise, he threatens to leave the community. This scenario exemplifies how individuals navigate the complex interplay between myth and fantasm, and when such negotiations fail, many choose to exit the action field altogether.

This is particularly evident among young LGBTQ+ individuals who may feel compelled to leave their hometowns, especially in rural areas, when the myths surrounding them are too rigid and resistant to re-negotiation (Annes & Redlin, 2012). Such examples underscore that the tension between myths and fantasms is a focal point of Cultural Psychology, a concept strongly supported by Boesch.

> This process of reciprocal assimilation of myth and fantasm probably lies at the core of interpersonal coordination of actions. Myths and my themes are collectively shared forms and contents of action, and to the extent that the individual is able to assimilate myths to his or her own fantasmic system on the one hand, and to integrate the fantasms with myths on the other, a process of socialization will take place in which the overarching goals of the individual will be transformed. Thus, action theory construes "individualization" (here: the assimilation of myths) and "socialization" (here: the assimilation and structuring of myths reciprocallly with fantasms) as taking place jointly and leading to the socialized individual. (Boesch, 1991, p. 125)

The significance of the myth<>fantasm cleavage has inspired the development of the model presented in Fig. 2.5. This model aims to illustrate that the interaction between myths and fantasms constitutes a unique psychological phenomenon that

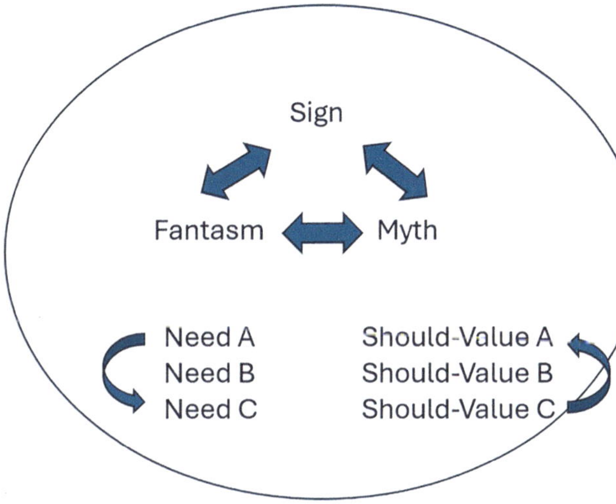

Fig. 2.5 Sign-making through myth<>fantasm interaction (taken and adapted from von Fircks, 2023e)

transcends the mere contents of each. The examples discussed throughout this chapter serve as evidence of this intricate interplay.

In relation to Fig. 2.5, we define a sign as a framework for social and personal meaning-making that can be applied across various contexts. This framework encapsulates the complexities inherent in the myth<>fantasm interaction, highlighting how individuals navigate and negotiate their personal aspirations (fantasms) within the constraints and expectations set by their social environments (myths).

Importantly, the sign facilitates the individual's connection to their Self or psychic system. For instance, when a person contemplates what to study, their fantasms act as a unique sign field, revealing their fundamental motivations for a given subject. This sign is inherently both social and personal, representing a higher function that reconciles previously antagonistic elements.

However, to fully understand the complex interaction among myths, mythemes, and fantasms, we must also consider how personal needs and social needs (should-values) relate to one another. Thus, discussing myths and fantasms necessitates an exploration of the underlying motivations embedded within them, which are derived from both private and social needs.

The interplay of myth and fantasm regulates action, giving rise to a unique personal ground-theme, termed *Lebensanschauung*, within a particular Weltanschauung. By examining the intricate dynamics of myths and fantasms, we can delve into a critical area of psychology that transcends monistically oriented scientific perspectives, which often emphasize either the individual or the social environment in isolation. Our aim is not only to illuminate extrospective data—actions directed outward—but also to uncover how such actions are generated, particularly through the overarching meaning-making patterns at play.

In Fig. 2.6, I present a graphic summary of Boesch's Symbolic Action Theory, which has been applied in various social contexts (von Fircks, 2024d). This model seeks to unite introspection and extrospection, following Valsiner's (2017) call to make sense of actions and their meanings both socially and personally.

To illustrate this model, consider a person aiming to determine what she wants to study, which serves as the overarching goal. This goal can be subdivided into more manageable sub-goals, such as identifying personal interests, gathering information about potential career outcomes, and assessing her own talents and aptitudes. The achievement of the overarching goal is contingent upon the interplay of these sub-goals, each pursued through specific underlying actions. For instance, the individual might complete a psychological test to assess her interests, discuss potential career paths with relatives who have extensive experience in specific industries, and review academic certificates to identify her strengths and aptitudes.

Importantly, every sub-goal and action related to the overarching goal derives its motivational power from the interaction between myths and fantasms, reflecting the duality of private and collective needs. Discovering one's own interests serves as a significant fantasm, supporting the pursuit of a self-centered and meaningful life. However, the individual's action field may convey the message that personal interests should not solely focus on individual gain; peers may assert that one's interests ought to benefit the larger community.

A similar dynamic can be observed regarding the sub-goal of gathering information about potential career outcomes. In this case, the individual's parents might

Fig. 2.6 Symbolic Action Theoretical Scheme (modified after von Fircks, 2024d)

argue that financial motivations should not be paramount, while the individual seeks to ensure a level of status and luxury through her chosen profession.

The necessary actions taken to pursue one's goals and sub-goals will be adapted and transformed based on the stance the individual adopts concerning the myth-fantasm cleavage. This interplay represents a dynamic feature of Boesch's Symbolic Action Theory, highlighting the constant negotiation between personal aspirations and societal expectations.

However, it is insufficient to investigate myths and fantasms in isolation. On the contrary, fantasms and myths are deeply interrelated, revealing both a distinct fantasmatic structure and a myth-like structure that warrant exploration. Thus, we must first unravel the interconnectedness of fantasms before examining the interaction between fantasms and myths.

For instance, the particular fantasm of leading a self-centered and meaningful life intertwines with the fantasm of acquiring status, power, and luxury, establishing a unique fantasmatic ground-theme for the individual. Similarly, the myth-like structure within the action field suggests that peers convey a message not merely about contributing to the community, but rather about doing so with the intent of enhancing the lives of others, rather than for financial gain. This interconnectedness of myths creates a distinctive social ground-theme that the individual must confront, requiring her to take a stance informed by her own fantasmatic structure. This exploration led me to revise my Action-Theoretical Scheme, which is depicted in Fig. 2.7.

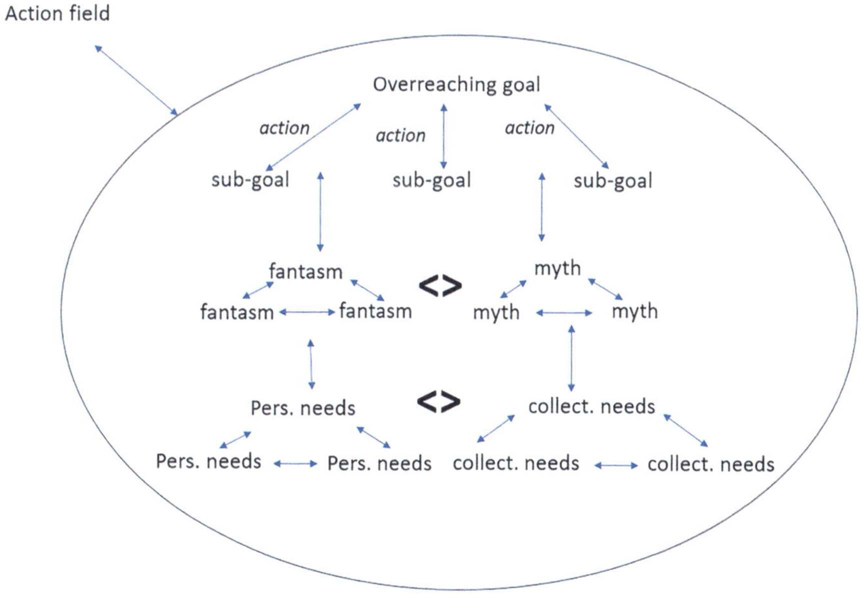

Fig. 2.7 Interconnected symbolic action-theoretical scheme

Applying Boeschian Cultural Psychology to the Study of Leadership

To clarify how Boesch's Symbolic Action Theory can be applied to the study of leadership, consider a concrete example involving a person starting a new job at a supermarket. In this scenario, the store manager assigns one of the more experienced employees to guide the newcomer in learning the job. The overarching goal can be defined as performing the job adequately. This goal can be further divided into specific sub-goals, which include working diligently and meticulously, completing tasks efficiently, and interacting with customers in a socially agreeable manner. The transition from these sub-goals to the overarching goal is facilitated by concrete actions, such as carefully filling the supermarket shelves while also maintaining a brisk pace and greeting customers politely as they inquire about products.

These actions, which are essential to goal attainment, are mediated by the specific myths present within the supermarket's action field. The store manager repeatedly emphasizes that employees should not only be courteous but also helpful and respectful toward customers and their various needs. This illustrates the myth-like interconnectedness of the supermarket environment, which can be identified through the store manager's discourse or the supermarket's official website.

In this context, the experienced employee, serving as the leader, is tasked with guiding the newcomer to adhere to the should-values articulated within the supermarket's action field. More importantly, the leader should help the new employee identify how these should-values resonate with his personal fantasms and private needs. This approach allows the leader to facilitate a person-centered appropriation of the myth-like structure within the supermarket environment. For example, if the new employee expresses a preference for non-anonymous, family-like jobs or reveals expertise in delicatessen products, the experienced employee gains insight into the newcomer's fantasmatic ground-theme, which involves establishing personal connections with customers through high-quality products.

The experienced employee can then discuss the personal qualities and private needs of the new employee with the store manager. This dialogue might lead to a practical intervention: after the training phase, the new employee could be assigned to manage the delicatessen section, becoming the go-to person for gourmet product inquiries.

Based on Boesch's Symbolic Action Theory (Ghazi & von Fircks, 2024), it is essential for leaders to recognize the fantasmatic ground-theme of their employees and how these themes relate to the myth-like structures in their action fields. The leader is called upon to assist employees in reconciling their private needs with the social needs of their immediate or broader action field. This reconciliation not only solidifies meaningful social meaning-making patterns but also enhances *the Lebensanschauung* of each individual, fostering motivation and commitment among employees.

However, it is crucial not to derive every aspect of leadership intervention solely from the interplay of myths and fantasms. Boesch's Symbolic Action Theory is rich in content, offering multiple dimensions for exploring leadership. Another fundamental aspect to consider is the notion of actions that bridge the gap between sub-goals and overarching goals. Not all actions are equally effective in achieving one's goals. For instance, if someone wishes to travel to a destination, they have various paths to consider. Their chosen route will depend on the interconnectedness of their sub-goals: do they want to arrive as quickly as possible, seek relaxation along the way, or meet someone during the journey? If speed is a priority, a detour through the forest may not be the best choice, while it might be ideal if relaxation is desired.

Similarly, in the context of interpersonal conflicts, not every approach is suitable for resolution. Resorting to yelling or insults may not facilitate a constructive outcome. The reconciliation of myths and fantasms does not guarantee the selection of appropriate actions that will assist individuals in achieving their goals and sub-goals. Even if an employee has internalized the myth-like structure of their environment in a personal and meaningful way, they may still struggle to translate that understanding into practice.

In our supermarket example, even if the employee has an interest in gourmet products and enjoys extensive customer interaction, this does not necessarily mean they possess the skills to effectively communicate with customers or sell products. The leader must assess whether the employee enjoys their work but lacks the necessary abilities. To address this gap, the leader could suggest customer training or similar initiatives to help build the required skills.

This highlights that a leader must not only assess social and personal meaning-making patterns in the workplace, which serve as important dispositions of directionality (*Richtungsdispositionen*), but they must also help employees orient themselves toward their goals (*Rüstungsdispositionen*) through the development of skills and competencies. The true value of Boesch's Symbolic Action Theory lies in its ability to integrate the study of social and private needs with the discussion of action, goals, and training. Consequently, Boesch's Cultural Psychology transcends being merely a phenomenological and descriptive tool for understanding personal and collective culture; it also generates intervention knowledge, which is a cornerstone of effective leadership (von Fircks, 2023f).

Having outlined the key principles of Boesch's Symbolic Action Theory and its application to the field of leadership, we can summarize the main points as follows:

A. *Action as a Dynamic I/World Balance*: An action serves as both a personal and social mechanism for creating a dynamic balance between the individual and the world. By achieving this I/World balance, a person can feel at ease and at home, as they make the world more aligned with their personal fantasms. However, fantasms do not exist in isolation; rather, they are intricately connected to the social ground-theme of the environment. This theme consists of specific myths that enable individuals to reconcile their private needs with the social needs of their immediate and broader social action fields. When a person successfully achieves this reconciliation, they enhance their own action potential while simultaneously contributing to the social meaningfulness of their environment. This, in turn, solidifies the myth-like structure of the action field and fosters a sense of belonging and identity within a particular group.

B. *Overarching Goals and Sub-Goals*: Boesch emphasizes that fantasms and myths, along with private and social needs, are not the only significant elements of Cultural Psychology. The Swiss psychologist places the individual at the center of his Symbolic Action Theory, encouraging contemplation of specific overarching goals. These overarching goals are subdivided into manageable sub-goals, and the interconnectedness of these sub-goals offers insights into the characteristics of the overarching goal itself. The transition from sub-goals to the pursuit of the overarching goal is mediated by concrete actions, highlighting a developmental perspective inherent in Boesch's Cultural Psychology. Thus, goals, sub-goals, actions, myths, fantasms, and needs are all crucial components within Boesch's framework. Importantly, Boesch, along with recent research (von Fircks, 2024d), shifts the focus from a fragmented study of these psychological categories to an integrated understanding of their interconnections.

C. *Leadership and Symbolic Action Theory*: The study of leadership benefits significantly from Boesch's Symbolic Action Theory. In this context, the leader's role can be characterized as facilitating the reconciliation of fantasms with myths. By doing so, the leader assists employees in discovering their private needs and understanding how these needs can be connected to the social needs (myths) of the action field. Central to this reconciliation process is the importance of dialogue and understanding what motivates each employee. A person-centered approach to leadership, while managing the responsibilities and duties of the organization, is a vital aspect of *Symbolic Action Leading* (Ghazi & von Fircks, 2024).

However, the leader's responsibilities extend beyond merely facilitating the personal appropriation of the myth-like structure of the action field. The leader must also be attuned to the employees' fantasms and the potential need for specific training and scaffolding to help them realize their fantasmatic structures within the action field. In other words, an employee's interest in a particular domain does not necessarily equate to their ability to excel in it. Therefore, the leader must focus not only on identifying interests and needs but also on assisting employees in developing the specific skills and abilities necessary to achieve a dynamic I/World balance.

Vygotsky's Cultural Historical Theory

What is missing in Lewinian field theory and in Boeschian Cultural Psychology is the specific mention of tools and signs. With the introduction of tool use, man alters his relationship towards himself as well as the environment:

> Man differs from animals in that he can make and use tools. (…) As a matter of fact, the tools used by man not only radically change his conditions of existence, they even react on him in that they effect a change in him and in his psychic condition. In the complicated

> inter-relations with his surroundings his organization is being differentiated and refined; his hand and his brain assume definite shapes, a series of complicated methods of conduct are being evolved, with the aid of which man adapt himself more perfectly to the surrounding world. (Luria, 1994, p. 46)

Tools serve as crucial resources for effecting change in one's environment, particularly in highly personalized ways. When individuals utilize tools, they aim to enact changes based on specific goals and sub-goals (Gillespie & Zittoun, 2010). This dynamic can be easily illustrated through everyday examples. For instance, if someone wishes to decorate and enhance the comfort of their home, they would not typically rely solely on their hands to accomplish this task. The process is inherently more complex.

Consider a person who aims to create a more inviting atmosphere by hanging pictures on the walls. In this scenario, they would utilize tools, such as a hammer and nails, to achieve their objective. The act of driving a nail into the wall is facilitated by the hammer, which serves as an extension of the individual, helping them to fulfill specific personal goals. However, the interaction with the tool also produces a feedback effect on the user's body and psyche. For instance, if the person does not position themselves correctly while using the hammer, they risk injuring themselves. This illustrates the dual nature of tool use: while the tool aids in reaching a goal, improper handling can lead to physical harm.

Literature on medicine provides numerous examples of how incorrect posture or improper tool use can result in health issues (Groszek et al., 2011). A notable case is *epicondylitis*, commonly referred to as tennis elbow, which is significantly impacted by occupational factors (Shiri & Viikari-Juntura, 2011). Such conditions highlight the importance of not only using tools effectively but also understanding the physical implications of tool use on the body. Consequently, the relationship between an individual and the tools they employ is multifaceted, encompassing both the achievement of personal goals and the necessity for mindful engagement to prevent adverse effects.

How Tool-Use Feeds Back onto the Person as a Whole

The interaction between individuals and tools extends beyond mere physical feedback loops; it encompasses significant psychological implications as well. For instance, research has demonstrated that reading on paper enhances retention of information compared to reading on screens such as smartphones or tablets (Jeong & Gweon, 2021). This finding suggests that tool use not only impacts physical processes but also profoundly impacts our psychological operations, or more broadly, our cognitive functions.

When we discuss tool use, it is essential to recognize that it alters the individual holistically, affecting both the body and the mind. Tools can be seen as extensions of the user, but in cases like reading, they also represent a curvature that shapes cognitive engagement and comprehension. Thus, the medium through which we engage with information—be it digital or analog—plays a crucial role in how we process and retain that information.

This perspective becomes particularly relevant when examining the introduction of digital devices in educational settings. For example, in Germany, the increasing use of digital tools in classrooms over the last decade necessitates a consideration of not only the advantages for teachers in preparing and delivering lessons but also how these tools affect the still-developing bodies and psyches of children and adolescents. The impact of digital devices on young learners goes beyond facilitating access to information; it also impacts their attention spans, memory retention, and overall cognitive development (Spitzer, 2018).

In summary, understanding tool use requires a comprehensive view that considers its effects on both the physical and psychological realms. By acknowledging how tools shape our cognitive processes alongside our bodily experiences, we can better appreciate the full scope of their impact on individuals.

> The transition to civilized habits of conduct is thus reduced to the alteration in the main scheme of behavior: instead of applying directly its natural function to the solution of a definite task, the [person] puts in between that function and the task a certain auxiliary means, a certain manner, by the medium of which the [person] manages to perform the task. (Luria, 1994, pp. 47–48)

Vygotsky and his colleagues (Vygotsky, 2003) shifted the focus of psychological study to the processes through which goals are pursued and needs are fulfilled. This approach emphasizes the strategies employed to satisfy these needs, whether they are acquired or innate (von Fircks, 2023g). By introducing specific tools or instruments to meet one's needs, individuals are liberated from mere stimulus-response behaviors (Vygotsky, 1994a). For instance, when a person feels the need to use the restroom, they do not simply relieve themselves wherever they happen to be; instead, they utilize a designated tool system (such as a bathroom and toilet) to address their needs in a hygienic manner.

This illustrates that the use of tool systems enables individuals to fulfill multiple personal and social demands simultaneously. Observing children as they learn to use the bathroom reveals that they are not merely mastering biological functions; they are also engaging in a cultural task (*Kulturaufgabe*). When a child can independently manage their biological and hygienic needs, they are more likely to integrate into broader societal contexts, alleviating parental concerns when the child wishes to sleep over at a friend's house.

This example demonstrates that tool systems are polyvalent, satisfying a range of needs and facilitating an individual's integration into a community that collectively recognizes the importance of these systems and their proper use. Mastering the use of tools enables a person to connect with the generalized social other (Vygotsky, 1994b). For instance, a person who learns to play tennis and effectively uses a racquet can join a tennis club, participating in matches with like-minded individuals and becoming part of a team that competes against others.

Vygotsky recognized the profound impact that appropriate tool systems could have, especially for marginalized groups. He argued that finding suitable tools for children with disabilities, such as those who are deaf or mute, could facilitate their transition from underprivileged to more privileged communities (Vygotsky, 1925). Vygotsky believed that individuals with limited biological functions could become full members of society through the discovery and co-construction of specific tool systems. This idea reflects Vygotsky's advocacy for a new type of individual who acts with greater freedom and justice—an instance where the philosophical Marxist Vygotsky articulated political implications stemming from his cultural-historical theory (Vygotsky, 1994c).

Sign-Systems Complementing Tool-Systems

While tool systems play a crucial role in guiding human conduct, they are complemented by what Gillespie and Zittoun (2010) refer to as semiotic resources. This introduces the realm of sign systems that assist individuals in adjusting and transforming their relationship with their own self or personality (Valsiner, 2014). Continuing with our example of a child learning to use the toilet, it becomes evident that the child not only masters a specific tool system to satisfy physiological needs but also engages with a corresponding sign system throughout this learning process.

As the child learns to navigate the bathroom independently, they rely on specific signs—both linguistic and pictorial—that provide guidance on how to proceed. For instance, parents may communicate to the child that they are old enough to go to the bathroom alone, thereby alleviating feelings of doubt or fear, such as the thought, "*I cannot do this on my own.*" They might further instruct the child to recall experiences when they were accompanied by their parents whenever feelings of uncertainty arise. In this way, the child utilizes a complex array of signs to navigate the task of using the bathroom.

Importantly, the use of signs extends beyond physical tasks like toilet training; it also encompasses more psychological operations, such as memory and self-regulation. The child may develop internal dialogues or mental images that help them remember the steps involved in using the bathroom properly. Thus, semiotic resources work in tandem with tool systems, facilitating not only practical skill development but also psychological growth and self-awareness. Through the interplay of these systems, children learn to navigate both their immediate physical environment and their internal emotional landscapes, fostering a more integrated sense of self.

> The child remembers by means of a geographical map or by means of a plan, a scheme or a summary, may serve as an example of such cultural development of memory. We have many reasons to assume that the cultural development consists in mastering methods of behavior which are based on the use of signs as a means of accomplishing any particular psychological operation. (Vygotsky, 1994a, pp. 56–57)

Vygotsky (1994a, b), along with Gillespie and Zittoun (2010), overlooked the interrelatedness of tool systems and sign systems in their analyses. For instance, a child learning to use the toilet engages with both semiotic resources to successfully navigate the environmental demands of this task. To fully understand this process, it is essential to analyze how the use of tools and signs interconnects, facilitating the transition from an undesired present state to a desired future state (Valsiner & Van der Veer, 2014).

In the context of toilet training, the child must utilize signs to learn how to operate the necessary tools, such as the toilet and washbasin. Parents might assist the child by creating specific mnemonic devices, such as a song that outlines the steps for using the bathroom. This song serves as a guiding sign system that aids the child in remembering how to position their body throughout the process, thereby enhancing their ability to use the tools effectively.

A similar dynamic occurs in my own work with children in tennis. To help them master the use of a racket, I employ metaphors that guide their handling of the tool. For example, I might instruct them to envision putting the racket in their rucksack, which symbolizes bringing the racket behind their head. This metaphor not only aids in their understanding of racket positioning but also illustrates how culturally and developmentally appropriate signs can facilitate tool use.

Furthermore, I establish specific play systems—essentially sign systems—on the tennis court that help children practice and improve their strokes. By introducing these sign systems, children experience fewer distractions and can follow instructions more easily. This approach enhances their relationship with various psychological functions, including memory, interest, and intelligence, all of which are central to goal-directed behavior. When individuals are placed in an adequately prepared mental state through a particular sign system, they are more likely to use the tools in the intended manner, thereby achieving their objectives more effectively.

> Expressing the idea in the most general form, the main promise lying at the root of this method is as follows: The child, in mastering himself (his behavior) goes on the whole in the same way as he does in mastering external nature, e.g. by technical means. The man master himself externally, as one of the forces of nature by means of a specific cultural 'technic of sign'. (Vygotsky, 1994a, p. 70)

The flexibility of sign systems is a crucial aspect of understanding their functionality. For instance, counting, as a particular sign system, serves multiple purposes beyond simple calculations, such as determining how much money one has left. It can also be employed in various contexts, such as helping individuals fall asleep by counting sheep, building courage before making a phone call by counting to three, or deciding how many times one can contact a friend before it becomes impolite (Toomela, 2021). This polyvalence indicates that sign systems are adaptable, allowing individuals to use them for a variety of self-directed purposes.

Vygotsky refers to his theoretical framework as cultural-historical, emphasizing that cultures play a significant role in shaping and over-determining the use of signs and tools across different contexts and time frames. While a specific sign or tool may serve various functions, its application is influenced by the cultural context in which it exists. This cultural over-determination assigns particular meanings to signs and tools, which can shift based on societal norms and practices (Valsiner, 2021).

Additionally, the historical transformation of tools and signs is essential to understanding their evolution. Vygotsky highlights that as individuals develop, their cognitive tools, such as egocentric speech, transition into more sophisticated forms, like inner speech, at certain developmental and cultural milestones (Vygotsky, 1972). This transformation is not arbitrary; rather, it occurs within a framework of historical and cultural significance.

For example, the youth movements of the 1960s did not create their vision for democratic education in isolation. Their proposals emerged in direct opposition to the authoritarian educational systems of the time, demonstrating that they were not only rejecting old paradigms but also transforming elements of the previous sign systems to create new ones that aligned with their goals. This illustrates how sign systems and tool systems are subject to metamorphosis, driven by purposefulness and contextual relevance. Therefore, understanding the interplay between history, culture, and the evolution of sign and tool systems provides valuable insights into their multifunctional roles in human behavior and development.

Applying Cultural-Historical Theory to the Study of Leadership

Having outlined the key aspects of Vygotskian Cultural-Historical Theory, we can now delve into its application within the context of leadership, drawing from my autoethnographic experiences working at a bank in Siegen, Germany. During the COVID-19 pandemic, our organization faced the imperative to evaluate and adapt our telework measures, also known as home office arrangements (von Fircks, 2021). This situation prompted a re-examination of work structures and the integration of various tools and signs to enhance operational efficiency.

In conducting a quantitative survey and in-depth interviews, I discovered that telework measures were positively correlated with improved work outcomes, particularly in terms of self-perceived job performance and job satisfaction (von Fircks, 2021). Employees reported increased concentration levels due to a reduction in distractions from colleagues and external noises. The absence of commuting times, often viewed as stressors, further contributed to their enhanced focus. Notably, the transition to online meetings facilitated a more efficient use of time, as employees no longer needed to navigate traffic or endure delays associated with in-person interactions.

However, the research also revealed a nuanced perspective regarding the efficacy of telework. Employees expressed that, while many tasks were suitable for remote execution, certain situations benefitted from face-to-face meetings—particularly those that required collaborative discussions or debates. This insight led management to formulate a strategy based on our findings. We produced an internal report summarizing the results of the quantitative and qualitative study and outlined recommendations for future telework practices, suggesting a potential policy to allow employees to work from home one day per week.

A key element of this transition was the shift in tool systems employed within the organization. Prior to the pandemic, the bank had limited reliance on online platforms for meetings and remote work. The urgency of the crisis necessitated a rapid adaptation, leading to an increase in telework setups while minimizing in-office presence. Initial concerns revolved around the potential negative impacts on social interactions and communication between employees and leaders.

Contrary to these fears, my findings indicated that teleworking employees experienced not only improved job-related outcomes but also enhanced well-being. This can be attributed to several factors. Many employees reported greater concentration levels when removed from the distractions inherent in an office environment. Given that Siegen is known for its greenery, numerous employees noted the calming effects of working with windows open and enjoying the soothing sounds of nature.

Interestingly, employees conveyed a preference for in-person meetings for specific purposes. They believed that while telework suited many operational tasks, it fell short in facilitating engaging discussions. For example, meetings where one or two colleagues presented developments without a dynamic exchange of ideas were often viewed as less effective online.

In response to these insights, our management team and I undertook a comprehensive evaluation of telework practices. We advocated for a balanced approach that considered the nature and objectives of meetings. For instance, we recommended conducting in-person meetings when collaborative discussions were essential. Furthermore, for online meetings that could not occur face-to-face, we initiated brainstorming sessions to explore strategies for making virtual discussions more interactive and engaging.

The integration of Vygotskian Cultural-Historical Theory into the study of leadership, particularly in the context of telework, reveals the intricate interplay between tool systems and social dynamics within organizations. This framework emphasizes the importance of understanding how cultural and historical contexts shape workplace practices and interpersonal relationships. By adopting a nuanced approach to telework—one that recognizes the benefits and limitations of different communication methods—leaders can foster a more adaptive and effective organizational culture that meets the evolving needs of employees.

Another significant contribution of this project was the recommendation letter we prepared for management and the staff council (von Fircks, 2021). This letter served as a sign system through which we could advocate for the future management of telework measures, tailored to the needs of both management and the council staff. In my understanding, research should function as a democratic sign system, enabling individuals to articulate and explain their perspectives, thus shaping the future of their work environments. The recommendation letter exemplifies the interconnection between sign and tool systems, highlighting the role of leadership from a Vygotskian perspective. Leaders are tasked with overseeing how specific tool systems are internalized and utilized to facilitate goal-directed conduct among employees. Additionally, leaders must consider the underlying motivations for the adoption of these tool systems and how they are internalized.

In this regard, leaders should scrutinize the processes involved in tool use, identifying potential challenges that arise during the appropriation and execution of the tool's functionality. They must also be attuned to the ways in which tool use impacts on the employees' physical and psychological well-being. Furthermore, leaders need to focus on how to enhance tool use by introducing specific signs that aid in interacting with the given tool. This concept aligns with what Valsiner (2014) describes as promoter sign fields, which impact how individuals approach and utilize tools sustainably. Understanding the intricate interplay between tool and sign systems is crucial for leaders, as this knowledge informs interventions that can facilitate the work process and enhance employees' motivation.

Connected to this point is the affective dimension of meaning-making in Vygotsky's work. Although Vygotsky did not have the opportunity to finalize his theory of emotions (Vygotskij, 1996) due to his untimely death, it is essential to recognize that he rejected organistic theories of emotions. Instead, Vygotsky argued for analyzing emotions in conjunction with an individual's psychological life and historical context. He emphasized that emotions are shaped by situational dynamics, illustrating this with the contrast between a medieval knight's mystical devotion to his lady and the gallant expressions of a seventeenth-century nobleman. Vygotskij (1996) urged researchers to examine the interplay of political, aesthetic, religious, and interpersonal dynamics that frame an individual's sense-making process, thereby impacting the affective dimension of meaning-making.

My interpretation of Vygotsky's insights on emotions is twofold. First, exploring the affective side of meaning-making can help researchers uncover what is significant for individuals in their specific contexts—for instance, a person who seeks to secure the love of another. Second, this significance is shaped by social norms and traditions, delineating the boundaries within which individuals pursue their interests. By examining the affective aspects of meaning-making, we gain insights into the personally meaningful social situations that individuals navigate, aligning with the notion that cultural-psychological theories must account for the interplay between personal and social domains.

In summary, the application of Vygotskian Cultural-Historical Theory to leadership reveals several key principles. First, Vygotsky's theory emphasizes the significance of sign and tool use, whereby tools serve as semiotic instruments for purposeful environmental change, while signs frame individuals' relationships with their own selves—what Vygotsky refers to as their psychic system (Vygotsky, 1985). Both tool and sign usage extend the individual's agency concerning their physical and psychological states. Thus, the introduction of specific sign and tool systems necessitates an exploration of the intrapersonal systemic consequences of their use.

Second, cultures shape and over-determine the use of signs and tools, establishing distinct meaning-making patterns and purposes. Nonetheless, this does not preclude the possibility of utilizing tool and sign systems for diverse personal objectives.

Third, tool and sign systems are intertwined in a temporal framework. The use of a tool often requires accompanying sign systems, as individuals may need guidance to navigate potential fears or risks associated with the tool's use. Thus, tool usage is frequently accompanied by verbal cues (sign systems) designed to promote and facilitate effective tool engagement.

Lastly, leaders can leverage Vygotskian theory productively by not only examining how tools are used but also by constructing and co-constructing sign systems that help employees navigate their psychological realities, including fears and anxieties related to work. In this sense, leadership involves more than merely introducing new tools, such as digital devices; these tools must be integrated into coherent sign systems that align with both employees' needs and the broader objectives of the organization.

Understanding Circumvention Strategies in Overcoming Affective Tensions

Before exploring a potential synthesis among Lewin, Boesch, and Vygotsky, it is essential to elaborate on some extensions of Vygotsky's theory of sign internalization, particularly those articulated by Valsiner, which are now encompassed under the concept of Cultural Psychology of Semiotic Dynamics (Valsiner, 2014, 2019, 2021). A key term that warrants examination in the context of our methodological and empirical inquiry into social leadership is "circumvention strategy," initially introduced by Josephs and Valsiner (1998).

To elucidate this notion, consider the example of an employee who expresses fear when advocating for a salary raise. This employee has scheduled a meeting with the human resources department and his supervisors. Specifically, he fears that his supervisors might perceive him as greedy, leading to feelings of embarrassment—an emotion he wishes to avoid, as he desires to be viewed favorably by others. Consequently, the employee faces a psychological tension characterized by the dilemma of demanding a raise versus refraining from doing so. Should the management board decline his request, the absence of a raise may translate into embarrassment, heightening the psychological tension within him, as he seeks coherence within his immediate and broader social networks while avoiding hyper-generalized anxieties.

In this scenario, the employee must develop a strategy to circumvent the anticipated embarrassment resulting from an unsuccessful request for a raise. Here, the team leader can intervene, assisting the employee in formulating a circumvention strategy that allows for a reappraisal of the tension in a more constructive manner. Through dialogue, the team leader and the employee can explore whether the employee genuinely needs to experience embarrassment or if there are alternative emotional responses to consider. For instance, the team leader might share a personal experience, arguing that rather than feeling embarrassed, the employee should focus on taking responsibility for his future—a sentiment that, while potentially burdensome, can lead to empowerment. By framing the situation in this way, the team leader seeks to negotiate a circumvention strategy that alleviates the initial tension rooted in the dichotomy of raise versus no raise and embarrassment versus non-embarrassment, aligning with the individual's broader emotional aspirations.

The tension experienced arises from the psychological barrier created by the negative feelings associated with the initial opposition, necessitating a circumvention strategy for the employee to continue pursuing his goals and fulfilling his needs. In this fictitious scenario, dialogue is crucial because the individual is unable to navigate this tension independently; he finds himself at the threshold of a psychological barrier. The employee can benefit from the suggested circumvention strategy offered by his team leader, which he can internalize by assessing its compatibility with his emotional landscape. Consequently, the employee may internalize and implement this circumvention strategy, enabling him to overcome the barrier and move closer to his objective of requesting a salary increase. As articulated by Josephs and Valsiner (1998):

> Regulators of the relationship between meaning complexes are what we call circumvention strategies; these are semiotic organizers of dialogic (and autodialogic) relations between meaning complexes. They change the "outcome" of the person's reasoning (e.g., co duct, internal feelings) regardless of whether the established meaning itself changes. For example, in "I am generally sad, but today the sun is shining!" the meaning is maintained, but the person has circumvented the meaning by distancing himself or herself. In this process, a "fragile" meaning can (but need not) be strengthened by a circumvention strategy, or alternatively can be overcome. Circumvention strategies are related to the goals constantly and instantly established by the person in the here-and-now context of life; because of this, we call them strategies. (p. 71).

A Semiotic Understanding of Internalization and Externalization

In this context, it is essential to expand on the concept of circumvention strategies by discussing the notion of internalization. This model of internalization is informed by Valsiner's work (2014), which situates an individual's meaning-making at the intersection of internalization and externalization of specific signs that regulate actions in the present while anticipating and constructing future experiences. Figure 2.8 illustrates this complex model of human meaning-making, navigating through three distinct layers triggered by environmental demands, which we can label as ecological determinants of human meaning-making.

For instance, consider a scenario where my wife enters my current life-space with the proposition that we need to plan our vacation for the upcoming summer. Our conversation begins with light small talk about pleasant weather and various locations that promise sunshine (first layer: externalization). This casual discussion is only loosely connected to the underlying hyper-generalized fantasms represented in Layer III. As we deliberate the type of vacation we are preparing, we weigh the

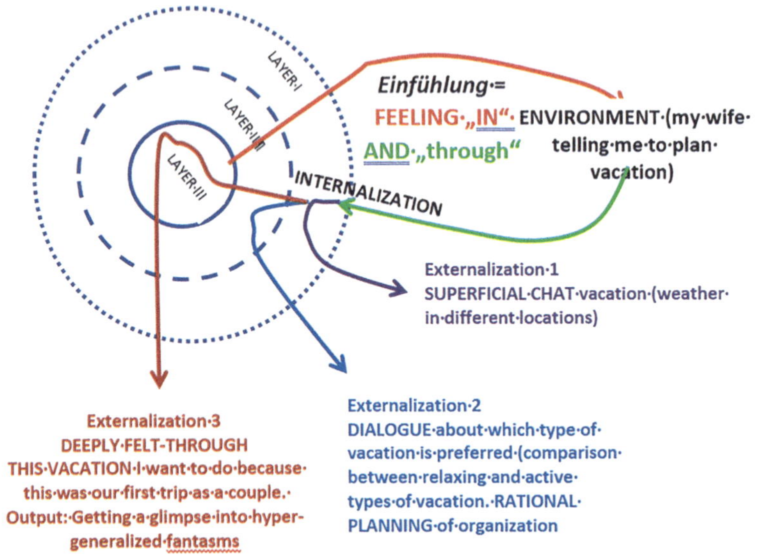

Fig. 2.8 Internalization model based on three different layers (after Valsiner, 2021)

pros and cons of city versus beach trips. This rational planning allows us to infuse the vague cognitive field of vacation with meaning through dialogue, aiming to find common ground for our anticipatory plans.

However, at this point, we have yet to agree on a specific destination and are still exploring our options. Suddenly, I recall our first vacation together and the overwhelming emotions associated with that experience. Inspired by this memory, I suggest revisiting that location, which my wife readily agrees to, as she, too, has fond memories of our time there. Thus, we embark on planning this romantic vacation (layer two), coordinating our hyper-generalized fantasms (layer three) while also considering the favorable weather at that destination (layer one). In this instance, meaning-making and its actualization emerge through dialogue and are driven by our shared hyper-generalized fantasms, demonstrating how they can be coordinated between multiple individuals.

The question that arises regarding leadership is what transpires when two individuals (in this case, the couple) do not agree on vacation planning (layer two) because their divergent hyper-generalized fantasms (layer three) are difficult to reconcile. If such coordination fails to materialize, particularly within a partnership, the relationship can face significant strain. It is, therefore, unsurprising when couples seek the assistance of a counselor to address difficulties in coordinating actions rooted in their underlying fantasms. In subsequent Chaps 5 and 6, we will examine empirical examples of what occurs when individuals cannot align their directions due to conflicting hyper-generalized fantasms and the implications of such a situation.

For the time being, we will set aside hypothetical examples and focus on concrete leader-follower interactions that can illuminate everyday situations, such as the couple's disagreement about vacation plans. Through this exploration, we gain preliminary insight into how meaning transforms through affective tensions via circumvention strategies and how internalization and externalization are structured across different personal layers. This understanding provides a glimpse into the cognitive-affective unities that can overwhelm individuals at times, shaping their experiences and interactions.

Synthesizing a Cultural-Psychological Model for the Study of Leadership

Upon examining the chapter as a whole, several important insights emerge for the study of leadership. Every socio-psychological or cultural-psychological theory illuminates the dynamic aspects inherent in leadership. Lewin's contributions are particularly notable as he shifts the focus toward the dynamic intra- and interpersonal processes that derive their power from an individual's need hierarchy and their expectations of the social other's intentions. This perspective is further enriched by Boesch's concept of action, which is regulated through the interaction of fantasms and myths, reflecting a potentially explosive division between private and social needs. Boesch posits that individuals need not be consciously aware of how their personal needs relate to the social needs present in their action fields. In this context, the leader's role extends beyond merely reconciling private and social needs; it involves assisting individuals in becoming cognizant of their pressing need hierarchies and guiding them in assessing the structure of their fantasms.

From a Vygotskian perspective, individuals not only encounter interpersonal barriers arising from conflicts between their fantasms and the myths of their environment, but they may also lack the knowledge necessary to execute specific actions aimed at effecting change in their external circumstances. Here, the introduction of tools into the psychological discourse becomes pivotal. Vygotsky illustrates that the appropriation of a tool can be facilitated through the promotion of sign systems that help individuals build the skills and abilities crucial for mastering their jobs. Consequently, barriers can manifest as psychological obstacles that can be circumvented through appropriate sign systems, or as physical barriers that necessitate the introduction of a particular tool system.

The works of Valsiner and Josephs further emphasize the necessity of circumvention strategies in addressing affective tensions, which are essential for reducing ambiguity and constructing future experiences despite the barriers that may limit actions. Our meaning-making processes can lead to self-imposed limitations, thereby necessitating the development of effective circumvention strategies to transcend these constraints. Josephs and Valsiner (1998) shed light on how actions are regulated when individuals face affective tensions while striving for need fulfillment. Importantly, when individuals come together to coordinate their work actions, they may not only be motivated by divergent hyper-generalized fantasms but may also struggle to grasp the complex hyper-generalization processes that drive both agents. Therefore, effective leadership requires an understanding of the layers in which leaders and followers operate, along with an awareness of whether they permit genuine externalization of their hyper-generalized fantasms. It is crucial to note that not every utterance correlates with the inner core of an individual's psyche, and thus, leaders must be sensitive to the meaningfulness or lack thereof in a follower's comments.

In Fig. 2.9, a synthetic model is presented that integrates the insights of Lewin, Boesch, and Vygotsky, striving to synthesize their fundamental concepts in a dynamic manner. This model adheres to Lewinian visualization principles, given that both Boesch and Vygotsky explicitly reference field theory (Boesch, 1991; Vygotsky, 1972) and advocate for a dynamic psychology in the study of leadership. The leader's role becomes clear in this context: first, the leader assists individuals in assessing the underlying structure of their fantasms, helping them recognize what motivates them (their needs); second, the leader aids individuals in developing circumvention strategies when confronted with myth-like structures that act as barriers to fulfilling their needs or when there is a knowledge gap regarding tool usage; third, the leader helps individuals evaluate the feedback loops arising from their engagement with particular sign or tool systems, particularly concerning their bodily and psychic functions.

This model aligns with our initial appeal in Chap. 1, where we sought to develop cultural-psychological axiomata of leadership that are inherently social, dialogical, and interpretative. By incorporating insights from Lewin, Boesch, Vygotsky, Valsiner, and Josephs, the model emphasizes the dynamic and socially embedded nature of leadership, highlighting the importance of understanding both leader and follower perspectives. Moreover, it operates in a dynamic manner, as mentioned in

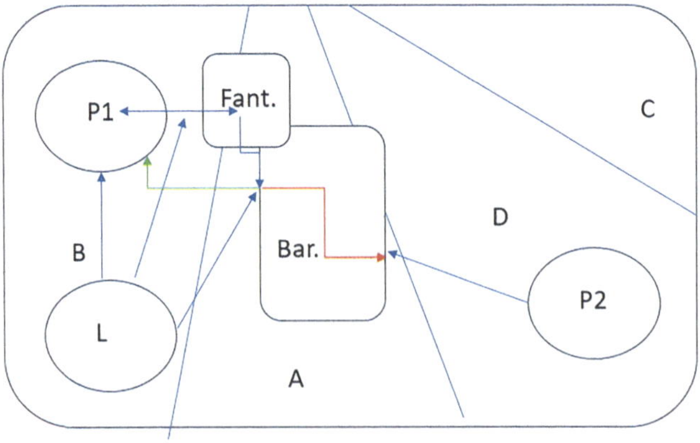

Fig. 2.9 Integrative Cultural-Psychological Model of Leadership (P = person, L = leader, fant. = fantasm, bar. = barrier, blue arrows = psychological forces based on needs, red arrow = circumvention strategy, green arrow = feedback loops of using sign and tool system)

the introduction to this chapter, and sheds light on how different individuals experience the field-theoretical situation, framing action in a microgenetic manner (see below).

In keeping with Lewin's field theory, we propose to analyze leader-follower interactions from a dynamic perspective, focusing on how each party experiences the field and how these experiences shape the action-theoretical constellation within the real field. This means we will explore the spatial and psychological dynamics of leadership, considering how the physical and emotional distance between individuals impacts their actions and interactions. In doing so, we aim to understand how these actions, embedded in their specific field contexts, lead to the actualization of new experiences in the subsequent present moment.

We might refer to this integrated approach as "Small Act Psychology"(SAP). SAP allows us to trace the nuanced micro-level interactions between leaders and followers, capturing the evolving dynamics of their experiences and actions within specific contexts. By analyzing how small, everyday actions contribute to larger leadership dynamics, SAP provides a comprehensive framework for understanding leadership as an ongoing process of meaning-making, shaped by the continuous interplay between personal, social, and environmental factors.

Small Act Psychology as Applied to a Hypothetical Example

Small Act Psychology (SAP) offers a nuanced framework for understanding everyday leader-follower interactions, using a dynamic and field-theoretical approach to analyze these interactions as they unfold in real time. A common situation that many employees and supervisors encounter can illustrate the key tenets of SAP: the process of an employee asking for a salary raise. This seemingly straightforward action becomes complex when we consider the underlying psychological and social dynamics at play.

Asking for a raise is an action that carries different meanings depending on the individual's internalized motivations and *hyper-generalized fantasms*—deep-seated, generalized expectations that shape how a person perceives and acts in the world. For example, one employee may request a raise because they need to provide for their family, another might do so seeking recognition for their contributions, while yet another may be driven by a competitive desire to out-earn their colleagues. These motivations reflect different personal needs, but they all manifest in the same outward action: requesting a salary increase. In this way, the employee's decision to ask for a raise is refracted through the lens of personal fantasms and desires, which regulate the emotional and cognitive significance of their actions.

However, the employee does not act in isolation. The interaction occurs within a social and organizational field that is influenced by the *should-values* internalized by the boss or supervisor. The boss represents the interests of the enterprise and must balance the personal needs of the employee with the broader goals of the organization. In this context, the supervisor cannot simply grant every request for a raise, as their decision-making is constrained by the company's financial priorities and policies. Thus, the boss constructs barriers that the employee must navigate—these barriers represent the values and expectations that have been internalized by the supervisor as they act on behalf of the organization.

For example, the boss may tell the employee that a raise will only be granted if they can demonstrate their ability to increase the company's revenue or add significant value to the business. This barrier, grounded in the company's should-values, becomes a challenge that the employee must overcome. In Boeschian terms, this obstacle reflects the larger myths and values that govern the enterprise, which the leader must apply in the specific context of this leader-follower interaction.

At this stage, the leader's role extends beyond merely presenting the barrier. They must also collaborate with the employee to develop a *circumvention strategy*—a method by which the employee can navigate the barrier and move closer to their goal of obtaining a raise. The negotiation of this strategy involves a dynamic process, wherein both the leader and follower explore potential solutions to the problem at hand. For instance, the employee may suggest increasing their efforts, but the boss might respond by requiring those efforts to translate into measurable outcomes, such as acquiring new clients or boosting revenue. Here, the leader helps the follower refine their strategy to align their personal motivations with the enterprise's needs.

The leader's responsibility continues after this initial negotiation. They must evaluate whether the employee is effectively implementing the circumvention strategy. If the strategy proves unsuccessful—if the employee's efforts fail to generate the desired results, for example—the leader must intervene and guide the employee toward alternative approaches. Throughout this process, the leader remains attuned to the underlying motivations that initially prompted the employee to seek a raise, reinforcing their efforts by acknowledging the personal needs driving their actions. For instance, the leader might remind the employee of their desire for success, encouraging them to stay persistent despite setbacks. This ongoing dialogue between leader and follower fosters an evolving relationship where both parties are engaged in a continuous process of adjustment and feedback.

SAP also highlights the importance of considering how successfully achieving a goal, or failing to do so, alters both the individual and the leader-follower dynamic. If the employee succeeds in circumventing the barrier and obtaining the raise, the outcome may shift their status within the company, potentially increasing their confidence and motivation. On the other hand, if the employee fails to reach their goal, this could lead to frustration or dissatisfaction, requiring further negotiation or intervention by the leader to restore the relationship's equilibrium.

This holistic approach provided by Small Act Psychology offers a comprehensive way to analyze everyday leadership challenges. It considers the personal, social, and organizational factors that shape leader-follower interactions and emphasizes the need for leaders to be sensitive to both individual motivations and broader social constraints. Through the dynamic negotiation of barriers and circumvention strategies, SAP provides a robust framework for understanding how individuals navigate complex social fields, how their actions are regulated by both internal and external factors, and how leaders can facilitate this process by fostering meaningful dialogue and strategic adaptation.

In subsequent chapters, this model will be applied to a range of empirical case studies, providing further insight into its practical implications. By doing so, we aim to refine the model and develop a broader understanding of how SAP can be applied not only to leadership scenarios but to other areas of applied psychology, making it a versatile tool for understanding the complex dynamics of human interaction and motivation.

1. What is the basic goal that an employee/follower wishes to reach? On which actions does he or she rely in order to reach that goal? By which fantasms and needs are those actions regulated or motivated?
2. What are the barriers, social should-values with which the employee is confronted? How does he or she intend to circumvent the barrier?
3. How does the leader try to negotiate the most adequate circumvention strategy in order for the follower to overcome the barrier?
4. How does reaching one's goal field alter the relationship between employee or follower and his or her boss? How does it change the employee him or herself?

In the following chapters, particularly throughout the empirical section of the manuscript, this model will be applied to a variety of leader-follower interactions. By putting Small Act Psychology into practice, we will observe and analyze how the model holds up in real-world scenarios, revealing insights that may guide necessary revisions and refinements. This iterative process of testing and adjusting will allow us to develop a more comprehensive understanding of the dynamics at play in leadership contexts. Ultimately, the goal is to synthesize a holistic psychological model that extends beyond leadership to inform other branches of applied psychology, offering broader relevance and applicability to various social and professional settings.

Pathways for an Action-Oriented Microgenesis

The book title reveals that we refer to our theory and methodology as microgenetic. But what does this entail? Microgenesis represents a historical tradition aimed at analyzing the process of meaning-making from psycho-physically neutral phenomena (Valsiner, 2000). The microgenetic method places special emphasis on both the process and substance of meaning formation (Wagoner, 2009, 2010). In other words, both the outcome and the process of meaning-making are central in the microgenetic tradition (Diriwächter, 2009). Here, the holistic phenomenological orientation of the microgenetic method is essential, involving an integrative analysis of a phenomenon that includes cultural-historical (social), emotional, and cognitive components (Wagoner, 2009). Historically, the microgenetic method evolved from actual genesis, which, in the second Leipzig school, was largely perceptually based (Sander, 1928).

In the following chapters, however, we aim to explore an action-oriented microgenesis, focusing on the process and structure of actions and how these might be coordinated between different individuals within a cultural-historical context. This action-oriented microgenesis is novel in the scientific discourse of microgenesis and actual genesis, analyzing how actions emerge in a social space. Our aim is to examine not only ecological field determinants but also personal purposes (phantasms) of the individual as part of the analysis. Thus, the genesis of action is not only mediated by social inhibitors and promoters but also by personal agency rooted in the fantasms of the individual. These processes play a significant role in both the planning and execution of actions, impacting the path leading to the final action and encouraging subsequent actions within a given field. In other words, action is mediated socially and personally, yielding a distinctive spectrum of outcomes that lay the groundwork for further actions or for the co-construction of actions from other perspectives. This interaction between personal and social forces also serves as an evolution from the traditional microgenetic focus on directionality. Directionality (i.e., the personal orientation of action) does not occur in a social vacuum but is accompanied, constrained, or reinforced by cultural-historical forces inherent to the individual.

The co-construction of meaning, accompanying the process of meaning-making, is an important criterion in recent microgenetic research (Psaltis, 2015), a feature our action-oriented microgenesis affirms. It is curious that Lewin's field theory has not yet been connected with microgenetic research, given that analyzing field forces in their dynamic transformation more than fulfills the central criteria of historically grounded microgenesis. Not only the genesis of meaning, which informs action, is crucial in microgenesis—as interpreted by Wagoner (2009)—but also the transformation of meaning, which any methodology aspiring to be called microgenetic should address. For our action-oriented microgenesis, this means: Why was an action reoriented? Why was the action intensified? Why were alternative tools consulted to complete the action? These are essential elements in the re-actualization of actions that encounter resistance or barriers, initiating an action's transformation. The emphasis here is on qualitative changes in the action, which also retroactively impact the organism. This retroactive influence of action is a central characteristic of action transformation: it is not only about reorienting actions in response to resistance or barriers but also learning how to handle future challenges through reorientation. In other words, reorienting an action also indicates a reorientation of the entire person—a qualitative change in their person and in the psycho-physical resources they deploy. These feedback processes of action impacting the individual are an underestimated topic in both Lewin's field theory and the scientific tradition of microgenesis. *In short: Field-Theory is action-oriented microgenesis.*

With this, we conclude our discussion of microgenesis and how our updated field theory integrates with it. However, before doing so, I would like to capture the insights gained from examining field theory in light of microgenesis and the consequences of this analysis in a tabular format (see Table 2.1). This table will examine two aspects: first, to what extent our action-oriented microgenesis (updated field theory) meets and advances the criteria of general microgenesis (e.g., as outlined in

Table 2.1 Comparing classic microgenesis with an action-oriented microgenesis

Classic microgenesis (after Wagoner, 2009, 2010)	Action-oriented microgenesis within field-theory
Unity of mind: Developing a wholistic model of the mind including the analysis of cognitive, social, and emotional processes	Unity of mind and action: Shifting the analysis not solely on a wholistic model of the mind but on how action comes into being. Including the analysis of resistances/barriers of action
Individual-environment-relationship: Meaning emerges in a context that is refracted through personal and social forces	Actions that are based on meaning are co-constructed by other people and feed back onto the psychic system of the person. Field-theoretical microgenesis wants to include an analysis of those feedback processes
Directedness: Persons are centers of teleology (finality) and construct their own past and future	Persons do not simply construct their own past and future, but they also coordinate this past and future with other people—Noticeably through dialogue. The interpersonal coordination of action is central for the emergence of actualized meaning
Temporal unfolding of meaning making: Analysis of the process that leads to meaning	Shifting the focus onto the psycho-physical forces of the person that are used within the process to generate meaning and action. What does happen if the psycho-physical forces are actualized/changed for the emergence of meaning?

Wagoner, 2009, 2010). Here, we will highlight not only the relevance of action-oriented microgenesis within leadership contexts but also appeal to researchers to ground the foundation of microgenesis in the core of action. This approach aims not only to enrich microgenetic research but also to establish methodological guidelines for employing a field-theoretical microgenesis—specifically for the analysis of leadership phenomena within this manuscript.

References

Adelman, C. (1993). Kurt Lewin and the origins of action research. *Educational Action Research, 1*(1), 7–24. https://doi.org/10.1080/0965079930010102

Annes, A., & Redlin, M. (2012). Coming out and coming back: Rural gay migration and the city. *Journal of Rural Studies, 28*(1), 56–68. https://doi.org/10.1016/j.jrurstud.2011.09.001

Ash, M. G. (1992). Cultural contexts and scientific change in psychology: Kurt Lewin in Iowa. *American Psychologist, 47*(2), 198. https://doi.org/10.1037/0003-066X.47.2.198

Ash, M. G. (1998). *Gestalt psychology in German culture, 1890–1967: Holism and the quest for objectivity*. Cambridge University Press.

Boesch, E. E. (1975). *Zwischen Angst und Triumph: über das Ich und seine Bestätigungen*. Huber.

Boesch, E. E. (1991). *Symbolic action theory and cultural psychology*. Springer.

Boesch, E. E. (1996). The seven flaws of cross-cultural psychology. The story of conversion. *Mind, Culture, and Activity, 3*(1), 2–10. https://doi.org/10.1207/s15327884mca0301_2

Boesch, E. E. (1998). *Sehnsucht: Von der Suche nach Glück und Sinn [longing: On the search of joy and meaning]*. Huber.

Boesch, E. E. (2005). *Von Kunst bis terror: Über den Zwiespalt in der Kultur [from art to terror: On the cleavage of culture]*. Vandenhoeck & Ruprecht.

Boesch, E. E. (2006). *Konnotationsanalyse: zur Verwendung der freien Ideen-Assoziation in Diagnostik und Therapie*. Privater Nachdruck. (Original work published in 1977).

Boesch, E. E. (2021). *Musik, Sprache und die Sehnsucht nach dem Paradies*. Psychosozial-Verlag.
Diriwächter, R. (2009). Idiographic microgenesis: Re-visiting the experimental tradition of Aktualgenese. In J. Valsiner, N. Chaudhary, M. C. D. P. Lyra, & P. C. M. Molenaar (Eds.), *Dynamic process methodology in the social and developmental sciences dynamic process methodology in the social and developmental sciences* (pp. 319–352). Springer.
Fircks, E. (2022a). Interdependence and cultural resources to mediate change: What was missing in Engeström's third generational activity theory. *Human Arenas, 1-13*. https://doi.org/10.1007/s42087-022-00246-y
Fircks, E. (2022b). Setting the seeds for a normative expansion of Lewinian field theory for cultural-psychological practitioners. *Human Arenas, 1–21*. https://doi.org/10.1007/s42087-022-00247-x
Fircks, E. F. (2023a). Cultural resources for leadership: When a banana is more than a banana. *Human Arenas, 6*(3), 444–461. https://doi.org/10.1007/s42087-021-00256-5
Fircks, E. (2023b). Enhancing and inhibiting: Framing of innovation in educational encounters. *Possibility Studies & Society.*, Advance Online Publication. https://doi.org/10.1177/27538699231201014
Fircks, E. (2023c). Eine kurze kulturpsychologische Anleitung für zukünftige Freunde. *cultura & psyché, 4*(2), 277–291. https://doi.org/10.1016/j.jrurstud.2011.09.001
Fircks, E. (2023d). The hero-villain-fool narrative construction method: Assessing hidden organizational phenomena. *Integrative Psychological and Behavioral Science, 1–25*. https://doi.org/10.1007/s12124-022-09613-3
Fircks, E. (2023e). Understanding the power of mindfulness from a cultural-psychological perspective. *Culture & Psychology*, Advance Online Publication. https://doi.org/10.1177/1354067X231201387
Fircks, E. F. (2023f). The fully objectified Catathymic imagery method (FOCI): Assessing the Amorphian inner at work. *Human Arenas, 1–18*. https://doi.org/10.1007/s42087-022-00256-4
Fircks, E. (2023g). Geštalt TERAPIJA IZVAN POTREBA: Kako UPOTREBA ALATA UTIČE NA OSOBU I OKRUŽENJE. *Geštalt Zbornik*, (10), 46–59. https://www.ceeol.com/search/article-detail?id=1201024
Fircks, E. (2024a). Towards a theoretical understanding of culture and leadership [Manuscript submitted for publication]. In E. von Fircks (Ed.), *Culture and leadership: From approximation towards Symbiosis*. IAP.
Fircks, E. (2024b). Between Lewin and Vygotsky: Understanding leader-follower interactions through a cultural psychological lens [manuscript submitted for publication]. In E. von Fircks (Ed.), *Culture and leadership: From approximation towards Symbiosis*. IAP.
Fircks, E. (2024c). Culture and leadership: A Lewinian perspective of organizational problem solving. *Hu Arenas, 7*, 1–14. https://doi.org/10.1007/s42087-021-00256-5
Fircks, E. (2024d). *Conservativism: A cultural-psychological exploration*. Springer.
Fircks, E. (2024e). *Learning with William Stern. Personology for future*. IAP.
Ghazi, A., & von Fircks, E. (2024). From an emotional autoethnography towards a theory of symbolic action leading (SAL) [manuscript submitted for publication]. In E. von Fircks (Ed.), *Culture and leadership: From approximation towards Symbiosis*. IAP.
Gillespie, A., & Zittoun, T. (2010). Using resources: conceptualizing the mediation and refective use of tools and signs [pre-refereed version]. *LSE Research Online*, 1–41. http://eprints.lse.ac.uk/38708/1/Using_resources_conceptualizing_the_mediation_and_refective_use_of_tools_and_signs_%28LSERO% 29.pdf
Groszek, M., Babula, G., Nagraba, Ł., Stolarczyk, A., & Mitek, T. (2011). Risks connected with a wrong sitting position. *Arthroscopy and Joint Surgery, 7*(3–4), 50–61. https://doi.org/10.5604/.969148
Janet, P. (1929). *L'évolution psychologique de la personnalité*. Edition Chahine.
Jeong, Y. J., & Gweon, G. (2021). Advantages of print reading over screen reading: A comparison of visual patterns, reading performance, and reading attitudes across paper, computers, and tablets. *International Journal of Human–Computer Interaction, 37*(17), 1674–1684. https://doi.org/10.1080/10447318.2020.1775692

Josephs, I. E., & Valsiner, J. (1998). How Does Autodialogue Work? Miracles of Meaning Maintenance and Circumvention Strategies. *Social Psychology Quarterly, 61*(1), 68. https://doi.org/10.2307/2787058

Koffka, K. (1922). Perception: An introduction to the gestalt-theorie. *Psychological Bulletin, 19*(10), 531–585.

Leeper, R. W. (1949). *Lewin's topological and vector psychology: A digest and critique*. University of Oregon. https://doi.org/10.1037/14168-000

Leont'ev, A. (1978). *Activity, consciousness, and personality*. Prentice-Hall.

Lewin, K. (1917). Kriegslandschaft [War landscape]. *Zeitschrift Für Angewandte Psychologie, 12*(5), 440–447.

Lewin, K. (1926). *Vorsatz Wille und Bedürfnis: Mit Vorbemerkungen über die psychischen Kräfte und Energien und die Struktur der Seele*. Springer.

Lewin, K. (1933). Environmental forces. In C. Murchison (Ed.), *Handbook of child psychology* (pp. 591–625). Oxford University Press.

Lewin, K. (1935). *A dynamic theory of personality*. McGraw-Hill.

Lewin, K. (1936). *Principles of topological psychology*. McGraw-Hill.

Lewin, K. (1982a). Formalisierung und Forschritt in der Psychologie. In C. F. Graumann (Ed.), *Kurt Lewin Werkausgabe: Feldtheorie* (Vol. 4, pp. 41–73). Klett-Cotta.

Lewin, K. (1982b). Konstrukte in der Feldtheorie. In C. F. Graumann (Ed.), *Kurt Lewin Werkausgabe: Feldtheorie* (Vol. 4, pp. 73–87). Klett-Cotta.

Lewin, K. (1982c). Mathematische Konstrukte in Psychologie und Soziologie. In C. F. Graumann (Ed.), *Kurt Lewin Werkausgabe: Feldtheorie* (Vol. 4, pp. 87–99). Klett-Cotta.

Lewin, K. (1982d). Feldtheorie des Lernens. In C. F. Graumann (Ed.), *Kurt Lewin Werkausgabe: Feldtheorie* (Vol. 4, pp. 157–187). Klett-Cotta.

Lewin, K. (1982e). Forschungsprobleme der Sozialpsychologie II: Soziales Gleichgewicht und sozialer Wandel im Gruppenerleben. In C. F. Graumann (Ed.), *Kurt Lewin Werkausgabe: Feldtheorie* (Vol. 4, pp. 237–291). Klett-Cotta.

Lewin, K., Lippitt, R., & White, R. K. (1939). Patterns of aggressive behavior in experimentally created "social climates." The Journal of Social Psychology, 10(2), 269–299. https://doi.org/10.1080/00224545.1939.9713366.

Lonner, W. J., & Hayes, S. A. (2007). *Discovering cultural psychology: A profile and selected readings of Ernest E. Boesch*. IAP.

Luria, A. (1994). The problem of the cultural behavior of the child. In R. Van Der Veer & J. Valsiner (Eds.), *The Vygotsky reader* (pp. 46–57). Blackwell.

Marrow, A. J. (1969). *The practical theorist; the life and work of Kurt Lewin*. Basic Books.

Marsico, G. (2016). The borderland. *Culture & Psychology, 22*(2), 206–215. https://doi.org/10.1177/1354067X15572038

Psaltis, C. (2015). Genetic social psychology: From microgenesis to ontogenesis, Sociogenesis… and Back. In C. Psaltis, A. Gillespie, & A.-N. Perret-Clermont (Eds.), *Social relations in human and societal development* (pp. 71–94). Palgrave Macmillan. https://doi.org/10.1057/9781137400994_5

Rogers, C. R. (1995). *On becoming a person: A therapist's view of psychotherapy*. Houghton Mifflin Harcourt.

Sander, F. (1928). Experimentelle Ergebnisse der Gestaltpsychologie [experimental results in gestalt psychology]. In E. Becher (Ed.), *Bericht über den X. Kongreß der Gesellschaft für experimentelle Psychologie in Bonn 1927* (pp. 23–88). Fischer.

Schönpflug, W. (1992). Kurt Lewin–eine biographische Skizze. In *Kurt Lewin–Person, Werk, Umfeld. Historische Rekonstruktionen und aktuelle Wertungen aus Anlaß seines hundertsten Geburtstages* (pp. 13–28).

Shiri, R., & Viikari-Juntura, E. (2011). Lateral and medial epicondylitis: Role of occupational factors. *Best Practice & Research Clinical Rheumatology, 25*(1), 43–57. https://doi.org/10.1016/j.berh.2011.01.014

Simão, L. M. (2001). Boesch's symbolic action theory in interaction. *Culture & Psychology, 7*(4), 485–493. https://doi.org/10.1177/1354067X0100700405

Simon, H. A. (1955). A behavioral model of rational choice. *The Quarterly Journal of Economics, 69*(1), 99. https://doi.org/10.2307/1884852

Spitzer, M. (2018). *Die Smartphone-Epidemie: Gefahren für Gesundheit, Bildung und Gesellschaft*. Klett-Cotta.

Stern, W. (1906). *Person und Sache. System des Kritischen Personalismus System der philosophischen Weltanschauung*. J.A. Barth.

Stern, W. (1923). *Person und Sache: Die Menschliche Persönlichkeit* (3rd ed.). J.A. Barth.

Stern, W. (1924). *Person und Sache: System des Kritischen Personalismus (Wertphilosophie)*. J.A. Barth.

Stern, W. (1935). *Allgemeine Psychologie auf personalistischer Grundlage*. Martinus Nijhoff.

Tateo, L., & Marsico, G. (2021). Signs as borders and borders as signs. *Theory & Psychology, 31*(5), 708–728. https://doi.org/10.1177/09593543211034534

Toomela, A. (2021). *Culture, speech and myself*. Porcos ante Margaritas.

Valsiner, J. (1997). The Saarbrucken tradition in cultural psychology, and its legacy. *Culture & Psychology, 3*(3), 243–245. https://doi.org/10.1177/1354067X970030030

Valsiner, J. (2000). *Culture and human development*. Sage.

Valsiner, J. (2014). *An invitation to cultural psychology*. Sage.

Valsiner, J. (2017). *From methodology to methods in human psychology*. Springer.

Valsiner, J. (2019). *Ornamented lives. Advances in cultural psychology*. IAP.

Valsiner, J. (2021). *General human psychology*. Springer.

Valsiner, J., & van der Veer, R. (2014). Encountering the border. In A. Yasnitsky, R. van der Veer, & M. Ferrari (Eds.), *Cambridge handbooks in psychology. The Cambridge handbook of cultural-historical psychology* (pp. 148–174). Cambridge University Press.

von Fircks, E. (2021). *Telework Measures at the Workplace during Covid 19: Assessing local effectiveness in a regional bank*. Privatdruck.

Vygotskij, L. S. (1996). *Die Lehre von den Emotionen. Eine psychologiehistorische Untersuchung. (Fortschritte der Psychologie, Bd. 15)*. Lit.

Vygotsky, L. S. (1925). Principles of social education for deaf and dumb children in Russia. In *International Conference on the Education of the Deaf* (Vol. 70, No. 5, pp. 227–235).

Vygotsky, L. S. (1972). *Denken und Sprechen [thinking and thought]* (4th ed.). S. Fischer Verlag.

Vygotsky, L. S. (1985). Die psychischen System. In J. Lompscher (Ed.), *Lew Wygotsky: Arbeiten zur theoretischen und methodologischen Problemen der Psychologie* (pp. 319–353). Pahl-Rugenstein Verlag.

Vygotsky, L. S. (1994a). The problem of the cultural development of the child. In R. Van Der Veer & J. Valsiner (Eds.), *The Vygotsky reader* (pp. 57–73). Blackwell.

Vygotsky, L. S. (1994b). The problem of the environment. In R. Van Der Veer & J. Valsiner (Eds.), *The Vygotsky reader* (pp. 338–355). Blackwell.

Vygotsky, L. S. (1994c). The socialist alteration of man. In R. Can der Veer & J. Valsiner (Eds.), *The Vygotsky reader* (pp. 175–184). Blackwell.

Vygotsky, L. S. (2003). Dynamik und Struktur der Persönlichkeit des Jugendlichen. In J. Lompscher (Ed.), *Lew Wygotsky: Arbeiten zur Entwicklung der Persönlichkeit* (pp. 624–659). Pahl-Rugenstein Verlag.

Wagoner, B. (2009). The experimental methodology of constructive microgenesis. In J. Valsiner, N. Chaudhary, M. C. D. P. Lyra, & P. C. M. Molenaar (Eds.), *Dynamic process methodology in the social and developmental sciences* (pp. 99–121). Springer.

Wagoner, B. (2010). Remembering methodology: Experimenting with Bartlett. In A. Toomela & J. Valsiner (Eds.), *Methodological thinking in psychology, 60 years gone astray?* (pp. 145–187). IAP.

Wertheimer, M. (1938). *Gestalt psychology. Source book of gestalt psychology*. Harcourt, Brace and.

Chapter 3
Toward Alternative Validity Criteria for the Qualitative Study of Leadership

The Domination of Quantitative Psychology in the Study of Leadership

In previous chapters, we argued for the necessity of a social, dialogical, and interpretive theory of leadership, grounded in Social and Cultural Psychology (von Fircks, 2024a, b). Drawing from the works of Boesch, Lewin, and Vygotsky, we developed a synthesized model aimed at analyzing leadership phenomena dynamically. This model aligns closely with Lewin's field theoretical methodology (Lewin, 1982a) and serves as a qualitative tool designed to explore how individuals make meaning in the workplace.

The central question driving our research remains: How can we situate the leader within a field-theoretical context, considering the broader organizational system that requires leadership? Our focus is on how leaders and followers co-construct meaning-making patterns and interact within their shared experiential action fields.

This model firmly places us within the realm of qualitative leadership research (see Klenke, 2008a, 2008b). There is already significant work highlighting the potential of qualitative approaches in leadership studies (Klenke, 2008c). Therefore, we aim to position our approach within this body of qualitative leadership literature. In doing so, we will also examine the advantages of qualitative methods compared to the more traditional, quantitative approaches, which continue to dominate much of the leadership research landscape (Klenke, 2008c, 2008d).

In order to contextualize our qualitative approach, it is essential to briefly discuss the historical roots of leadership research, which quickly became dominated by quantitative psychology. This will provide a foundation for understanding the benefits and necessity of a qualitative framework in the study of leadership.

> Historically, leadership research has been grounded in the objectivist, positivist, quantitative paradigm, since the inception of leadership studies as a field of scholarly inquiry. (…)

E. Freiherr von Fircks, *Studying Leadership from a Microgenetic Perspective*, Methodologies in Developmental Sciences,
https://doi.org/10.1007/978-3-031-90214-7_3

> During the history of the discipline, research has relied heavily, at times almost exclusively, on the traditional social science repertoire of quantitative methodologies to help us identify and understand leadership problems and develop solutions that can be scientifically tested, verified and replicated. (Klenke, 2008a, p. 3)

When examining the most prominent leadership theories (Kauffeld, 2019), we observe the dominance of transactional and transformational leadership (Kuantan, 2015). Interestingly, transformational leadership was originally developed using qualitative methodologies, rooted in Downton's (1973) study of revolutionary leadership and Burns' (1978) work as a presidential biographer. Burns, in particular, helped popularize transformational leadership within the broader research community. A political scientist influenced by the Civil Rights Movement and prominent leaders like Franklin D. Roosevelt and John F. Kennedy, Burns viewed transformational leaders as those who sought to reshape the meaning of work, promoting shared values and higher visions to motivate their followers (Bass, 1999).

Bass (1985) later adapted this concept by creating a questionnaire to measure both transformational and transactional leadership. He refined transformational leadership into a four-factor model, which included the scales of *Intellectual Stimulation, Individualized Consideration, Idealized Influence*, and *Inspirational Motivation* (Bass & Avolio, 1993). The introduction of this questionnaire allowed management and research scholars to measure leadership through a positivist lens, correlating leadership styles—such as transformational and transactional leadership—with job-related outcomes like job satisfaction, performance, commitment, and well-being (Dumdum et al., 2013; Wang et al., 2011).

What becomes clear from these developments is that Burns initially approached leadership through a qualitative lens, analyzing the lives and works of specific political figures in a holistic manner. However, Bass, a quantitative psychologist, appropriated this work to measure leadership on a broader scale. He created a questionnaire based on Burns' qualitative insights but relied on factor analysis and statistical consistency to validate the results. While this approach allowed for large-scale measurement, it also distanced the research from its original qualitative roots, which were focused on understanding leadership within specific historical and contextual settings.

The Qualitative Turn in Leadership Research

With the introduction of leadership questionnaires, qualitative research on leadership did not disappear but was largely relegated to the background within the broader leadership research domain (Conger, 1998). This shift is somewhat surprising, given the inherent limitations of quantitative approaches in capturing the complexity of social phenomena like leadership. As Klenke (2008a) notes, quantitative methods often fall short in fully addressing the nuanced, dynamic, and context-dependent nature of leadership interactions.

> Although quantitative methods are ideal for testing hypotheses, especially with large samples, permitting the development of sophisticated causal models and allowing for replicability across settings, they are poorly suited to help us understand the meanings leaders and follower ascribe to events in their lives and the success or failure in organizations. As a result, until fairly recently, qualitative studies in leadership remained relatively rare (at least as measured by published journal articles) (…). Instead, the paradigm that still guides leadership research is the quantitative model heavily subscribing to survey and questionnaire research as the dominant data collection. (p. 4)

The issue with the quantitative approach to leadership research can be understood as follows: First, it predominantly adheres to the hypothetico-deductive model of science. In this approach, researchers postulate a specific potential relationship—such as between transformational leadership and self-reported job performance—based on pre-existing theories (Bono & Judge, 2004). Those studies have often shown that transformational leadership correlates strongly with self-reported job performance, providing incremental value over transactional leadership.

The typical methodology involves administering pre-defined items in specific organizational settings, such as a factory or business, where followers evaluate their supervisors' leadership style and report on factors like well-being and job satisfaction. Researchers often rely on standardized questionnaires, which have been validated through various measures such as factor and convergent validity, and tested for reliability. As a result, these questionnaires are widely used without significant adjustments to fit the unique context of each study.

This reliance on standard instruments, such as the *Multifactor Leadership Questionnaire (MLQ)*, often leads to a one-size-fits-all approach. Researchers adopt the questionnaire to fit their hypotheses, but rarely tailor the items to the specific leadership context under investigation. In other words, the assumed clarity and applicability of the questionnaire items are taken for granted, regardless of the nuances or specificities of the leadership environment.

For example, if we wanted to investigate the relationship between transformational leadership and employee commitment, we might distribute the MLQ (e.g., Rowold, 2005) in a given organization. The participants would then respond to standardized items, which may or may not capture the full range of their experiences or the specific characteristics of leadership within that organization. Below is given an extract of questions from the MLQ:

My leader helps me to develop my strengths
My leader provides appealing images about what we can do.
My leader lets me know how I am doing.
My leader helps me find meaning in my work.
My leader gives personal attention to others who seem rejected.

The issue with surveys and questionnaires is that participants often have highly personal interpretations of the items presented to them (Rosenbaum & Valsiner, 2011). In my earlier quantitative research (von Fircks, 2020), I found that participants frequently asked whether specific experiences aligned with the meaning of a particular item. This indicates a desire to negotiate the meaning of the items and engage in an open dialogue with the researcher to explore and transform their own meaning-making patterns. However, standard quantitative research practice discourages such dialogue. Researchers are advised not to get personally involved or clarify participants' questions (Bühner, 2011). As a result, researchers typically respond by telling participants to answer as best they can, relying on their initial interpretation of the item. This approach, however, assumes that all participants will understand the questionnaire items in a clear and uniform way, which is highly unlikely (Valsiner, 2017).

In fact, every question is inherently ambiguous (Bruner, 1986) and can be interpreted from multiple perspectives. Meaning is dynamic and emerges through the translation from one meaning-making pattern to another (Bruner, 1996, 1997). For example, when a wife asks her husband whether he has cleaned the house, the question is ambiguous. The husband may respond that he has, yet the wife's follow-up question, "What did you do?" implies that his cleaning efforts were insufficient. The question contains a subtext: a layer of meaning that goes beyond the literal words. Similarly, if a follower asks their leader for more help, the subtext implies dissatisfaction with previous support. The request isn't just for more assistance, but also carries an expectation that the leader should understand where previous efforts fell short.

In cases like these, meaning is negotiated through dialogue, as the ambiguity of the question invites both parties to reflect on their interpretations. For a researcher to fully capture this process, they must engage with the ambiguity and help the participants unpack the underlying meanings. This is where Cultural Psychology of Semiotic Dynamics becomes crucial (Valsiner, 2014, 2019, 2021). In this framework, research is designed to illustrate how meaning-making emerges between multiple agents. The researcher can play an active role in facilitating this process by helping participants become aware of their habitual interpretation patterns. This is achieved through the creation of "meta-signs," or reflective tools that allow participants to step back and examine their current perspectives, fostering deeper understanding between themselves and others.

By recognizing and embracing the inherent ambiguity in questions, qualitative research can facilitate a richer, more meaningful exchange between leaders and followers, allowing for a more dynamic investigation of leadership phenomena than rigid, pre-defined questionnaires typically permit.

Let's consider a leadership example to illustrate this point. Take the item: "My leader helps me to develop my strengths." The meaning of each word—"help," "develop," and "strength"—is inherently open to interpretation and must be negotiated. The complexity of psychological operations is best understood through dialogue (Mead, 1934/2015). For instance, the participant might answer affirmatively, stating, "Yes, my leader helps me develop my strengths." However, they might also express, "But what I truly want from my leader is fair and equal pay," indicating a shift in their personal priorities (von Fircks, 2020). This reflects the interplay between the external roles assigned to a person (the leader helping with strengths) and the individual's personal appropriation of those roles, as described by Dialogical Self Theory (Hermans, 1999, 2001).

In this example, while the participant agrees that their leader helps them develop strengths, their primary concern may not be about strength development at all. Rather, it is about their unmet needs and goals, such as equitable compensation. The original question, meant to explore leadership in terms of personal development, is transformed into a dialogue about the broader conditions of leadership, including fairness in pay. The participant might view strength development as hypocritical, asking, "Why develop strengths if those strengths aren't financially appreciated?" As a result, the question shifts to an investigation of developing strengths under fair and equal working conditions.

A researcher, in this scenario, must be sensitive to the participant's transformation of meaning and explore why the original question was reframed. Understanding this shift is vital for producing context-sensitive, interventional knowledge. By following the participant's line of thought, the researcher may uncover crucial preconditions for effective leadership, such as the fact that followers only take leadership actions seriously once fundamental conditions, like fair compensation, are met.

This dynamic approach allows for a more comprehensive study of interconnected psychological functions—leadership, compensation, frustration, and disappointment—which together form a complex web of experiences. These functions cannot be fully understood in isolation. Rather, their interrelatedness must be examined if leadership is to be sustained and meaningful in real-world settings. Such a holistic perspective provides deeper insights into how leadership unfolds in practice, beyond the scope of standardized questionnaires.

The Dialogical Nature of Research Emphasized

In the context of hypothetical or real dialogue, we can observe how various psychic functions—such as disappointment, frustration, emotions, and appraisal mechanisms—interact and impact each other. These elements collectively contribute to broader psychological processes. A dialogical approach enables us to study the person holistically, rather than reducing them to isolated psychological operations. By exploring why a person perceives their leader as only valuing their strengths when they align with economic interests, we can generate targeted interventional knowledge. This approach considers the individual's specific situation and cultural context, rather than detaching the psychological phenomenon from its social and cultural origins—a common practice in quantitative psychology (Valsiner, 2017).

In the quantitative approach, the context in which a survey item is interpreted is often ignored. Items are presented in isolation, bracketing out the crucial social and cultural background that informs the psychological operation in question. This is problematic, as all psychological functions have social roots (Valsiner, 2014, 2019, 2021), a reality often overlooked in traditional psychological research. Even individuals who withdraw from society, such as ascetics, maintain some form of dialogue—whether with nature, the cosmos, or spiritual texts like Laozi's (von Fircks, 2023a, 2023b, 2023c). Therefore, experience is always embedded in a cultural and social context, which is a complex but essential element of understanding psychological phenomena.

By disregarding these contextual dimensions, quantitative methods risk producing knowledge that is disconnected from the natural environment in which person-centered psychological processes unfold (von Fircks, 2024c). Once we understand the complexity of a psychological experience within its social and cultural setting, leaders and followers can engage in a meaningful dialogue to negotiate a shared narrative. This narrative will shape their future actions and experiences together (Raia, 2020). Meaning, in this sense, is always a product of negotiation between multiple individuals, evolving over time as circumstances change.

This understanding leads to the conclusion that we must exercise great caution when using quantitative methods, especially in context-sensitive fields like leadership. Quantitative approaches are not designed to account for the nuances of specific situations, which is a significant flaw given that all psychological phenomena are inherently context-bound (Bruner, 1986). This is particularly true in organizational settings, where leaders and followers must continually adapt to changing market conditions and adjust their conduct accordingly (as discussed in Chap. 1).

In raising these critiques, I align with others in the field, such as Klenke (2008a), who has noted similar limitations with quantitative methods in leadership research.

> However, quantitatively generated leadership descriptors often fail to lead to an understanding of the deeper structures of the phenomenon we study. (…) Qualitative leadership studies, when conducted with the same degree of rigor and concern for validity and quality, have several distinct advantages over quantitative approaches by offering more opportunities to explore leadership phenomena in depth, do so longitudinally and answer 'why' types of questions as opposed to 'what' and 'how' types of questions answered by quantitative research. (p. 5)

Having highlighted the limitations of quantitative research, we can now attempt to define the nature and significance of qualitative research in the study of leadership. Our hypothetical example, in which we deconstructed a survey item and used it as a starting point for an open interview, illustrates that qualitative research is fundamentally situated within the realm of meaning-making (see also Bruner, 1996, 1997). This meaning-making process is critical because it interrelates with other psychic functions of the individual, emphasizing the interconnectedness of these functions. This interconnectedness shapes not only present actions but also future ones.

In essence, qualitative research focuses on investigating how meaning is negotiated, understood, and transformed. This approach is particularly important in leadership studies, where the negotiation of meaning often involves multiple individuals or systems. Leadership settings are inherently complex, with leaders and followers constantly interacting and impacting one another. Thus, qualitative research allows for the exploration of how meaning is co-constructed and evolves in these dynamic interpersonal and organizational environments.

In short, qualitative research goes beyond merely identifying relationships between variables; it seeks to understand the deeper, context-specific processes that drive human conduct, making it an invaluable tool for studying leadership in a more nuanced and holistic way.

Qualitative Research Can Establish Psychological Lawfulness

In the realm of qualitative research, our objective extends beyond merely understanding or making sense of participants' conduct and experiences. We can also deduce intra-systemic laws that govern these phenomena. The traditional dichotomy that contrasts qualitative and quantitative research—where only the latter is viewed as capable of establishing psychological laws based on the hypothetico-deductive model of science (positivism)—is a misleading oversimplification. Researchers over the past few decades (Lamiell, 1998, 2003, 2024; von Fircks, 2024d) have demonstrated that methods such as experiments, interviews, and field studies—often involving only a few participants or even a single individual—can contribute to the construction of psychological laws.

This misconception has led to a false association: qualitative research is seen solely as a means to understand psychological phenomena, while quantitative research is viewed as the domain for establishing lawfulness. However, as Lamiell (2024) and other scholars (Valsiner, 2017) argue, psychological laws must be explored within in-depth settings that typically include a limited number of participants. For instance, notable findings within Cultural Psychology, such as the Dialogical Self Theory (Hermans, 1999, 2001), reveal that the human Self comprises multiple I-positions that interact based on environmental triggers. Hermans and his colleagues have successfully demonstrated that individuals use interpersonal dialogue for intrapersonal purposes.

What is particularly striking about these findings, and others in Cultural Psychology, such as Valsiner's exploration of the semiotic structuring of experience, is that they do not rely on large sample sizes or population generalizations derived from hypothesis testing. Instead, researchers like Hermans (2001), Marsico (Español & Marsico, 2021), Tateo (2018), and Valsiner (2021) focus on psychological phenomena in their natural contexts, allowing them to investigate the interconnectedness of psychological functions with a smaller participant base.

To illustrate this point, Lewin (1927) argued that establishing the law of gravitation does not require dropping a stone a thousand times; rather, observing the same stone a few times is sufficient. A similar approach can be applied to the study of leadership, where we seek to identify intra-systemic and inter-systemic laws that guide the interactions between leaders and followers in their daily experiences. Our focus is on the interconnected psychological functions that shape experiences and impact the actions taken, which can have significant implications for the leader-follower relationship.

Every personal experience yields consequences not only for the individual's self but also for the interpersonal system to which they belong (Lang, 1992, 1993). As demonstrated in previous chapters, research approaches such as field theory (Lewin,

1982b) can elucidate the unique tensions arising between intra-personal and interpersonal systems, potentially leading to the identification of lawful principles for the study of leadership and beyond.

Qualitative Research and Alternatives to Validity and Reliability: Trustworthiness and Authenticity

Yet, we must acknowledge that quantitative research has become widely established due to its clearly defined criteria for validity (Bühner, 2011). These criteria enable researchers to adhere to scientific protocols that guide their inquiries over time. As a result, quantitative researchers can follow basic rules to ensure quality standards, which reinforces the credibility of their scientific undertakings. The primary criteria for quantitative research include objectivity, reliability, and validity (Hughes, 2018). Additionally, within the realm of validity, quantitative researchers propose various notions, such as factor validity, content validity, and convergent validity, among many other forms of validity (Bühner, 2011). Major textbooks on quantitative research designs and statistics (Bortz & Schuster, 2010) provide clear-cut scripts that offer guidelines on how to ensure the validity of scientific inquiries.

However, the criteria for validity in qualitative research are somewhat underdefined. There is no consensus on how qualitative research should be conducted validly within the scientific community, leading many different communities to interpret the term in various ways (Klenke, 2008b). While the criteria for quantitative psychology are clear and accompanied by illustrative instructions, qualitative psychology lacks agreement on how to define validity. Consequently, we also miss the necessary scripts and instructions for conducting qualitative research to high-quality standards. This necessitates that any form of qualitative research in psychology must redefine its validity criteria and justify them against its theoretical orientation. While we can draw inspiration from different qualitative research strands and paradigms, we must also adjust them to meet the goals of our specific research undertaking. Among the major qualitative quality criteria are authenticity and trustworthiness, which deserve attention in this chapter. These two quality criteria draw inspiration from psychological research within constructivism (Rolfe, 2006), which rejects the importance of positivist criteria of validity and reliability.

What do these terms mean, and how can we use them in our present study? This implies that we should not only become aware of the underlying assumptions regarding what constitutes credible science for our research but also how we might strive to achieve those standards throughout our study. Furthermore, we are compelled to link these quality criteria to our theoretical orientation—specifically, field-theoretical and cultural-psychological frameworks—to investigate how they interrelate.

> Drawing from the epistemological assumptions associated with constructivism (…) [a]ccording to the authors, the idea of discovering truth through measures of reliability and

> validity is replaced by the idea of trustworthiness. (...) Research reports aiming at [trustworthiness] must address the following issues: (1) the theoretical positioning of the researchers which includes the ontological, epistemological assumptions as well as the values (axiology), motives and personal history he or she brings to the study; (2) the congruence between method and methodology; (3) strategies employed to establish rigor and quality; and (4) the analytic lens through which the data are examined (...). (Klenke, 2008b, pp. 38–39)

These are critical criteria for a qualitative study within the domain of leadership. A researcher seeking to investigate leadership from an in-depth perspective must consider these various criteria. In the second chapter of our exploration of potential meta-theories suitable for an intensive study of leadership, we identified several cultural-psychological models, including Boesch's Symbolic Action Theory (Boesch, 1991, 1998, 2005). Analyzing leadership interactions from a symbolic action theoretical perspective necessitates the following considerations: our theoretical positioning regarding leadership interactions is grounded in cultural-psychological premises. With this in mind, our theory of reality (ontology) is semiotic, meaning that meaning is co-constructed based on shared social meaning-making patterns that are personally appropriated.

This perspective is complemented by a specific theory of knowledge, particularly emerging knowledge (epistemology). Here, Symbolic Action Theory, as inspired by Boesch (1998), seeks to gain insight into everyday interactions among multiple individuals, emphasizing the significance of introspection (experience) in relation to observable forms of conduct (extrospection) (von Fircks, 2024e). Therefore, it is essential for a cultural-psychological meta-theory to analyze experience and conduct in conjunction, a fundamental value (axiology) that must be respected in research aimed at capturing the complexity of human leadership. The personal history of the researcher (in this case, myself) reflects discontentment with the predominant research traditions in the field of leadership, which often overlook the individual and their quest for meaning and meaningfulness.

As we have not yet reached the methods and methodology section of our study, we will refrain from elaborating on these criteria extensively. This detailed exploration will be conducted in the subsequent chapter of the manuscript. Our aim here is to illustrate how qualitative research can adhere to quality criteria for robust science and how these differ from traditional quantitative quality criteria, such as validity and reliability. This approach can also be applied to other criteria. For instance, the discussion of the analytical lens through which data are examined—identified as the fourth criterion by Klenke (2008b)—is rooted in a cultural-psychological framework. We might explore how a psychoanalytic lens would interpret the same data, discussing the convergences and divergences that arise. This approach allows for a holistic interpretation of the data and highlights potential blind spots associated with the meta-theory applied to the analysis. Moreover, it may lead to the integration of cultural-psychological and psychoanalytic research traditions, ultimately contributing to a unified methodology for future studies in the domain of leadership. This serves as another example of how validity criteria can be applied in ways fundamentally different from those in quantitative psychology, which we will examine more explicitly in the following chapters.

However, trustworthiness and its various pillars are not the only quality criteria essential for conducting rigorous qualitative research. We must also address the concept of authenticity, which plays a significant role in constructivist research traditions.

> [A]uthencity as a quality criterion is consistent with the relativist view that research accounts do not more than represent a sophisticated but temporary consensus of views about what is considered to be true. Authenticity, according to the authors, demonstrated whether researchers can show that they have represented a range of different realities, also known as fairness defined as balanced view that represents all constructions and the values that undergird them (…). Research should also help members of the scholarly community to develop more sophisticated understandings of the phenomenon being studied (*ontological authenticity*), be shown to have helped members appreciate the viewpoints of others than themselves (*educative authenticity*) leading to improved understanding of constructions of others, to have stimulated to some kind of action (*catalytic authenticity*) providing value to practitioners and facilitating the practical use of research findings, and to have empowered members to act (*tactical authenticity*). (Klenke, 2008b, p. 39, original emphasis)

Klenke (2008b), in alignment with other researchers such as Rolfe (2006), emphasizes that trustworthiness is not the only critical criterion for qualitative studies. Klenke does not merely list the essential pillars of authenticity; she also provides guidelines for researchers on how to ensure authenticity as a quality marker in qualitative research. In this section, we will focus on two of these quality markers and explore them in relation to our cultural-psychological theoretical framework. While we will not address every criterion in detail—reserving that for the methodology section in the upcoming chapters—our goal is to illustrate how we can enrich our understanding of the phenomenon under investigation through the lens of leader-follower interactions.

Applying our cultural-psychological meta-theory is likely to challenge and refine our theoretical orientation, making it essential to adapt our framework for future studies. This approach allows us to deepen our understanding not only of the scientific phenomenon but also of the cultural-psychological lens we apply, potentially enhancing its utility for subsequent researchers and their inquiries (ontological authenticity).

Furthermore, in adhering to the criterion of catalytic authenticity, we must examine the consequences of our research, specifically whether our findings have prompted any actions. For instance, we may discover that a leader fails to help an employee recognize their own fantasms and understand how these fantasms connect to the myth-like structure of the working environment. This realization might lead to various outcomes: the employee could confront the leader to request a different type of guidance, choose to leave the organization, or be transferred to another department to work under a new supervisor. Such insights empower the employee to act more strategically in fulfilling their needs, which aligns with the pillar of tactical authenticity in qualitative research.

These examples illustrate that qualitative research does not operate under the premise of *"anything goes"* regarding quality criteria. Instead, it is entirely feasible to uphold scientific rigor and quality markers in qualitative research within the realm of leadership. However, achieving this requires researchers to make their criteria explicit and engage in thorough discussions about them—an undertaking that is often overlooked in qualitative leadership studies (Klenke, 2008b, 2008c). We will address this in greater detail in the methodology section of the present work.

> Taken together, [the discussions of quality criteria within qualitative research] are intended to promote the understanding of the ontological and epistemological bases of qualitative research methodologies, their interrelationships, and linkages to research methods and the concomitant ethical issues that arise from qualitative research. Overall, the aim of qualitative research is to understand how the world is socially constructed by its participants and what meanings they ascribe to them. The notion of the world being socially constructed implies that individuals inhabit a social, personal and relational world that is complex, layered and can be constructed from multiple perspectives. (Klenke, 2008b, pp. 53–54)

Beyond the Use of Questionnaires: Conducting Valuable Leadership Research from a Qualitative Perspective

Having outlined some of the major premises of qualitative research in the study of leadership, we can draw several conclusions:

A. Quantitative research in the leadership domain primarily operates within the positivist paradigm, meaning that researchers adhering to this scientific tradition rely on the hypothetico-deductive model. In this framework, the rejection or non-rejection of hypotheses takes center stage, often stifling the potential for open and iterative research processes. One of the primary methods employed in quantitative psychology is the use of questionnaires, where researchers present items without taking a stance or answering questions posed by participants. This approach precludes meaningful dialogue that could facilitate in-depth exploration and transformation of meaning-making patterns. Given that leadership is a highly context-sensitive and social phenomenon, it becomes essential to negotiate meaning. Thus, the qualitative research paradigm may be more suitable for studying leader-follower interactions.

B. Qualitative research is not only pivotal for understanding psychological phenomena but also for establishing some degree of lawfulness within psychology, particularly at the intersection of psychology and leadership. Lawfulness is not exclusive to quantitative inquiry; it can also emerge from in-depth studies of psychological phenomena. Cultural Psychology and the Dialogical Self Theory are notable examples that demonstrate this potential. By integrating this cultural-psychological research tradition, leadership studies can leverage the tension between inter-systemic and intra-systemic psychological operations. Qualitative leadership research and the establishment of psychological laws are not mutually exclusive concepts.

C. It is important to note that qualitative research in the leadership domain does not operate under the premise of "anything goes." Instead, qualitative studies adhere to established criteria for good and appropriate science, incorporating various facets of validity and reliability derived from quantitative psychology. However, qualitative research in leadership can also employ concurrent quality markers such as trustworthiness and authenticity, which are informed by social constructivism. These terms come with adaptable guidelines for ensuring rigor and scientific quality that must align with the chosen meta-theory. For instance, to ensure authenticity in a qualitative study of leadership, researchers must consider how their data might empower participants to enact change in their life-space (experiential unit), thereby significantly altering leader-follower interactions. A notable issue in previous qualitative leadership research has been the reluctance of researchers to adopt explicit quality markers or to do so only implicitly.

In this chapter, we have illuminated some potential advantages of qualitative research in the study of leadership compared to quantitative approaches. We have also set the stage for our empirical study by presenting quality criteria that we intend to adhere to throughout the empirical sections of this book. This foundational understanding will be further developed in the methodology chapter, where we will explore how to effectively implement these quality markers. For now, we recognize that qualitative research enables us to study context-sensitive phenomena such as leadership in depth, and it can be conducted from a rigorous scientific perspective that does not need to rely solely on quantitative validity criteria.

References

Bass, B. M. (1985). *Leadership and performance beyond expectations* (1st ed.). New-York Free Press.

Bass, B. M. (1999). Two decades of research and development in transformational leadership. *European Journal of Work and Organizational Psychology, 8*(1), 9–32. https://doi.org/10.1080/135943299398410

Bass, B. M., & Avolio, B. J. (1993). Transformational leadership and organizational culture. *Public Administration Quarterly, 17*(1), 112–121.

Boesch, E. E. (1991). *Symbolic action theory and cultural psychology*. Springer.

Boesch, E. E. (1998). *Sehnsucht: Von der Suche nach Glück und Sinn [Longing: On the search of joy and meaning]*. Huber.

Boesch, E. E. (2005). *Von Kunst bis Terror: Über den Zwiespalt in der Kultur [From art to terror: On the cleavage of culture]*. Vandenhoeck & Ruprecht.

Bono, J. E., & Judge, T. A. (2004). Personality and transformational and transactional leadership: A meta-analysis. *Journal of Applied Psychology, 89*(5), 901.

Bortz, J., & Schuster, C. (2010). Faktorenanalyse. In J. Bortz & C. Schuster (Eds.), *Springer-Lehrbuch. Statistik für Human- und Sozialwissenschaftler* (pp. 385–433). Springer-Verlag.

Bruner, J. (1986). *Actual minds, possible worlds. The Jerusalem-Harvard lectures*. Harvard University Press.

Bruner, J. (1996). *The culture of education. Harvard University Press*. https://doi.org/10.2307/j.ctv136c601

Bruner, J. (1997). *Sinn, Kultur und Ich-Identität*. Carl Auer.

Bühner, M. (2011). *Einführung in die Test-und Fragebogenkonstruktion* (Vol. 4033). Pearson Deutschland GmbH.

Burns, G. P. (1978). *The principles of leadership*. ERICH.

Conger, J. A. (1998). Qualitative research as the cornerstone methodology for understanding leadership. *The Leadership Quarterly, 9*(1), 107–121. https://doi.org/10.1016/S1048-9843(98)90044-3

Downton, J. V. (1973). *Rebel leadership: Commitment and charisma in the revolutionary process*. Free Press.

Dumdum, U.R., Lowe, K.B. and Avolio, B.J. (2013), "A Meta-Analysis of Transformational and Transactional Leadership Correlates of Effectiveness and Satisfaction: An Update and Extension", Transformational and Charismatic Leadership: The Road Ahead 10th Anniversary Edition (Monographs in Leadership and Management, Vol. 5), Emerald Group Publishing Limited, Leeds, pp. 39-70. https://doi.org/10.1108/S1479-357120130000005008

Español, A., & Marsico, G. (*2021*). Psychology of borders: An integral proposal to understand border phenomena in human life. *Theory & Psychology, 31*(5), 665–674. https://doi.org/10.1177/09593543211002561. Anniversary edition (Vol. 5, pp. 39–70). Emerald Group Publishing Limited.

Fircks, E. (2024a). Towards a theoretical understanding of culture and leadership [Manuscript submitted for publication]. In E. von Fircks (Ed.), *Culture and Leadership: From Approximation Towards Symbiosis*. IAP.

Fircks, E. (2024b). Between Lewin and Vygotsky: Understanding leader-follower interactions through a cultural psychological lens [Manuscript submitted for publication]. In E. von Fircks (Ed.), *Culture and leadership: From approximation towards symbiosis*. IAP.

Fircks, E. (2024c). *Learning with William Stern. Personology for future*. IAP.

Fircks, E. (2024d). Raising Questions with Lamiell about future research directions of critical personalism: A book review essay. *Integrative Psychological and Behavioral Science*, 1–11.

Fircks, E. (2024e). *Conservativism: A cultural-psychological exploration*. Springer.

Hermans, H. J. (2001). The construction of a personal position repertoire: Method and practice. *Culture & Psychology, 7*(3), 323–366. https://doi.org/10.1177/1354067X0173005

Hermans, H. J. M. (1999). Dialogical thinking and self-innovation. *Culture & Psychology, 5*(1), 67–87. https://doi.org/10.1177/1354067X9951004

Hughes, D. J. (2018). Psychometric validity: Establishing the accuracy and appropriateness of psychometric measures. In *The Wiley handbook of psychometric testing: A multidisciplinary reference on survey, scale, and test development* (pp. 751–779). Wiley.

Kauffeld, S. (2019). *Arbeits-, Organisations-und Personalpsychologie für Bachelor*. Springer.

Klenke, K. (2008a). Qualitative research as paradigm. In K. Klenke (Ed.), *Qualitative research in the study of leadership* (pp. 3–29). Emerald.

Klenke, K. (2008b). Qualitative research as paradigm. In K. Klenke (Ed.), *Qualitative research as a method* (pp. 31–55). Emerald.

Klenke, K. (2008c). Case studies in leadership research. In K. Klenke (Ed.), *Qualitative research as a -method* (pp. 57–84). Emerald.

Klenke, K. (2008d). Epilogue. In K. Klenke (Ed.), *Qualitative research as a -method* (pp. 367–384). Emerald.

Kuantan, P. (2015). Transactional or transformational leadership: Which works best for now. *International Journal of Industrial Management, 22*(89), 28–26. https://doi.org/10.1142/S0219649215500144

Lamiell, J. T. (1998). 'Nomothetic' and 'Idiographic' contrasting Windelband's understanding with contemporary usage. *Theory & Psychology, 8*(1), 23–38. https://doi.org/10.1177/0959354398081002

Lamiell, J. T. (2003). *Beyond individual and group differences: Human individuality, scientific psychology, and William Stern's critical personalism*. Sage.

Lamiell, J. T. (2024). *Primer in critical personalism: A framework for reviving psychological inquiry and for grounding a socio-cultural ethos*. Routledge.

Lang, A. (1992). On the knowledge in things and places. In M. von Cranach, W. Doise, & G. Mugny (Eds.), *Social representations and the social basis of knowledge* (pp. 76–83). Hans Huber.
Lang, A. (1993). Non-Cartesian artefacts in dwelling activities: Step towards a semiotic ecology. *Schweizerische Zeitschrift Für Psychologie, 52*(2), 138–147. Retrieved from http://www.lang-papers.org/pap2/1993-01noncartesartefact.htm
Lewin, K. (1927). Gesetz und Experiment in der Psychologie [Law and experiment in psychology]. *Symposion, 375–421.*
Lewin, K. (1982a). Formalisierung und Forschritt in der Psychologie. In C. F. Graumann (Ed.), *Kurt Lewin Werkausgabe: Feldtheorie* (Vol. 4, pp. 41–73). Klett-Cotta.
Lewin, K. (1982b). Konstrukte in der Feldtheorie. In C. F. Graumann (Ed.), *Kurt Lewin Werkausgabe: Feldtheorie* (Vol. 4, pp. 73–87). Klett-Cotta.
Mead, G. H. (2015). *Mind, self & society*. The University of Chicago Press. (Original work published 1934).
Raia, F. (2020). The temporality of becoming: Care as an activity to support the being and becoming of the other. *Mind, Culture, and Activity, 27*(3), 292–312. https://doi.org/10.1080/10749039.2020.1774609
Rolfe, G. (2006). Validity, trustworthiness and rigour: Quality and the idea of qualitative research. *Journal of Advanced Nursing, 53*(3), 304–310.
Rosenbaum, P. J., & Valsiner, J. (2011). The un-making of a method: From rating scales to the study of psychological processes. *Theory & Psychology, 21*(1), 47–65.
Rowold, J. (2005). Multifactor leadership questionnaire. *Psychometric properties of the German translation by Jens Rowold. Redwood City: Mind Garden.*
Tateo, L. (2018). Affective semiosis and affective logic. *New Ideas in Psychology, 48*, 1–11. https://doi.org/10.1016/j.newideapsych.2017.12.004
Valsiner, J. (2014). *An invitation to cultural psychology*. Sage.
Valsiner, J. (2017). *From methodology to methods in human psychology*. Springer.
Valsiner, J. (2019). *Ornamented lives. Advances in cultural psychology*. IAP.
Valsiner, J. (2021). *General human psychology*. Springer.
von Fircks, E. (2023a). Understanding The Process of Taoistic-Informed Mindfulness from a Meadian Perspective. *Integrative Psychological & Behavioral Science*. Advance online publication. https://doi.org/10.1007/s12124-023-09805-9
von Fircks, E. (2023b). Understanding the power of mindfulness from a cultural-psychological perspective. *Culture & Psychology*. Advance online publication. https://doi.org/10.1177/1354067X231201387
von Fircks, E. (2023c). The dialogical self of taoistic dynamics: How scientists and practitioners can trigger the discovery of a harmonious self. *Integrative Psychological & Behavioral Science*. Advance online publication. https://doi.org/10.1007/s12124-023-09807-7
von Fircks, E. (2020). Populismus als mehrdimensionales Konstrukt: Entwicklung und Validierung eines Fragebogens zur Erfassung des populistischen Denkstils. Universität Luxemburg..
von Fircks, E. F. (2020). Existential humanistic leadership (EHL) as a dialogical process: Equality of the non-equality in organizations. *Integrative Psychological and Behavioral Science, 54*(4), 719–741. https://doi.org/10.1007/s12124-020-09550-1
Wang, G., Oh, I. S., Courtright, S. H., & Colbert, A. E. (2011). Transformational leadership and performance across criteria and levels: A meta-analytic review of 25 years of research. *Group & Organization Management, 36*(2), 223–270. https://doi.org/10.1177/1059601111401017

Chapter 4
Case Studies, Autoethnographies, and Ethnographies: Insights for Qualitative Leadership Research

In the theoretical chapters of this work, we have explored our social, dialogical, and interpretative theory of leadership, culminating in a field-theoretical model that synthesizes Boesch's Symbolic Action Theory and Vygotsky's Cultural-Historical Theory. To this end, we have integrated the primary tenets of Boesch's and Vygotsky's theories into a field-theoretical operationalization of leadership, inspired by Kurt Lewin, thereby illuminating the social role of the leader. In the present chapter, we reiterate the research questions that guide our search for appropriate methods and methodology.

Our theoretical elaboration of leadership, grounded in a cultural-psychological perspective, has identified specific social tasks associated with leadership. We are particularly interested in whether empirical studies corroborate our field-theoretical model of leadership. However, our objective extends beyond mere confirmation; we aim to examine how the empirical material enables us to revise the model and enhance our understanding of the social functions of leadership. This iterative approach aligns with the definition of science as a continually evolving process (Elliott, 2012).

Building on the works of Boesch, Lewin, and Vygotsky, we assert that the social role of leadership encompasses several interpersonal functions: First, leaders can help employees become aware of their fantasms—essentially, their underlying inter-connected need structures. Second, leaders can assist employees in selecting appropriate sign- and tool-systems to navigate physical and psychological barriers in their work. Third, leaders play a crucial role in facilitating the monitoring of how the use of signs and tools affects both the body and mind of the individual.

Our study does not merely seek to validate a theoretical framework; it also incorporates an exploratory approach to the qualitative study of leadership. In previous chapters, we laid the groundwork for qualitatively analyzing leadership interactions over time, aiming to illuminate the complex interplay between personal and social dimensions of leadership. Thus, it is essential to elaborate on our methodological

E. Freiherr von Fircks, *Studying Leadership from a Microgenetic Perspective*, Methodologies in Developmental Sciences,
https://doi.org/10.1007/978-3-031-90214-7_4

approach, which aligns with our theoretical orientation. This holistic understanding of validity encompasses the convergence of phenomena and methods that are suitable for comprehensively understanding and measuring those phenomena.

As discussed earlier, this manuscript draws on multiple case studies from both autoethnographic and ethnographic perspectives, featuring two distinct studies. The first study employs an autoethnographic approach to qualitative leadership research, while the second adopts an ethnographic framework. Both studies operate under the principle of method triangulation, where multiple methods are utilized in the empirical exploration of social leadership.

This chapter is organized as follows: First, we will define the autoethnographic case study that has informed the empirical research, arguing for validity criteria that differ from classical psychometric standards within the quantitative social sciences. Second, we will define the ethnographic case study and elucidate its unique validity criteria, which are comparable to those of the autoethnographic approach. Third, we will discuss how the ethnographic and autoethnographic studies have been integrated into a multiple-case study analysis. This three-fold approach will provide two methodological protocols detailing how data were sampled, analyzed, and interpreted from both autoethnographic and ethnographic perspectives, guiding the empirical study's unfolding.

Case Study Research in the Domain of Leadership

We will start to illuminate the notion of *case study* while referring to some of the literature being performed in this domain. The goals of the case study seem to fit our previous operationalization of the social function of leadership. According to Klenke (2008a), we can denote the following:

> It [the case study] is driven by the desire to understand complex social phenomena because the study method allows investigators to retain the holistic and meaningful characteristics of real-life events such as leadership processes. (…) [Yet], [c)ase study research requires clear research questions, a thorough understanding of the extant literature, a well-formulated research design resting on explicit paradigmatic assumptions[.] (Klenke, 2008a, p. 59)

Case study research is particularly well-suited for investigating context-sensitive phenomena, such as leadership (Bryman, 2011; Klenke, 2008a; Parry et al., 2014). This approach enables researchers to understand the dynamics between agents and their specific environments (Cousin, 2005; Stake, 1995). As Boesch (1975) posits, it is essential to unravel ecological and personal determinants to comprehend psychological phenomena. However, case study research does not operate under the premise of anything goes (Gerring, 2006). Instead, it presents a more complex landscape, requiring researchers to navigate various challenges when conducting studies in the social sciences.

Klenke (2008a), along with other scholars (e.g., Stake, 1995), emphasizes that case study researchers must synthesize substantial amounts of data from diverse research methods to achieve a holistic understanding of both intra-personal and inter-personal systems. This often includes longitudinal elements (Eisenhardt, 1989), which allow for an examination of the transformation of psychological phenomena over time. However, research designs that incorporate longitudinal features are typically resource-intensive and place specific demands on the researcher (Klenke, 2008a).

To address these challenges, one effective strategy is to articulate the cognitive, emotional, and motivational strains experienced during the conduct of case studies. This approach enables researchers to adopt a meta-perspective on their roles within the research process. For instance, a researcher engaged in autoethnography may reflect on the emotional burdens they encounter, allowing them to express complex emotions freely and potentially alleviate psychological tension within themselves.

Such a perspective can facilitate future research efforts, aiding in the refinement of methodological protocols for subsequent case studies. After all, the methodological protocol is a key component of any scientific endeavor. In our study, we conceptualize this protocol not as a means to facilitate replication—an almost impossible task in qualitative research (Stroebe & Strack, 2014)—but rather as a framework that elucidates the underlying assumptions guiding our empirical inquiry.

Case-Study Research: Between a Multitude of Definitions

When attempting to scientifically define case studies within the social sciences, researchers encounter a plethora of definitions (Yin, 2012). While acknowledging the significance of these diverse definitions, we find Stake's (1995) approach particularly relevant for this manuscript. Stake differentiates between two types of case studies: *intrinsic case studies* and *instrumental case studies*.

In an intrinsic case study, the researcher aims to gain a deep understanding of a specific historical phenomenon, such as the emergence of leadership in a tennis club over time through various actions and interactions. This approach is inherently idiographic, as researchers strive to explore how leadership unfolds within a unique social and historical context.

Conversely, the instrumental case study seeks a broader understanding of the underlying theories that govern psychological approaches beyond the specific social and historical context in which leadership is examined. This perspective links equally to the concept of *idiographic Wissenschaft* (Stern, 1911), where researchers are encouraged to explore the development of concrete personal and social cases. In this sense, the case study serves an instrumental purpose by elucidating general leadership processes that may contribute to the formulation of leadership theories and generalizations, while still providing an idiographic understanding of leadership behavior in particular social situations.

Lamiell (2024) contends that idiographic research and lawfulness are not inherently opposed; rather, illuminating specific social and personal cases can also lead to the generation and transformation of theoretical frameworks. Thus, as Klenke

(2008a) suggests, there is potential to combine intrinsic and instrumental case studies, enriching the methodological approach to studying leadership.

> Most definitions agree that case studies accomplish a variety of purposes: to provide an in-depth description of a phenomenon, test theory or generate theory. (…) [Researchers argue that] the ultimate aim of case study research is the construction of middle-range explanatory theory where the researcher disaggregates complex contexts into more discrete, carefully defined chunks, and then reintegrates these parts with an explicit analysis of their context. (Klenke, 2008a, p. 60)

The present manuscript seeks to utilize both intrinsic and instrumental approaches to gain a comprehensive understanding of a leadership setting within a specific context while also striving for insights that extend beyond the immediate environment. This dual approach is exemplified by our goal to enhance the theoretical understanding of leadership, particularly through the revision of Lewin's model based on concrete empirical data.

This methodological stance is rooted in the historical context of W. Stern's differential psychological approach—specifically, the psychographic perspective—which emphasizes the study of an individual over time, taking into account various dispositions and their directionality, as well as the scaffolding that impacts these dispositions (see Fig. 4.1). Stern characterizes this form of study as idiographic; however, we align with Lamiell (2024) in asserting that the qualitative analysis of an individual within a defined historical context can also lead to the establishment of specific laws. Thus, the dichotomy between idiographic and nomothetic approaches is artificial. Both scientific objectives can be pursued within a single case study, as demonstrated in Chaps. 5, 6, and 7 of this manuscript, which encompass both the historical understanding of an individual and the underlying lawful principles that inform this understanding.

Nonetheless, Stern's notion of idiographic study lacks an exploration of how dispositions emerge, interact with one another, and transform over irreversible time. His graphical representations tend to be static and present a non-developmental

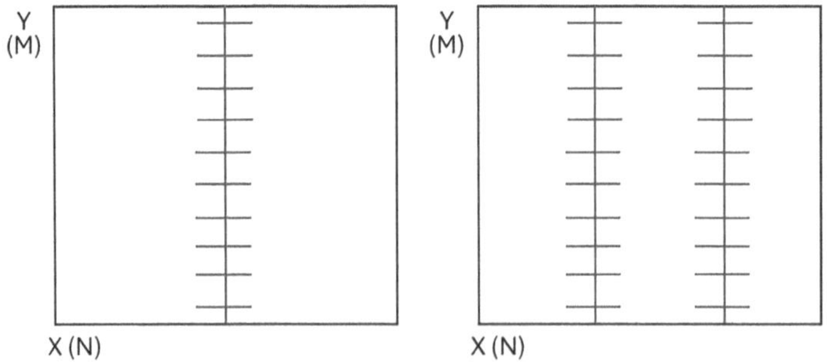

Fig. 4.1 Stern: Stern's notion of idiographic science (Y = axis, M = disposition, X = axis, N = subject)

view of dispositions and their actualization[1]. In this manuscript, we aim to transcend this static perspective by investigating how dispositions arise and become interconnected with existing personal attributes and semiotic resources. This aligns with a microgenetic perspective, as articulated by Wagoner (2009), which focuses on the unfolding of both psychological and non-psychological functions—and which we called action-oriented microgenesis in Chap. 2.

Consequently, it is insufficient to merely illustrate specific dispositions of directionality and scaffolding, as this would result in a superficial analysis of individuals within their contexts. A critical question that must be addressed is how these dispositions emerge in response to the environmental challenges faced by the individual. An individual cannot be understood in isolation from a particular context (Stern, 1911; Eco, 2002). Therefore, psychology and applied psychology must strive to demonstrate how context is incorporated into the analysis and interacts with the individual's intrinsic forces.

The present manuscript centers on the exploration of how theory and methodology can address the challenge of studying leadership in a context-sensitive manner, moving beyond mere scientific utopia. This endeavor directly engages with Valsiner's notion of single-instance analysis, which highlights that generalizations can emerge not solely from individual case studies but rather from the examination of specific situations (Valsiner, 2017).

To achieve this, it is essential to study how the internal system—characterized as inherently open—actualizes itself in response to the influx of environmental field forces. This includes an analysis of how these field forces are personally processed and subsequently externalized, thereby transforming the environment in distinctive ways. Axiomatic to our approach is the recognition that we aim to include the study of context by investigating which environmental field forces interact with the individual being studied, and how these forces are made meaningful or digested on a personal level.

In this framework, we do not seek to analyze merely a single case or instance; rather, we focus on the interplay between the individual (the case) and the specific event or situation. This holistic study of the individual is visually represented in Fig. 4.2. For example, consider the act of eating: food, which exists in the external environment, is consumed by the personal system and then digested. The unique characteristics of the individual—such as allergies, intolerances, and preferences—affect how this food is processed, resulting in specific personal outcomes that can alter the environment in significant ways (e.g., segregation, physical reactions like headaches).

---

[1] It comes not unsurprising that Otto Lipmann (as a friend and colleague of Stern) has used Stern's static conceptualization of psychographic research when investigating psychological and physiological aptitudes for a given job. Here, Lipmann developed so-called Berufspsychogramme, in English work psychograms that he put together by asking employees and supervisors which traits might be best for this or that job. Which resulted in rather static trait lists for specific jobs (Lipmann, 1926). How those dispositions come into being and might be trained was a rather under-estimated question by Lipmann and applied psychology.

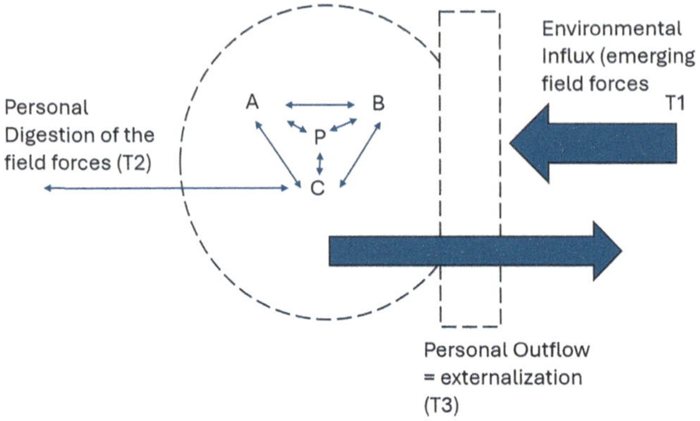

Fig. 4.2 Single case and single event in interaction (A, B, C = elements of the personal system, P = person, T = time) modified after Valsiner (2017, p. 81)

A parallel can be drawn to leadership dynamics. For instance, when a leader instructs a follower to complete a task such as copying documents, the success of this request hinges on the follower's understanding of the task (e.g., knowledge of the copy machine) and their skills in using it. Only when the demand to copy is successfully internalized and linked to the follower's personal system (e.g., "I know where to copy and how to do it") in relation to their own responsibilities (e.g., "I will do it after finishing this project") can the task be externalized effectively. If the follower struggles with the copying process, it may lead to errors that could frustrate the leader, potentially threatening their relationship.

Figure 4.2 illustrates the construction and co-construction of field forces that the individual must navigate. In other words, the individual is portrayed as an active agent, making sense of various field forces and arranging them in a uniquely personal manner. This perspective seeks to challenge monistic doctrines within psychology—specifically, historically materialistic worldviews that reduce the individual to a mere "internalizer" of external forces, which purportedly shape their internal experiences (Leontiev, 1978). Instead, our approach emphasizes the active role of individuals in processing and responding to their environments.

The Role of Theory in the Qualitative Study of Leadership

In this section, we examine the role of theory within qualitative research focused on leadership. As Klenke (2008a) notes, along with several other researchers (George & Bennett, 2005; Woodside & Wilson, 2003), the function of theory must be clearly articulated within the methodological framework employed by a researcher. The significance of theory can differ markedly among researchers (Klenke, 2008a) and across various research traditions (Valsiner, 2017).

For instance, the Grounded Theory approach is often characterized by its empirical orientation, focusing primarily on data collection and analysis without being anchored in stringent theoretical frameworks (Strauss & Corbin, 1994). This exploratory nature allows researchers to derive theory organically from the empirical material itself, often necessitating the bracketing of pre-existing theoretical assumptions (Klenke, 2008b). Conversely, another approach incorporates theory as a tool to evaluate and potentially falsify existing models or hypotheses, aligning closely with positivist methodologies (Johansson, 2007) that test hypotheses through case studies.

Between these two extremes lies a middle-ground methodological approach that recognizes the value of theory while simultaneously leveraging empirical findings to refine theoretical constructs through an iterative process (Klenke, 2008a). In this context, theory serves as a framework for data interpretation (Eisenhardt, 1989), allowing for continuous theory reconstruction based on the insights gained from empirical studies. Klenke (2008a) refers to the former as a purist methodology that views psychological phenomena from a tabula rasa perspective, while the latter is characterized as a generative approach that integrates both theory and empirical findings.

Our methodological approach is fundamentally theory-driven, inspired by the principles of field theory and Cultural Psychology as elaborated in earlier sections. However, we seek to define case study not merely as a tool for confirming or rejecting a predefined model, but as a means to assess whether the empirical study prompts us to revise or extend our initial framework. Consequently, this study can be classified as both theory-driven and iterative, potentially culminating in a new and refined conceptual framework for understanding leadership from a cultural-psychological standpoint. Many researchers view this iterative process as the ultimate objective of case studies: to illuminate historical and social phenomena while also producing a conceptual framework that is applicable across various contexts (Eisenhardt, 1989). As Klenke (2008a) emphasizes:

> The motivation of the use of theory in the earlier stages of a case study is to create an initial theoretical framework which takes into account previous knowledge and which creates a theoretical basis to inform the topics and approach to the early empirical work. (…) Although theory can provide a valuable initial guide, it limits the researcher to focusing on the concepts embedded in the theory, which stifles potential new issues and avenues of exploration. The concept of constant comparison encourages qualitative researcher to preserve a considerable degree of openness to the field data and willingness to modify initial assumptions and theories. (p. 61)

To limit the dangers of a too narrow-minded perspective when examining the empirical data, contradictory findings were incorporated into the interpretation and discussion sections while juxtaposing them with data that aligned more closely with the theoretical orientations previously articulated. Consequently, contradictory findings were particularly emphasized and presented to the audience, discussing their implications for the theory-driven approach. Regarding the notion of theory, we could report that our study was theory-driven while also allowing some space for revising the initial leadership model introduced in the introductory chapters of this manuscript. We acknowledge that we leaned toward a theoretical perspective on qualitative research while attempting to mitigate potential pitfalls when sampling, reporting, analyzing, and interpreting data from a singular standpoint. Thus, our approach can be characterized as both theory-driven and iterative.

However, we must further define the notion of case studies. We are called to clarify our stance on whether the case study was conducted as a single case study, a longitudinal one, or multiple case studies that are compared. While the initial studies within the qualitative domain of leadership were predominantly conducted as single case studies, recent years have witnessed a trend toward more longitudinal case studies and between-case study designs (Antunes & Franco, 2016). In other words, the leadership research domain has become more complex over time, incorporating more sophisticated research designs that extend beyond simple cross-sectional case study approaches (Zheng et al., 2010). This complexity was particularly important for the present manuscript, as we aimed to understand the development and transformation of leadership over irreversible time. Thus, our research did not simply utilize multiple cases—the first autoethnographic and the second ethnographic—but was also inherently longitudinal. This is why we classified our approach as a multiple, longitudinal case study design.

Having clarified the nature of our research design, we now turn to an important pillar of conducting rigorous qualitative research within the study of leadership, which is the selection of cases. For Klenke (2008a), this is a crucial aspect of conducting leadership studies with high-quality standards, and the researcher needs to be explicit about the selection criteria employed. Given that our approach was inherently qualitative in nature, we could not apply the same selection or sampling criteria as those used in positivist research designs (Yin, 2003, 2009). This runs counter to the very definition of qualitative research, which is interested in understanding dynamic social phenomena. Instead, we adopted a structural approach to the selection of case studies (Valsiner & Sato, 2006). According to Klenke (2008a):

> Case selection relies on theoretical or purposive sampling strategies; in other words cases are selected because they may contribute to the emergent theory the investigator is attempting to build, or (...) they may be chosen to fill theoretical categories and provide examples of polar types of or extreme situations. (...) Finally, case study selection is influenced by resources in contacting case participants, traveling to their locations, transcription of interview data, and other practical issues of importance. (Klenke, 2008a, p. 64)

Purposive sampling is thus a critical objective of qualitative research within the domain of leadership studies. This entails our interest in phenomena that could enhance our theoretical understanding of leadership, as elaborated in the introductory chapters of the manuscript. In other words, we aimed to study leader-follower interactions that aligned with our operationalization of leadership as a social, dialogical, and interpretative phenomenon. A significant consideration, as emphasized by other researchers (Yin, 2009), is the accessibility of the field (Bergman Blix & Wettergren, 2015). Such accessibility is crucial for unraveling the depth of the phenomenon we are investigating. Therefore, our approach aimed to provide insights into the structure of interactions within which leaders and followers operated under the premises we identified as vital for any form of leadership.

Indeed, this indicates that we did not intend to sample incidents where leaders and followers reflected on each other separately—such as after an interaction had occurred—but rather to observe contexts in which concrete actions were negotiated to address organizational issues within an enterprise. This focus was central to our current research design; we selected cases to which we had in-depth access, a prerequisite for any contextual study of leadership (Riese, 2019). With this in mind, we employed a case study research design informed by the first author's autoethnographic experience as a tennis instructor.

Autoethnography and the Critical Incident Technique

Before defining autoethnography, I would like to highlight some core features of my job experience. I began my role as a tennis instructor several years ago and changed enterprises twice. Consequently, I was guided by three different leaders in my position. My aim was to illuminate the social, dialogical, and interpretative features of leadership as I experienced them in these three organizations. To scientifically unravel complex leadership conduct and its psychological consequences for the employee (myself in this instance), I reported five critical incidents involving interactions with my leaders (all three of them). These incidents shed light on not only the social, interpretative, and dialogical dimensions of leadership but also how these features evolved over time and across different leaders. After reporting and analyzing the critical incidents within each organization, I conducted comparisons between them, which is an essential characteristic of case study research in the field of leadership (Klenke, 2008a).

The critical incidents were documented using the Critical Incident Technique (CIT) (Chell, 1998; Flanagan, 1954), framed from an autoethnographic perspective. The selection of these incidents adhered to several criteria. First, they were chosen based on their relevance to our objectives, focusing on social, dialogical, and interpretative phenomena of leadership. Additionally, the first criterion of the CIT stipulates that the incidents reflect situations in which success or failure was particularly significant. Second, the critical incidents had to demonstrate an impact on performance; specifically, how they altered the framework for actions related to critical work outcomes. For this study, we aimed to show how the incidents influenced the follower's attitude toward the leader and how they contributed to resolving issues or achieving goals. Third, each incident was observed and described phenomenologically, ensuring clear differentiation between description and analysis. This description required accuracy and detail. Fourth, we included a variety of incidents to diversify the range of scenarios, encompassing both successful and unsuccessful types of leadership in our current study.

Having outlined the general nature of the present study, which comprises multiple case studies that are compared while employing the Critical Incident Technique within an autoethnographic framework, we now need to define autoethnography to fully establish its methodological significance.

> Autoethnography is a research approach that strives to describe personal experience and to analyze it systematically wanting to understand cultural experience as a whole (...). Researchers use premises of autobiography and ethnography when doing autoethnography. Hence, autoethnography describes a method, a process as well as a product of research. (Ellis et al., 2010, p. 345, author's translation)

Numerous autoethnographers (Adams et al., 2015) report that they tend to write retrospectively. In other words, the autoethnographer seeks to reflect on critical moments in their life—or work, in the context of this manuscript—while not only describing those moments but also analyzing and explaining them from both theoretical and practical perspectives (Chang, 2016). The rationale behind this approach is that the autoethnographer aims to make their experiences comprehensible to outsiders of the culture being investigated, as well as to derive systemic generalizations about a cultural-psychological phenomenon (Ellis et al., 2010). This method can be labeled as narrative autoethnography, where past experiences are narrated in a story-like fashion (Adams et al., 2015).

By combining the narrative autoethnographic stance with the Critical Incident Technique (CIT), we described critical leader-follower interactions from a retrospective perspective while attempting to illuminate some developmental aspects within those interactions. Importantly, we distinguished the description phase of the autoethnographically reported critical incidents from the analysis phase, addressing the critique encountered during earlier autoethnographic studies (von Fircks, 2023a, 2023b). Reviewers argued that autoethnography must separate analysis from description, emphasizing the need for researchers to clarify how the analysis was conducted and the premises guiding it. Furthermore, they suggested that the analysis should be structured around specific categories to allow for transparent comprehension of the analytical process. While it is essential that autoethnographies present rich and detailed descriptions in their descriptive phase (Ellis et al., 2010), the analysis must also be guided in a clear and concise manner.

In line with the theoretical frameworks discussed in previous chapters, we developed the following analytical categories to guide the interpretation of the autoethnographic descriptions within the critical incidents. In Table 4.1, we present the autoethnographic analysis scheme, which is informed by the theoretical orientation of this manuscript as outlined in the introductory chapters. The problems and issues could be readily identified from the rich, detailed autoethnographic descriptions—consistent with the CIT—leading to a summary of the overarching goals for the individuals involved. This was complemented by examining the underlying needs of the autoethnographer in a given situation (personal needs), contrasted with the social needs of the organization or leader. This methodological triangulation also

Table 4.1 Autoethnographic analysis scheme

Problem/ Issue	Personal need (follower's needs)	Social needs (organizational needs)	Interactional patterns	Tool-/ Sign-systems	Solution	Feelings

included interview data from colleagues and textual data available on the respective tennis clubs' websites. Interactional patterns, tool and sign systems, as well as solutions and emotional responses, could again be deduced from the autoethnographic reports regarding the critical incidents.

These analytical categories aided us in reliably and validly filling in the field-theoretical models, which we deemed crucial in the introductory chapters of the manuscript, allowing us to dynamically interpret leader-follower interactions. In accordance with Stake (1995), we engaged in a categorical aggregation analysis while striving to unravel the dynamic interrelationships between our categories and how they shaped actions in subsequent moments, as understood through field theory. Furthermore, we aimed to investigate the extent to which the field-theoretical models exhibited development or non-development and the implications of these findings.

Lastly, we interpreted the case study through two trajectories (Stake, 1995). First, we sought to evaluate whether our findings aligned with the existing literature, particularly our theoretical framework, and whether any discrepancies were present.

As discussed in the previous chapter, positivist criteria for conducting rigorous science do not apply to our qualitative understanding of leadership. Consequently, we were motivated to articulate concurrent quality markers for conducting rigorous science within the qualitative study of leadership. We identified two distinct yet interrelated criteria: trustworthiness and authenticity (Klenke, 2008c). This involved a discussion of our theoretical and analytical lens through which the data were analyzed, as well as comparisons to other potential meta-theories that make sense of the psychological phenomena, and a reflection on the method and methodology employed, alongside strategies for ensuring scientific rigor.

To enhance trustworthiness, the findings were interpreted from an existential perspective within the discussion section of the present manuscript, illustrating where other analytical lenses converged or diverged from our employed meta-theory. We then discussed the extent to which quality markers of scientific rigor were adhered to, such as the separation of autoethnographic description and analysis.

Regarding authenticity, we examined how the findings contributed to revising our Lewinian model of dynamic leadership (ontological authenticity), a discussion presented in the manuscript. We also illuminated how the research facilitated an understanding of multiple perspectives, generating insights for the various participants involved in the multiple case studies (educative authenticity) and how the research empowered participants to strategically alter their actions (catalytical and strategic authenticity). This evaluation included a reflective sub-chapter within the general discussion of the manuscript. Specifically, to trigger reflection and facilitate the digestion of the empirical findings, we employed a constructivist method—writing a letter to the future self (Chishima et al., 2021; Wetzler & Feltner, 2021). In Table 4.2, I summarize the quality criteria for conducting rigorous scientific research in the domain of qualitative leadership research, outlining how and when we evaluated those criteria.

Table 4.2 Quality markers for the qualitative study of leadership and how to ensure quality

Quality Marker for Qualitative Studies in Leadership	Sub-Criteria	How and When to Evaluate
Trustworthiness	Comparison of analytical meta-theories Scientific Rigor	Comparison of analysis between cultural-psychological, psychoanalytical, and existential theories (interpretation and discussion section) Did the study separate description and analysis of critical incidents and how? (discussion section)
Authenticity	Ontological Authenticity Educative Authenticity Catalytical and Strategic Authenticity	Did the empirical findings help to revise the underlying theory? (Discussion section). Did the research help the participant to gain insight into the phenomenon? (Discussion section via reflection sub-chapter) Did the research help the participants implied to adjust their actions and how? (discussion section via sub-chapter on reflection of the findings)

The Role of Introspection in Our Methodological Design

Discussing ethnography naturally leads us to the inquiry of introspection. Broadly defined, introspection involves looking into oneself with the goal of assessing internal perception (Walach, 2015). In the tradition of the Würzburg School of introspection (Danziger, 1980), I consider certain premises more significant than others. Wundt, for example, emphasized the distinction between internal perception and its observation, the latter of which he termed self-observation. Internal perception refers to subjective feelings, such as feeling good while reading a book, while self-observation involves a conscious recognition of the reasons behind those feelings, such as acknowledging that it is one's favorite book. Wundt was cautious about conflating these concepts, as failing to separate them could distort the nature of internal perception. Furthermore, Wundt's concept of introspection emerged within the context of external stimuli (e.g., visual stimuli presented through a tachistoscope), which were used to assess objective reactions (physiological measures) in his experimental designs.

Later, the Würzburg School of introspection sought to modify Wundt's more dogmatic understanding by shifting the experimental focus. Their premises centered on the importance of retrospection, the use of introspective reports, and not solely on objective experimental measures (e.g., response time). This approach allowed for the qualitative exploration of psychological operations such as feelings, tastes, and memories, which were clarified through dialogue with the researcher to better understand the phenomenon at hand.

In our present methodology, we primarily adhered to the Würzburg School's approach while utilizing autoethnography and retrospective accounts of interactions between leaders and followers on and off the tennis court. A specific event served as the focal point of this introspective account, acting as an external stimulus that triggered retro-introspective reflection. Our goal was to shed light on the quality of the event as thoroughly as possible. This process was further complemented by an intra-psychological dialogue between the researcher as a participant and the researcher in a scholarly capacity. The field-theoretical interpretation of the event stimulated dialogue between the naïve research participant and the researcher as an analyst. Chapter 7 serves as a compelling example of this objective, where the researcher writes a letter to their future self, guiding their roles as leader and follower.

Importantly, we focused not only on the qualitative introspective report and its outcomes but also on the emergence of psychological and non-psychological phenomena throughout the report—a concept that can be termed idiographic microgenesis (Diriwächter, 2009). The application of field theory served as a scaffolding that facilitated the interpretation of autoethnographic (introspective) reports. Here, we align with the origins of introspection (from a more Wundtian perspective), arguing that introspective reports necessitate interpretation. By employing field theory as an interpretational tool, we aimed to understand interpersonal events from an introspective account, thus expanding the scope of introspective research. Taking introspection beyond the confines of classical experimental laboratories exemplifies a more flexible understanding of the concept, contrasting with a traditional Wundtian interpretation (see Valsiner, 2017), a perspective also embraced by the Hamburg School of Introspection (Kleining, 2010).

Having discussed the criteria for rigorous qualitative research within the qualitative study of leadership for the autoethnographic approach, we can summarize the methodological protocol we employed for the first study.

A. The first study utilized a multiple case study research design from an autoethnographic perspective, drawing on critical incidents and events to transcend the artificial dichotomy between individual case and event analysis. The case and event study became multiple, encompassing different critical incidents within one enterprise as well as across various enterprises. We compared these critical incidents both within and between cases to understand the dynamics of leadership and leader-follower interactions. These comparisons were informed by the field-theoretical models introduced in the manuscript's introductory chapters.

B. The autoethnography was conducted in a narrative and reflexive manner. To this end, we divided the autoethnographic description and analysis into two distinct phases, addressing critiques that autoethnography tends to conflate analysis with description. For the analysis, we developed an interpretative scheme that allowed us to filter the necessary and interrelated categories of social, dialogical, and interpretative leadership. This perspective was further complemented by situating our autoethnographic approach within a flexible understanding of introspection, relating introspective accounts to external events, examining developmental changes within the introspective report, utilizing interpretational tools (field theory), and focusing on the quality of psychological functions.

C. Finally, we discussed quality markers for conducting excellent qualitative research in the study of leadership, enlivening alternative validity criteria such as trustworthiness and authenticity, which were later evaluated within the empirical section of the study. Additionally, we developed a framework detailing how and when these criteria could be assessed, demonstrating that qualitative research can be conducted rigorously within the domain of leadership studies.

Ethnographic Study: Toward a Holistic Ethnographic Research Protocol for the Study of Leadership

In our ethnographic study, we employed a methodological approach similar to that of the autoethnography. Before elaborating on the protocol employed in the second study, it is essential to discuss the nature of ethnographic studies and their defining characteristics. There is a lack of consensus regarding the criteria that determine whether a study qualifies as ethnographic (Klenke, 2008b). Some researchers assert that ethnographic studies hinge on the researcher's direct access to the field, fostering a cohabitation between the researcher and participants (Conklin, 1968; van Maanen, 1979). Others contend that the temporal aspect—specifically, conducting research over a span of at least one year—marks a study as ethnographic (Klenke, 2008b). Notably, ethnographies culminate in ethnographic reports that elucidate the meaning-making systems of specific groups or cultures (Chilcott, 1987; Gold, 1997). According to Klenke (2008b), ethnography is the following:

> a description and interpretation of a social group or system. It involves immersion in the social context being studied. The ethnographer examines the group's observable and learned patterns of behavior and grounds their research in ethnographic fieldwork. As a process, ethnography involves extended observation of the group typically through participant observation, in which the ethnographer is immersed in the day-to-day lives of the people, or through one-to-one interviews with members of the group. Ethnographers study the meanings of behaviors, language, and interactions of members of the culture (p. 200).

It is crucial to note that ethnography is more of an approach than a rigidly defined set of methods (Klenke, 2008b). This flexibility allows the ethnographer the freedom to select appropriate methods tailored to the phenomenon under investigation. Thus, ethnographic methods are inherently open and can depend on the researcher's creativity in identifying the best ways to study the natural conduct of individuals within a particular environment or group. A consensus among various definitions of ethnography is that it employs an in-depth methodological approach using a triangulation of methods, which may include participant observation, interviews, and the analysis of archival data, among other sources (Okely, 2020).

While we do not subscribe to rigid definitions of ethnography based solely on duration (such as requiring a one-year time frame), we believe that incorporating longitudinal elements is essential for qualifying a study as an in-depth ethnographic method. This entails that interviews, observations, and other data sources should be consulted multiple times—at least more than twice—to meet the criteria of ethnography. Additionally, the process of extended observation or participation in the field must access the inner world of the participants, often facilitated through interviews, leading to the production of an ethnographic report. This report serves as the primary data source for a rich and detailed description of the community or group under study, which can then be utilized for concise data interpretation. Effective data collection is achieved through the juxtaposition and combination of multiple data sources (Klenke, 2008b); yet again, there are no pre-defined methodologies that govern this step in the ethnographic approach.

In summary, the methodological protocol for our ethnographic study involved the researcher engaging in prolonged immersion within the leadership context being studied. This included active participation in relevant activities and observation of day-to-day interactions among leaders and followers. The data collection methods employed participant observation, where the researcher participated in leadership meetings, training sessions, and informal gatherings to capture the dynamics of leader-follower interactions in real time. In-depth interviews were conducted with leaders and followers to gather their perspectives on leadership practices, challenges, and successes, utilizing both open and semi-structured formats to facilitate open-ended responses. Archival data analysis was also performed, reviewing organizational documents, meeting minutes, and other relevant materials to gain insights into the historical context and operational frameworks that shape leadership practices.

Data was collected over an extended period, ensuring that multiple interactions and events were captured, thereby providing a deeper understanding of leadership dynamics. Follow-up interviews and observations were conducted to monitor changes over time. The culmination of the study resulted in a comprehensive ethnographic report that detailed the cultural and behavioral norms of the leadership context. This report served to interpret the findings and offered a narrative that captured the complexities of leadership as experienced by participants. The integration of different data sources—observational notes, interview transcripts, and archival materials—allowed for a robust analysis, helping to validate findings and uncover patterns across various contexts and interactions. By adhering to this holistic ethnographic research protocol, we aimed to develop a nuanced understanding of leadership that accounts for the intricate social interactions and cultural contexts shaping leader-follower dynamics. This approach not only enriches our theoretical frameworks but also provides actionable insights that can inform leadership practice.

Selection of the Research Site

The selection criteria for the research site were largely influenced by the accessibility of the field for our ethnographic research design. Keeping this in mind, we chose to study the leadership dynamics within a bakery where we had established personal relationships with most of the employees. This familiarity facilitated the first author's seamless integration into the environment, allowing for the organic observation of leadership phenomena without the researcher becoming a hindrance to the employees' interactions. Our research schedule involved visiting the bakery once a month during morning shifts. We positioned ourselves in a corner with a newspaper, enabling us to discreetly observe the interactions among employees, particularly in situations where problems arose or issues required resolution.

In this context, we utilized the *Critical Incident Technique*, categorizing incidents based on the presence of specific keywords that emerged in overheard conversations, such as "help," "problem," "issue," "look," "come," and "do not know." These keywords indicated a negotiation of a problem or goal. When we encountered such keywords, we took field notes under the overarching questions of what had transpired (e.g., the issue, conflict, or goal) and how the employees led one another in addressing the situation (the solution) and the means they employed (tools and signs). This process allowed us to assess interactional patterns that might have crystallized into a generalized systemic leadership conduct. The critical incidents were reported according to the criteria we had established.

Following each observation, we conducted brief interviews with the employees to gain insights into their experiences regarding the issues or conflicts that had emerged during their work. After sampling incidents from five ethnographic field observations conducted over a five-month period, we compiled an ethnographic field report summarizing these incidents. Our approach for the report leaned toward a descriptive account of the leadership conduct observed in the bakery, deliberately suspending initial interpretations.

Once the report was drafted, we visualized the leadership interactions based on our field-theoretical models, aiming to identify microgenetic developments within these interactions or generalized patterns present across all models. Acknowledging that "there are no formal rules for analyzing ethnographic data" (Klenke, 2008b, p. 204), we chose not to produce a conventional descriptive vignette of general leadership conduct within the bakery. Instead, we sought to distill the essence of our field-theoretical analysis into an action-oriented policy brief intended for the bakery employees. This policy brief was presented to one of the bakery's sellers, who was asked for her feedback on the content, specifically regarding any aspects she felt were missing or could be improved. This intervention was aimed at fulfilling the criteria of authenticity and trustworthiness, which are crucial in conducting qualitative research within the leadership domain (Klenke, 2008c, 2008d).

The methodological protocol for the ethnographic study is detailed in Table 4.3. It is important to note that steps 2 and 3 of the protocol were repeated five times over the course of one month. Through this ethnographic protocol, we aimed to systematize an approach to leadership research that meets essential quality markers for rigorous qualitative inquiry. To the best of our knowledge, this represents one of the first ethnographic protocols designed to guide researchers in assessing leadership conduct from a field-theoretical perspective while satisfying alternative validity criteria that are central to qualitative research inquiries.

We do not intend to summarize our writings in bullet points, as we believe that Table 4.3 speaks for itself. In conclusion, we compared the field-theoretical models derived from both the autoethnographic and ethnographic studies, examining their

Table 4.3 Ethnographic protocol for the second leadership study

Steps and concepts	Actions being undertaken	Alternative validity criteria
1 Gaining access to the field	Obtaining consent for observation. Looking for an appropriate spot from which to observe leadership conduct. Checking whether one interferes with the work the employees do in their shift.	Multi-perspectivity (trustworthiness)
2 Observing in-vivo leadership conduct to unfold	Observing, listening, and taking field notes of critical leadership incidents if keywords have been verbalized during a conversation between employees leading each other.	Authenticity
3 Interviewing one or more employees about their experience and the meaning of the leadership situations	Conducting a short unstructured interview about the meanings attributed to the leadership situations.	Method triangulation (trustworthiness)
4 Write-up of the ethnographic report for the leadership conduct within the bakery	Describing the leadership conduct between employees and how they solved issues cooperatively at the workplace.	Separating description and analysis (trustworthiness and authenticity)
5 Analysis based on field-theoretical model	Analyzing and interpreting the data based on field-theory	Trustworthiness/authenti city
6 Creation of a short policy brief with intended actions for changing the leadership situation within the bakery	Deducing concrete action strategies of how to improve the leadership situation in the bakery.	Authenticity (catalytical and strategical)
7 Confronting one or more employees with the policy brief	Looking for the employee's perspective onto the researcher's interpretation and potentially complementing the policy brief from the perspective of the employee	Authenticity

development over time. This comparison involved assessing convergences and divergences and discussing these findings comprehensively to meet the requirements of a multiple case study design. Furthermore, we juxtaposed the reflection chapter of the autoethnography with the policy brief generated from the ethnographic study. This juxtaposition aimed to explore how the analysis facilitated strategic insights and actions, as well as to determine whether these insights and actions exhibited differences or convergences.

We recognize that the methodological design may appear complex. To aid understanding, we have chosen to visualize the methodological steps in a graphic model (see Fig. 4.3). This visual representation is intended to clarify the intricate connections and processes involved in our research methodology, thereby enhancing the comprehensibility of our findings and their implications.

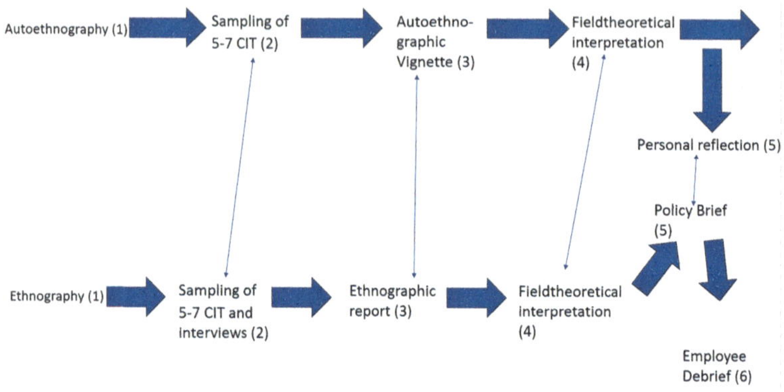

Fig. 4.3 Visualized research plan (Step 2 is repeated in the ethnographic and autoethnographic design, double-sided arrows indicate comparison opportunities)

References

Adams, T. E., Jones, S. L. H., & Ellis, C. (2015). *Autoethnography*. Rese.

Antunes, A., & Franco, M. (2016). How people in organizations make sense of responsible leadership practices: Multiple case studies. *Leadership & Organization Development Journal, 37*(1), 126–152. https://doi.org/10.1108/LODJ-07-2013-0086

Bergman Blix, S., & Wettergren, Å. (2015). The emotional labour of gaining and maintaining access to the field. *Qualitative Research, 15*(6), 688–704. https://doi.org/10.1177/1468794114553622

Boesch, E. E. (1975). *Zwischen Angst und Triumph: Über d. Ich u. seine Bestätigungen*. Huber.

Bryman, A. (2011). Research methods in the study of leadership. In A. Bryman, D. Collinson, K. Grint, B. Jackson, & M. Uhl-Bien (Eds.), *The SAGE handbook of leadership* (pp. 15–28). Sage.

Chang, H. (2016). *Autoethnography as method* (Vol. 1). Routledge.

Chell, E. (1998). Critical incident technique. In G. Symon & C. Cassell (Eds.), *Qualitative methods and analysis in organizational research: A practical guide* (pp. 51–72). Sage Publications Ltd.

Chilcott, J. H. (1987). Where are you coming from and where are you going? The reporting of ethnographic research. *American Educational Research Journal, 24*(2), 199–218.

Chishima, Y., Huai-Ching Liu, I. T., & Wilson, A. E. (2021). Temporal distancing during the COVID-19 pandemic: Letter writing with future self can mitigate negative affect. *Applied Psychology: Health and Well-Being, 13*(2), 406–418. https://doi.org/10.1111/aphw.12256

Conklin, H. C. (1968). Lexicographical treatment of folk taxonomies. *Readings in the Sociology of Language, 1968*, 414–433.

Cousin, G. (2005). Case study research. *Journal of Geography in Higher Education, 29*(3), 421–427. https://doi.org/10.1080/03098260500130438

Danziger, K. (1980). The history of introspection reconsidered. *Journal of the History of the Behavioral Sciences, 16*(3), 241–262. https://doi.org/10.1002/1520-6696198007

Diriwächter, R. (2009). Idiographic microgenesis: Re-visiting the experimental tradition of Aktualgenese. In J. Valsiner (Ed.), *Dynamic process methodology in the social and developmental sciences* (pp. 319–352). Springer. https://doi.org/10.1007/978-0-387-95922-1_15

Eco, U. (2002). *Einführung in die Semiotik*. utb GmbH.

Eisenhardt, K. M. (1989). Building theories from case study research. *Academy of Management Review, 14*(4), 532–550. https://doi.org/10.5465/amr.1989.4308385

Elliott, K. C. (2012). Epistemic and methodological iteration in scientific research. *Studies in History and Philosophy of Science Part A, 43*(2), 376–382. https://doi.org/10.1016/j.shpsa.2011.12.004

Ellis, C., Adams, T. E., & Bochner, A. P. (2010). Autoethnografie. In A. Mey & S. Mruck (Eds.), *Handbuch qualitative forschung in der psychologie* (pp. 345–357). VS Verlag für Sozialwissenschaften.

Flanagan, J. C. (1954). The critical incident technique. *Psychological Bulletin, 51*(4), 327–358.

George, A. L., & Bennett, A. (2005). *Case studies and theory development in the social sciences*. MIT Press.

Gerring, J. (2006). *Case study research: Principles and practices*. Cambridge University Press.

Gold, R. L. (1997). The ethnographic method in sociology. *Qualitative Inquiry, 3*(4), 388–402. https://doi.org/10.1177/107780049700300402

Johansson, R. (2007). On case study methodology. *Open House International, 32*(3), 48–54. https://doi.org/10.1108/OHI-03-2007-B0006

Kleining, G. (2010). Erleben eines Bahnhofs. In T. Burkart, G. Kleining, & H. Witt (Eds.), *Dialogische Introspektion* (pp. 64–75) VS Verlag.

Klenke, K. (2008a). Case studies in leadership research. In K. Klenke (Ed.), *Qualitative research in the study of leadership* (pp. 57–84). Emerald.

Klenke, K. (2008b). Grounded theory, ethnography and historiometry. In K. Klenke (Ed.), *Qualitative research in the study of leadership* (pp. 185–213). Emerald.

Klenke, K. (2008c). Qualitative research as paradigm. In K. Klenke (Ed.), *Qualitative research in the study of leadership* (pp. 3–29). Emerald.

Klenke, K. (2008d). Qualitative research as a method. In K. Klenke (Ed.), *Qualitative research in the study of leadership* (pp. 31–55). Emerald.

Lamiell, J. T. (2024). *Primer in critical personalism: A framework for reviving psychological inquiry and for grounding a socio-cultural ethos*. Routledge.

Leont'ev, A. N. (1978). *Activity, consciousness, and personality*. Prentice-Hall.

Lipmann, O. (1926). *Grundriß der Arbeitswissenschaft und Ergebnisse der arbeitswissenschaftlichen Statistik*. Gustav Fischer.

Okely, J. (2020). *Anthropological practice: Fieldwork and the ethnographic method*. Routledge.

Parry, K., Mumford, M. D., Bower, I., & Watts, L. L. (2014). Qualitative and historiometric methods in leadership research: A review of the first 25 years of the leadership quarterly. *The Leadership Quarterly, 25*(1), 132–151. https://doi.org/10.1016/j.leaqua.2013.08.002

Riese, J. (2019). What is 'access' in the context of qualitative research? *Qualitative Research, 19*(6), 669–684. https://doi.org/10.1177/1468794118782641

Stake, R. E. (1995). *The art of case study research*. Sage.

Stern, W. (1911). *Die differentielle Psychologie in ihren methodischen Grundlagen*. J.A. Barth.

Strauss, A., & Corbin, J. (1994). Grounded theory methodology: An overview. In N. K. Denzin & Y. S. Lincoln (Eds.), *Handbook of qualitative research* (pp. 273–285). Sage Publications, Inc.

Stroebe, W., & Strack, F. (2014). The alleged crisis and the illusion of exact replication. *Perspectives on Psychological Science, 9*(1), 59–71. https://doi.org/10.1177/1745691613514450

Valsiner, J. (2017). *From methodology to methods in human psychology*. Springer.

Valsiner, J., & Sato, T. (2006). Historically Structured Sampling (HSS): How can psychology's methodology become tuned in to the reality of the historical nature of cultural psychology. *Pursuit of meaning. Advances in cultural and cross-cultural psychology*, 215–251.

Van Maanen, J. (1979). The fact of fiction in organizational ethnography. *Administrative Science Quarterly, 24*(4), 539–550.

von Fircks, E. (2023b). Categorizing personal appropriation processes of cultural givens and investigating their personal and collective functions. *Human Arenas*, 1–14. https://doi.org/10.1007/s42087-023-00350-7.

von Fircks, E. F. (2023a). Reasoning with Vygotsky: Semiosis between everyday and scientific concepts. *Human Arenas*, 1–17. https://doi.org/10.1007/s42087-023-00345-4.

Wagoner, B. (2009). The Experimental Methodology of Constructive Microgenesis. In J. Valsiner, N. Chaudhary, M. C.D.P. Lyra, & P. C. M. Molenaar (Eds.), Dynamic Process Methodology in the Social and Developmental Sciences (pp. 99–121). Springer.

Walach, H. (2015). Reflexion über Introspektion, *EWE, 26*(1), 60–62.

Wetzler, E. L., & Feltner, D. T. (2021). A proflective writing assignment in advanced general psychology for leaders: Letter to the future self. In *Teaching and learning the west point way* (pp. 72–77). Routledge.

Woodside, A. G., & Wilson, E. J. (2003). Case study research methods for theory building. *Journal of Business & Industrial Marketing, 18*(6/7), 493–508. https://doi.org/10.1108/08858620310484023

Yin, R. K. (2003). Designing case studies. In L. Bickman & D. J. Rog (Eds.), *The SAGE handbook of applied social research methods* (pp. 229–259). Sage.

Yin, R. K. (2009). *Case study research: Design and methods, 5*, sage.

Yin, R. K. (2012). Case study methods. In H. Cooper, P. M. Camic, D. L. Long, A. T. Panter, D. Rindskopf, & K. J. Sher (Eds.), *APA handbook of research methods in psychology, Vol. 2. Research designs: Quantitative, qualitative, neuropsychological, and biological* (pp. 141–155). American Psychological Association. https://doi.org/10.1037/13620-009

Zheng, W., Khoury, A. E., & Grobmeier, C. (2010). How do leadership and context matter in R&D team innovation? –A multiple case study. *Human Resource Development International, 13*(3), 265–283. https://doi.org/10.1080/13678868.2010.484352

Chapter 5
Cross-Sectional and Longitudinal Interpretations of Ethnographic Leadership Patterns

In the following section, we will explore the description, analysis, and interpretation of ethnographic vignettes related to prevailing leadership patterns. This will be done using the same premises applied in the examination of the autoethnographic vignettes. As outlined in the Methodology Chapter (Chap. 4), our aim is not to replicate the findings, but rather to assess whether our analytical and interpretative framework—field-theoretical and cultural-psychological—can effectively capture and elucidate leadership patterns. This approach holds potential for yielding novel insights within the domain of qualitative leadership and for further actualizing the cultural-psychological theory of leadership developed in the introductory chapters (Chaps. 1 and 2).

First Ethnographic Vignette: Cooperative Counting of Returned Goods

It was a typical Tuesday afternoon when I decided to visit one of my favorite bakeries and cafés in my hometown. My motivation for this visit was twofold: to enjoy a cup of coffee while relaxing and to observe leadership dynamics in real time. Upon entering the bakery, I exchanged pleasantries with the employees and engaged in some casual small talk. Afterward, I settled into a corner where I had a good view of the counter and could observe the interactions between the employees and customers. However, from this position, the employees couldn't easily see me. I had brought some books along to give the impression that I was simply studying, so as not to make the employees feel as though they were under constant

We start with the ethnographic study as it helps the reader to get acquainted with the theory and methodology we presented in the introductory chapters.

E. Freiherr von Fircks, *Studying Leadership from a Microgenetic Perspective*, Methodologies in Developmental Sciences,
https://doi.org/10.1007/978-3-031-90214-7_5

observation—something I was keen to avoid. Nonetheless, I remained attentive to any critical incidents, as outlined in the methodology chapter.

From prior visits, I knew that the employees didn't find my presence unusual, as I had spent considerable time in the café before beginning my observations. Consequently, they wouldn't have suspected any difference between my studying habits and my intent to observe their interactions. Before delving into the first critical incident, it is important to provide some background information on the two employees working the morning shift. These two workers, who are the usual staff for the bakery's morning schedule, share more than just a professional relationship—they also have a friendship that extends beyond working hours. Based on personal conversations, I know that they socialize at least once a month with a larger group of friends and have a shared sense of humor that is both cheeky and direct. During my two-hour observation, what struck me was the number of jokes they exchanged with each other, which seemed to lighten the atmosphere.

With this context in mind, we can now focus on the critical incident I observed. During the beginning of my observation, there was a rush of customers, which required the two employees to work quickly and separately to meet customer needs. They divided the waiting line so that both could serve customers simultaneously, streamlining the process. When I later inquired about this, they explained that these kinds of rush hours were typical, particularly in the afternoon when people finished work and stopped by on their way home.

After the rush subsided, the employees did not take a break but continued to focus on other tasks. This was when something particularly noteworthy caught my attention. One of the employees asked the other for assistance in preparing the returns for the evening—a process that involved counting the remaining baked goods and entering the figures into the computer system. They divided this task efficiently: one employee stood by the computer to input the data, while the other counted the goods. Employee A, who was managing the computer, guided employee B on which products to count first. They also communicated carefully, repeating the names of the products to ensure that the correct quantities were being recorded for each item. For instance, the conversation went as follows:

Employee A:	How much of the spelt bread?
Employee B:	20 spelt breads
Employee A:	How many multigrain breads?
Employee B:	10 multigrain breads
Employee A:	How many brown breads?
Employee B:	5 brown breads.

During the counting process, new customers arrived, prompting the employees to momentarily interrupt their task to attend to them. After serving the customers, the employees seamlessly returned to their previous task, picking up exactly where they had left off. This pattern of alternating between serving customers and continuing their counting process persisted until all the baked goods were accounted for and the corresponding numbers were entered into the system. When I later inquired about what happens if customers purchase some of the already-counted goods, the employees explained that the system automatically adjusts for those sales by deducting the amount from the recorded returns. What stood out during these interruptions was the way the employees re-engaged with their original task. After serving a customer, one of them would prompt the other by asking whether they had additional numbers to input, effectively signaling a return to the task at hand. This informal check-in facilitated a smooth transition back to the counting process. Once they completed the returns procedure, the employees discussed what task to undertake next, thereby initiating a new cooperative activity.

Analyzing the First Ethnographic Vignette

Analyzing the first ethnographic vignette from a psychological perspective reveals several layers of interaction and leadership dynamics. The primary issue identified in this incident is the need for cooperation between the employees to efficiently complete the task of counting the returns. Although this task could theoretically be accomplished by one person, the employees clearly preferred a cooperative approach, as it increased efficiency. If conducted alone, the process would have required more time and effort, involving both counting the baked goods and manually entering the data into the computer, all while frequently shifting between different locations. Thus, the need for cooperation arises from the desire to complete the task as efficiently as possible.

From a social standpoint, it is evident that accuracy is crucial for this task, as the count of returned goods informs the bakery's future production adjustments. The interaction pattern between the employees is noteworthy for its dual nature. On the one hand, the employees maintain a friendly but problem-focused dialogue, characterized by short exchanges tied to the task at hand. On the other hand, the interaction between employees and management remains somewhat distant, with management providing overarching directives—such as the use of the computer system—while leaving the specifics of task execution to the employees.

In terms of the tools and signs utilized during this interaction, we observe a dynamic form of guidance between the two employees. The repetition of instructions, such as the verification of product counts, is particularly important. This serves to ensure the accurate entry of data, with the system of communication emphasizing efficiency and precision. Their brief exchanges, often stripped off verbs, suggest a highly routinized and efficient process focused on completing the task with minimal error.

A further point of interest is the employees' method of resuming their task after serving customers, facilitated by the use of simple prompts such as "Do you have additional numbers?" These questions serve as cues to re-engage with the original task, reinforcing the rhythm of cooperation that had been established. This suggests that the employees have internalized the process to such a degree that they do not need to renegotiate or alter it, highlighting the presence of an established, effective routine. The lack of observable emotional engagement during this routine can be described as emotional indifference, or *Nicht-Gestimmtheit*, indicating that the task had become so habitual that it no longer demanded emotional investment.

In sum, this vignette reveals leadership dynamics at two levels. First, management exerts leadership by establishing procedural guidelines for counting and data entry. Second, leadership emerges between the employees themselves, as they initiate and sustain a cooperative workflow that successfully overcomes interruptions and ecological challenges (e.g., attending to customers). These two forms of leadership (vertical and horizontal leadership) operate in tandem, shaping the overall structure of the task while reflecting a harmonious interaction of top-down and peer-level leadership. Table 5.1 provides a summary of our psychological analysis based on the scheme being developed in Chap. 4.

Field-Theoretical Interpretation of the First Autoethnography

In the field-theoretical interpretation of the first ethnographic vignette, we observe a more intricate psychological landscape than in the autoethnographic scenarios (Fig. 5.1). This complexity arises because two employees are both navigating a specific challenge in their respective life-spaces. Both employee 1 and employee 2 face a barrier, yet they express a mutual willingness to overcome it and move toward their shared goal. This is demonstrated by their cooperative signals, which indicate their intention to work together in resolving the issue at hand. Cooperation between the employees is a key strategy for circumventing the barrier and reaching their objective.

Management plays a secondary but significant role in shaping the employees' psychological field. While management sets up the constraint—represented by the task of counting returns and entering the data into the system—this constraint is not rigidly defined. Instead, management allows the employees the freedom to

Table 5.1 Analysis scheme for counting the returned goods ethnographic vignette

Problem/ Issue	Personal need (follower's needs)	Social needs (organizational needs)	Interaction patterns	Tool-/ Sign-systems	Solution	Feelings
Counting the returned goods	Doing it in a rapid manner	The counting needs to be done accurately.	Between employees: direct, short, solution-oriented. Between employees and management: remote, distanced	Repetitive signs, cooperative signs, accuracy signs	Cooperative counting, perseverance of cooperative counting despite hindrances	Objectual attunement for the given situation.

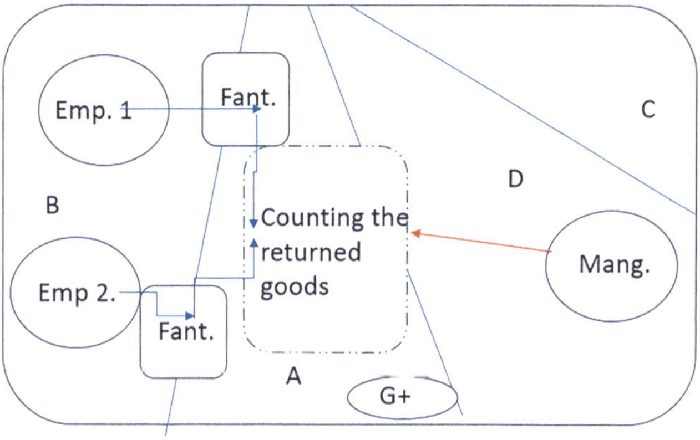

Fig. 5.1 Life-space of employees (Emp.) regarding their intentions and the expected intentions of management (Mang.)

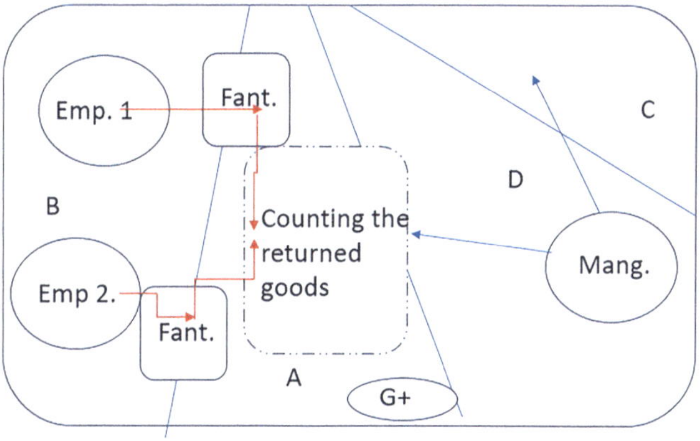

Fig. 5.2 Life-space of management regarding its intentions and the expected intentions of the employees

resolve the issue in their own way, provided they achieve the desired result. Thus, the managerial directive remains somewhat in the background of the employees' psychological attention during the task, serving more as a general guideline than a detailed set of instructions. For Employee 1 and Employee 2, the cooperative activity becomes the most effective means of meeting the managerial demands, and they instinctively recognize this need for collaboration. Consequently, their life-space transforms as they begin to work together, forming a unified psychological position, a "We-Position."

In Fig. 5.2, the psychological field of management is depicted. Here, we see that management initiates the constraint but then moves on to focus on other zones of interest. After establishing the barrier in Zone A, management expects the employees to find a way around the obstacle without direct supervision, trusting that they will meet the expectation. This allows management to redirect its attention and psychological resources to other pressing issues in different zones, such as Zones C and D. Thus, management's role is two-fold: first, to define the constraint and set its parameters, and second, to entrust the employees with solving the problem while management shifts its focus to more urgent concerns elsewhere. This pattern underscores a form of decentralized leadership, where management delegates responsibility for specific tasks, relying on the employees' capacity for autonomous problem-solving.

Ultimately, this field-theoretical interpretation highlights the dynamic interplay between management's broad oversight and the employees' collaborative initiative, revealing how leadership can emerge organically within the confines of delegated tasks.

In the sociological analysis (Fig. 5.3), we observe an intriguing dynamic between individual roles and collective action. The two employees in the vignette form a "We-Position" through which cooperative activity is initiated and sustained. However, this cooperative identity does not eliminate their individual roles and responsibilities. Despite their collaboration to overcome the barrier and move closer to their respective goals, they remain distinct individuals with separate duties. This is evident in the way they periodically interrupt their cooperation to serve different customers at separate counters.

What emerges is a cyclical process in which the employees alternate between cooperative activity and individual tasks. They initiate cooperation, pause to perform competing or individual actions, and then resume cooperation using semiotic cues, such as the repetitive signs described earlier. This process is essential for regulating their movement between different life-spaces and action fields, governed by specific sign systems that facilitate their return to the original task. The use of repetitive signs also enhances the accuracy of their work, which satisfies both personal and organizational needs—particularly the need for precise accounting of returned goods.

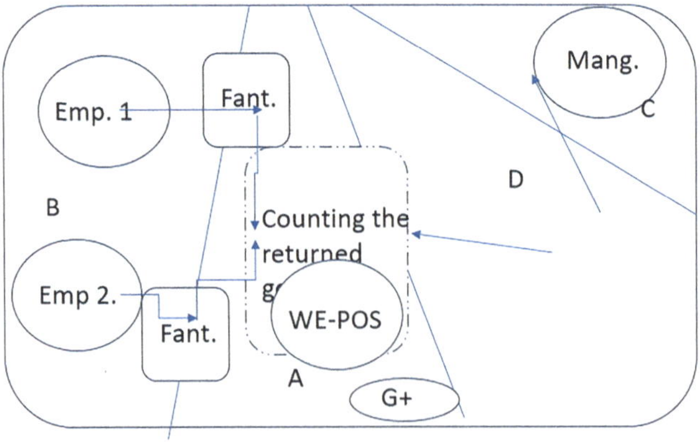

Fig. 5.3 Sociological analysis of the action field when counting the returned goods

Despite the distance and limited direct involvement of management in this specific interaction, management plays a pivotal role by establishing the boundaries and constraints that the employees must navigate. This highlights management's unique power position: while not immediately present in the employees' psychological field, management sets up the structural framework—through barriers and rules—that governs employee actions. This places management in a delicate situation, as their authority to impose constraints can sometimes conflict with the actual needs or preferences of the employees. In the case of this vignette, however, organizational and personal needs align to a significant degree, so the managerial constraint does not pose a substantial threat to the employees' sense of self or their work satisfaction. Nonetheless, the underlying power dynamic underscores the potential for tension between employee autonomy and managerial control, even when the two are aligned in practice.

When we intend to put the above-mentioned in an equation, we might depict the following:

$$\mathrm{L}(\mathrm{f}) = \mathrm{N}(\mathrm{F}) * \mathrm{N}(\mathrm{l}) = \mathrm{Circ}\left(\mathrm{WePos}^{*}\mathrm{Rep} - \mathrm{Signs}\right) * \mathrm{Bar} \rightarrow \mathrm{g} +$$

Leadership in this context emerges as a process of uniting the needs of both the leader and the follower within a shared "We-Position," enabling them to navigate barriers and move closer to their collective goal. The cooperation that arises between the employees is maintained through the use of repetitive signs, which serve as a stabilizing mechanism for their collaboration. In this framework, leadership is defined as a specific, context-driven action that occurs both within the immediate situation and as part of broader organizational dynamics.

In this case, the focus is on leadership happening within the situation, where both employees demonstrate leadership in addressing the task at hand. This is done while operating within the larger constraints set by management. Hence, the analysis takes into account the dynamics of vertical (management<>followers) and horizontal (followers becoming leaders) leadership. The employees act as leaders in their own right, using cooperative strategies to meet both their own needs and the organizational demands. Through their collaboration, they effectively navigate the structural barriers imposed by management, demonstrating how leadership can be fluid and situational, emerging from collective action rather than residing in a single individual.

Second Ethnographic Vignette: Debate About Ingredients

A month later, I returned to the bakery, this time observing a different dynamic as my friend was working alongside another colleague. I was present during the early morning shift, which is typically busier as customers purchase items for their work and lunch breaks. As expected, there was a rush, and I noticed that the employees were visibly more stressed than usual. Their interactions were louder, and they occasionally expressed frustration, particularly directed toward management. This atmosphere of heightened tension intrigued me, and I decided to move closer to the counter to better understand the situation.

One particular incident stood out. A customer approached the counter asking for a type of bread I hadn't previously encountered in the bakery. It soon became clear that this was a new product that had recently been added to the bakery's offerings. The customer's inquiry led to the following exchange between them and the seller:

Customer: What's this new bread?
Seller: This is the 57 bread.
Customer: What does it contain?
Seller: 57 water.
Customer: What else? Which type of flour?
Seller: (long pause) Honestly, I do not know.
Customer: (long pause) Well, I take it and will try it out.
Seller: Okay. Should we cut the bread?
Customer: Yes, but thin, please.
Seller: Okay, no worries.

After having served the customer and while the customer was on their way out, I overheard the ongoing conversation between the employees.

Employee A: Honestly, I feel bad about not being able to tell my customers what this new bread is.
Employee B: No, this is not good.
Employee A: I will phone management asking them about this particular bread and see whether I can get some information.
Employee: B Okay, great.

After discussing the issue and reaching a consensus on how to address it, employee A decided to contact a responsible person in management. She went to the back office to make the call, preventing me from overhearing their conversation. Meanwhile, a similar scenario unfolded at the counter when another customer inquired about the new bread and requested additional information.

Later, I had the opportunity to ask employee A about her conversation with management. She shared her experience, stating, "*I asked management about the bread, but they couldn't answer my question. They kept stumbling over their words and only mentioned that there is 57 water*[1] *in it. When I pressed for more details, they went silent.*"

Upon her return from the back office, similar situations continued to arise. Some customers chose to buy the bread without any further information, while others refrained from purchasing it due to a lack of clarity or concerns about potential allergic reactions. After the fifth or sixth incident, employee A resorted to inventing some of the ingredients when customers asked. When I inquired about her reasoning, she explained, "*It's important not to appear unprofessional in front of customers.*"

[1] 57 water is a specific type of water in a German region.

Later, during a break, she expressed her frustration with management's passive role in this process, lamenting, "*Unfortunately, this type of situation is typical for the bakery.*"

Analyzing the Second Ethnographic Vignette Psychologically

From a psychological perspective, the analysis of the situation reveals a significant lack of communication and information, which prevents employees from adequately responding to customer inquiries. This deficiency carries serious negative emotional implications, as the employees are concerned about appearing unprofessional. Such concerns directly conflict with their fundamental goal of providing excellent service to customers. In essence, the employees' ability to fulfill their roles effectively is undermined by the inadequate communication between them and management. Conversely, management's overarching objective is to encourage employees to sell the new bread and make it appealing to customers, thereby increasing overall product awareness and sales.

The ethnographic vignette highlights the remote and distanced nature of interactions between employees and management. This relationship exhibits a taken-for-granted pattern, where management assumes that simply introducing a new product is sufficient for its success. This presumption overlooks the necessity of effective communication regarding the product's details and benefits.

To deepen our understanding of the situation, we must explore the sign system at play in the vignette. The lack of communication permeates both the core and periphery of the employees' life-space and examining the employed sign system can elucidate the roots of this communication breakdown. Here, we encounter a unique interconnectedness of signs, specifically the absence of certain signs and the presence of others that the employees interpret.

For example, management conveys economic signs that indicate the new bread needs to be sold, combined with pressure signs urging employees to effectively market the product. However, these economic and pressure signs are further complicated by the absence of specific, product-related signs that provide essential information about the bread. This absence creates a stressor for employees, as they find themselves in a position where they must sell a product without adequate knowledge about it.

In their attempts to address this issue, employees actively seek to engage management in order to clarify the absent signs and alter the existing relationships between the various signs. Unfortunately, despite these proactive efforts, employees find themselves unsuccessful, leading to feelings of frustration and dissatisfaction.

In Table 5.2, I have summarized this analysis, and in Fig. 5.4, I have illustrated the sign system employed by management in the context of this autoethnographic study.

Table 5.2 Analysis scheme for the lack of communication ethnographic scheme

Problem/Issue	Personal need (follower's needs)	Social needs (organizational needs)	Interaction patterns	Tool-/ Sign-systems	Solution	Feelings
Lack of communication about a new type of bread to be sold	Serving the customer as good as possible (and as detailed as possible)	Selling the new product	Remote and distanced	Economic, pressure, and lack of objective signs combine with each other.	Employees contact management to illuminate the nature of the absent sign	Frustration

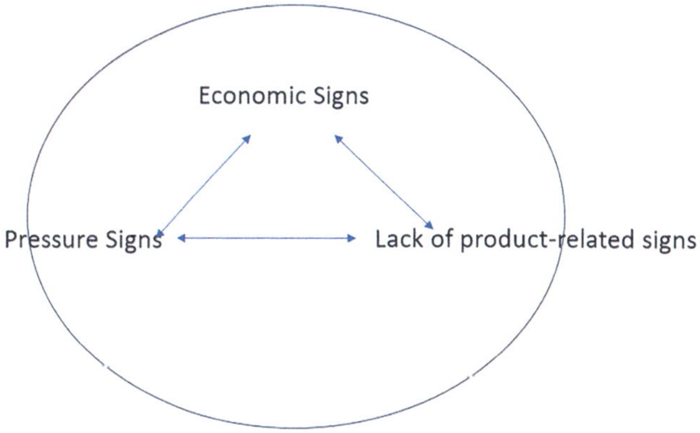

Fig. 5.4 Peculiar sign system as employed by management within the given autoethnography

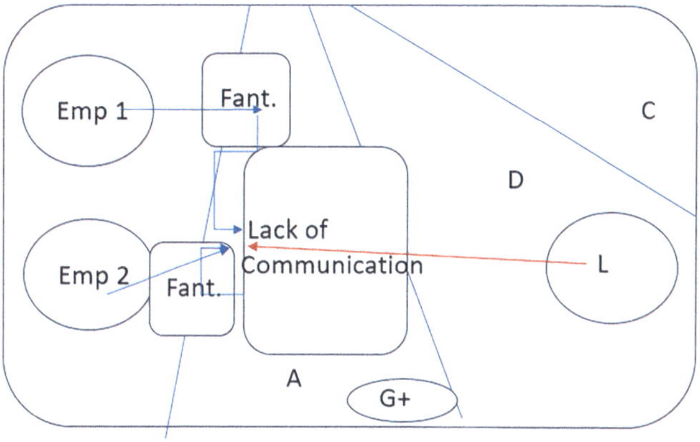

Fig. 5.5 Experiential unit of the employees regarding the conflict lack of communication

Field-Theoretical Interpretation of the Second Ethnographic Vignette

In Fig. 5.5, the general life-space of the employees is depicted in relation to the conflict at hand. The employees experience a pronounced lack of communication regarding the ingredients used in the new bread, leaving them ill-equipped to respond to customer inquiries effectively. They are acutely aware of past situations where customers were interested in purchasing the new product but were left without answers due to the lack of information. This uncertainty engenders anxiety as the employees struggle to reconcile their professional responsibilities with their own internal standards for performance (fantasm).

Consequently, the employees encounter stressors on both personal and social levels. Socially, they feel incapable of promoting the new bread and engaging with customers professionally, while personally, they grapple with the inability to meet their own job-related standards due to insufficient communication. Nevertheless, the employees are determined to escape this uncomfortable position and seek resolution. They aim to approach management, hoping to develop a circumvention strategy to address the barriers they face and alleviate the negative impact on both their professional lives and the bakery's success. Their expectations of management revolve around a desire for more active involvement in addressing the emerging conflict and supporting them in navigating this challenging situation.

When we examine the experiential unit of management, specifically the individual representing management on the phone, we can depict the following, as illustrated in Fig. 5.6. Management considers the barrier to be essentially permeable. They believe that the employees can navigate through the barrier to reach their goal field. Regarding their own intentions, management adopts a remote stance toward the issue at hand. With this in mind, management intends to position themselves at the periphery of the barrier to ensure an economic rationale for placing new products in the various bakeries. Once this is accomplished, they plan to redirect their psychological focus to other pressing issues. Thus, management moves closer to the periphery of the bakery, but after achieving this, they intend to move away, reallocating their psychological resources to different needs.

When we take a closer look at the action field (sociological reality) of the employees and management, a peculiar picture emerges (see Fig. 5.7). Employee 2 remains focused on her zone, attending to customer demands. However, for some of these demands, she lacks the necessary information and cannot address specific job-related issues. In cooperation with Employee 2, Employee 1 decides to approach management (L) and moves closer to the zone in which management operates (by phone). This indicates that both employees are moving (or not moving)

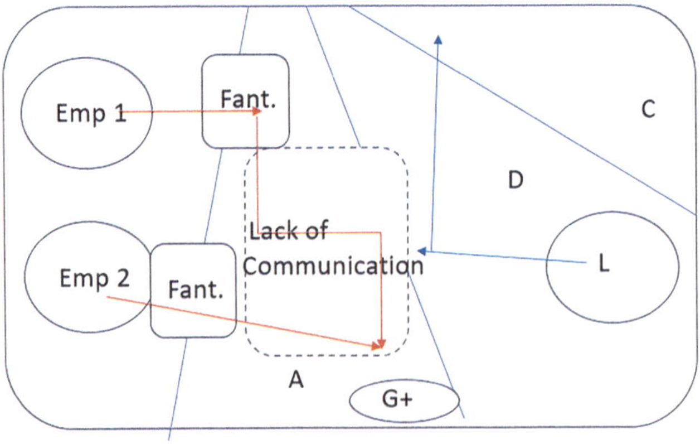

Fig. 5.6 Experiential unit of management regarding the conflict lack of communication

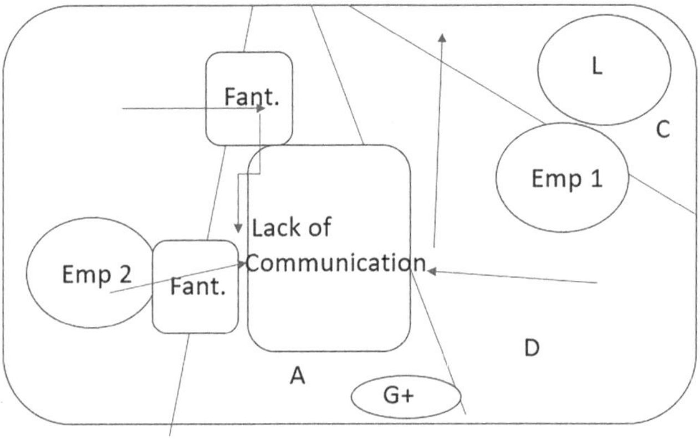

Fig. 5.7 Sociological reality (action field) of the follower regarding issue lack of communication

independently of their intended actions, as previously explored in their psychological realities (life-spaces). The actions of the employees do not align with their life-spaces, necessitating a step outside their psychological realities to approach management and proactively seek a solution. In short, the employees bridge the physiological distance between themselves and management through the phone call.

However, even with this attempt to bridge the distance, the situation remains unresolved, as management fails to engage in effective cooperation. Management simply reverts to their initial circumvention strategy, which has already proven ineffective. This unsuccessful reapplication of the circumvention strategy, which does not address customer-related demands, frustrates the employees, as they are unable to resolve the issue effectively. Consequently, a second barrier emerges: the sense of being abandoned by management when specific issues arise. This perception becomes hyper-generalized, confirming the already prevalent sentiment of neglect, as illustrated by the quotes in the autoethnographic vignette.

If we want to formulize our writings, we might depict the following.

$$-L(f) = N(F) * \text{Bar} \neq N(l) * \text{Bar} \rightarrow \text{Circ}(N_L) * \text{Bar}$$
$$\text{DIA}(N_F + N_L) = \text{Circ}(N_L) \neq g+$$

In other words, a lack of leadership emerges as a result of the followers' needs being negatively interrelated with the leader's needs regarding the barrier at hand. Specifically, management, as the leader in this context, fails to consider the demands and needs of the employees when devising a circumvention strategy. The autoethnography further illustrates that the employees actively attempt to renegotiate this strategy, as it does not assist them in overcoming their job-related challenges. However, despite two individuals communicating, a genuine dialogue with management does not materialize. This is because management does not intend to actualize its circumvention strategy based on the input of the employees.

Third Ethnographic Vignette: How to Fill Bread Rolls

Several weeks later, I decided to conduct another ethnographic visit to the bakery. I settled into my usual corner, equipped with my books and field journal, waiting for critical incidents to unfold. As I observed the employees completing their morning shift, I noticed that I had arrived after both employees had already worked together for two hours. For about twenty minutes, there was a rush as customers, primarily workers purchasing food for breakfast or their lunch breaks, lined up at the counter. During this time, I did not observe any significant in-depth cooperation between the employees; both were focused on serving the customers as quickly as possible.

However, once the rush subsided and the customers were served, I overheard a conversation between the employees that indicated a critical incident. They were expressing dissatisfaction with a recent measure introduced by management. Intrigued by their comments, I approached the employees and decided to conduct a spontaneous interview with them. Below is the protocol of the interview:

Interviewer: Explain to me this new measure management decided to come up with.
Employee: They force us to fill the bread rolls according to some filling plan (Belegplan).
Interviewer: What does that mean?
Employee: During the morning, we need to fill some bread rolls for people buying their breakfast or stuff for their lunch break. Now, management prescribes how to do that and by which quantity.
Interviewer: How did you do it before?
Employee: We have some experience what our customers want and like eating. Hence, we do it in a manner to satisfy the customer-related demands. That's why we did it based on our own personal experience.
Interviewer: And now what does management want you to do?
Employee: They want us to fill the bread rolls according to their system.

Unfortunately, the interview was interrupted by some customers wanting to buy some baked goods. Hence, I decided to go back to my observational corner and pause for a minute with the interview. Once the customers had been served by the employees, there was some time for me to re-approach the employee with whom I did the initial interview.

Interviewer: What do you think about their system regarding the filling of the bread rolls?
Employee: I mean, I think they want that every bakery does it more or less the same way. That is okay. But they want us to photograph the counter in order to check whether we did it their way.
Interviewer: How does that make you feel?
Employee: I feel that (name of the bakery) they do not trust us.
Interviewer: And some other things?

During the interview with one of the employees, new customers approached the counter, eager to be served. However, the other employee signaled to the person I was interviewing that she could manage the customers on her own. This allowed us to continue the interview without interruption. Fortunately, the counter's L-shaped arrangement provided some privacy, enabling me to conduct the interview somewhat out of sight from the main area of the employees' action field.

Employee:	I think that this measurement is not good for us nor for the other bakeries.
Interviewer:	Why?
Employee:	Because we know what our customers want; management does not know so.
Interviewer:	Okay, that is enough. I will let you do your job as of now. Thanks for having this kind of conversation with me.

After the interview, I returned to my observational corner, reflecting on the experiences of the employees. Occasionally, I overheard them discussing the new management measure, openly expressing their complaints about it. After observing for about 30 minutes without any significant incidents occurring, I decided to conclude my ethnographic field study and returned home.

Analyzing the Third Ethnographic Vignette Psychologically

From a psychological perspective, analyzing the third ethnographic vignette reveals a significant issue regarding how employees anticipate the filling of the bread rolls. The employees, as discussed in the ad-hoc interview, demonstrate a particular need to rely on their personal experiences when addressing customer demands. They attempt to navigate the bread-filling task using a unique strategy based on their individual perspectives. This approach starkly contrasts with the social needs dictated by the organization, as highlighted by management's specific directives. Management requires the employees to fill the bread rolls according to a prescribed scheme, crucial for maintaining uniformity across different bakery locations. This uniformity is intended to enhance customer experience, guiding customers to perceive the various stores in a similar manner.

The interactional pattern present in this vignette is particularly noteworthy. Management communicates its expectations distantly, relying on a group chat on WhatsApp to relay the necessary guidelines. This mediated interaction creates a disconnect between management's intentions and the psychological and sociological realities of the employees. From a semiotic standpoint, these guidelines are perceived as non-negotiable, leaving the employees feeling alienated. Management, particularly the individual responsible for sending the guidelines, operates based on interconnected signs that they introduce into the employees' ecological environment. These signs consist of a fantasm for uniformity across stores, which is linked to themes of dependence and control, while also integrating economic

Table 5.3 Analysis scheme for the lack of communication ethnographic scheme

Problem/ Issue	Personal need (follower's needs)	Social needs (organizational needs)	Interaction patterns	Tool-/ Sign-systems	Solution	Feelings
Filling the bread rolls independent from the follower's experience	Followers have the need to be consulted when being confront with a new measurement	Making the different stores more similar with each other	Remote and distanced (via WhatsApp)	Economic pressure signs, customer anticipation signs, absent signs of consulting the employee's experience.	Top-Down solution	Frustration. anger.

considerations. The rationale is that consistent customer experience will foster comfort and increase willingness to spend time and money within the bakery.

Despite the employees' active attempts to illuminate the absent signs and infuse them with meaning, a viable solution remains elusive. This lack of resolution leads to frustration among the employees, who connect this situation with previous experiences, reinforcing the hyper-generalized belief that management does not value their insights. Notably, the employees engage in discussions among themselves to navigate the emotional fallout from this conflict, striving to regulate the negative emotional implications of the event. This hyper-generalization allows them to make sense of their experiences, even if it results in negative emotional consequences. In Table 5.3, I have summarized my analysis of the third ethnographic vignette.

Field-Theoretical Interpretation of the Third Ethnographic Vignette

From a field-theoretical perspective, the situation can be interpreted as follows (see Fig. 5.8): The life-space of the employees highlights their prioritization of personal experience in the process of filling the bread rolls. They engage in discussions about how to approach this task, collaborating based on various determinants, including the day of the week and the weather, among other criteria. This indicates that the employees perceive the barrier as primarily permeable, allowing them to utilize a circumvention strategy effectively.

In this context, the employees expect management to refrain from interfering in their processes and to focus on other operational areas. Their desire for management to maintain a distance reflects an aspiration for autonomy (fantasm); they believe that their previous experiences equip them to handle the situation competently.

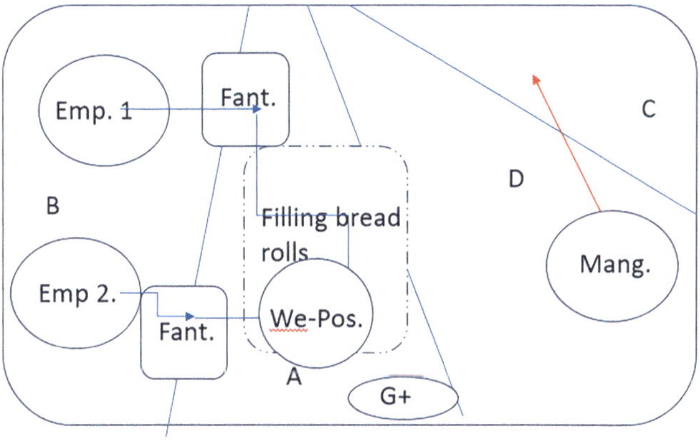

Fig. 5.8 Experiential unit of the followers regarding the task of filling the bread rolls

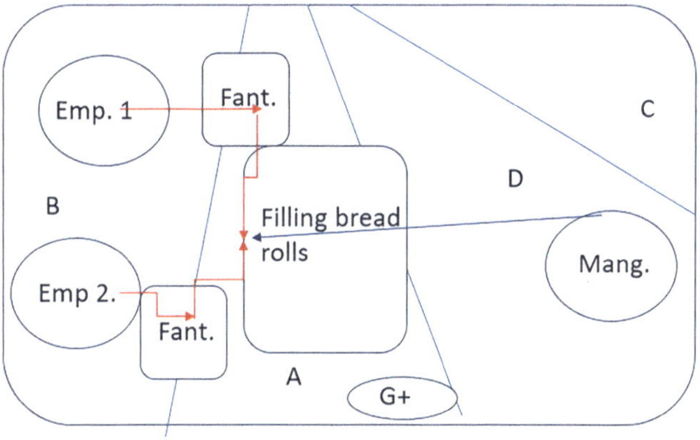

Fig. 5.9 Experiential unit of management regarding filling the bread rolls

Essentially, they wish to exercise control over the filling process without external oversight, relying on their established knowledge and skills to navigate the task at hand.

Focusing on the experiential unit (life-space) of management, an opposite pattern emerges (see Fig. 5.9). In this scenario, management views the border as impermeable, intending for the employees to approach the boundary of this barrier while awaiting further instructions. Management's goal is to guide employees with specific suggestions on how to fill the bread rolls in accordance with their established plan. Consequently, the barrier is deemed permeable only when employees have internalized this prescribed circumvention strategy.

To facilitate this process, management communicates with the employees via WhatsApp, presenting their circumvention strategy and providing directions on its application. Essentially, management expects the employees to advance toward

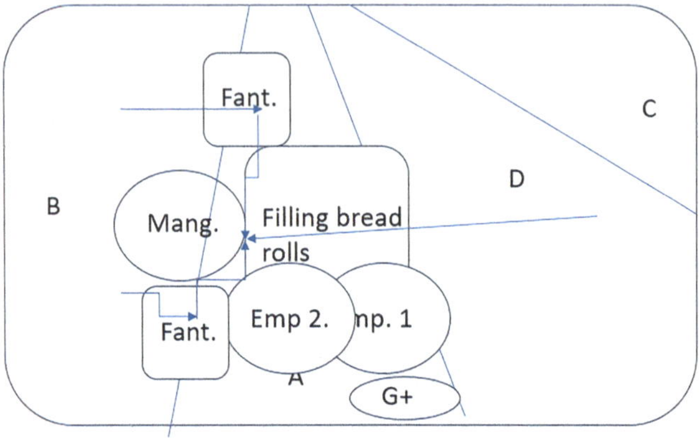

Fig. 5.10 Action-theoretical analysis regarding filling the bread rolls

their goal field only when they adhere to the suggested circumvention strategy, effectively inhibiting any competing or prior approaches.

Taking a closer look at the action-theoretical (sociological) analysis of the action field (see Fig. 5.10), we observe that the employees have already moved into the zone to achieve their goals, effectively penetrating the barrier with their own strategies. However, management views this approach as incorrect. Conversely, management has also relocated to a different zone, positioning itself closer to the employees in order to demonstrate how to navigate through the barrier. Despite the reduced distance between management and employees, a gap still exists—one that contradicts management's overall intentions.

Further analysis of the life-spaces of both management and employees reveals that management expects the employees to step back, distancing themselves from the goals they have already achieved, as they have not adhered to the prescribed circumvention strategy. This backward movement is negatively interpreted by the employees and contributes to the hyper-generalization of management's approach, which inhibits the employees' ability to derive meaning from their experiences.

While management does not deny that the employees have reached relevant goals, it re-prioritizes the importance of uniformity across stores—aiming for a consistent customer experience. The expectation for employees to revert is not inherently negative; rather, it becomes so because employees feel excluded from the development of an alternative circumvention strategy that better aligns with their needs. Though moving backward to advance collectively could be feasible for the employees, this is not the case, as management insists on the internalization of a specific meaning-making pattern (circumvention strategy).

It is therefore not surprising that the employees comply with management's directives only reluctantly, often expressing their dissatisfaction—not out of conviction, but due to the pressure to conform.

With this elaboration, we might come up with a summary of the ethnographic vignette put into a Lewinian field equation:

$$-L(f) = CVS^{*}N(1) \neq CVS^{*}N(F) \neq g +$$
$$CVS^{*}N(1) * N(1) = CVS^{*}N(1)^{2} \neq CVS^{*}N(F)$$

In this context, leadership manifests destructive effects on the employees' psychological well-being, as two circumvention strategies—reflecting the needs of both management and employees—are at play but perceived as incompatible. These circumvention strategies fail to converge into a unified solution or framework. Management emphasizes the importance of their own circumvention strategy, driven by a variety of organizational needs, while simultaneously disregarding the strategy employed by the employees. This disconnection leads to a lack of cohesion and understanding, ultimately undermining the employees' ability to effectively navigate their roles and responsibilities within the organization.

Fourth Ethnographic Vignette: Does the Counter Look Attractive?

During my fourth visit to the bakery, I settled into my usual corner one afternoon to observe the employees' interactions, anticipating potential insights into leadership conduct. For the first 90 min, however, nothing particularly noteworthy occurred regarding leadership dynamics. A few customers entered the bakery, made their purchases, and quickly left. The employees performed their tasks as usual, largely working independently of each other. Notably, during this calm period, the two colleagues engaged in amicable conversations, sharing personal anecdotes and joking about their weaknesses, all while maintaining a positive atmosphere. Their ability to seamlessly switch between friendly interactions and a more professional selling demeanor was particularly striking.

However, a critical incident arose when one of the employees decided to take a bathroom break. In this bakery, employees must leave the premises and use the bathroom facilities of an adjacent supermarket. Upon returning, the employee paused in front of the display counter and examined the baked goods. Her colleague observed her intently, and after a few moments, the employee remarked, "*The counter looks good.*" The colleague then inquired whether she was completely satisfied. The employee nodded in response, and they both proceeded to tackle other pressing tasks.

Following this incident, I continued my observations to see if any additional critical moments might emerge. Ultimately, the only notable task was the counting of returned goods, where the employees employed the same strategy, I had noted in the previous ethnographic vignette. After nearly three hours of observation, I decided to conclude my study and return home.

The seemingly minor incident of commenting on the counter's appearance lingered in my mind. Days later, I asked the employee about her comment, and she explained that she aimed to check in with her colleague to see if she was also satisfied with their work. When I probed further about the specific nature of this work, she clarified that her intention was to make the counter visually attractive to customers.

Analyzing the Fourth Ethnographic Vignette Psychologically

When analyzing this situation within our previously established framework, several key insights emerge. The primary issue at hand is the employees' need to ensure that the counter remains attractive to customers. By undertaking this action, they pursue multiple objectives. First, they aim to perform their duties adequately and anticipate customer preferences, thereby establishing a sense of customer proximity. Second, it is essential to consider the social needs dictated by management, which instruct employees to undertake specific actions regarding the presentation of the counter. Management seeks to guide the customer experience, intending for customers to perceive the richness of the product range. Importantly, the personal goals of the employees align with the social objectives of management, as both parties aim to foster positive customer experience.

From a psychological perspective, the interactional pattern between the employees is friendly, informal, and personal. Notably, negotiation concerning the counter's attractiveness occurs within a matter of seconds. The employee who had just returned from the bathroom momentarily stands in front of the counter, considering it from the customer's perspective. This demonstrates an empathetic approach that warrants psychological attention. Employee A employs empathetic signs in her conversation with her colleague. Importantly, she does not merely assume the customer's viewpoint; she also takes into account the expectations set forth by management, striving to adhere to their overarching guidelines that facilitate a rich product experience. In essence, the signs of customer empathy intertwine with management directives, creating a unique sign strategy that seeks to fulfill both customer and supervisory demands.

Employee B plays a significant role in this co-construction of meaning by reinforcing employee A's assessment, allowing her to re-evaluate the situation. Consequently, the employees collaboratively negotiate a crucial sign strategy—a circumvention strategy—pertaining to the issue at hand. In this context, customer-focused signs, management guidelines, and re-assessment indicators converge into a cohesive sign field that empowers the employees to enhance customers' experiences with the bakery's offerings. This alignment reflects a positive interrelation between the employees' needs and those of management.

The feelings that arise while implementing this circumvention strategy are notably positive, as evidenced by the smiles exchanged between the employees during their discussion. This suggests that they both perceive the situation as satisfactorily resolved.

Table 5.4 Analysis Scheme for Counter Issue

Problem/ Issue	Personal need (follower's needs)	Social needs (organizational needs)	Interaction patterns	Tool-/ Sign-systems	Solution
Does the counter look attractive?	Employees want to ensure a positive experience customer-wise	Management wishes to allow the customers to experience the full range of products.	Between employee A and B, amical, informal, personal	Employee A constructs customer-related and management-related sign field while employee B co-constructs this sign field with re-assessing signs.	Co-constructive signs are employed to the conflict, successfully (positive emotions)

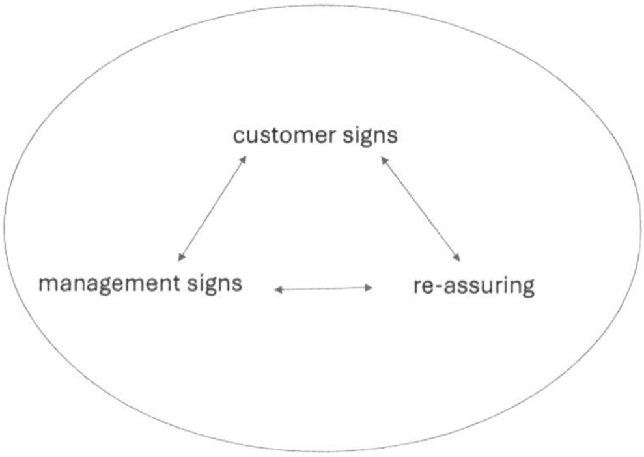

Fig. 5.11 Co-constructed sign field (anticipatory sign field)

Table 5.4 summarizes the psychological analysis of the fourth ethnographic vignette, while Fig. 5.11 illustrates the co-constructed sign field utilized as a circumvention strategy to address the issue at stake.

What remains crucial to highlight regarding Fig. 5.10 is not only the power of co-construction in relation to the sign field but also how the various signs address the differing demands of multiple stakeholders. For instance, management-related signs are essential for enhancing the economic productivity of the bakery, ensuring that operations align with organizational goals. Simultaneously, the customer-related signs enable employees to cater to individual customer needs effectively. Both employees are motivated to perform their jobs competently, which is why they also utilize re-assessment (reassuring) signs. These signs reflect their need for self-regulation and control, ensuring that their actions meet both personal and organizational expectations.

Interpreting the Fourth Ethnographic Vignette Field-Theoretically

When we contemplate the experiential unit of employee A, we can depict a nuanced scenario (see Fig. 5.12). Employee A seeks to move closer to the barrier, but her approach is grounded in the client's perspective, particularly in how the client views the counter. Her intended actions are refracted through fantasms and themes related to performing her job adequately. A notable aspect of employee A's life-space is the central role of the client, imagined from the perspectives of both employees. The client's potential perceptions of the counter they are preparing become pivotal in their psychological reality, which employee A acknowledges wholeheartedly.

Management also plays a role in resolving the issue, as it pursues its interests and establishes loose boundaries aimed at preserving economic objectives. In this context, employee A perceives management in the background of her life-space, which creates a distance between the employees and management. Thus, the dynamics of leadership between the employees themselves become more significant amid the broader, more loosely defined leadership style of management. It is essential to recognize that employee B's expected intentions are also a consideration for employee A. Specifically, employee A seeks employee B's assistance in evaluating whether the counter looks attractive. In this regard, employee B assumes a more critical role in the assessment process than management, which is only vaguely represented in the background of employee A's life-space. Figure 5.11 illustrates the life-space of employee A concerning the conflict at hand, highlighting the general distance between management and employees, as well as between employees and the generalized customer.

Turning to employee B's life-space, we observe that she also wishes to address the conflict while considering her own needs and those of the customer (see Fig. 5.13). Employee B exhibits confidence in employee A's intended actions,

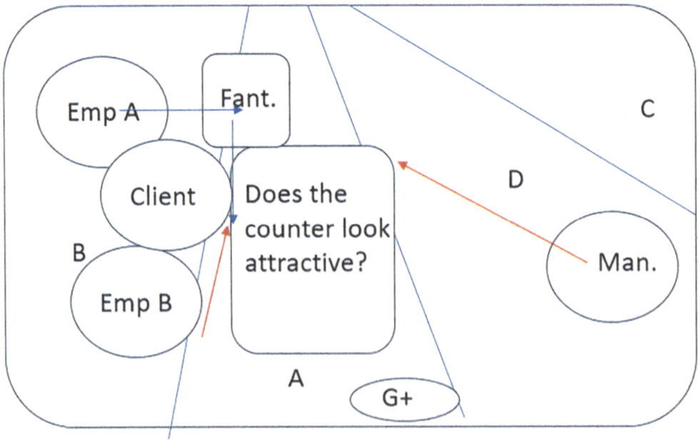

Fig. 5.12 Experiential unit of employee A regarding the issue of whether the counter looks attractive or not

recognizing their shared focus on the client's perspective. Similar to employee A, employee B situates management in the background, maintaining that it does not play a direct role in their immediate interactions. As such, I will refrain from depicting the life-space of management, as it would not contribute further relevant insights for illuminating the sociological dynamics at play. Instead, I will proceed with an analysis of the sociological aspects of this scenario.

In the sociological analysis from an action-theoretical perspective (see Fig. 5.14), both employees engage in actions that reflect their intentions. By putting themselves in the client's position, they develop a unique circumvention strategy to neutralize the existing barriers. This interaction suggests that while their psychological realities exhibit some overlap, the employees are able to synthesize and negotiate a strategy that addresses both their own needs and those of the client.

The negotiation of signs occurs within the context of three distinct life-spaces, which also consider the more distant needs of management. This circumvention

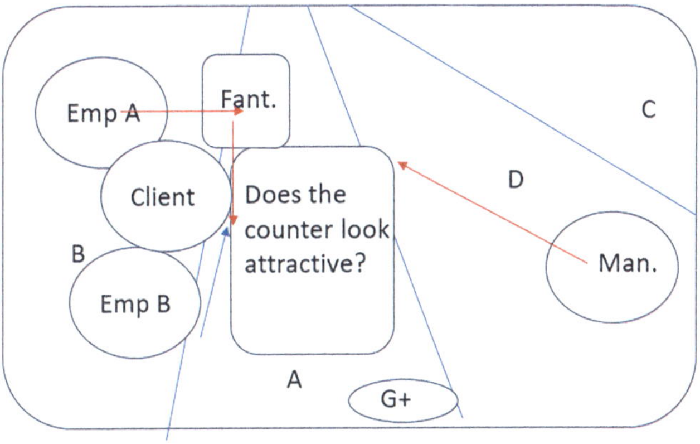

Fig. 5.13 Experimental unit of employee B regarding the issue of whether the counter looks attractive or not

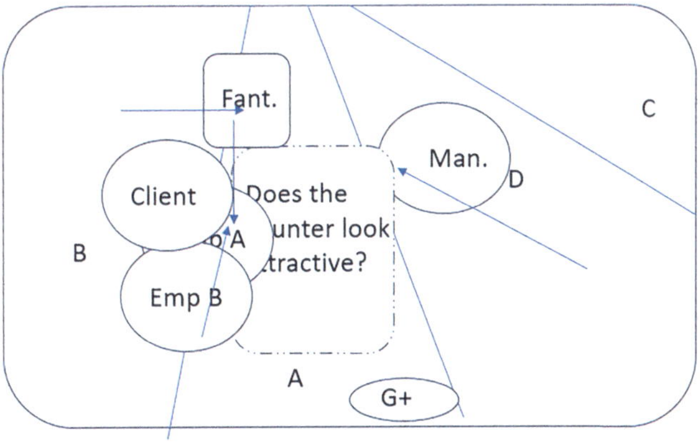

Fig. 5.14 Action-theoretical analysis (sociological analysis) within the conflict does the counter look attractive

strategy is informed by the interplay of these life-spaces, leading to the construction and co-construction of a sign field. For example, employee A's empathetic perspective toward the customer generates customer-related signs, while employee B's desire for reassurance creates controlling signs. Additionally, generalized client preferences and management's economic objectives contribute further layers to this sign field. This pluralistic circumvention strategy, emerging from the convergence of these diverse life-spaces, ultimately renders the barrier permeable. Consequently, the employees are able to navigate through these barriers toward their respective goals, while management remains somewhat in the background of this sociological analysis. The employees effectively guide one another toward a more nuanced understanding of the conflict at hand, leading to action that is catalyzed by the predominant needs of all actors involved, culminating in a unified circumvention strategy.

However, it is important to note that, despite the existence of a joint circumvention strategy, not all signs hold equal validity. The dominance of customer-related signs is particularly evident, reflecting a core theme in the employees' work: the establishment of customer proximity. This example illustrates that leadership extends beyond the hierarchical relationship between management and employees; it also occurs among the employees themselves. In this dynamic environment, the roles of leader and follower can shift rapidly, demonstrating that leadership can be a collective endeavor among employees. Furthermore, this form of leadership not only addresses immediate, tangible needs but also considers generalized, imagined needs, as seen in the employees' hypothetical construction of the client's perspective.

In this context, we can advocate for a multi-level leadership approach that comprehensively addresses the complexities of the situation faced by both employees and management. This ethnographic vignette primarily highlights the dynamic leadership patterns that emerge among employees themselves. Recognizing this, we can formulate the following equation to encapsulate the psychological nature of the ethnographic vignette:

$$L(f) = \text{Empl}(\text{ACirc}) * N(F), N(\text{manag.}), N(\text{Cust.}) = \text{Empl}(A \rightarrow \text{Empl}(1)) * \text{Bar} = g +$$

In this scenario, employee A assumes a leadership role by integrating the needs of her colleagues, management, and customers into a cohesive circumvention strategy. Leadership, therefore, manifests as a process of unifying diverse needs through a collaboratively negotiated framework. Central to this strategy is the concept of imagined dialogue, which allows the employees to internalize the customers' needs and preferences.

This circumvention occurs within a meaning-making pattern—a sign system—that interconnects these various needs. Consequently, the equation illustrates that leadership is not a static function but rather an evolving process defined by actions taken in response to the context. This dynamic understanding of leadership emphasizes the fluidity of roles among employees and highlights the importance of collaboration and communication in addressing the complexities of their work environment.

Fifth Ethnographic Vignette: An Employee Needs To Do Some Work She Is Not Paid For

During my fifth visit to the bakery, I had the opportunity to observe the morning shift, where the dynamics between the employees unfolded in an intriguing manner. Both employees, who were not only colleagues but also good friends outside of work, exhibited a strong rapport. Their interactions reflected a level of comfort and familiarity that suggested a deeper connection beyond their professional roles.

What stood out during this observation was the candidness with which the employees discussed management and its recent developments. They engaged in a critical dialogue, openly expressing their dissatisfaction with certain actions taken by management. This conversation revealed a growing consensus between them, as they collectively painted a negative portrait of management's approach.

In the following sections, I will present excerpts from their dialogue that highlight the specific issues the employees faced, showcasing their shared concerns and frustrations regarding management practices. This exchange not only illuminates their perspectives on the workplace dynamics but also sheds light on the broader implications of employee management relationships in the bakery context.

Employee A: Did you already hear about what happened with X (name of employee)?
Employee B: You mean with management?
Employee A: Yes, with management.
Employee B: Yeah, sort of.
Employee A: What is your take on that?
Employee B: I think it's not fair. She does all the work but is not paid well enough.
Employee A: They should not do that.
Employee B: They shouldn't but will they change?
Employee A: I do not think so. I mean it's still enterprise X (name of enterprise).

After overhearing a conversation between the employees, I approached employee A following her shift to clarify what I had heard. I asked her to help me understand the details of their discussion, and she kindly agreed to explain.

She began by explaining that management had been searching for a new store manager but had initially struggled to find a candidate willing to take the role. This vacancy had persisted for several months. Eventually, another employee expressed interest in the position, which prompted management to offer her a small raise as an incentive. However, they required her to trial the role in a neighboring store, a condition she ultimately rejected.

Despite her initial enthusiasm for the role, the two parties could not reach an agreement. Consequently, even though the responsibilities of the store manager still needed to be fulfilled, management pressured her to carry out those tasks temporarily without providing a salary increase. I inquired whether there was a possibility for this situation to change in the future. Employee A expressed skepticism, indicating that the current arrangement was advantageous for management, as they effectively had someone performing the store manager's duties without incurring additional costs.

Psychological Analysis of the Fifth Ethnographic Vignette

In analyzing the fifth ethnographic vignette from a psychological perspective, we first identify a central issue: one colleague is required to perform work without compensation, which triggers feelings of unfairness and injustice. This dynamic reveals the underlying needs of the employees, particularly the need to be treated fairly within the workplace. Both employees appear to share a consensus on this interpretation of their situation, feeling aggrieved by management's actions.

On the other hand, management's needs are primarily practical—they require someone to fulfill the store manager's duties on a daily basis until a suitable replacement can be found. This necessity compels them to pressure an employee into temporarily taking on responsibilities without the promise of additional (significant) pay, which exacerbates the tension between management's requirements and employees' expectations.

When we consider the interplay of the employees' and management's needs, it becomes clear that their interests are not merely opposed but deeply contradictory. This contradiction creates significant psychological tension within the employees' mental frameworks. In seeking to make sense of the situation, the employees engage in symbolic interpretations, categorizing the event in a way that affords its meaning and context.

Notably, the interaction between the employees reveals a pattern characterized by remoteness and a degree of secrecy, as their dialogue about management's shortcomings remains hidden from managerial oversight. This suggests a level of detachment from management and indicates that their frustrations are not subject to direct scrutiny.

To understand how these interpretations develop, we observe the convergence of various signs within their discussions. Regularity signs indicate that they are still operating within the context of "enterprise X," while signs of unfairness emerge as they express their feelings of injustice. Additionally, signs of non-adaptation signify a resignation to the current circumstances, leading to a sign system characterized by an exploitive status quo. This system becomes evident in the employees' dialogue, particularly highlighted in the final remarks made during the ad-hoc interview, which are charged with negative emotions and a sense of hopelessness (see Fig. 5.15).

In summary, the psychological analysis of this vignette illustrates the complex interplay of fairness, managerial expectations, and the resulting emotional responses

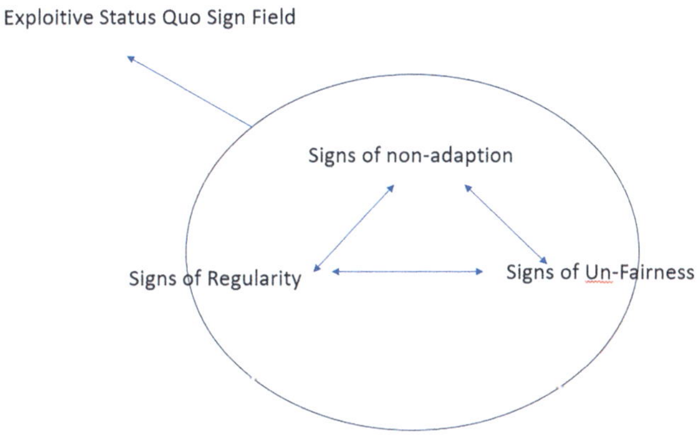

Fig. 5.15 Interrelated sign field regarding the issue of unfairness

Table 5.5 Analysis Scheme for Unfairness Issue

Problem/Issue	Personal need (follower's needs)	Social needs (organizational needs)	Interaction patterns	Tool-/ Sign-systems	Solution
A colleague needs to do some work she is not paid for by management and how to organize the store without a store manager.	Followers wish that she is paid justly.	Management is content that someone is doing the job	Remote, distanced, separated, hidden	Exploitive status quo sign field based on lower order signs (signs of regularity, signs of unfairness, signs of non-adaptation.	A negative sequence of events is given some meaning in order to make it tangible.

among employees. This analysis underscores the significance of perceived justice in the workplace and its profound impact on employee morale and interactions (Table 5.5).

Field-Theoretical Interpretation of the Fifth Ethnographic Vignette

In conducting a field-theoretical interpretation of the fifth ethnographic event, we examine the life-space of the employee considered for promotion—referred to as employee A. In contrast, employee B encompasses those employees who observe the situation from a more passive perspective (see Fig. 5.16). Within this framework, it becomes evident that employee A anticipates support from employee B regarding her aspirations to assume the role of store manager. This support validates

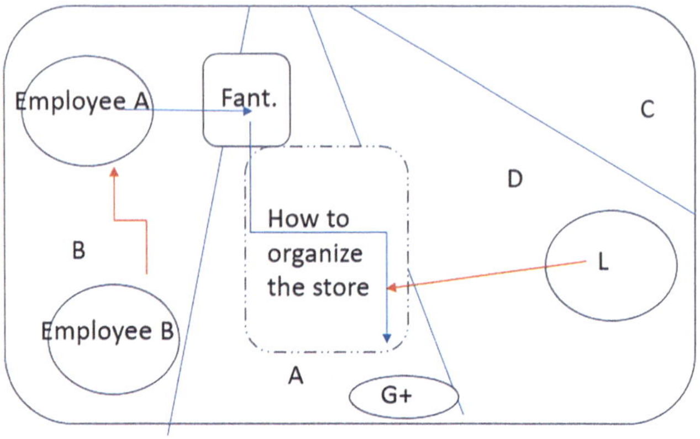

Fig. 5.16 Experiential unit of the employee who was keen to get the promotion and wanted to become the store manager of the bakery

employee A's intentions and reinforces her confidence in pursuing this new responsibility.

Employee A's wish to become the store manager is enhanced by her personal fantasms—her internal motivations and aspirations—which allow her to envision the challenge meaningfully. These fantasms instill in her a sense of self-trust that she can meet the demands of the position. She believes that she possesses the skills and commitment necessary to fulfill the responsibilities associated with being a store manager.

Additionally, employee A hopes that management will recognize and support her efforts. She seeks validation from management, desiring acknowledgment of her dedication and capability to take on the new role. This anticipation reflects her understanding of the dynamics at play within the organization, where both peer support and managerial endorsement are critical for her progression.

This interpretation highlights the interplay between personal aspirations, peer support, and managerial expectations within the workplace. It illustrates how the life-space of employee A is impacted and the overarching organizational context. Employee A's journey toward potential promotion is characterized by a complex interplay of internal motivations and external determinants.

Focusing on the experiential unit of management (L), we can identify several key elements regarding their perspective on employee A's potential promotion (see Fig. 5.17). Management seeks to assess employee A's capabilities as a store manager by placing her in a different store, thus relocating her to a new area outside her home bakery zone. This relocation serves a dual purpose: it allows employee A to gain critical experience in a different environment while simultaneously enabling management to evaluate her readiness for the position.

In this context, management expresses a desire to assist employee A in this transition, demonstrating their willingness to support her development. They aim to collaborate with her as she navigates the challenges of the new store, fostering an

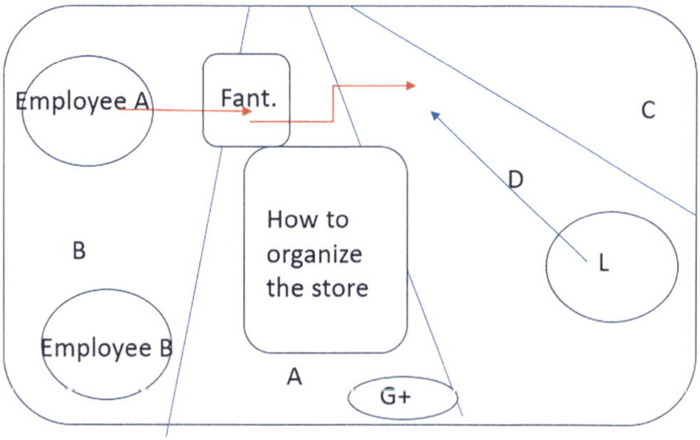

Fig. 5.17 Experiential unit of management who was responsible for the potential promotion of the employee

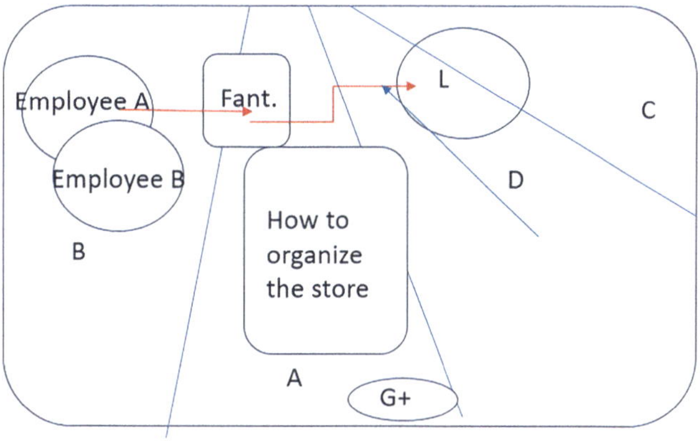

Fig. 5.18 Action-theoretical analysis of how to organize the store

environment where both parties can evaluate their performance and potential. Through this approach, management not only seeks to gauge employee A's capabilities but also emphasizes their commitment to her professional growth within the organization.

In the action-theoretical analysis of the situation, we observe the following dynamics (see Fig. 5.18): Employee A decides against moving to the alternative store due to her fear that management may attempt to retain her there permanently. Despite her initial enthusiasm for the promotion, this apprehension leads her to refrain from taking further actions.

Conversely, employee B chooses to approach employee A to ascertain the outcome of the situation and determine whether the conflict has been resolved. Upon investigation, employee B discovers that while management has indeed encouraged employee A to relocate, the proposed location does not align with the collective needs and goals of the employees as a team. This discrepancy highlights a potential misalignment between management's objectives and the desires of the employees, contributing to the ongoing tension within the workplace.

Management finds itself in a peculiar position, having attempted to implement their intended actions yet realizing they are alone in this effort. Employee A has not arrived at the alternative location suggested by management, leading to a scenario described as movement into the void (*Bewegung ins Leere*). This indicates that management's proposed circumvention strategy has not been accepted, and instead, it has encountered resistance. Consequently, management cannot resolve the conflict, as a minimal level of cooperation between the employees and management is essential for any resolution. However, such cooperation is absent, leaving the conflict unresolved.

Despite this, the store still requires a supervisor, prompting the employees to manage the store to the best of their ability without support from management. This situation brings forth the next experiential unit. Rather than depicting these units individually, I will summarize the essence of the diagrams. The employees realize that management is unwilling to move toward them, necessitating that they operate the store without a designated manager. This lack of leadership is generalized and negatively interpreted by the employees. Even though they cannot circumvent the barrier due to management's refusal to engage further, the employees maintain a sense of agency, interpreting the situation and allowing that interpretation to circulate within the bakery. This is a critical step for them, enabling them to adjust their subsequent actions despite the organizational shortcomings.

Management, however, remains largely unaware of this interpretation. This lack of awareness prevents them from constructing a counter-narrative to the events unfolding in the store.

We can encapsulate this leadership example with the following equation: non-leadership arises when management and employees fail to agree on a circumvention strategy to address the barrier present in their respective action fields. Each party expects the other to adopt their interpretation of the barrier, with minimal negotiation occurring. In this scenario, management opts to move in a direction that does not align with employee needs, leading employee A to conclude that staying put is the more favorable option. While employee A has demonstrated the capability to tackle the barrier, her strategy contradicts management's objectives, which is why they resist it. Consequently, the barrier remains impermeable to both management and employees.

As the conflict remains unresolved, the struggle for dominance over the interpretation of events escalates. The employees quickly develop powerful connotations regarding what has transpired, illustrating that the failure of guidance carries significant symbolic capital that could undermine the reputation of specific individuals, particularly management. To reduce the complexity of this interpretation, we can summarize the situation as follows:

$$-L(f) = \mathrm{Circ}(F) * N(F) \neq \mathrm{Circ}(1) * N(1) \neq g+ = \mathrm{BAR}(-)$$

In this scenario, the circumvention strategies do not merely contradict one another; rather, they actively obstruct each other's implementation. This mutual hindrance is the reason the barrier remains unaddressed and chronically open. The barrier continues to be a significant concern within the life-space and action field of both employees and management. As a result, the only recourse available to both parties is to interpret the event, making it more palatable, particularly for the employees.

Management now faces two pressing issues: first, how to resolve the primary concern of appointing the next store supervisor, and second, how to counteract the symbolic narrative that the employees may construct, which assigns blame to management. If management becomes aware of this narrative, it may further complicate their situation.

Consequently, within the life-space of management, two barriers emerge: the original barrier concerning the lack of a store supervisor, and a secondary barrier arising from the unsuccessful attempts to circumvent the first. This example powerfully illustrates the potential consequences of unresolved conflicts, as they can lead to compounded issues that complicate the organizational landscape.

Longitudinal Leadership Trends Within the Ethnographic Vignettes

When analyzing the ethnographic vignettes from a longitudinal perspective, it becomes evident that leadership is a dynamic quality. This understanding suggests that leadership can emerge among employees themselves, independent of formal hierarchies where management is directly considered the leader. For instance, in the first ethnographic vignette, leadership manifested as a dynamic and dialogical quality between two employees, with the role of leadership preserved through the use of specific, repetitive signs. A crucial element of this dynamic quality of leadership is the unwritten agreement that specific actions reflect the needs of both agents. Consequently, cooperation between management and employees emerged because both parties recognized that they were generally aligned in their goals.

This experience, as interpreted, enabled employees to generalize meaningful patterns, such as the ability to manage multiple job-related demands autonomously while flexibly assigning leadership responsibilities. Essentially, employees strengthened the hyper-generalization of their autonomous leadership conduct, where management played a passive role, leading to what can be described as an inside leadership pattern. This experience was critical, as employees realized they could circumvent several barriers without the need for management's mediation.

However, a thematic shift becomes apparent in the second autoethnography. In this instance, followers struggled to resolve an issue independently and found themselves in desperate need of assistance from management. Interestingly, despite their need for management intervention, the followers were reluctant to relinquish their autonomy. They desired a collaborative circumvention strategy that would allow them to maintain their leadership conduct in future situations. Therefore, the followers sought management's involvement but wished to ensure that management did not solely dictate the terms. They wanted management to negotiate the subsequent actions to address the issue, thereby fostering their understanding of flexible leadership. Nevertheless, management's failure to engage in this collaborative process led to powerful, negative interpretations among employees regarding management's leadership style, culminating in a hyper-generalization of leadership conduct.

This hyper-generalization was further solidified in the third ethnographic vignette, where management imposed a new strategy onto the employees' existing circumvention approach. In this case, employees had already successfully neutralized a barrier but were obstructed by management from continuing their efforts. Management's insistence on reverting to their strategy, which ignored employee needs, exacerbated tensions. As management emphasized their economic needs in the dialogue with employees, it became clear that they were prioritizing their agenda over the pressing concerns of staff members. Consequently, employees evaluated this situation negatively, reinforcing their critical view of management's leadership style.

As a result, an antagonism emerged between the leadership exercised by management and that applied by the staff, which can be categorized as an inside versus outside leadership pattern. Employees were convinced that management failed to recognize the possibility of an additional, flexible leadership conduct being exercised by the team.

This antagonism appeared to be further entrenched in the fourth ethnographic vignette, where followers resolved an issue independently while considering the needs of all parties involved. Imagined dialogue with both the customer and management proved crucial in this context. Here, leadership became a dynamic quality that was primarily assigned to the staff, enabling them to synthesize a position that accommodated multiple needs. The employees' ability to solve problems autonomously while distributing flexible leadership roles was a testament to the highly dynamic nature of the inside leadership pattern. This experience reinforced the staff's potential for leadership, demonstrating that they could lead effectively while acknowledging management's role.

In the final ethnographic incident, the hyper-generalization of management's neglect of employee needs became even more pronounced, reflecting a consistent trend in management's leadership patterns. Management sought a new store supervisor but insisted that the designated candidate prove herself in another location, which conflicted with the needs of the employee willing to take on the role. Consequently, she ultimately declined the position. However, the responsibilities of the store supervisor did not disappear; they were assigned to the same employee without compensation. This situation exemplified a disconnect between management and the employee regarding the terms of her new role, as she was left to fulfill supervisory duties without the corresponding title or pay.

Employees interpreted this situation within the framework of the hyper-generalization, perceiving management as disinterested in their needs, which led to a destructive interpretation of the leadership style. This resulted in a recurring theme throughout the ethnographic vignettes: management operates apart from the employees rather than in conjunction with them. Despite this disconnection, it is noteworthy that employees developed an inside leadership pattern that management appeared unaware of, according to the employees' perspective.

When we wish to sum up our writings from a longitudinal perspective, we might come up with the following:

(A) There exists a dynamic inside leadership style employed by the staff within the bakery. In this context, leadership becomes a fluid feature as employees lead one another, integrating various needs into a common circumvention strategy. This approach enables employees to resolve issues autonomously and adaptively.

(B) Management appears to overlook this dynamic inside leadership patterns concerning several challenges that arose during the observational phase. Specifically, management seems to disregard the dynamic qualities of the staff—most notably, their pressing needs that emerged in response to customer demands. As a result, management undermines the staff's leadership power and attempts to impose several circumvention strategies onto the employees' psychological landscape, denying their ability to address conflicts independently.

(C) An antagonism arises between inside and outside leadership patterns—specifically, a conflict between management and staff. Management remains unaware that staff has developed their own leadership strategies that assist them in navigating challenges autonomously. Consequently, the imposition of management's leadership style stifles the effective leadership patterns cultivated by the staff.

(D) This situation leads to a hyper-generalization among the staff that management fails to consider their needs, which have been crystallized within their inside leadership perspective. Consequently, staff develops a negative interpretation of the leadership style practiced by management, perceiving it as undermining their carefully constructed leadership dynamics in real time. However, this interpretation enables employees to better cope with the existing conflict.

Table 5.6 gives an overview of the ethnographic vignettes.

Table 5.6 Overview of the ethnographic leadership vignettes

Number of Vignette	Issue	Leadership Equation and Explanation
1	Counting the returned goods Leadership emerges between employees—management only plays a passive role during that process.	$L(f) = N(F) * N(l) = Circ(WePos^{*}Rep - Signs) * Bar \rightarrow g+$ Where leadership becomes a function of uniting the needs of the follower and the leader within a particular We-Position that circumvents the barrier in order to move closer to the goal-field. Yet, the cooperation being established is preserved or hold constant through repetitive signs.
2	Sellers do not dispose over background information regarding a new product. There appears to be a lack of communication.	$-L(f) = N(F) * Bar \neq N(l) * Bar \rightarrow Circ(N_L) * Bar \rightarrow DIA(N_F + N_L) = Circ(N_L) \neq g+$A lack of leadership comes into being as a function of the follower needs—regarding the barrier at hand—when those needs are different and negatively interrelated to the leader's needs. In other words, the leader—or management in our example—does not take into account the follower-related demands (and thus needs) when coming up with a respective circumvention strategy. However, management dialogue does not come into being despite two people talking with each other because management does not intend to actualize its circumvention strategy based on the follower's or employee's input.
3	Filling bread rolls according to some generalized plan	$-L(f) = CVS^{*}N(l) \neq CVS^{*}N(F) \neq g+$ $CVS^{*}N(l) * N(l) = CVS^{*}N(l)^{2} \neq CVS^{*}N(F)$ Leadership unfolds rather destructive effects upon the psychic system of the employees as two circumvention strategies are used—regarding the needs of management as well as regarding the needs of the employees—and which are perceived as incompatible. Here, the circumvention strategies are not flowing into a joint solution or framework while management stresses heavily the importance of their circumvention strategy due to a variety of their needs (the reason why we square the needs of management) while equally ignoring the circumvention strategy as applied by the followers.

4	Question emerges whether the counter looks attractive to the customer	$L(f) = Empl(ACirc) * N(F), N(manag.), N(Cust.) = Empl(A \rightarrow Empl(l)) * Bar = g+$ Here, employee A becomes the leader in the given situation while incorporating the needs of the followers, the management, and the customers in a joint circumvention strategy. Hence, leadership comes into being as a matter of uniting different needs within a jointly negotiated circumvention strategy. For that strategy, imagined dialogue seemed to be the key while interiorizing the needs of the customer.
5	A colleague needs to do some work she is not paid for	$-L\ (f) = Circ(F) * N(F) \neq Circ\ (l) * N(l) \neq g+ \ = BAR\ (-)$ where the circumvention strategies do not simply contradict each other but hinder each other from being put into practice which is the reason why the barrier does not become circumvented and remains chronically open. The barrier as such remains in the life-space and action field of the employees and management, and the only thing the employees and management can do is to make sense of the event which makes it more digestible at least for the employees.

Chapter 6
Cross-Sectional and Longitudinal Interpretations of Autoethnographic Leadership Patterns

This section presents twelve separate autoethnographic vignettes, each offering insights into leadership. These twelve vignettes are structured such that the author shares four distinct experiences from each of the three enterprises, culminating in a total of twelve auto-ethnographic accounts. After providing descriptions, analysis, and interpretation of each, longitudinal trends emerging from the autoethnographies will be examined.

First Autoethnography: Delivering My First Tennis Class

One of the earliest incidents that left a lasting impression on me occurred when I began my job as a tennis instructor. I was hired without formal training in tennis instruction, as my former boss believed I could learn on the job. I agreed, recognizing that I had strong interpersonal skills, a connection with children, and a deep passion for tennis, having played the sport for over twenty years. Transitioning from being a tennis player to an instructor felt relatively smooth. Initially, I was tasked with teaching for three hours a week, stepping in for a colleague who could no longer teach due to scheduling conflicts.

On my first day, I felt nervous. I didn't know the clients and was unsure how they would react to me. I questioned whether I could perform the job without formal training, something my boss had never directly addressed. I arrived at the court and prepared what I believed was important for the lesson. My boss had informed me that my first clients were beginners, so I introduced myself, asked for their names, and inquired about what they had previously learned. They mentioned they had practiced some groundstrokes (forehand and backhand) during feeding sessions with their former instructor. I decided to continue working on those skills, and they agreed.

E. Freiherr von Fircks, *Studying Leadership from a Microgenetic Perspective*, Methodologies in Developmental Sciences,
https://doi.org/10.1007/978-3-031-90214-7_6

I sought to establish a connection with the students. To me, tennis is a personal endeavor, with each person having their own reasons for learning—whether to play with friends and family, learn a new sport, or find work-life balance. The students shared that their motivation was simply to learn a new and interesting sport. I acknowledged their experiences and tried to bridge a connection by asking about their occupations—one was a student, and the other was doing an apprenticeship. I believe getting to know the person across from you is important, as learning a new sport can make one feel vulnerable, with failure being a necessary part of the process.

When they missed the ball and became visibly frustrated, I reassured them that this was part of learning and encouraged them not to worry. They smiled, appreciating the reassurance. After spending some time feeding them balls, I asked if they had played together before. They hadn't, so I suggested they try. Their first attempts were poor—the balls flew all over the court, but not where they needed to be. I remained calm, reminding them that patience was key and that this was a normal part of the process. Eventually, they managed to play decently, considering they had just started. I was pleased with how the lesson went, not for my own sake, but because I had shown them that they were already capable of playing with each other.

For me, this is the essence of tennis. While some might prefer to focus on perfecting every stroke before playing, I realized that people begin to find tennis engaging and dynamic once they can actually play with someone else. After the lesson, I felt satisfied, not just because of the progress I had facilitated, but because the students had experienced tangible improvement.

Afterward, I approached my boss, who was teaching a class nearby. I don't recall why exactly I went to speak with him, but it likely wasn't related to tennis, as we often discussed various topics. We had a good relationship, as he had been my instructor for over a decade. After our conversation, he gave me feedback on the lesson I had just taught. He appreciated that I had fed the balls by hand, but he noted that I was throwing the balls incorrectly. He explained that throwing the ball from top to bottom was less effective because the ball would bounce more easily when thrown from the bottom. I hadn't considered this before, assuming there wasn't a wrong way to feed balls. But his point made sense, and I agreed.

His feedback made me feel uneasy about the lesson. I began to question the quality of the entire session, particularly the parts my boss had not commented on. I found myself ruminating over whether the training had been bad overall and wondered why my boss hadn't offered more comprehensive feedback. I was eager for any input and left the court feeling even more insecure than when I had arrived, hoping for more feedback in the future, but receiving none.

Analyzing the First Autoethnography

From a psychological perspective, this autoethnography reveals several key insights. First, the protagonist faces a clear problem: he experiences visible difficulties in preparing for the tennis lesson, which he has taken over from a colleague. His sense of insecurity stems from not knowing how to structure the lesson, even though his desire to perform the job well is evident throughout the account. This tension prompts him to seek guidance from the absent colleague, asking the participants about their prior lessons. This step reveals the clients' primary need—to improve their basic tennis skills.

Additionally, the autoethnography highlights the social need of the leader or supervisor, who aims to maintain a certain standard of quality in the training. The tennis instructor personalizes the lesson by attempting to establish rapport with the clients, inquiring about their personal backgrounds. Furthermore, the instructor places significant importance on having the clients play with each other, a reflection of his personal priorities for the lesson. However, the autoethnography makes clear that the instructor received little guidance regarding how to conduct the lesson or the clients' developmental progress. There was no direct communication with the colleague about the group's general characteristics or skill level, resulting in a lack of smooth transition between the instructors.

From an analytical standpoint, we must acknowledge that the interaction between the leader (supervisor) and follower (tennis instructor) is shaped by their personal backgrounds. However, the interaction to resolve the technical issue—specifically, how to feed the ball correctly—is brief and lacks openness. The leader does not ask the follower why he throws the ball from the top rather than from the bottom, as recommended. Instead, the leader simply instructs the follower to change his technique, without exploring the reasoning behind the follower's initial approach.

Another noteworthy element in this autoethnography is the follower's evident desire for feedback. The instructor's sense of insecurity is intensified, even dramatized, after the interaction with the supervisor. This is partly due to the way the issue is resolved: from the leader's perspective, the follower must follow the supervisor's instructions on how to feed the ball. Although the supervisor validates the follower's general method of feeding the ball, this validation is insufficient for the follower, who yearns for a more comprehensive evaluation of the lesson.

Ultimately, the follower wishes for a more holistic debriefing with the leader, but this need remains unmet, leaving him to ruminate over the lesson without further guidance. Table 6.1 summarizes this analysis according to the framework presented in the Methodology Chapter.

Interpreting the First Autoethnography from a Field-Theoretical Perspective

Figure 6.1 depicts the visual interpretation of the autoethnography from a field-theoretical perspective. Here, we have depicted the experiential unit of the follower: The follower becomes aware of his underlying fantasms—that is to become aware of his needs.

Table 6.1 Analysis scheme for the first tennis instruction lesson

Problem/ Issue	Personal need (follower's needs)	Social needs (organizational needs)	Interactional patterns	Tool-/ Sign-systems	Solution	Feelings
How to structure one's tennis class?	To do the job appropriately and personally. To get holistic feedback about teaching the class	Substitute the colleague and ensure continuation with some quality in the training	Short personal leader intervention what the employee did wrong	Some appreciative language but major focus on criticism	Follower needs to adapt to the leader's advice	In-secureness

This scheme (Table 6.1) equips us with the necessary material to illuminate our field-theoretical models according to our introductory chapters.

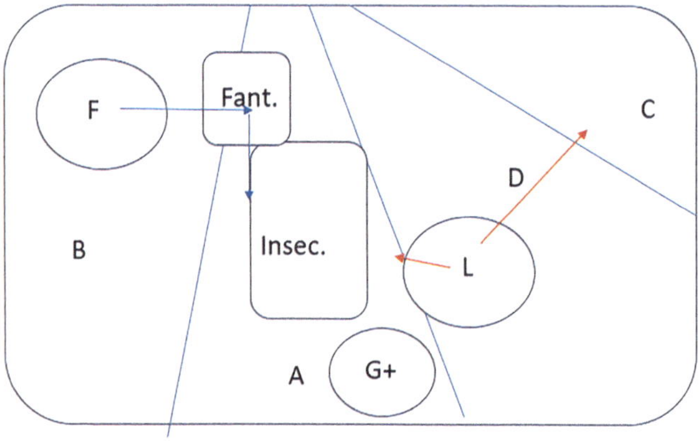

Fig. 6.1 Field-theoretical interpretation of the experiential unit by the follower perspective (F = follower, Insec. = insecurities, g + = goal field, L = leader, blue arrows = intended actions, red arrows = expected actions

In other words, the follower aims to deliver a high-quality tennis lesson, helping clients improve (such as facilitating their ability to play with each other). However, the follower exhibits significant insecurity, which serves as a barrier to effectively achieving this goal. This insecurity hinders his ability to deliver the lesson with confidence and to gauge whether he has successfully met the desired standard, preventing him from reaching his goal. What the follower seeks from the leader is assistance in overcoming this barrier, specifically through feedback on the quality of the lesson. The follower expects the leader to actively engage in the process by providing feedback that would alleviate his insecurity and enable him to improve his performance. Therefore, the follower wants the leader to be an active participant in helping him navigate and circumvent this barrier.

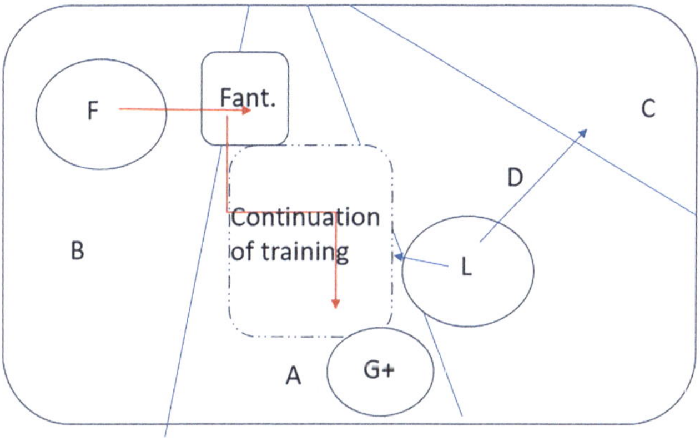

Fig. 6.2 Field-theoretical interpretation of the experiential unity by the leader perspective

From a field-theoretical perspective, the leader's experiential unit (Fig. 6.2) reveals a different psychological reality. The leader's emergent need is primarily focused on ensuring the continuation of the training program. This priority is likely driven by economic concerns, as the leader would have had to cancel the classes if a replacement instructor had not been found, potentially damaging his reputation. The leader's main goal, therefore, is to find someone capable of maintaining the training schedule. This urgent need leads the leader to entrust the follower (the new tennis instructor) with the class, fulfilling his immediate requirement to keep the program running.

Consequently, the leader and the follower face different barriers within their respective experiential units, rooted in their divergent needs. The follower's barrier is personal insecurity, which hinders his ability to achieve professional growth and confidence. Meanwhile, the leader's primary concern is logistical and reputational, revolving around ensuring the continuity of the training program. These differing priorities shape the dynamics of their interaction.

What stands out in the analysis of the leader's and follower's action fields is the absence of a common goal. As a result, both the leader and the follower construct separate psychological realities, each shaped by their immediate pressing needs (life-spaces). These divergent needs lead the leader and the follower to not only develop distinct psychological perspectives but also to prepare actions within their own specific and separate action spheres. Thus, rather than engaging in a shared sociological reality—where real actions are jointly taken—they remain confined to their individual realities. This division requires that we analyze their actions separately, rather than considering them as part of a unified dynamic.

From the follower's perspective, it becomes evident that the leader has distanced himself from the follower's needs and expectations (represented by the distance to the follower's fantasms). Furthermore, the leader has moved away from the follower's perceived barrier—the insecurity that the follower hoped the leader would help neutralize. Consequently, the follower is left to face this barrier alone, and he

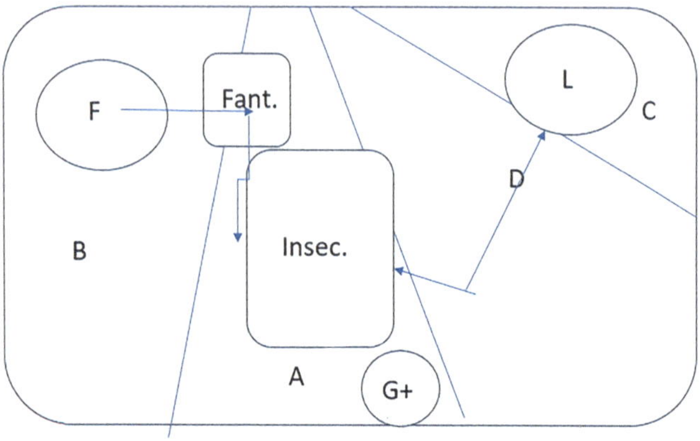

Fig. 6.3 Sociological analysis within the action sphere of the follower

fails to overcome it successfully (as illustrated in Fig. 6.3). This separation in psychological realities leaves the follower unsupported in achieving his goal, and the barrier remains unaddressed.

Since the leader remains too distant to assist the follower in resolving the key issue—namely, overcoming the feeling of insecurity—the follower becomes stuck with a chronically unmet need. This need, being unresolved, starts to solidify in the follower's need hierarchy, further intensifying the situation. The follower becomes acutely aware that he cannot address the problem on his own, which causes the barrier to grow and become more formidable. The leader's critique of specific elements in the tennis class, instead of providing constructive guidance to manage the follower's insecurity, exacerbates the barrier, making it feel even more insurmountable.

As a result, the lack of a proper circumvention strategy from the leader dramatizes the barrier even further. Through our field-theoretical lens, we observe that the barrier transforms: it not only grows in magnitude but is also dramatized due to the absence of any effective strategies to bypass it. This escalation underscores the importance of timely and appropriate interventions, as the barrier's expansion directly correlates with the leader's failure to address the follower's core need.

The sociological analysis of the leader's action field (or more accurately, action sphere) presents a contrasting image (Fig. 6.4). In this view, the leader saw the follower as having successfully ensured the continuation of the tennis training sessions. From the leader's perspective, the follower fulfilled the minimal expectations by arriving on time and delivering the lesson for the agreed-upon duration. This represents the minimal consensus achieved by the follower, which the leader considered sufficient.

This analysis sets the stage for the next experiential unit, where the leader perceives the follower as having met his own economic and social needs. However, the follower's experience is quite different. The follower feels disconnected from the leader because, while the leader sees the situation as a successful collaboration

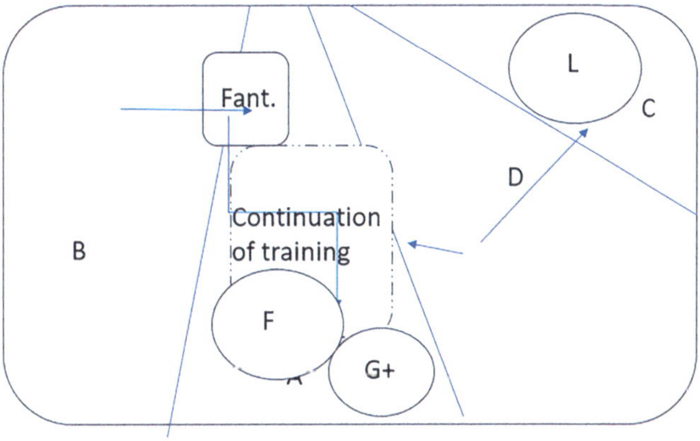

Fig. 6.4 Sociological analysis within the action sphere of the leader

(achieving the goal of continuing the lessons), the follower has entirely different goals. Specifically, the follower not only wanted to give a lesson but also wanted to structure and execute it successfully. The lack of support from the leader in this area left the follower feeling unsupported.

The leader, therefore, operates within an action sphere focused on practical and logistical goal attainment—securing the training schedule—while the follower operates in an action sphere centered on the desire for guidance and feedback to address feelings of insecurity. The follower perceives the leader as being in a different action sphere, as the leader did not provide the necessary support or feedback to help circumvent the follower's feelings of insecurity. The leader's proximity (being on the next court) did not translate into psychological support or leadership.

Leadership as a social function could not emerge in this situation because the leader and the follower were operating in distinct psychological realities. Both were acting in different action spheres that were not interconnected. The conditions for effective leadership—based on shared goals or a jointly constructed framework—were absent. Ideally, the continuation of training could have occurred within a supervised framework, allowing both the leader and the follower to experience a shared action sphere. However, this critical autoethnographic incident illustrates that they not only perceived themselves as operating in separate action fields but also took action within distinct action spheres.

The lack of leadership, as described in the autoethnographic account, arose from the misalignment of needs and goals, which placed the leader and the follower in different action fields and action spheres. This may stem from the absence of a clearly formulated joint goal. The sociological analysis in Figs. 6.3 and 6.4 illustrates that the leader imposed his own priorities—ensuring the continuation of training—without considering whether these priorities aligned with those of the employee. In other words, the leader used the employee to meet his own objectives without taking an interest in whether these objectives matched the employee's needs.

While there was a physical proximity between the leader and the follower, as they conducted tennis classes next to each other, there was no psychological rapprochement. The key takeaway from the autoethnographic report and its analysis can be encapsulated in the following equation:

$$-\mathrm{L}(\mathrm{f}) = \mathrm{l}(\mathrm{R}) \neq \mathrm{F}(\mathrm{R}): \text{The non}-\text{emergence of leadership is a function of the leader reality unequal to the follower reality} \ (\mathrm{L} = \text{leadership}, \mathrm{f} = \text{function}, \mathrm{l} = \text{leader}, \mathrm{F} = \text{follower}, \mathrm{R} = \text{Reality})$$

Regarding Figs. 6.3 and 6.4, we can conclude that leadership within the context of the autoethnographic field report requires the establishment of a shared reality as a prerequisite for the emergence of a collaborative field of action. In instances where this shared reality cannot be established, the emergence of leadership as a social fact is unlikely. As illustrated by the examples provided, leadership as a social fact can only materialize within a joint framework defined by a common goal that necessitates both the leader and the follower to operate within the same action sphere.

Second Autoethnography: Dealing with Ungratefulness

A second significant incident that I vividly recall pertains to my experiences both on and off the tennis court. I was required to teach some classes in a smaller town adjacent to my hometown, which necessitated a drive of approximately 30–40 min from my apartment. The initial twenty minutes of the journey involved traveling on the highway, followed by another twenty minutes through small villages to reach the tennis courts in that town. I particularly enjoyed the latter part of the drive, as it offered a scenic view of beautiful nature. During the summer months, everything was lush and vibrant, and I felt fortunate to have a job that allowed me to engage with nature.

The tennis club where I was to conduct my lessons was small, and my boss had been approached by the club president with a request for him to provide lessons at their courts. Due to his unavailability, he suggested that I take over. However, he specified that it was only worthwhile for me to come if I had at least three consecutive classes scheduled. The club agreed to this stipulation, leading to the enrollment of not only children but also adults interested in tennis lessons. Consequently, my boss sent me to the club.

During the first hour, I conducted a class for children on the verge of adolescence (ages 11–12). Unfortunately, the class was over-enrolled, resulting in reduced costs for the participants, as expenses were divided among them. All of the participants were amateurs with no prior experience, and I found myself managing six participants in this first class—an arrangement that proved to be more challenging than it may appear. Course instructors typically agree that the optimal number of participants is four; exceeding this number complicates the training process significantly.

For the first six to eight weeks, participants had the opportunity to use racquets provided by my boss (borrowed for the initial sessions). However, my boss later informed them that they needed to bring their own racquets or equipment. This decision was crucial for the participants, as it encouraged them to consider their commitment to the sport; purchasing a racquet signifies a deeper investment in tennis. My boss offered some racquets for sale to the young participants and provided test racquets *(Testschläger)* to facilitate their decision-making. According to him, this approach would assist participants in evaluating whether a particular racquet was appropriately sized or too heavy, with my guidance.

He sold the racquets at a fair price of 80 euros, which is relatively favorable compared to other options. Participants tested the racquets for one or two hours before making their choices. All those without an adult racquet ended up purchasing one, and I assisted them in assessing whether they could handle the racquet appropriately without hindering their performance while hitting balls with the test racquets. I had no doubts in providing this guidance.

During the sales process, some participants received test racquets that were essentially new, having been used only once or twice. For my boss, this was not a concern, as he had previously engaged in similar practices without complaints. He argued that even minimal use does not diminish a racquet's status as a new item, and I concurred with this perspective. The children were visibly happy to acquire their own racquets, exhibiting pride and increased concentration in their play. I was also satisfied with how the situation unfolded, as our objective was not merely to sell equipment but to aid participants in making informed decisions about their racquet choices.

My boss and I felt that we had executed our responsibilities well. Additionally, we offered grip tape for free with each racquet purchase, which could be perceived as a courteous gesture. After completing all three classes, I returned to my hometown, feeling fulfilled. The ride back was enjoyable; as dusk approached, I reflected on the positive aspects of teaching tennis—not only do children engage in physical activity, but they also have the opportunity to forge friendships. Despite some challenges throughout the day, particularly with this group, I concluded that I liked my job and appreciated the day's events.

Upon arriving home, I contemplated taking a bath and relaxing for a few hours before getting a good night's sleep, as more classes awaited me the following day. While checking my phone for a message from my sister, I noticed another message from a mother of a young participant. She expressed her confusion regarding the racquet purchase, stating that she had expected a new racquet for 80 euros rather than a test racquet. She attached a photo showing minor abrasions on the racquet frame, likely incurred when the children accidentally dropped the test racquets during play. Although these abrasions were barely visible, they were present. I felt a surge of anger upon reading her message, perceiving her response as ungrateful. I began to question whether our efforts had been in vain, as her conduct seemed to disregard my role as a course instructor.

Moreover, I considered whether alternative approaches might have been more effective. We could have suggested that participants purchase a racquet from a sports shop, foregoing the extensive guidance we provided. However, our approach aimed to be informative and supportive, ultimately facilitating successful tennis engagement and ensuring participants made informed racquet choices. As I processed this message, I experienced conflicting emotions, feeling compelled to respond to the mother in an offensive manner. However, an unknown restraint held me back.

Instead of replying directly to the mother, I composed a message to my boss, explaining the incident and including a screenshot of our conversation. Twenty minutes later, he called and asked if I had time to discuss the matter. I agreed. He explained, *"Now you are deeply involved in the issues I have faced for a long time. I deal with these matters almost every day. This is not surprising. People do not see what we do; they simply do not understand the nature of our work."* I expressed my frustration, stating, *"I am so angry because this does not appreciate what we did for the child, nor does it acknowledge our efforts. We provided quality racquets and valuable information that they are unlikely to receive in a sports shop, where sales assistants are not familiar with the participants' skill levels or playing styles."* I conveyed that this incident impacted me deeply and led me to doubt the purposefulness of my job.

My boss attempted to reassure me, explaining that such complaints were commonplace for him and that I would learn to cope with them over time. He emphasized that those who complain often lack awareness of the background context of our work, meaning they do not understand what we do beyond the courts. I agreed with his interpretation and felt somewhat relieved. He concluded the call by advising me not to take the incident too seriously. He offered to provide a new racquet for the child and recommended that I resolve the conflict as swiftly as possible.

After the call, I took my bath and went to sleep. While I was dissatisfied with my boss's proposed solution, feeling it suggested a sense of guilt, I also appreciated that he had helped me interpret the incident in a way that allowed me to cope better with my negative emotions. Although I struggled to fully embrace his interpretation, my boss offered a pathway to relieve my distress and handle my feelings appropriately.

The following day, I informed the mother that I would be acquiring a new racquet for her child, refraining from expressing any disappointment or negativity. We resolved the issue as objectively as possible and continued with the training as planned. I chose not to send my original message to the mother, and ultimately, I felt at peace with that decision.

Analyzing the Second Autoethnography

When analyzing the situation from a psychological perspective, we can draw several conclusions. The protagonist of the autoethnographic field report expressed enjoyment in his job, which relates to his underlying hierarchy of needs. He does not engage in work solely for financial gain; rather, he seeks to find fulfillment through interactions with others and a connection to nature. This presents a particular interconnection of the individual's needs, wherein engagement with nature, physical activity, and professional fulfillment converge into a unique synthesis described as performing one's job both socially and cosmologically. This fundamental need hierarchy serves as a source of motivation and meaning in his work, as illustrated at the beginning of the autoethnographic field report.

However, a significant issue arose in the middle and at the end of the report when the protagonist faced criticism from a mother regarding the purchase of a racquet for which he, along with his boss, was responsible. The concern extended beyond the clients' dissatisfaction with the racquet's quality; it was the protagonist's perception that this critique undermined the purposefulness of his role. The incident led him to reevaluate his contributions when assisting the client in making a racquet purchase. The crux of the problem lies not merely in managing workplace criticism but in the symbolic meaning attached to the event, specifically the perceived devaluation of the protagonist's efforts in light of this feedback.

The social and organizational needs in this context are relatively straightforward. Participants and their parents sought assurance that they would receive quality materials to succeed in tennis, while the protagonist's boss aimed to foster the parents' and children's commitment to the sport. The interactional dynamic between the participants (and their parents) and the protagonist was characterized by helpfulness and courtesy, evident through extra-role behaviors, such as providing grip tape, which anticipated potential issues for the clients. Additionally, the interaction between the protagonist and his supervisor could also be described as friendly, collegial, understanding, and supportive.

Examining the sign and tool systems utilized, it becomes apparent that the supervisor employed specific communicative strategies to mitigate the emotionality of the situation. He structured the conversation in a way that validated the protagonist's emotions while also conveying that such incidents are inherent to the job. In this manner, the leader attempted to implement a normalization strategy aimed at calming the protagonist and assisting him in reappraising the situation.

This reappraisal enabled the protagonist to manage the negative emotions stemming from the incident and to respond to the client in a manner that was objective rather than emotional. Thus, the leader's normalization strategy equipped the protagonist with a more rational perspective regarding the issue at hand, framing the forthcoming interaction with the mother. This approach not only addressed the client's concerns but also benefited the protagonist himself.

Notably, the normalization strategy employed by the leader in the autoethnographic field report relied on a distinctive sign system. During their conversation, the leader utilized various symbolic signs, including expressions of similarity ("it happened to me too"), empathy ("I understand your reaction"), informational statements ("they do not know what we do outside the courts"), and regularity ("this happens to me almost every day"). Consequently, this sign system of normalization was constructed through the interplay of signs representing similarity, regularity, information, and empathy. This framework facilitated the creation of a supportive normalization climate, enabling the protagonist to reevaluate his response to the client (the mother).

An interpretation of the autoethnographic report is summarized in Table 6.2.

Field-Theoretical Interpretation of the Second Autoethnography

In Fig. 6.5, I have depicted the field-theoretical experiential unit of the follower and its interpretation regarding the expected intentions of the leader.

What the field-theoretical visualization illustrates is that the follower encounters a significant barrier when attempting to navigate toward the goal field. This goal can be conceptualized as the need (fantasm) to understand how to manage feelings of ungratefulness or de-appreciation in the workplace. In this context, the follower faces considerable resistance, manifested through the parent's critique, which fails to acknowledge the effort invested in the child's training. What is particularly intriguing in the autoethnography is the protagonist's uncertainty in addressing such criticism—specifically, how to counter this resistance and progress toward the goal field despite the impediments encountered. This situation reveals a pronounced lack of circumvention strategies for effectively navigating the ecological challenges that arise in the course of his work.

The absence of these resources engenders a negative feedback loop that adversely affects the individual as a whole. Consequently, the protagonist clearly suffers from a deficit of circumvention strategies, leading to a chronically unresolved need that he is unable to fulfill independently. This struggle prompts him to question the purposefulness of his job and, by extension, the entirety of his value system. The deficiency in effective circumvention strategies for addressing ecological challenges results in a negative cascade of self-doubt regarding both his identity and his professional role. Thus, the lack of adequate circumvention strategies transforms the individual as an open system, compelling him to reassess his teleological and general activities.

Figure 6.5, however, does not depict the transformation that occurs when an individual is unable to neutralize a barrier within their life-space. As such, the F-field in Zone B is dynamically altered. The follower seeks support from the leader, though there is uncertainty about whether this support will effectively help neutralize the barrier. By sending a private message to the leader, the follower expresses a hope for assistance in developing or adjusting circumvention strategies to manage the encountered barrier. At this point, the leader still maintains some distance from the issue, as he is unaware of the events that transpired during and after the training. Nevertheless, the message serves as a promoter sign,[1] inviting the leader to draw closer to the follower's experiential unit.

---

[1] Promoter signs were scientifically established by the work of Valsiner (2014, 2019, 2021) in loose tradition to the action theory of Pierre Janet (1929). Here, the promoter sign becomes a secondary action regulating a first-order action wholistically. In other words, the promoter sign promotes

Table 6.2 Analysis scheme for the racquet conflict case

Problem/Issue	Personal need (follower's needs)	Social needs (organizational needs)	Interactional patterns	Tool-/Sign-systems	Solution	Feelings
How to react to de-appreciation? How to deal with ungratefulness?	To do one's job socially and cosmologically	Getting appropriate racquets for one's kids and defending one's claim to get that	Friendly phone call clarifying the issue	Normalization Sign System: interconnected signs of similarity, regularity, empathy, and information	Provide the child with a fresh racquet	First anger and disappointment, then relief

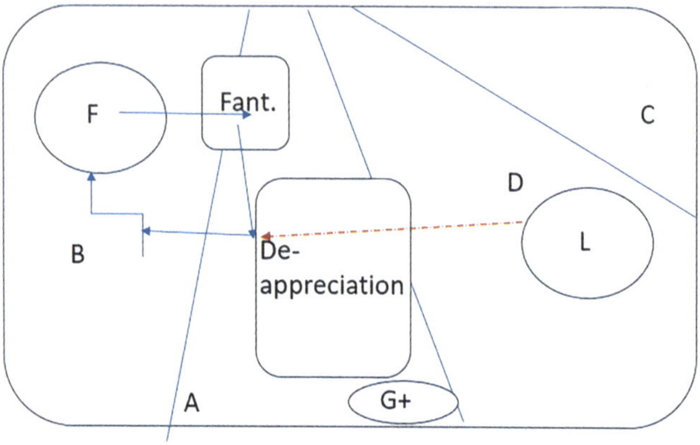

Fig. 6.5 Field-theoretical experiential unit of the follower within the conflict of de-appreciation (g = goal field, red arrow = expected intentions of the leader as experienced by the follower)

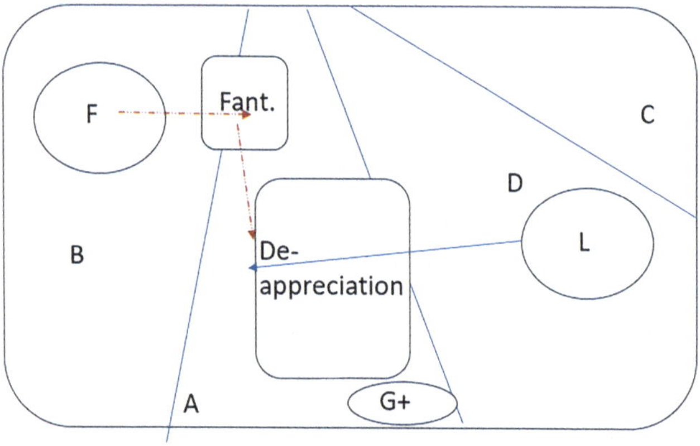

Fig. 6.6 Field-theoretical experiential unit of the leader within the conflict of de-appreciation (g = goal field, red arrow = expected intentions of the follower as experienced by the leader)

In Fig. 6.6, the life-space of the leader is depicted alongside the follower's experiences and anticipated intentions.

Upon receiving information regarding the conflict at hand, the leader seeks to assist the follower in overcoming the barrier to facilitate the employee's goal attainment. To this end, the leader shares similar experiences and endeavors to move closer to the follower's zone in order to provide support. Within his experiential unit, the leader perceives the follower's eagerness to resolve the conflict and advance toward the goal field. This determination is evident in the follower's decision to

action to be regulated in a specific manner or direction. For example, if I am tired while finishing my thesis, the deadline works as a promoter sign to continue my work and to fight my tiredness.

message the leader—an important indicator for the leader that the follower is genuinely seeking assistance.

In summary, the follower desires for the leader to approach his zone and aid in neutralizing the barrier, while the leader, recognizing the seriousness of the follower's request for help (notably, the message was sent after official working hours), is motivated to draw nearer to the follower. Consequently, in Fig. 6.7, we can encapsulate the findings of our sociological analysis of the respective action field.

Interestingly, both the leader and the follower have engaged with one another, establishing a mutual understanding of the seriousness of the conflict. Consequently, their psychological realities (or needs) align, facilitating the creation of a joint field of action. The circumvention strategy that emerges during the communication between the leader and the follower draws upon a normalization strategy, through which the leader demonstrates to the follower that such incidents are quite common in the social field of action of a tennis instructor. In other words, the leader endeavors to encourage the follower to re-appraise the barrier, arguing that such occurrences are integral to the role of a tennis instructor. He invites the follower to avoid taking the issue or conflict too personally, without, however, invalidating the follower's experience.

Importantly, the follower not only feels a sense of relief as his experience is shared and contextualized within a similar interpretive framework, but the internalized circumvention strategy also aids the follower in moving closer to the actual goal field. In simpler terms, the follower internalizes the normalization strategy and applies it to his current issue with the mother, who has devalued his efforts on the tennis court. By employing this normalization strategy—an effective form of circumvention—the follower does not merely neutralize the barrier to facilitate smoother progress toward the goal field; he also reconstructs the barrier itself.

As the follower acts upon the barrier using the internalization strategy suggested by the leader, he transforms the barrier, which in turn allows for a more adaptive

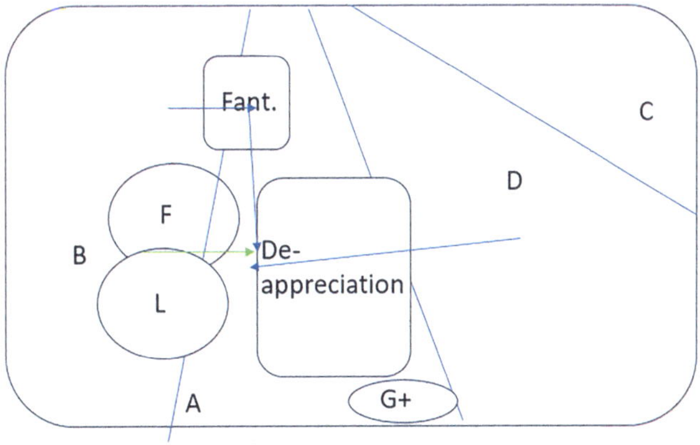

Fig. 6.7 Sociological analysis of the action field when facing a barrier (green arrow = suggested circumvention strategy by the leader)

movement toward the goal. For instance, the informative sign field (i.e., "they do not understand all the work we do" and "they are unaware of our background efforts") reframes the barrier from one of de-appreciation to a nuisance, which can be viewed more objectively—as a misunderstanding rooted in differing prioritizations of needs (see Fig. 6.8).

Thus, we observe that through the application of the circumvention strategy, the barrier is reconstructed. While it does not entirely disappear, it becomes modified, allowing the follower to address the altered barrier independently. In our example and its analysis, we see that the barrier is reconstructed, leading the follower to feel more at ease in resolving the issue autonomously. The leader's involvement in resolving the conflict becomes unnecessary; instead, by assisting the follower in transforming the barrier through a specific circumvention strategy, the leader has equipped the follower with the tools needed to address the issue at hand independently (see Fig. 6.8).

Importantly, the leader did not resolve the problem for the follower; rather, he provided essential assistance by offering a circumvention strategy to help the follower navigate the barriers and resistances encountered on the path to goal attainment. Our field-theoretical analysis can be succinctly summarized by the following equation:

$$\text{Leadership}(L)\text{ is a function }(f)\text{ of providing a circumvention strategy }(CVS)\text{ to one's follower }(F)\text{ — depending on his needs }(Nf)\text{ — in order to locomote more autonomously toward one's goal field }(g+)$$

$$L(f) = CVS^{*}N(F) \rightarrow g+$$

Regarding Figs. 6.7 and 6.8, we can conclude that leadership—within the context of the autoethnographic field report—functions as a form of guidance that facilitates not only a more unobstructed progression toward the goal field but also

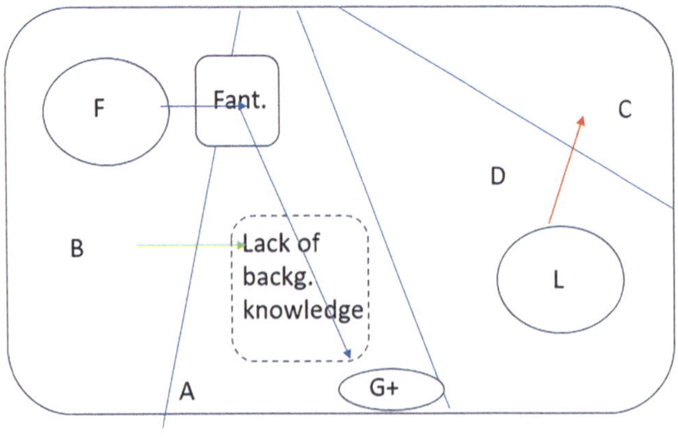

Fig. 6.8 Field-theoretical experiential unit of the follower after restructuring a barrier

enables individuals to independently navigate the challenges encountered along the way. This does not imply that the leader is inactive; rather, the leader plays an assistive role in helping the follower transform the barrier using the provided circumvention strategy, thereby empowering the follower to manage the barrier autonomously.

Third Autoethnographic Report: Dealing with the Cancellation of One's Class

An incident arose while I was teaching for my former boss that pertained to the absence or cancellation of classes by a former client. To provide context, I had been coaching a 16-year-old client who was notably shy and introverted. Despite his reserved nature, he was motivated to attend classes. I could observe this motivation during our matches; he often pushed himself to the limit and came close to winning against me. Each time he fell short, he expressed frustration but managed to smile. Over the course of my instruction, he made significant progress, which instilled a sense of pride in me regarding his development.

After instructing him for more than eight or nine months, I felt positive about our training relationship. While he may not have been the most passionate tennis player, his commitment to my classes was evident; he rarely missed a session. However, establishing a personal rapport was challenging due to his shyness and introversion. I often found myself needing to invite him to share aspects of his life, with varying degrees of success. Nevertheless, I was confident that I had done everything I could, and even in moments of failure, I did not question my abilities as an instructor or as a person.

One day, as I was preparing to leave my apartment for the tennis courts, I received a WhatsApp message from my boss. The message read: "*Person XY is not coming to classes anymore. Please come an hour later.*" I was taken aback by this communication. My mind raced with questions: *Why had he stopped attending my classes? Why didn't he reach out to me directly? Why was my boss withholding further information about the situation?* These questions led me to grapple with significant self-doubt. I found myself wondering if my client had discontinued lessons because he had suddenly developed a dislike for my teaching style or if I had inadvertently said something that offended him. I replayed our recent sessions in my mind, searching for any signs or clues that might explain his decision. However, I could not find any answers. This situation was unprecedented for me, and while I could not change the reality of it, I chose to undress and continue reading the book I had been engaged with prior to my departure.

Upon arriving at the tennis courts, I noticed that my boss was giving lessons next to me. He greeted me as usual, yet he did not mention the earlier message as if nothing had transpired. This behavior left me feeling perplexed and confused. I wondered why he had not felt compelled to explain the situation to me. The incident left me feeling intimidated, and I lacked the courage to inquire about the details that my boss had deemed unimportant to share. I proceeded with my classes, but the self-doubt continued to gnaw at me, proving difficult to dispel.

Several days later, I confided in a colleague, seeking any background information regarding the incident, as I still lacked the courage to approach my boss directly. She speculated that my client had likely stopped attending due to the need to focus on school. Yet, this explanation did little to satisfy my lingering questions. Even now, I remain uncertain about the reasons for his discontinuation. My dissatisfaction stemmed not only from the incident itself—recognizing that individuals often stop participating in activities for various reasons—but also from my boss's lack of transparency regarding the situation.

Analyzing the Third Autoethnography

From a field-theoretical perspective, several patterns emerge in this situation. First, we must identify the core issue at stake: the protagonist of the autoethnographic account is grappling with a conflict in his life-space. Specifically, the follower is seeking an explanation for the cancellation of one of his classes. It is clear that he wishes to understand the reasons behind the client's discontinuation of lessons, as this information would help him adjust his future actions as an instructor. Notably, the boss does not provide a rationale in the WhatsApp message, leaving the follower in a state of confusion and uncertainty.

The follower's motivation is rooted in a desire to perform his job to the best of his ability and to facilitate the client's progress. He aims not only to foster improvement in the client's skills but also to ensure that the client remains motivated to participate in tennis. This intent is reflected in the structure of the follower's classes, which incorporate competitive exercises to engage the client effectively. Thus, the problem is not merely the cancellation of the class but rather the lack of a rationale for this decision, which exacerbates the follower's internal conflict.

The communication regarding the class cancellation seems to serve as a solution from the leader's perspective. He provides the follower with the necessary information about the class cancellation and its implications for the schedule, viewing this as a sufficient resolution to the matter. This is evidenced by the leader's choice not to discuss the incident further upon the follower's arrival, indicating a more distant interactional pattern. The leader's use of WhatsApp to convey this information also contributes to the impersonal nature of the communication.

The predominant reliance on informative signs in the leader's message lacks the inclusion of rationale or reason signs, which would help the follower understand the context behind the cancellation. As a result, the leader's solution—a mere restructuring of the follower's work schedule—leaves the follower with little to adapt to, except for the logistical changes. While this adaptation does not inherently breed frustration, the absence of an explanation fosters negative emotions during this critical incident.

Before presenting Table 6.3, it is important to reflect on the sign system employed by the leader in this situation. By sending a concise message instructing the follower to come later than usual, the leader emphasizes logistical information necessary for the smooth continuation of classes. However, he neglects to provide any rationale for the change, leaving the follower in a void of uncertainty and questioning his own coaching abilities. This drive for meaning-making becomes particularly evident when the follower arrives at the court, expecting a discussion with the leader that would clarify the reasons behind the cancellation. While the leader focuses solely on the informative aspect of scheduling, the follower interprets the event through a different lens, yearning for a deeper understanding beyond the mere factual information.

The absence of rationale or reason signs places the follower in a precarious position, leading him to question the quality of his work and contribution as an instructor. This situation underscores the leader's unawareness of the emotional implications of withholding certain signs. The follower is left with a chronically open need for understanding, which translates into negative emotions stemming from this lack of clarity.

Field-Theoretical Interpretation of the Third Autoethnography

We can now look at the field-theoretical visualization and its interpretation and gain some further insights into the leadership setting within the autoethnographic report (see Fig. 6.9).

In the field-theoretical visualization, it becomes evident that the follower anticipates the leader to move toward his experiential field, assisting him in making sense of the complex situation surrounding the cancellation of a class. The core issue for the follower lies in his inability to identify appropriate circumvention strategies to address this unexpected development. This creates a palpable need for leadership to help decipher the symbolic meaning of the event. Essentially, the follower desires the leader to adopt a similar perspective on the barrier, reflecting his own understanding of the situation.

This pattern crystallizes poignantly when the follower arrives at the tennis court, expecting guidance from his leader, who ultimately fails to provide it.

When we examine the leader's experiential unit (as depicted in Fig. 6.10), we encounter a divergent life-space. It is critical to recognize that the leader does not perceive the same barrier as the follower. Instead, the leader confronts a different form of resistance within his own experiential unit: the need to restructure the work schedule. His intention is to assist the follower by delivering the necessary information—specifically, that the class has been canceled. The leader hopes that this guidance will enable the follower to adjust his work schedule accordingly and return to teaching the respective classes an hour later.

This discrepancy highlights that the leader and the follower possess different needs and goals within their respective experiential units. While the follower aims

Table 6.3 Analysis scheme for the class cancellation case

Problem/Issue	Personal need (follower's needs)	Social needs (organizational needs)	Interactional patterns	Tool-/Sign-systems	Solution	Feelings
Cancellation of a Class and its Symbolic Meaning	To do one's job appropriately	Class Schedule needs to be updated	Short, informative digital message	Inform. Signs, Absence of Reason/Rationale Signs	Updated class schedule for follower	Frustration

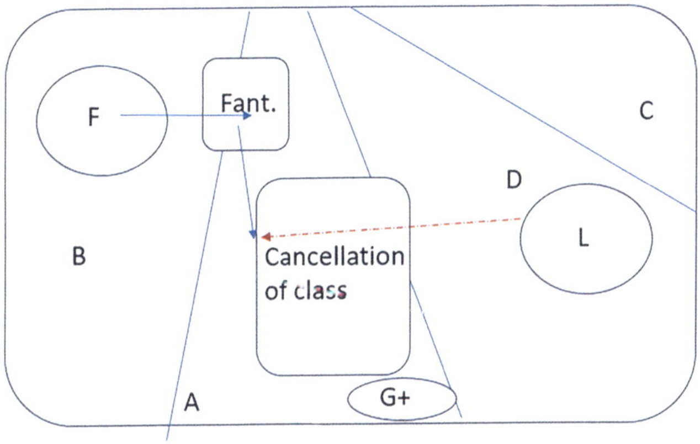

Fig. 6.9 Field-theoretical experiential unit of the follower encountering the barrier of the classes' cancellation

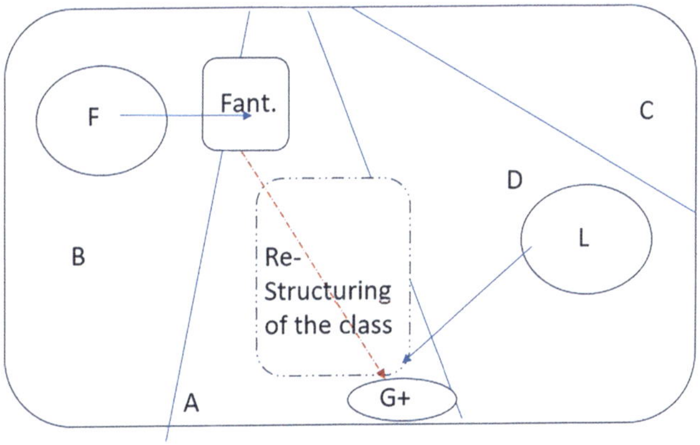

Fig. 6.10 Field-theoretical experiential unit of the leader encountering the barrier of restructuring one's class schedule

to conduct his classes as effectively as possible, grappling with the symbolic ambiguity surrounding the class cancellation, the leader focuses on restructuring the follower's schedule and requires his compliance to facilitate this change. Thus, we observe a significant divergence between their life-spaces: each perceives distinct goals and pressing needs that lead to the emergence of different barriers on the path toward goal attainment.

For example, the leader perceives the barrier as permeable for the follower, believing that adjusting one's schedule does not necessitate complex circumvention strategies. Consequently, he does not offer guidance during this process. Conversely, the follower views the barrier as non-permeable and feels compelled to develop a circumvention strategy to transform the barrier, thus allowing him to navigate more freely toward the goal field.

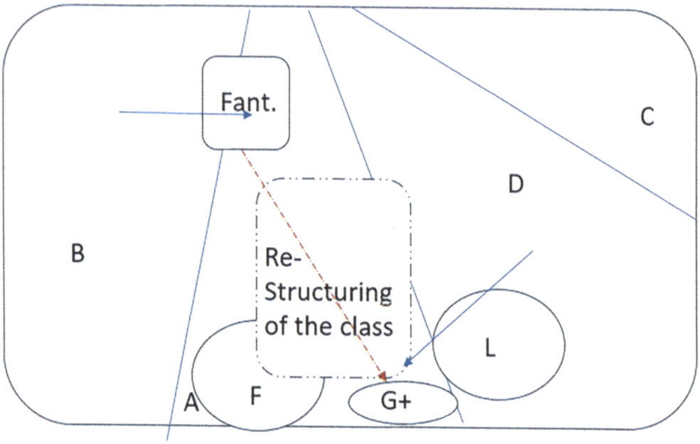

Fig. 6.11 Sociological analysis of the leader's action field

As both the leader and the follower fail to agree on a shared definition of the goal field and perceive distinct barriers in their respective paths toward that goal, they navigate different psychological spaces. The leader's perspective is represented in the sociological analysis depicted in Fig. 6.11. In this framework, the leader assists the follower in restructuring his work schedule by providing essential information. The follower, in turn, agrees to adjust his working hours according to the leader's needs. From the leader's viewpoint, this adjustment signifies that the barrier has been successfully circumvented, leading to a psychological and physiological rapprochement between the leader and the follower. Conversely, the sociological analysis of the follower's action field reveals that he is unable to circumvent the barrier on his own. He grapples with self-doubt as a result of this inability (see Fig. 6.12). Consequently, the barrier takes on secondary meaning, becoming dramatized and laden with additional symbolic weight due to the follower's lack of effective circumvention strategies. This transformation indicates that the absence of specific signs and tools to address the barrier not only alters the barrier itself but also dramatizes it on a personal level. The follower does not merely experience the leader as estranged due to the lack of mediation; rather, this estrangement extends to the differing underlying needs, goals, and actions of both parties. While the leader actively supports the follower in restructuring his work schedule, he does so from a psychological reality that does not center on the follower's lived experience. This analysis underscores that experiences are multi-layered and deeply personal. Additionally, it suggests that psychological realities are complex and layered, shaped by individual perspectives. The absence of semiotic mediation within the follower's action field—specifically, the lack of reason or rationale signs—leads to the follower's suffering. He finds himself unable to navigate a barrier essential for performing his job, which in turn transforms and dramatizes the barrier itself.

With Figs. 6.11 and 6.12, we gain a deeper understanding of the absence of leadership, which cannot be solely explained by the differences in psychological experiences and realities between the leader and the follower. The lack of leadership

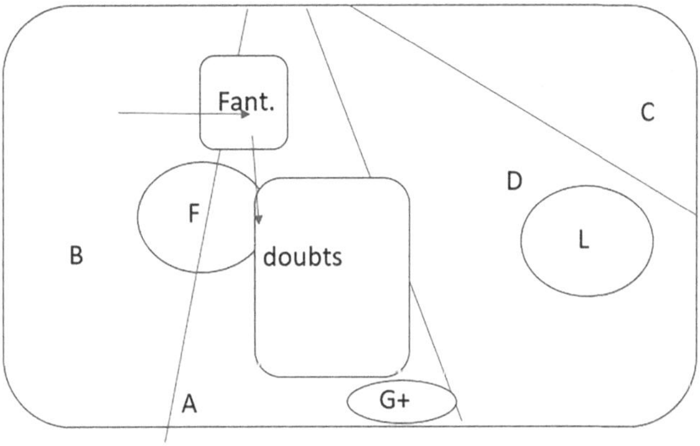

Fig. 6.12 Sociological analysis of the follower's action field

extends beyond this equation. It becomes clear that the absence of leadership cannot simply be attributed to the differing psychological realities and experiences of the leader and the follower. As both psychological realities manifest in their environment, distinct circumvention strategies are employed to address the barriers they perceive, which are fundamentally different. The leader provides the follower with a circumvention strategy rooted in his own psychological and sociological reality, while the follower requires a concrete circumvention strategy tailored to the barrier he faces in his action field.

When discussing the lack of leadership in the context of autoethnography, it is essential to highlight the absence of specific signs and tools directed at the follower's unique experience and action reality. This absence of particular sign mediation within the follower's psychological and sociological reality arises because the leader remains unaware of the follower's distinct goals and needs, which contribute to the divergence in their psychological and sociological realities. Thus, the lack of leadership is not characterized by a total absence of signs and tools, but rather by the lack of signs and tools that hold specific relevance for the follower's psychological and sociological reality.

Leadership in this critical autoethnographic incident must assist the follower in negotiating the necessary circumvention strategies tailored to his psychological and sociological context. Consequently, we can summarize the insights gained from our autoethnographic report.

Lack of Leadership$(-\mathrm{L})$comes into being by the unequalness of Leader's$(1)$and Follower's(F)psychological and sociological reality(R)which makes the leader suggest circumvention strategies(CVS)unequal to the quality of the follower's perceived and real barrier(B)

$$-\mathrm{L}(\mathrm{f}) = \mathrm{l}(\mathrm{R}) \neq \mathrm{F}(\mathrm{R}) = \mathrm{CVS}(\mathrm{L}) * \mathrm{B}(\mathrm{F})$$

In short, we can conclude from the autoethnographic report that leadership must employ the appropriate circumvention strategies, where "appropriate" refers to those strategies necessary for addressing the real and experienced barriers within the follower's action field. The findings suggest that different life-spaces, or experiential units, create distinct sociological spaces, or action fields. Lewin's analysis of conflicts, such as that between a husband and wife, posited that a researcher could utilize a shared sociological reality, a principle that holds true in the context of effective leadership. However, this concept could not be substantiated in our analysis and interpretation of the lack of leadership evident in the autoethnographic field reports.

Fourth Autoethnography: How to Learn Playing a Particular Stroke

For the last autoethnographic incident from my initial experience as a tennis instructor, I'd like to highlight a smaller illustration. This event occurred during the summer months. It was warm outside, with no clouds in the sky and no rain in sight. I felt good as I had three classes lined up in a row, which suited me fine because it allowed me to engage in other activities before and after the sessions. The first class, however, turned out to be more challenging than expected. I was faced with an adolescent who could play quite well. To start the lesson, we began hitting some balls together, focusing on rhythm training. This exercise aimed to help him keep the ball in play for as long as possible, a crucial drill for players who can hit regularly but struggle with concentration or proper footwork. After about ten minutes, I wanted to shift focus, but during this time, I noticed something unusual in my pupil's technique. While he had good timing and hit the ball at hip level—a key factor for striking the ball in the sweet spot of the racquet—he was unable to generate topspin. Instead, the ball was rotating sideways or even backward.

Topspin is essential for a player to control the ball and achieve greater length in their groundstrokes. Recognizing this deficiency, I pondered how to help him develop an adequate topspin, but I struggled to come up with a solution. I was aware of some exercises suited for younger clients, especially when combined with games, but I lacked suitable drills tailored for adolescents and adults. As I continued hitting with him, I thought about how to create an exercise that would facilitate his learning of topspin. Fortunately, my boss was on the court next to me, playing with another client. I decided to approach him after my exercise and ask for advice on how to teach topspin.

Once we finished the drill, I instructed my pupil to pick up the balls and take a water break. While he did that, I approached my boss and asked him what I should do to teach topspin. He explained that developing topspin is a complex process that requires patience from both the trainer and the pupil, so I shouldn't expect him to master the skill in just one or two lessons. I agreed with this assessment. My boss then outlined several exercises, starting simply by putting the balls aside. He suggested that the client should imagine hitting the ball while at the net and use his racquet to wipe over his shoulder. In other words, he recommended doing dry runs initially to demonstrate how the body and racquet movement should work. Once my client had executed the dry runs successfully, I would begin including ball-hitting into our practice. My boss advised me to start by feeding him balls from my hand and, as he internalized the movement, gradually moved backward to increase the complexity of the drill. Once my client had successfully mastered this, we could transition to playing on the smaller T-field of the tennis court. He emphasized that many players struggle with topspin and that I shouldn't expect quick results. I agreed with him and expressed gratitude for his guidance. I felt relieved returning to my court with a clearer plan for how to proceed with the lesson in a way that would benefit my client in the long run. I genuinely wanted my players to progress and improve their foundational skills.

I was pleased that my boss communicated the exercises swiftly, as my client had already picked up the balls and taken a refreshment by the time I returned. This timing was crucial because I didn't want my pupil to feel like our training session was merely an opportunity for me to chat with my boss. After explaining the new exercise to him, we continued with our class. I slightly adapted the session to incorporate exercises for both his forehand and backhand, with the overarching goal of developing topspin. Reflecting on the class, I noted some small improvements during the exercises I had discussed with my boss, but I was also aware that I had more work to do for the remainder of the summer term with this pupil. Overall, I felt we were on the right track as I identified some weaknesses in his general groundstrokes and received valuable suggestions from my boss on how to address them. It felt gratifying to know that I genuinely cared about his progress and wanted him to benefit from our sessions.

I was also appreciative of my boss's approach; he did not impose his ideas rigidly on my training. Instead, he consistently emphasized that I was responsible for planning the sessions autonomously while merely suggesting exercises I could incorporate. This openness allowed for personal modifications, enabling me to bring in my ideas. Thus, this incident reinforced my appreciation for my boss's teaching style, which was characterized by flexibility and a willingness to help rather than dictate.

Analysis of the Fourth Autoethnography

Analyzing the autoethnographic field report from a psychological perspective reveals several key insights. First, we must identify the central issue that arose during the tennis session. The protagonist realizes that his client struggles with a crucial aspect of his groundstrokes: the inability to generate topspin. However, the instructor finds himself at a loss regarding how to help the client improve this specific technical skill. This highlights a fundamental challenge in the report: the instructor's lack of knowledge about which exercises would effectively assist the client in enhancing his topspin.

When considering the personal needs of the follower—in this case, the instructor—it's clear that he wants the client to derive maximum benefit from the sessions, thereby ensuring that the client feels he is getting value for his investment. Consequently, progress becomes a significant personal need driving the narrative of the autoethnographic report. On a broader level, the social or organizational needs can be articulated as the instructor's goal to provide quality sessions that enable clients to improve as tennis players. This is evident when the boss emphasizes that the ultimate aim of tennis lessons is not to create dependence on the trainer but to empower players to play autonomously and confidently on their own. Intriguingly, the personal and social/organizational needs of the instructor align, suggesting a cohesive direction for guiding the tennis sessions. This congruence implies a shared psychological and sociological reality, facilitating a more effective learning environment.

The interactional dynamics between the leader and the follower are particularly noteworthy. The leader gains insight into the follower's experiential unit, which allows him to introduce relevant signs into their conversation. This interaction is marked by personal engagement, characterized by an open and approachable atmosphere. A closer examination of the sign system employed by the leader reveals the nuanced interactions at play in the autoethnographic field report. The leader begins the conversation using validation signs, establishing a foundation for their dialogue. Additionally, he incorporates scaffolding signs by demonstrating the exercises that can be implemented. Importantly, the leader does not impose these exercises on the follower; instead, he presents them as suggestions. This approach fosters a negotiable framework in which the follower can adapt the exercises to fit his unique teaching style.

As the leader allows the follower the freedom to modify the exercise for different strokes, he acknowledges the follower's autonomy in personalizing the lesson and adapting the structure of his class. Thus, the semiotic mediation between the leader and the follower is constructed as an open dialogue. While the follower primarily accepts the sign and tool mediation as proposed by the leader, it remains a personal adaptation that reflects his ownership of the lesson.

Another intriguing aspect is the interplay of multiple signs, which function collectively. The leader utilizes the interconnectedness of validation signs to initiate the conversation while also drawing on scaffolding and suggestive signs to introduce a practical tool system that may aid the follower in addressing his challenges. This interplay of lower-order signs creates a framework of higher-order signs, establishing a specific leadership theme within the context of the leader-follower interaction. The resolution of the issue transcends mere internalization of the sign and tool system; it also encompasses the follower's adaptation of these elements, even if the adjustments are minor in this particular example (see Fig. 6.13).

Positive emotions arise not only from resolving an organizational challenge but also from achieving this resolution collaboratively and personally. This shared experience enhances the learning environment, fostering a sense of progress and

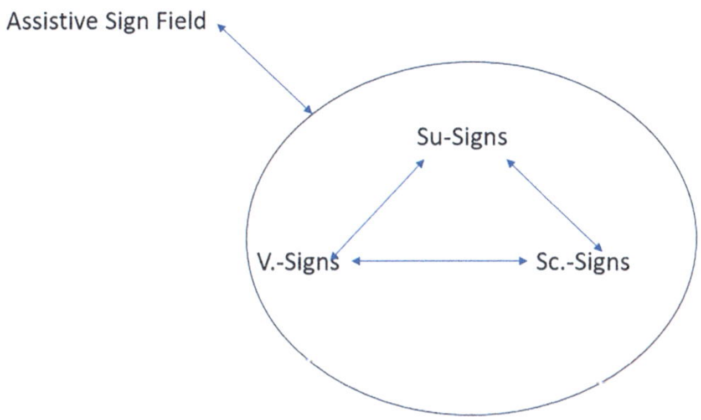

Fig. 6.13 Assistive sign field comes into being due to the interrelationship of suggestive signs (Su), Validation signs (V), and signs of scaffolding (SC)

Table 6.4 Analysis scheme for the class cancellation case

Problem/ Issue	Personal need (follower's needs)	Social needs (organizational needs)	Interactional patterns	Tool-/ Sign-systems	Solution	Feelings
How to help the client improving his topspin? Lack of knowledge how to do that	Players should improve	Clients should receive a high-quality training	Personal, next to each other	Signs of Validation, Signs of Scaffolding, suggestive signs	Adjusted Training	Feelings of Mastery Relief Proud

achievement for both the leader and the follower. In Table 6.4, I have depicted the field-theoretical analysis scheme for the autoethnographic report, encapsulating these insights and observations.

Interpreting the Fourth Autoethnography Field-Theoretically

Interpreting the fourth autoethnography from a field-theoretical perspective highlights the intricate relationship between leadership and followership through the lens of semiotics. Leadership, when viewed through this framework, reveals how signs are constructed by a specific agent (the leader) and subsequently reconstructed by the follower for their own purposes. This dynamic creates a shared space that transcends a simple one-dimensional sign for the follower or a unique sign for the leader.

When examining the field-theoretical visualization and interpretation (see Fig. 6.14), we can identify the experiential unit of the follower. The follower faces a significant barrier: he does not know how to teach his pupil to generate topspin, which is an essential skill for any tennis player. Consequently, he seeks ideas or inspiration from his leader on how to neutralize this barrier. In essence, the follower expects the leader to engage with him actively and assist him in overcoming the obstacle he is encountering. This expectation is evident when he approaches the leader, signaling a desire for the leader to step into his zone and provide support.

The follower's request highlights his need for concrete tools and signs that can help him navigate his challenges—specifically, how to address his problem of teaching topspin. This circumvention strategy is vital for the follower, enabling him to move more freely and quickly toward the goal of helping his player improve. The interaction underscores the importance of leadership in facilitating the follower's growth and development, as it provides the necessary resources and guidance to overcome obstacles within the learning process.

Thus, this field-theoretical interpretation emphasizes that effective leadership involves not only the construction of signs but also their thoughtful mediation, which allows followers to adapt and apply these signs in ways that support their unique contexts and needs. The interplay between the leader and the follower becomes a co-constructive process, enriching both parties' experiences and fostering an environment conducive to growth and improvement.

If we examine the leader's experiential unit—his life-space—we observe a parallel pattern. The leader recognizes the issue as valid and is eager to assist the follower in neutralizing the barrier. He intends to enter the follower's zone with specific ideas on how to transform the obstacle. Consequently, the leader anticipates that the follower will take the situation seriously and be motivated to solve the problem, as indicated by the expected intentions (red arrow).

In this dynamic, the leader expects some level of motivation or willingness from the follower to address the issue at hand. If the follower demonstrates this

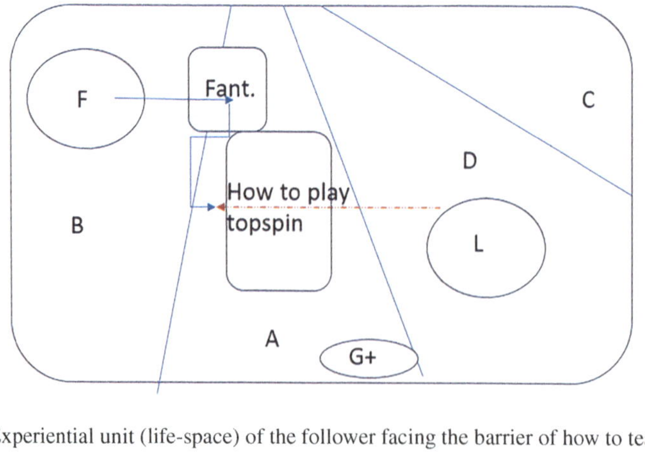

Fig. 6.14 Experiential unit (life-space) of the follower facing the barrier of how to teach topspin

willingness, the leader, in turn, is inclined to move toward the follower's zone, motivated by his own organizational needs. This mutual motivation facilitates a collaborative effort, allowing the leader to effectively support the follower in overcoming the barrier they face (see Fig. 6.15).

The interplay between the leader and the follower highlights the importance of shared intentions and commitment in navigating challenges, illustrating how both parties can work together to foster a productive and supportive learning environment.

In the sociological analysis of the autoethnographic field report (see Fig. 6.16), we can identify several key points. First, it is important to note that the expected intentions and self-intentions align within both the life-space of the follower and that of the leader. This alignment indicates that both the follower and the leader accurately anticipate each other's intentions and adjust their actions accordingly in response to the social context.

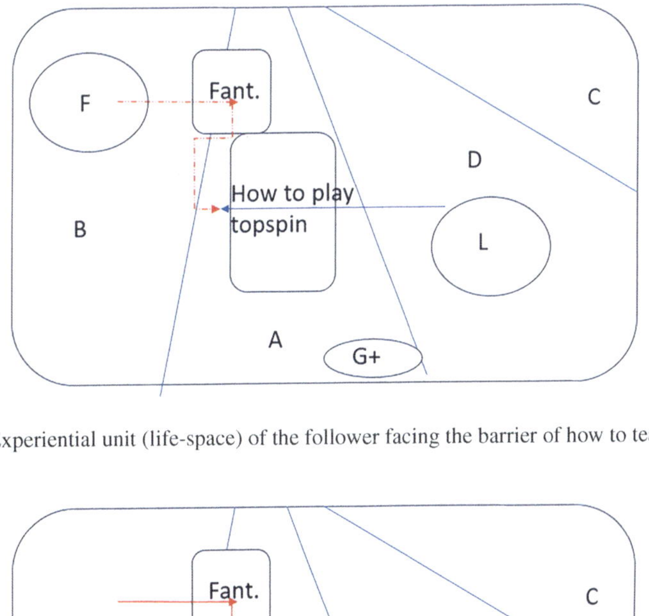

Fig. 6.15 Experiential unit (life-space) of the follower facing the barrier of how to teach topspin

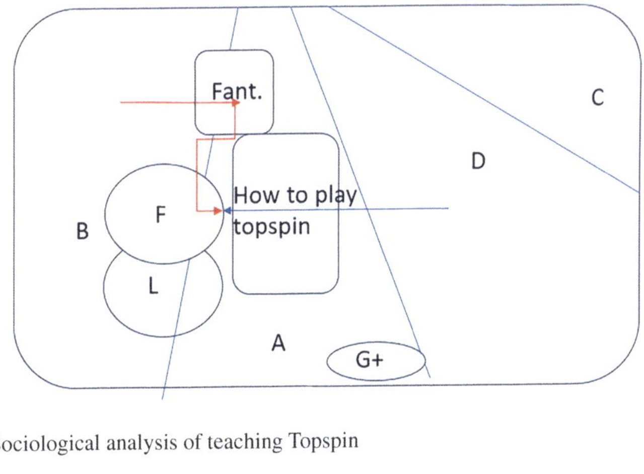

Fig. 6.16 Sociological analysis of teaching Topspin

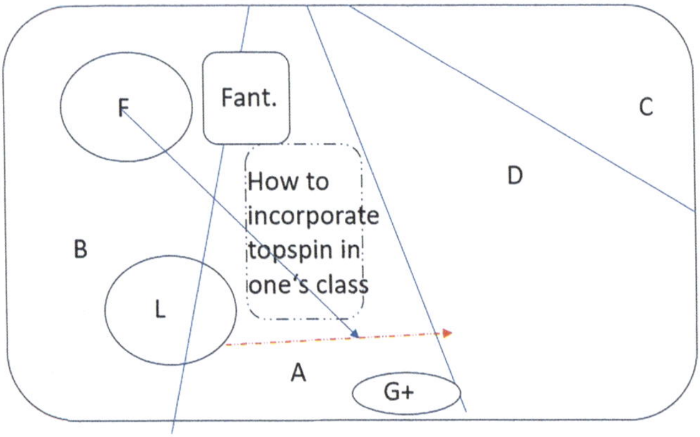

Fig. 6.17 Experiential unit of the follower after having received some ideas about potential circumvention strategies

As a result, this mutual understanding enables the leader to step into the follower's zone and offer specific circumvention strategies for teaching topspin to the client. Once the leader demonstrates which exercises the follower could implement, the follower feels adequately equipped to return to his training and restructure the class. This collaborative dynamic enhances the learning experience, empowering the follower to effectively address the technical challenge presented by the pupil.

Importantly, the leader comes up with a specific sign and tool system that the follower does not need to rigidly adopt but can adapt for his very own self-purposes. Hence, the interiorization does not come into being due to force but due to some kind of adaptive freedom. This is an important asset as such an intervention allows the exercise to be personally transformed and owned by the respective follower—here within the autoethnography. I conclude that this is also the reason why the follower feels some positive emotions because it is not his boss solving the issue but him under the guidance of his boss. With the adoption and adaption of the circumvention strategy within the experiential and sociological reality of the leader and the follower interactions, the barrier becomes transformed (see Fig. 6.17) and the person experiences himself capable of actually moving through the barrier that has now become not simply how to teach topspin but how to incorporate the new exercises in the whole of the class. For this purpose, the follower does not experience the leader as necessary figure anymore as he feels that he can circumvent this barrier on his own.

On the other hand, the leader experiences a similar perspective (Fig. 6.18) and does not feel the need to monitor whether the follower can successfully navigate toward his goal field. The leader seems to trust the follower's abilities and skills, which have been enhanced through the suggestion and negotiation of tool and sign systems functioning as circumvention strategies. This trust allows the leader to step back into his own zone while expecting the follower to autonomously reach his goal field. The events described in the autoethnographic field report reinforce this

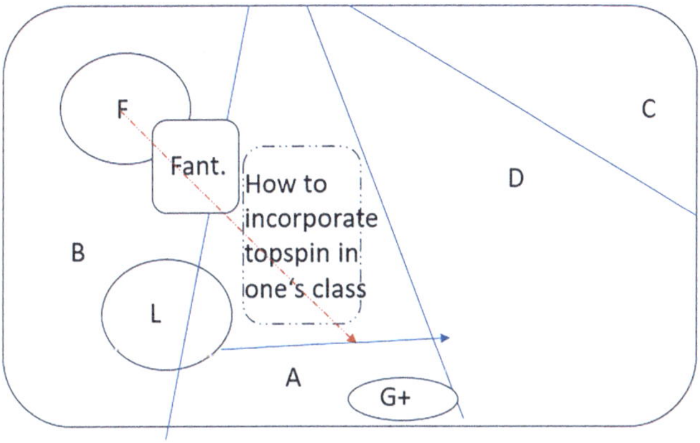

Fig. 6.18 Experiential unit (life-space) of the leader after transformation of the barrier

observation, eliminating the necessity for an additional sociological visualization of the situation.

A potential interpretation of our analysis of the autoethnographic field report suggests that leadership functions as a negotiation of a circumvention strategy that reflects both the needs of the follower and those of the organization (the leader's needs). This process is essential for enabling the follower to navigate toward his goal field, which is also crucial for the organization as a whole, thereby fulfilling the leader's responsibility toward the enterprise.

$$\begin{aligned}
&L(f) = N(F), N(l) = CVS^{*}\, N(F), N(l) \rightarrow g + (\text{where } L = \text{leadership},\\
&n = \text{negotiation}, N = \text{needs}, f = \text{Function}, l = \text{leader}, F = \text{Follower},\\
&CVS = \text{circumvention strategy}, N = \text{needs}, g+ = \text{goal field with}\\
&\text{positive valence}). \text{It is to be noted that } CVS^{*} N(f), N(l) \text{ happens to}\\
&\text{come into being by dialogical back} - \text{and} - \text{forth processes.}
\end{aligned}$$

Fifth Autoethnography: How to Structure a Class with Young, Talented Kids?

I changed enterprises when I realized that my boss was not fully honest with me regarding some matters of money. While I did not really care about the financial aspect, this dishonesty represented a central violation of my value system. We had a friendly relationship, and I had often supported him by stepping in as an instructor when he needed help. Dishonesty and lack of transparency are core values that he failed to respect in our interactions. I learned this retrospectively when clients disclosed information that revealed his questionable practices. This was the main reason I decided to leave the enterprise and work under a new boss. My former boss attempted to persuade me to stay by promising to offer me more money, but as I mentioned, that was not the reason for my departure. Consequently, I left my former boss's enterprise, which he did not understand.

When I began teaching under my new supervisor, I felt quite nervous. Although I knew him somewhat beforehand, we hadn't had extensive contact. Prior to committing fully to his enterprise, I had worked at both my former boss's and my future boss's establishments, which made the transition smoother for me. My new boss assigned me three initial lessons, with the last one being for his children. I felt honored to teach his kids because they were talented, and I sensed a significant responsibility to deliver quality instruction. They were good kids; they listened carefully and followed my directions. Moreover, they were funny, had their own personalities, and enjoyed playing tennis, which is one of the aspects I love about my job. When students are genuinely passionate, they appreciate the effort I invest in their training.

Given my sense of responsibility, I wanted to provide exceptional instruction, particularly because these were my boss's children, and they required a different kind of training. Therefore, I spent considerable time thinking about how to structure their class effectively. Before I started, my new boss approached me personally while delivering his children to the training session. He suggested that I could do some drill sessions focusing on forehand, backhand, and serve, followed by matches between the kids. He also mentioned that I could incorporate my own elements into the class. I agreed and proceeded with the training.

During the class, I implemented the drill sessions and had the children play points against each other. I also included a volley exercise and a drill on how to attack the opponent strategically. I felt that the training went well; the children laughed continuously and remained highly concentrated. When their mother arrived at the court, she asked me whether they had misbehaved. She seemed surprised when I told her that her kids were well-behaved and had followed my instructions without issue. Looking back, I considered this a positive indicator of success. Additionally, my (future) boss continued to send his kids for training week after week, which I took as a sign of appreciation for my classes.

Analyzing the Fifth Autoethnography Psychologically

If we analyze the situation from a psychological viewpoint, we can depict the following: First, we need to note that the protagonist of the autoethnographic report is confronted with a peculiar problem or issue. Here, he is questioning to what extent he should plan and structure the training as he deals with highly talented young kids. The protagonist's central needs can be easily described as a desire to do justice to the responsibility he feels toward the kids as well as his boss. What the leader wants to ensure is quality training that improves the kids' general technique as well as their competitiveness. Hence, we can argue that leader and the follower have needs that converge and point in a similar direction. This direction is the unfolding of competitive training through which the children are likely to develop their repertoire of skills. The interactional pattern needs to be described as personal, as the boss established a face-to-face conversation with the follower to brief him about the background of his children, particularly what they would benefit from during the class.

Sign-wise, the boss relies on suggestive signs, which means that he does not superimpose his training scheme onto the follower but only suggests what the kids would benefit from. The leader begins the conversation with "you can," allowing for some degree of free appropriation of the leader's suggestion. Hence, the leader does not simply rely on suggestive signs but combines them with ideal (inspirative) signs. This is further complemented by the leader arguing that the follower is allowed to deviate from this scheme and come up with his own ideas—not so much in the direction of reorganizing the total scheme of the class but to alter it personally where it might fit. In other words, the leader encourages the follower to deviate from the scheme personally, but only within a given framework. Here, the leader draws on invitational-deviation signs that help the follower make the class necessarily personal. Thus, we are confronted with the interconnectedness of specific signs that unfold power over the leader-follower interactions. Suggestive signs, ideal (inspirative) signs, and invitational-deviation signs combine into a specific leadership sign field that can be described as open leading. This open leading pattern becomes appropriated by the follower and filled with life—the alteration of the class's scheme based on introducing some volley exercises and introducing the children to new strokes. The follower concludes that he has reached some accomplishments upon realizing that the children were more concentrated than usual—based on the conversation with the kids' mother. Hence, we are confronted with a feeling of appreciation that rounds off the class as a whole. In Table 6.5, I have summarized the interpretation of the analysis based on the autoethnographic report. In Fig. 6.19, I have depicted the open leading sign field, which was the sign system employed by the respective leader.

Field-Theoretical Analysis of the Fifth Autoethnography

If we interpret the autoethnographic report from a field-theoretical perspective, we can depict the following: The follower encounters a barrier in his life-space—specifically, how to structure the class with young and talented kids. Importantly, this is a task for which he needs guidance, as the follower is also confronted with clients who are new to him (young, talented kids). It is essential to note that the follower wants to locomote to or through the barrier, feeling empowered by his aspirations and a sense of responsibility for delivering effective training (see Fig. 6.20).

For this purpose, he hopes for cooperation with his leader and expects him to move closer to his zone of action. In other words, the follower seeks the leader's assistance in overcoming the barrier he faces in his life-space. This support is

Table 6.5 Analysis scheme for how to structure a class with young talented kids

Problem/Issue	Personal need (follower's needs)	Social needs (organizational needs)	Interactional patterns	Tool-/Sign-systems	Solution	Feelings
How to structure a class with young, talented kids?	Responsibility for passionate young children	Ensuring the progress of young, talented kids	Personal, dialogical	Suggestive signs, ideal (inspirative signs), invitational-deviation signs	Appropriated and personally altered class scheme	Feelings of appreciation

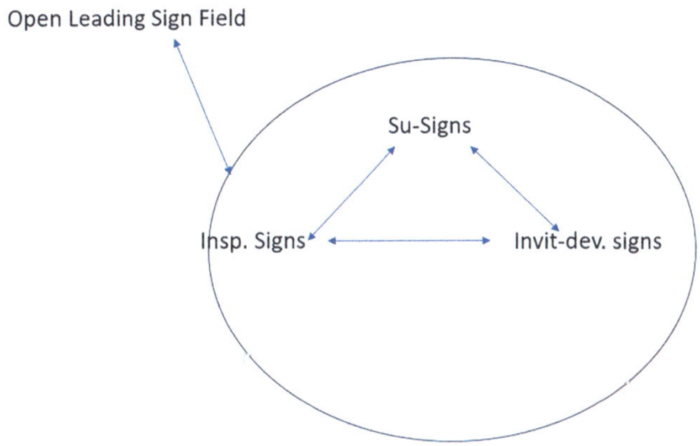

Fig. 6.19 Open leading sign field as employed by the leader to guide the follower

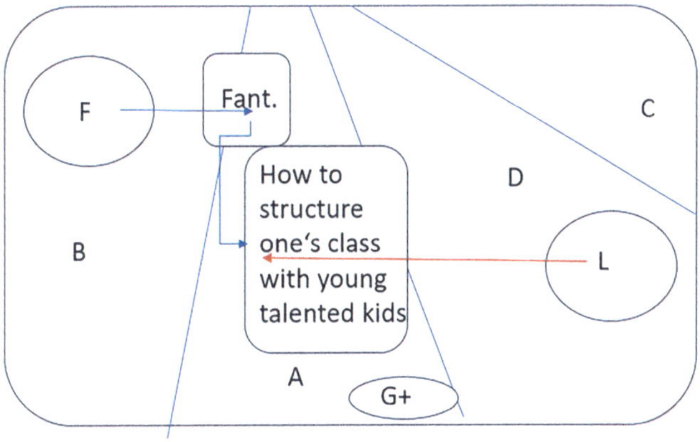

Fig. 6.20 Experiential unit of the follower (life-space) for structuring one's class with young talented kids

necessary for the follower to navigate freely toward his goal field, as discussed in our analysis scheme (see Table 6.5).

If we examine the life-space of the leader (experiential unit), we see a similar picture (see Fig. 6.21). The leader anticipates the follower's lack of knowledge in training young, talented kids—within the follower's zone. He expresses a desire to enter the follower's zone to assist him in overcoming the barrier that hinders his progress toward the goal field. In other words, the leader aims to help the follower confront the barrier. However, for this to occur, the leader requires certain prerequisites: specifically, that the follower demonstrates some convergence with the leader's own needs. Thus, the leader expects the follower to cooperate with him to successfully address the barrier. The leader further anticipates that the follower will not shy away from the barrier but will instead move toward it, despite not yet having an adequate circumvention strategy to manage the challenge.

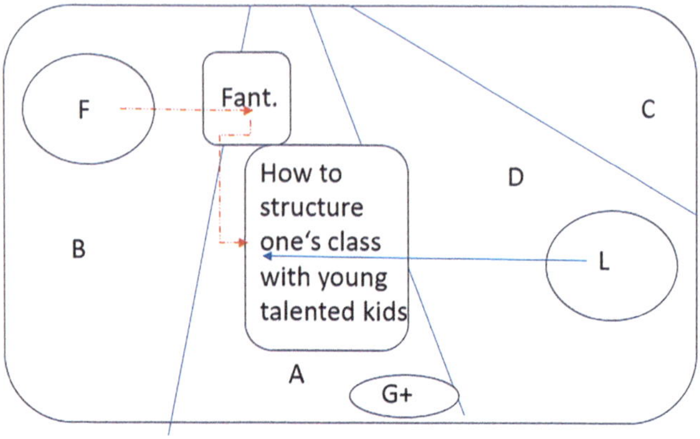

Fig. 6.21 Experiential unit of the leader (life-space) for structuring one's class with young talented kids

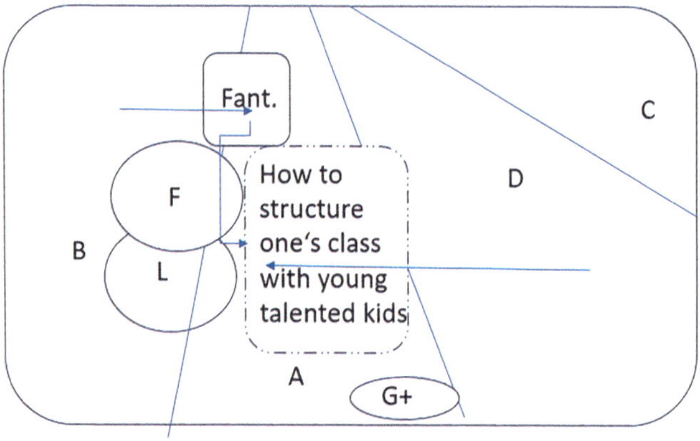

Fig. 6.22 Sociological analysis of the joint action field of the leader and the follower for the task of structuring one's class with young talented kids

Taking a closer look at the sociological analysis (Fig. 6.22), we can observe that the leader and the follower engage in a conversation (dialogue) through which they negotiate a circumvention strategy for the issue at hand. This negotiation emerges as the follower agrees with some elements that the leader deems important for the training session, while also having the opportunity to co-construct those elements based on his skills and abilities. Through this dialogical co-construction of circumvention strategies, the barrier that previously hindered the follower's progression toward the goal field becomes perceived as permeable. In other words, the jointly negotiated circumvention strategy enables both the leader and the follower to experience a shift in the permeability of the boundary, thus facilitating the actual application of the circumvention strategy. I have illustrated the follower's life-space after

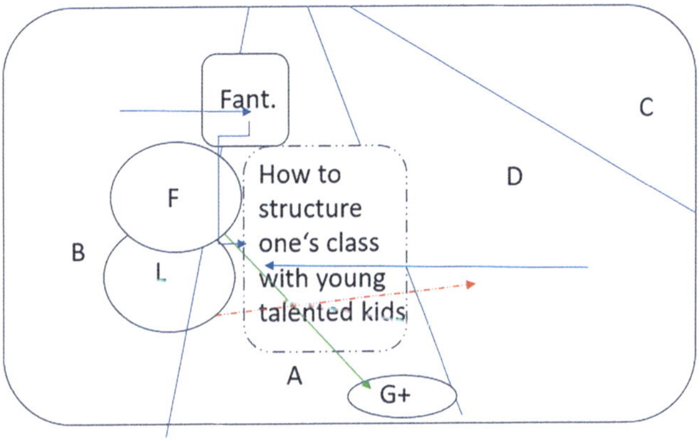

Fig. 6.23 Experiential unit of the follower (life-space) after negotiation of circumvention strategy

the joint negotiation of a circumvention strategy, which ultimately motivates the follower to navigate toward the goal field and neutralize the barrier (see Fig. 6.23).

With the analysis and interpretation of our autoethnographic critical incident, we can formulate a revised equation. Leadership can be defined as a function of the negotiation of a circumvention strategy that reflects both the needs of the follower and the needs of the organization. This circumvention strategy emerges exclusively through dialogue, enabling the follower to render the barrier permeable and facilitating movement toward the goal field.

$$L(f) = N(l), N(F) = CVS^{*}Dia\,N(F), N(l) = g+$$

$L = N(F), l, f = CVS^{*}\,N(f), N(l) \rightarrow g+$ (where L = leadership, n = negotiation, N = needs, F function, l = leader, f = follower, CVS = circumvention strategy, N = needs, Dia = dialogue $g+$ = goal field with positive valence).

Sixth Autoethnography: Preparing for a Class in a Gymnasium

An incident that stands out occurred when I had to conduct my first lessons for my new boss, shortly after the events described in the fifth autoethnographic incident. The setting was a gymnasium in my hometown, which required specific preparation to set up a tennis court. In particular, I needed to retrieve a net from a storage box and stretch it around the posts to create the proper tension. This task was not straightforward, and I was forewarned by my boss about its difficulty.

In anticipation of the challenge and with a strong desire for my first lesson to go smoothly, I arrived 30 min early to ensure that everything would be ready. My goal was to make sure the client would not lose valuable time due to any shortcomings in my preparations. Despite my early arrival and best efforts, I found myself unable to complete the task; it was simply too challenging to manage on my own. Unsure of what to do, I initially sought help from my boss, but he was unavailable due to his busy schedule. I also called my girlfriend, who, though responsive, could not assist effectively given her lack of visual context for the situation.

As desperation set in, I realized I needed external help. Although I had to abandon the task of setting up the net, I continued to prepare the other necessary elements for the class. Despite these efforts, I felt uneasy, knowing the court would not be fully ready. Eventually, the gymnasium's bell rang, signaling the arrival of the client and her father. After they changed, I instructed my client to warm up. At that moment, the father noticed my struggle with the net and kindly offered his assistance, doing so in a way that did not make me feel incompetent or embarrassed. He simply asked, in an objective manner, if I needed help.

Gratefully, I accepted his offer. While we worked together to fix the net, I explained the difficulties I had encountered. He agreed that it was indeed a difficult task to manage alone, which validated my frustration and gave me some relief. Together, we succeeded in setting up the net, and I was able to officially start the class with only a slight delay.

Despite this positive outcome, I was left feeling somewhat abandoned by my boss. Although I understood that he could not be present to help me with the net on that particular day, I believed he should have provided a demonstration of the setup beforehand, especially knowing how difficult the task would be for someone unfamiliar with it. A simple demonstration the week prior would have alleviated much of the stress I experienced. Nonetheless, I was profoundly grateful for the father's assistance, which allowed me to quickly resolve the issue and focus on conducting the class effectively.

Analyzing the Sixth Autoethnography

From a psychological perspective, the situation can be understood in terms of several key dynamics. First, the central issue is the follower's difficulty in fixing the net around the posts, a task he visibly struggles to complete alone. Despite the follower's strong motivation to prepare the class thoroughly, his efforts to resolve the issue independently prove unsuccessful. The follower's desire to provide a well-prepared class is clear, but his attempts to find a solution, such as reaching out to his girlfriend, fail because he requires immediate, in-field assistance with the net.

The leader, in this case, is absent and unavailable to offer support. Though it is apparent that the leader values the success of the class (as demonstrated by planning the session in the first place), he is physically and practically distanced from the situation. This leads to an interaction characterized by a lack of immediate guidance or monitoring, which is critical when unforeseen issues arise, particularly for someone in their first experience of managing the logistics of a new setting.

The absence of a sign system or tools to guide the follower is notable. There are no preparatory instructions or demonstrations provided to help the follower manage the physical setup of the net, which leaves him reliant on his own problem-solving methods. Although the follower actively seeks alternative solutions, first by attempting to fix the net himself and later by contacting his girlfriend for advice, these efforts do not yield success. The failure to provide adequate guidance, in this case, results in the follower having to invent a solution under pressure, which ultimately arrives in the form of assistance from the client's father.

The follower's sense of disappointment and frustration toward his leader is significant. His expectation that his leader should have anticipated this problem and provided a demonstration or guidance is unmet, leading to feelings of abandonment. These emotions are compounded by the fact that the follower, eager to perform well in front of the client, is left feeling embarrassed by the inadequacy of his preparation.

The absence of signs or instruction is crucial to the psychological analysis of this incident. The leader's failure to offer guidance in how to handle the net not only results in logistical failure but also affects the follower's self-presentation. The lack of leadership, in this case, translates into a personal and professional challenge for the follower, who must simultaneously manage the practical task and the potential judgment of the client. This absence of sign construction and co-construction between the leader and the follower results in frustration and a sense of vulnerability, both toward the leader and in the follower's interaction with the client. The follower is left feeling unprepared and exposed, as his ability to deliver a smooth class is compromised from the outset. In Table 6.6, I have summarized the analysis from a psychological viewpoint.

Table 6.6 Analysis scheme for how to prepare one's class in a gymnasium

Problem/ Issue	Personal need (follower's needs)	Social needs (organizational needs)	Interactional patterns	Tool-/ Sign-systems	Solution	Feelings
How to prepare one's class in a gymnasium? How to fix the net around the posts?	To prepare well the class and to deliver a perfect session	Ensuring that the training takes place	Distanced, remote	Absence of signs and tools	No leader guidance comes into being; independent solution	Frustration, desperation, embarrass-ment

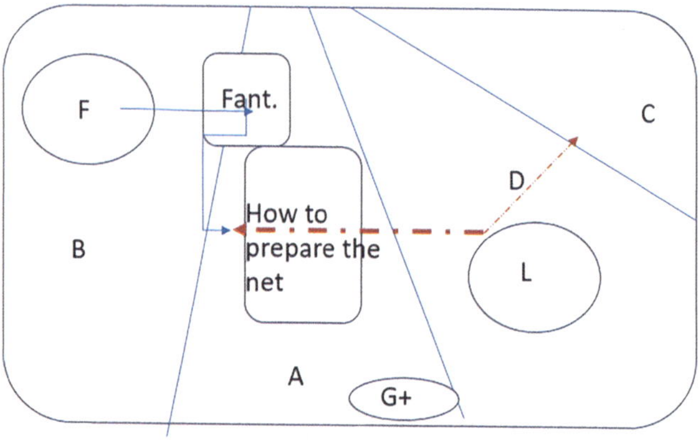

Fig. 6.24 Experiential unit (life-space) of the follower when wanting to prepare the net for his class

Field-Theoretical Analysis of the Sixth Autoethnography

From a field-theoretical perspective, the sixth autoethnography reveals a significant tension within the follower's life-space, which must be carefully examined. This tension arises from the discrepancy between the follower's expectations of the leader and his own personal wishes regarding the leader's actions (see Fig. 6.24). In this case, the follower understands that the leader is unavailable due to scheduling conflicts and is aware of the limitations imposed by this situation. Nevertheless, the follower harbors a strong wish for guidance, despite knowing that it will not be forthcoming.

This duality introduces a critical modification in our understanding of the follower's life-space. The autoethnography highlights not only the follower's awareness of the leader's constraints but also his inner need for support, creating a thick arrow of tension. This tension reflects the psychological struggle between the practical reality of the situation—wherein the leader cannot assist—and the follower's unmet need for leadership and direction.

In this sense, the life-space of the follower is marked by a contradiction between two sets of intentions: those he expects from the leader (i.e., absence due to the leader's other obligations) and those he wishes the leader would fulfill (i.e., providing guidance or a demonstration beforehand). This gap between expectation and desire creates a field of psychological tension, particularly as the follower faces a challenging task he is unprepared to handle on his own.

The tension within the experiential unit of the follower becomes more pronounced as the distance between these two sets of intentions increases. The further apart the expected actions of the leader are from the follower's wishes, the more intense the inner conflict and frustration become. This field-theoretical interpretation thus illuminates the dynamics of unmet expectations and their emotional impact on the follower, who, despite understanding the situation intellectually, remains

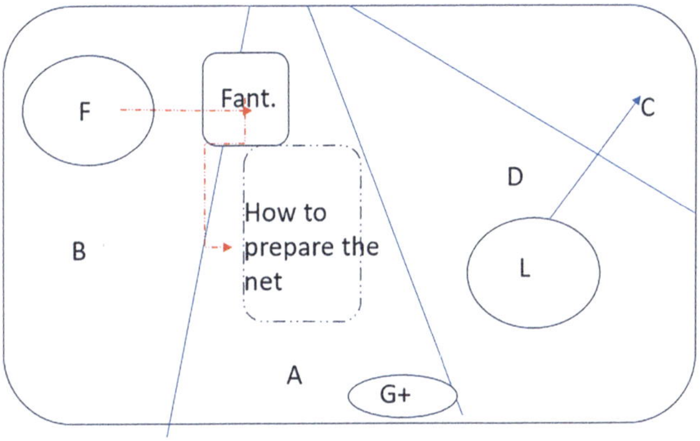

Fig. 6.25 Experiential unit (life-space) of the leader regarding the preparation of the class

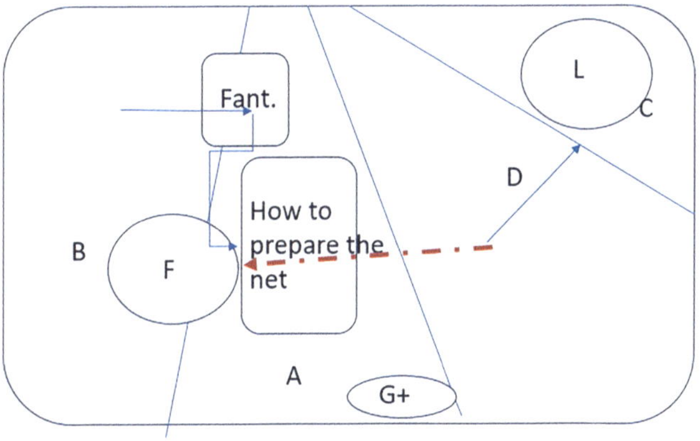

Fig. 6.26 Sociological analysis of the action field when preparing a class

emotionally and practically unfulfilled due to the absence of leadership in a crucial moment.

If we analyze the leader's experiential unit, we observe a divergent picture (see Fig. 6.25). In this case, the leader both expects and wishes (indicating a convergence between these two psychological functions) for the follower to confront the barrier and solve the issue autonomously. Consequently, the leader perceives the barrier as inherently permeable. Given this perception of the barrier as something the follower can overcome, the leader feels no need to provide direct guidance. Instead, he anticipates that the follower will approach and address the barrier independently, allowing the leader to focus on other areas.

In the sociological analysis (see Fig. 6.26), we observe an interesting pattern. The follower finds himself in a different zone, teaching tennis to other pupils at a separate location. Consequently, the leader becomes absent from the specific action sphere where the follower's problem has emerged, thus increasing the distance between the leader and the follower. This distance highlights a discrepancy between what the follower hoped for—guidance and support—and the leader's actual movement away from the situation. Additionally, the border or barrier that the follower faces does not become permeable in practice, as the follower is unable to solve the issue independently.

As a result, the follower experiences frustration from being unable to circumvent the barrier, while the leader remains unaware of this difficulty due to his physical and psychological distance from the problem. The sociological analysis clearly shows that tension arises within the follower, stemming from a need and desire for guidance that goes unmet. This unfulfilled need is a direct result of the leader's distance from the issue, making it difficult for the leader to recognize where and why the follower is struggling to overcome the barrier. The systemic or organizational tension building within the follower becomes proportional to the growing distance between the leader and the follower, who, though part of a jointly established action field, experience a disconnect in their approach to circumventing the barrier.

Regarding the analysis and interpretation of our autoethnographic field report, we can come up with a peculiar equation that might summarize our writings about this critical incident. Here, we can say that intra-systemic tension within the follower is a function of the distance between the wished and expected intentions for the leader as experienced by the follower:

$$\begin{aligned}&\mathrm{IST}_{\mathrm{f}}(\mathrm{f}) = \mathrm{D}(\mathrm{EIL}) - \mathrm{D}(\mathrm{WIL})\ \text{where the distance is proportional to the tension}\\&\text{felt within the follower's system}\ (\mathrm{ISTf} = \text{Intra} - \text{systemic tension follower},\\&\mathrm{D} = \text{Distance}, \mathrm{EIL} = \text{Expected Intentions Leader}, \mathrm{WIL}\left(\text{Wished Intentions Leader}\right).\end{aligned}$$

I will forgo sketching the third step in our Lewinian field-theoretical interpretation, which would involve a modified analysis of the life-space of both the leader and the follower. From the autoethnographic event, we observe that the follower receives assistance from a new individual entering and engaging with the field—this is the necessary guidance the follower requires to address the issue. Conversely, the leader does not recognize the situation as a problem and, as a result, remains in the zone to which he previously relocated.

Seventh Autoethnography: Revising One's Instruction Style

There is another critical incident that I would like to report regarding my experience with my second boss while working as a tennis instructor. This event elicited strong negative emotions toward him. I had been employed by my new boss for about a month to six weeks. The initial weeks were great because I retained my groups from my previous boss and simply continued working. My new boss did not interfere with my classes; he conducted his classes while I conducted mine. There was an unwritten agreement in place, and I was content with this arrangement.

I had a different approach to tennis compared to both my former and later bosses. While they undoubtedly possessed more tennis knowledge, they lacked interpersonal connections with their clients, in my opinion. They were very strict in their insistence that clients learn the fundamentals of tennis, which sometimes diminished the enjoyment and fun aspect of the sport. My approach, however, was somewhat the opposite. I aimed to demonstrate the enjoyment of the sport first and then focus on the precision of each stroke. I firmly believe that individuals need to experience the beauty of the sport before an instructor can enforce strict techniques. Once pupils experience the sport in action, they become motivated and passionate about mastering the intricacies of the game. I have witnessed many of my friends try tennis but ultimately stop playing due to the lengthy learning phase before they could actually play independently and enjoy rallies with friends or colleagues.

While teaching under my new boss, I blended the didactics of my former boss, my new boss, and my own self-taught methods. In my opinion, this approach worked quite well. Many of my pupils could play tennis within two or three months, a progress I did not observe when my former and new bosses were teaching. Their clients progressed more slowly, which I do not believe was due to a lack of talent but rather because their instructors aimed to maintain linear progress. I am also convinced that economic interests play a role here; if instructors keep the progress linear, they can work with the same client for four or five years. My approach was different; I taught my clients new strokes quickly and engaged them in real play (in vivo). After several months, my clients and I developed a training regimen that facilitated rapid progress, enabling them to play well with me or with friends.

However, one day my boss approached me and asked if I could attend one of his classes on the weekend. I agreed, even though I was puzzled by this request, given our unwritten agreement. Nonetheless, I thought the least I could do was listen to him. The weekend arrived, and I spent the morning enjoying the early summer in Frankfurt. When it was time, I drove back to my hometown and went directly to the tennis courts to meet my boss, who was preoccupied with giving a class to children. After a brief pause, he had time to talk with me. Following some initial small talk, he began demonstrating some strokes and how I should teach them. His methods differed from mine. I resisted and expressed that I believed my approach was more suitable for achieving particular goals. He listened attentively but was not swayed by my arguments.

My boss continued to show me how to teach other strokes, explaining his methods while referencing the guidelines of the International Tennis Federation (ITF) and his personal experience. I remained resistant, and we did not reach a resolution. Our discussions turned into minor debates about each stroke, as I was not convinced by his rationale. He also attempted to illustrate the disadvantages of my teaching methods by hitting the ball according to my instructions, demonstrating how this could lead to improper execution. I had consistent, observable evidence of the progress my clients were making.

I had assumed he recognized their advancements, but he did not seem to acknowledge them. I felt frustrated and disappointed, especially since my clients expressed satisfaction with my training. Almost every week, I was approached by others wanting to train with me, and I received support for my instructional style. Nevertheless, my boss insisted on lecturing me about what and how to teach. He explained that this was important for his overall enterprise; in other words, he sought to establish a unified teaching style among all his employees. While I understood his position, I did not agree with his teaching methodology.

Our conversation became increasingly uncomfortable, as it became evident that we could not reach an agreement. After several minutes of unproductive dialogue, I simply conceded to his explanations without committing to adopting his style. I asked how he would teach specific strokes, and he demonstrated and explained them to me. After he finished, I nodded and thanked him for the demonstration. I was cautious not to assert that I would strictly follow his methods, but I acknowledged his perspective. We then said goodbye and parted ways. Back in my car, I remained frustrated, yet I knew deep down that I would continue instructing as I had been.

Analyzing the Seventh Autoethnography

If we analyze the autoethnography psychologically, we observe that the protagonist is confronted with an issue not previously encountered in his life-space. The course instructor is prompted to reconsider his instructional approach, as his boss seeks to unify the teaching style within the enterprise. Consequently, a barrier emerges in the life-space of the autoethnography's protagonist: the need to alter his teaching style. This barrier stands in stark opposition to the instructor's personal needs or desires, which involve constructing his teaching in a manner that reflects his individuality. In other words, the protagonist has developed a personal need to instruct his clients based on his own experiences and the various supervisory influences he has encountered. Thus, we can argue that the instructor's personal needs are in conflict with the organizational needs represented by his boss, creating a form of tension between the instructor and the leader.

Examining the interactional pattern, we note that the leader and the follower engage in a personal interaction, meeting on the tennis courts. This interaction is not only personal but also in vivo, meaning that they engage in the actual field where the training occurs. Analyzing the sign system employed, we recognize that the leader relies on specific signs of expertise, referencing the guidelines of the largest tennis federation in the world, the ITF. However, this is not the only sign he uses to persuade the course instructor to adopt his teaching style. He also draws on signs of seniority based on his experience. Interestingly, these two types of signs are interconnected with plausibility signs, as the leader attempts to illustrate potential pitfalls in the follower's instructional methods. Therefore, we can conclude that expertise signs, seniority signs, and plausibility signs intertwine to form a given sign field, which can be described as an authority sign field. The interconnectedness of these different signs contributes to the overall authority of the sign field (see Fig. 6.27).

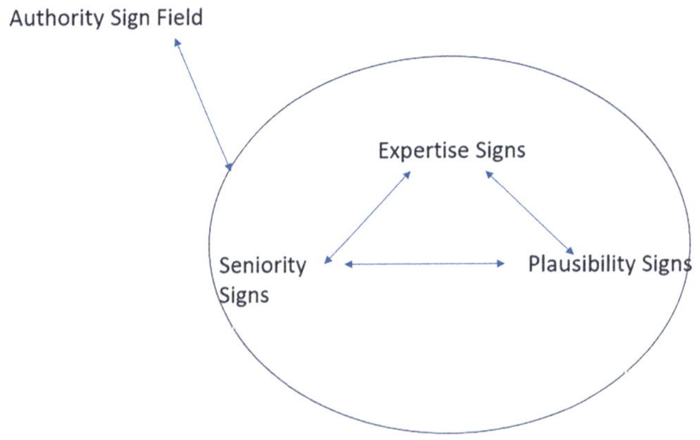

Fig. 6.27 Authority sign field as sign system employed within the autoethnographic field report

Table 6.7 Analysis scheme for unified teaching autoethnography

Problem/ Issue	Personal need (follower's needs)	Social needs (organizational needs)	Interactional patterns	Tool-/ Sign-systems	Solution	Feelings
Course instructor needs to revise his instructing style	Plan and carry out course instructions autonomously	Unification of different teaching styles	Personal, monological	Authority sign field based on expertise, seniority, and plausibility signs	Inhibition or blockage of sign field	Disappointing Frustration

What is particularly striking in the autoethnographic report is that the protagonist does not accept this sign field, as he is unable to co-construct it in a manner consistent with his own personal way of being. In other words, the sign field becomes closed because the leader does not allow for the co-construction of the sign based on the follower's life-space or experiential unit. The opposition to the sign field arises from the inability to contribute to it in a meaningful way. As a consequence, the instructor acknowledges the existence of the sign field but does not internalize it. The follower recognizes that this sign field exists, yet he blocks its internalization, preventing it from exerting its influence on his conduct. The result is a non-agreement between the leader and the follower (Table 6.7).

Field-Theoretical Interpretation of the Seventh Autoethnography

If we interpret the autoethnography from a field-theoretical perspective (see Fig. 6.28), we gain an intriguing insight into the follower's experiential unit. First, it is important to note that the follower is highly motivated in conducting his classes.

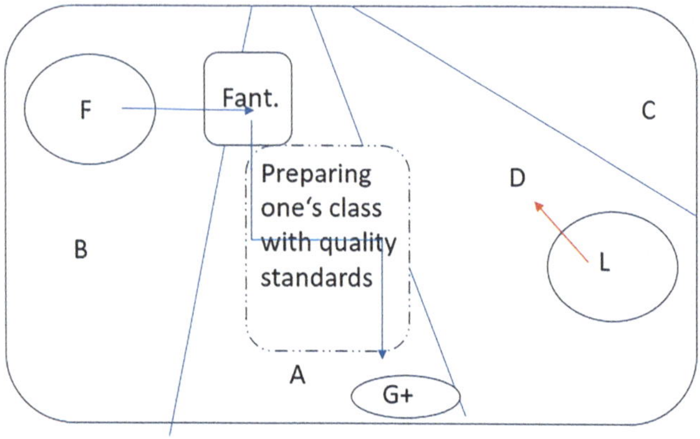

Fig. 6.28 Life-space (experiential unit) of the follower while preparing one's classes

This motivation can be explained by his underlying desires—to provide his pupils with quality instruction that allows them to quickly enjoy the benefits of the sport. He views his teaching style as more than adequate for this purpose, which leads him to experience the barrier as permeable. Thus, the follower perceives a barrier, but it does not present a significant problem for him; he believes it can be circumvented with his existing repertoire of skills.

In this context, it is also essential to consider how the follower views the leader, particularly regarding the follower's expectations about the leader's movement within his action field. The follower describes a sort of unwritten agreement, suggesting that he anticipates his leader will allow him autonomy in planning and conducting his classes. Consequently, he expects the leader to remain or operate solely within his distinct zone of action, without interfering in the pressing zones of the follower.

If we interpret the situation from the follower's perspective (see Fig. 6.29), we gain an intriguing glimpse into his life-space. Here, the leader does not simply want the follower to reach the goal of delivering his classes based on a certain quality standard; he also wants the follower to incorporate the essential sign field of doing so within a unified teaching style. Consequently, the barrier—quality standard—is linked to another emerging barrier that the leader deems important: the issue of unifying the teaching style (unified classes). From this perspective, the leader does not want the follower to prepare his classes autonomously but rather in alignment with the need to unify teaching approaches.

Thus, the leader perceives more barriers than the follower does concerning the successful delivery of classes. Furthermore, the leader is more attuned to the interconnectedness of these barriers and what they mean for the clients paying for the classes. What the leader hopes for is that the follower acknowledges this second-order barrier and agrees with the leader on its significance to develop specific strategies for circumventing it. In other words, the leader wants the follower to cease delivering classes in his preferred teaching style and encourages him to navigate to

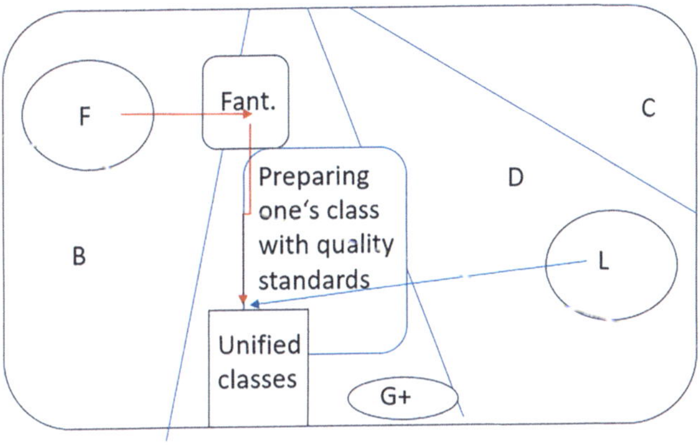

Fig. 6.29 Leader's life-space (experiential unit) regarding the matter of preparing one's classes based on a unified teaching style

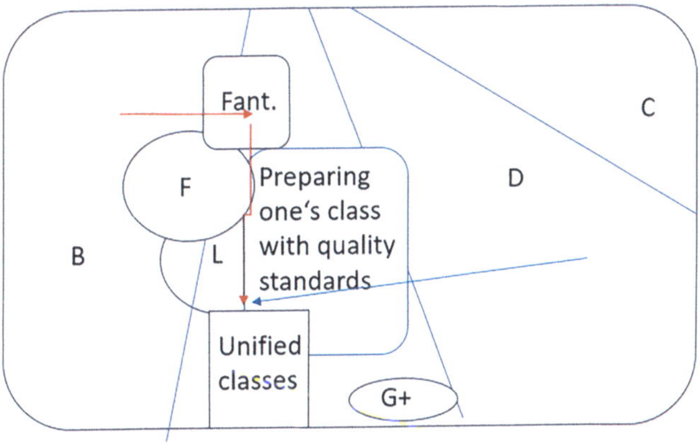

Fig. 6.30 Sociological analysis of the joint action field given the conflict between the leader and the follower based on a unifying teaching style

the intersection of both barriers, dictating how to address them through a single circumvention strategy.

Here, we need to emphasize that the leader aims for the follower to internalize the authority sign field, mediating his conduct to not only deliver classes with a high-quality standard but also to do so in a unified manner consistent with the approaches of the other trainers. Ultimately, the leader's insistence on a co-constructed sign system becomes the primary reason for the follower's rejection of the circumvention strategy.

If we take a look at the sociological analysis (see Fig. 6.30), the follower acknowledges the existence of the barrier. However, he rejects the importance of that very barrier. The leader wants the follower to internalize a specific strategy regarding how and why to teach in a particular manner. In this context, the leader effectively dictates how the instructor should teach. As a social fact, both individuals meet on the tennis court and engage with each other physically. While the follower listens to and observes the leader's suggestions, he ultimately rejects the internalization of the proposed tools and sign systems. This debate serves as empirical evidence of their conflict, highlighting the negative feelings that arise from the disagreement between the leader and the follower.

If we proceed to analyze the situation from a field-theoretical perspective and return to the analysis of the follower's life-space (experiential unit), we observe that the follower acknowledges the existence of the barrier, which was the reason he agreed to meet with the leader on the court. However, he denies the importance of this barrier for delivering quality training on the tennis courts. The follower is convinced that he can navigate around the second-order barrier established by the leader. In essence, the follower expects the leader to return to his zone, focusing on his own training and classes, while he wishes to continue progressing toward his goal field as he had previously done.

Because the follower believes the barrier can be circumvented, he dismisses its significance and maintains his previous approach to training (see Fig. 6.31). Despite rejecting the circumvention strategy and the importance of the barrier as suggested by the leader, the follower feels disappointed and frustrated. He perceives the leader's intervention as an unwelcome interference in his area of expertise.

On the other hand, the life-space of the leader—though not explicitly depicted—centers around his desire to revert to his own field while expecting the follower to adhere to the barrier he has imposed. Importantly, the leader does not establish any mechanisms to monitor whether the follower respects the implemented barrier or follows the suggested circumvention strategy. This lack of oversight contributes to the disconnect between the leader and the follower, further intensifying the feelings of frustration and disappointment experienced by the follower.

Bearing this in mind, we can say that the leader inhabits a peculiar power position through which he can impose barriers on the life-space (psychological

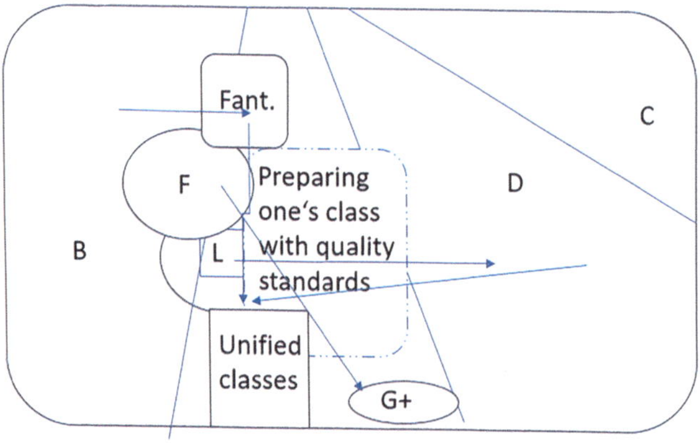

Fig. 6.31 Life-space of the follower after joint discussion of the issue at stake

reality) and the action field of the follower, while the follower can still block or inhibit the internalization of this barrier within his life-space or deviate from the suggested circumvention strategy dictated by the leader. Leadership, as understood from a cultural-psychological perspective analyzed by field theory, is not solely preoccupied with identifying specific promoter signs that help circumvent a barrier on which both the leader and the follower agree. It is also noteworthy that leadership considers the construction, suggested interiorization, and circumvention of a given barrier that can run counter to the general needs and goals of the follower.

The follower's acknowledgment of the barrier within his life-space and action field (psychological and sociological reality) is well illustrated in the autoethnography. Yet, the follower denies the importance of the barrier in assisting him to navigate through the first-order barrier. From the leader's perspective, it is interesting to note that the second-order barrier interacts with the first-order barrier, sharpening the thematic nucleus of the first-order barrier. This means that the construction of an additional barrier helps the leader channel the follower's motivation. The rejection of the additional barrier emerged within our analyzed autoethnography because the follower was not allowed to co-construct the circumvention strategy for the second-order barrier and was expected to act solely as the leader wanted him to act.

Leadership failed in this autoethnography not merely because the leader constructed a second-order barrier interacting with the first-order barrier, but because the leader did not allow any space for the follower to act on the barrier using his own means, thus hindering the co-construction process. For example, the follower was not consulted in the general scheme of unifying the classes or in sketching out a joint teaching program. Bearing this in mind, the barrier did not reflect the life-space of the follower because it was constructed solely based on the life-space of the leader. This resulted in the rejection of not only the importance of the barrier within the psychological and sociological reality of the follower but also in the failure to internalize the leader's suggested circumvention strategy. If we wish to summarize our analysis and interpretation formally, we might depict the following equation:

$$
\begin{aligned}
&-L(f)=(B1)*N(1),N(F)^{*}\,\mathrm{Cons}(B2)^{*}\,N(1)=B(1)^{*}\,\mathrm{Cons}\,B(2)^{*}\,N(1)^{2},\\
&N(F)=B(1,2)^{*}\,N(1^{2}),N(f)\neq g+\text{which shows a pre}-\text{domination of}\\
&\text{leader needs in contrast to follower needs (where the failure of}\\
&\text{leadership is a function}\,(f=\text{function})\,\text{of a jointly agreed barrier}\\
&(b=\text{barrier})\,\text{depending on the needs}\,(n=\text{needs})\,\text{of the follower}\\
&(F=\text{follower})\,\text{and the needs of the leader}\,(1=\text{leader})\,\text{while the}\\
&\text{leader constructs a second}-\text{order barrier based on his needs}\\
&\text{regardless of the needs of the follower in relation to the}\\
&\text{second}-\text{order barrier.}
\end{aligned}
$$

Eighth Autoethnography: Switching Tennis Courts in a Short Period of Time

For my second boss, I had to give lessons on multiple tennis courts in my hometown. Sometimes, I needed to switch courts within a period of 30 min. This was due to the fact that some clients preferred to play at club X rather than club Y. This caused a lot of stress for me because I had to pack my things and hurry to the other club. On Mondays, I typically had to give four classes at club X and two other classes at club Y. I really enjoyed playing at club X because it was a small club with only four courts. My boss taught classes nearby, and we often talked about tennis and other topics—like our private lives. This was nice because I could get to know my second boss more closely. Luckily, he did not lecture me about my classes or interfere with the way I taught tennis. We often chatted when our pupils needed to pick up the balls, and we joked around. It was a great time. The summer was beautiful, and the pupils were focused and attentive. I realized I had a great relationship with my boss despite a few disagreements.

While I was giving my classes, I received a message from one of my friends who had taken a lesson with me at club Y. He couldn't make it and canceled the class. I realized that I needed to switch courts for just one class—pack my things, drive to the other club, prepare for the class, and then teach it. I felt somewhat frustrated because changing courts for a single class seemed like a waste of personal and economic resources. When my pupils took a break to drink some water, I approached my boss. I had no clear intention when I approached him; I just wanted to talk. After several minutes of casual conversation, I shared that I was frustrated because a client had canceled last minute, and I had to switch courts for one class. My boss looked surprised and said, "Then you can give the class on this court." He was right. I had never thought about asking the client whether he could make an exception and play once at club X instead of Y. I messaged the client, and he agreed almost immediately. I felt relieved because I no longer had to worry about getting to club Y in time; I could just wait for my last client to arrive. I was grateful that my boss had suggested such a solution and wondered why I hadn't thought of it myself. Either way, I was happy that we had resolved the issue.

Analyzing the Eighth Autoethnography

If we analyze the situation from a psychological perspective, we can discern the following structure: First of all, it is important to highlight a peculiar issue emerging within the autoethnography. The protagonist experiences stress due to the need to change courts in a short amount of time. This is a resource-intensive endeavor, making it not worthwhile to switch courts for just one class. Because one client canceled at the last minute, the course instructor is forced to switch courts for that single class, which runs counter to his personal needs when giving tennis lessons. These personal needs can be described as follows: the course instructor wants to give classes while being well-prepared and having sufficient time to do so. The organization's needs (and, by extension, those of his leader) require that the instructor ensures the smooth operation of the tennis class. Thus, it is crucial for the instructor to be punctual and adequately prepare for the class. We can say that personal and organizational needs generally align, as both the leader and the follower want to move in a similar direction. Yet, the issue that emerged in the autoethnographic field report conflicts with the personal needs of the follower and the organizational needs of the leader. It is not surprising that the course instructor feels stressed when considering how to switch courts for just one class.

The solution to the conflict is particularly interesting. The leader and thee follower come together personally during the break when their pupils are picking up the balls. Here, the interaction is both personal and informal. The course instructor did not approach the leader with a specific intention to solve an issue; instead, he simply wanted to talk and enjoy the leader's company. During this informal conversation, the course instructor allows the leader to glimpse into his experiential unit and reveals what is on his mind. He invites the leader to consider his pressing needs within his life-space, not because he expects a solution but because he wants to share his thoughts and feelings. Yet, the leader recognizes that he can help and suggests a potential solution that is negotiated between them. To the course instructor's surprise, this solution becomes feasible once he messages his client and receives confirmation that the client can come to club X.

If we take a closer look at the sign system employed, we need to be aware of the interconnected signs that guide the conversation between the leader and the follower. First, both approach each other with informal signs (such as discussions about studies and the character of pupils) through which they share their feelings and thoughts about matters related to their private lives. Interestingly, the follower continues to share feelings about what is happening in his life-space regarding the structure of his tennis classes. He openly expresses his negative feelings about the cancellation of one of his classes and how it complicates his schedule. In other words, the follower introduces personal signs into the conversation, followed by professional-consequential signs that indicate what the cancellation means for the next moment in the course instructor's day.

In short, we see a unique interaction between the leader and the follower. The follower initiates the conversation, structuring it with informal, personal, and professional-consequential signs. On the other hand, the leader co-constructs these personal signs by asking about the follower's studies and engaging in informal talk. This shows that the leader does not simply agree with or respect the structure of the conversation that is important to the follower; he actively co-constructs it based on his own life-space. This co-construction enables the leader to suggest a potential solution for the professional signs the follower has introduced, ultimately leading to a resolution of the conflict at hand.

The sign field, based on these interconnected lower-order signs (informal, personal, and professional-consequential), can be labeled as invitational/revealing. Interestingly, before it becomes co-constructed, the follower initiates this sign field,

Table 6.8 Analysis scheme for unified teaching autoethnography

Problem/ Issue	Personal need (follower's needs)	Social needs (organizational needs)	Interactional patterns	Tool-/ Sign-systems	Solution	Feelings
Switching tennis courts in a short period of time	No hurry, no stress, protecting one's resources, preparing well one's classes	Smooth processing of tennis classes	Personal, friendly, informal	Personal signs, informal signs, professional-consequential signs based on the follower's initiative	Co-construction of follower's sign field (playing last hour in club X rather than Y)	Relief

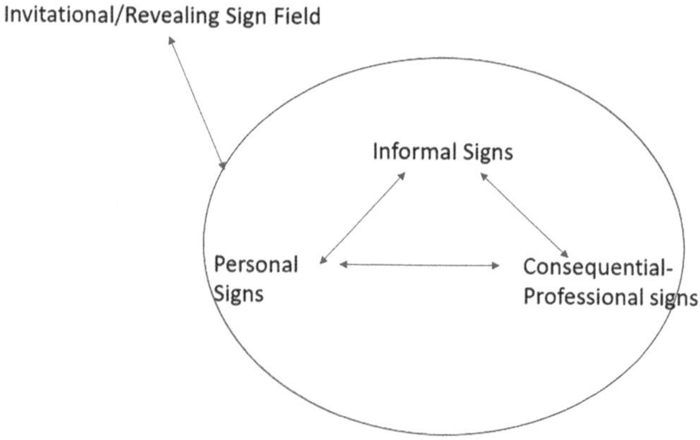

Fig. 6.32 Follower sign field that becomes co-constructed by the leader regarding the conflict of switching tennis courts in a short period of time

contrasting with other autoethnographic reports where the leader initiates it. Thus, the roles seem to be reversed in this particular sign system. The follower approaches the leader, initiating and structuring the conversation based on the invitational/revealing open sign field, which is then co-constructed by the leader. Because the sign field is openly structured, the leader feels free to appropriate and co-construct it from his perspective. As a result, he suggests that the follower can give the last class at club X rather than Y, significantly altering the professional-consequential sign.

The solution, based on the constructed and co-constructed sign field, reflects the needs of both the follower and the leader, bringing closure to the negative emotions experienced by the follower while paving the way for positive emotions, such as relief, as analyzed in the autoethnographic field report.

I have summarized the analysis in Table 6.8. In Fig. 6.32, I have depicted the invitational/revealing sign field that helped the leader gain insight into the life-space of the follower while co-constructing the sign field.

Field-Theoretical Interpretation of the Eighth Autoethnography

If we take a closer look at the experiential unit of the follower, we encounter a distinct life-space. Here, we recognize that the follower is indeed facing a significant problem: switching courts in a short amount of time. However, this problem contradicts his major fantasms—or, in other words, his primary personal needs. In seeking to resolve the issue, he feels largely alone. He does not perceive the leader as capable of helping him with this problem, which is why he does not approach him about it. Consequently, the leader aims to navigate the barrier of the problem independently, contemplating potential circumvention strategies to reach the other club. Meanwhile, the follower intends to approach the leader for something different—engaging in small talk—without any expectation of assistance in resolving the issue that is causing him distress. Thus, the follower perceives these events as unrelated.

In terms of the leader's expected intentions, the follower believes he will likely remain on his court, giving his classes. However, he also recognizes that the leader will probably respond to his small talk and come over to spend some time with him. This situation is illustrated in Fig. 6.33.

Looking at the experiential unit of the leader, we gain a distinct understanding of the issue at hand (see Fig. 6.34). The leader does not perceive the issue because he is not approached by the follower regarding this matter. Instead, he interprets the follower's approach as a desire to engage in their usual small talk. The leader aims to respond positively to the follower's expected intentions and consequently wishes to move toward the follower, who is approaching his zone. However, it is important to note that the leader is unaware of the follower's pressing issue concerning the cancellation of his class and the challenge of switching clubs in a short amount of time.

Looking at the sociological analysis (Fig. 6.35), we can see that the leader and the follower meet in the leader's zone (the leader's court). This aligns with the

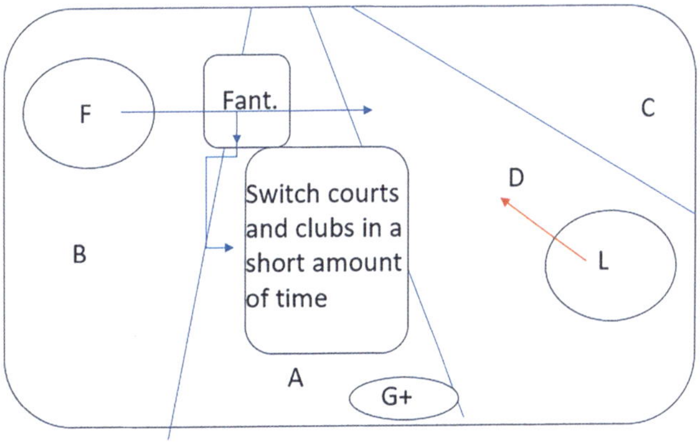

Fig. 6.33 Experiential unit of the follower who perceives himself as needing to solve the conflict on his own and approaches the leader for some small talk

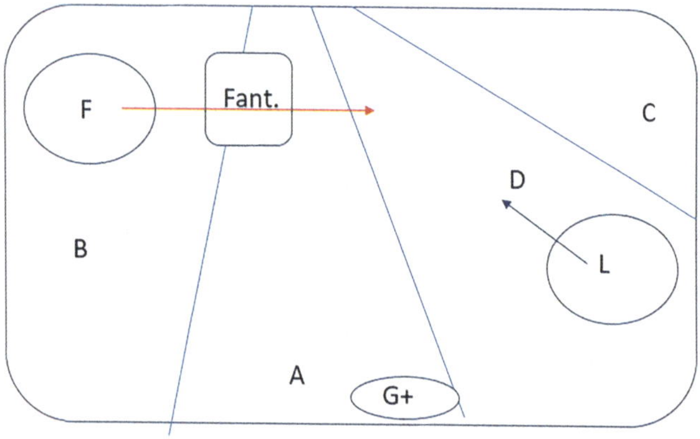

Fig. 6.34 Experiential unit of the leader who perceives the follower moving toward him but who does not know about the pressing, professional issue of the follower

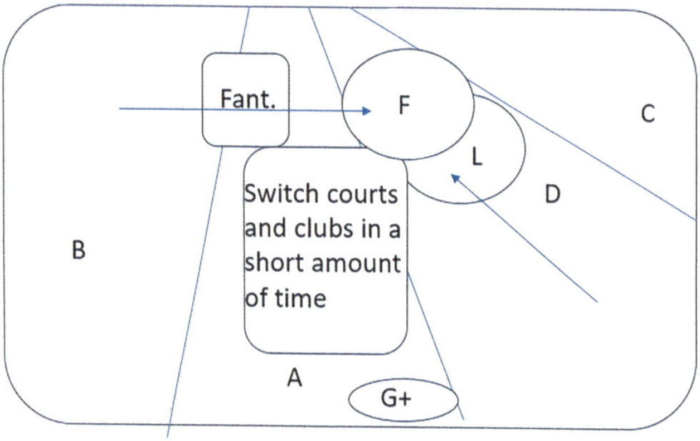

Fig. 6.35 Sociological analysis of the leader and the follower meeting for small talk

events described in the autoethnographic report, where the follower approached the leader for some small talk. During this interaction, both the leader and the follower shared not only informal and personal information but also casually discussed details regarding the upcoming present moment. Notably, the follower expressed some negative emotions related to the cancellation of his class. By doing so, he allowed the leader a glimpse into his life-space, enabling the leader to co-construct the sign and tool systems relevant to the barrier and the pressing need.

What the sociological analysis reveals quite illustratively is that the leader and the follower meet for some non-professional events in the leader's zone, and it is only by chance that the follower reveals his problems related to his job through the sharing of personal feelings. While both are together and the follower shares some of his personal thoughts informally, the leader gains the opportunity to glimpse into the follower's life-space and its barriers. This insight occurs due to the specific conversational style initiated by the follower, which we described as invitational and revealing. It is in this context that the leader recognizes the opportunity to assist the follower in resolving a pressing issue of which he was previously unaware, including the genesis of his thought process regarding which circumvention strategy to suggest.

As a consequence of this sociological situation, the follower internalizes the circumvention strategy proposed by the leader and applies it for his own purposes. Therefore, he reaches out to his last client to inquire whether he would object to switching courts in a short amount of time. Consequently, the follower realizes that the primary barrier he faced might be circumvented not simply by transforming it but by making a detour—based on the informal circumvention strategy discussed with his leader. Thus, the follower sees the opportunity to navigate around the primary barrier and reach his goal without directly confronting it. However, it is important to note that the negotiated circumvention strategy introduces a second barrier: the client must agree to play at club X instead of Y. To facilitate this, the follower considers concrete ways to persuade the client—such as arguing that this is only a one-time exception. For this reason, he does not require the leader's assistance and expects him to return to the center of his zone (D). This scenario is depicted in Fig. 6.36.

If we take a closer look at the experiential unit of the leader, we get a similar picture. Here, the leader wants to locomote back to his zone—or court, in our example—to continue giving his classes. Thus, he perceives that the small talk with the follower has concluded while simultaneously assisting him in navigating around the primary barrier he faced in his respective life-space. This aligns with the experiential unit of the follower (see Figs. 6.36 and 6.37).

The second sociological analysis reveals quite illustratively that the follower has penetrated the secondary barrier and locomotes to the goal field while the leader moves back to his respective zone or court (see Fig. 6.38).

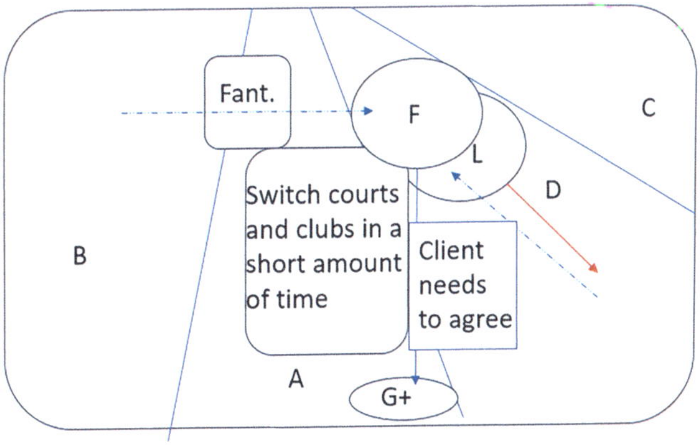

Fig. 6.36 Life-space of the follower after the informal meeting between the leader and the follower

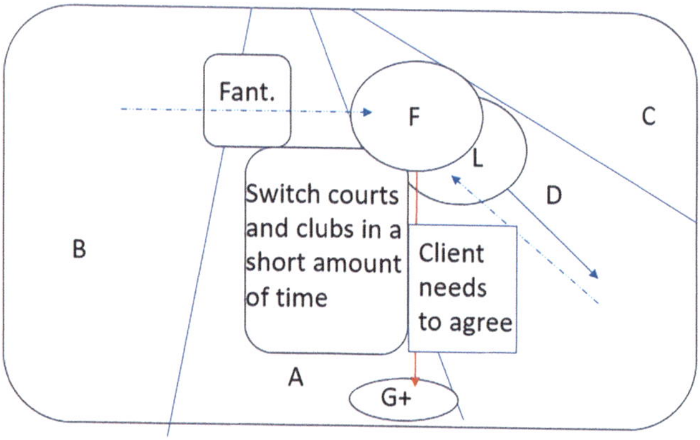

Fig. 6.37 Life-space leader after small talk and suggested circumvention strategy

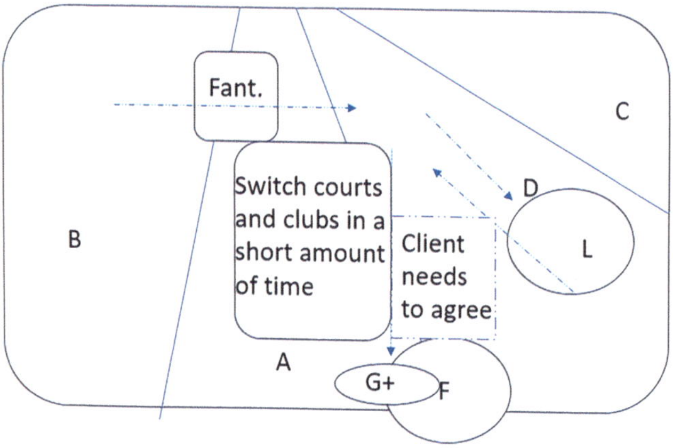

Fig. 6.38 Second sociological analysis after the leader and the follower have agreed informally on a circumvention strategy

What the analysis and interpretation reveal within this autoethnographic example goes beyond what we have previously depicted. We can assert that leadership in this instance could be initiated by a specific conduct of followership. Here, the follower facilitated the leader in providing a form of leadership based on an invitational/revealing followership sign field, which encouraged the leader to co-construct the sign field from his perspective. Thus, leadership emerged from the introduction of a specific follower sign field, allowing the leader to adopt and co-construct the sign field while incorporating suggested circumvention strategies to navigate the primary barrier the follower faced within his life-space.

This leads us to a second major finding worth elaborating on: the follower does not need to neutralize or transform the barrier, as seen in previous examples. Instead, with the negotiated circumvention strategy, the follower can move along a trajectory that detours the primary barrier. However, it is important to note that this new trajectory also reveals interesting barriers or resistances, which the follower can face and neutralize autonomously. Consequently, the negotiated circumvention strategy not only helps the follower make a detour around the primary barrier but also uncovers secondary barriers that the follower can manage independently. Therefore, making a detour does not necessarily imply that the follower is free from facing barriers; rather, it means that the follower can now engage more autonomously with secondary barriers while employing a suggested and co-constructed circumvention strategy. With this elaboration, we can summarize the interpretation of the autoethnography within a potential equation.

$$L(f) = \mathrm{Fol}(\mathrm{CoSign}) * N(F), N(1) = \mathrm{CVS}(F,1) * \mathrm{Bar}(F)$$

Here, we can capture that leadership requires, as a prerequisite, an active followership that emerges when the follower allows the leader to co-construct a given sign field based on the needs of both the leader and the follower. This co-construction can lead to a jointly negotiated circumvention strategy that the follower can autonomously apply to neutralize a given barrier (in this case, a second-order barrier).

Ninth Autoethnography: Irregular Payment

Upon changing jobs for a third time, I had already established a solid reputation as a tennis instructor in my hometown. Many clients approached me, preferring my approach over that of my supervisor. This development made me feel both proud and fulfilled. However, due to family obligations, I had to switch to another organization, and we moved to Austria. In Austria, I secured a position as a tennis instructor at a larger tennis organization. This environment was entirely new to me; I was now one of fifteen instructors. Some colleagues welcomed me warmly, while others barely acknowledged my presence. When entering the courts, some would greet me, while others were focused on teaching their own classes.

Before my first class, my supervisor showed me the storage room with all necessary equipment—balls, training materials, and so on. He also emphasized a few key rules, including punctuality, to which I readily agreed. After this brief introduction, he indicated that I was ready to start teaching. I began giving lessons, which went well as far as I could tell, with positive responses from both the clients and myself. I continued teaching over the subsequent days and weeks.

During this time, my supervisor asked for my bank account details for payroll. I provided the information, yet he did not specify a pay schedule. I assumed this was normal and continued teaching for another two months. Periodically, I checked my bank account to see if any payments had been made. I noticed a few deposits, though they only covered about 30% of the hours I had worked. I assumed the remaining balance would be paid at the end of the month, trusting that there was a logical reason for the partial payments.

At the end of the month, however, I checked my account again and found no additional transactions. Still, I reassured myself that there must be an explanation and continued teaching, confident that the issue would resolve itself. Yet, by the third month, with a significant amount owed to me, my confusion deepened. Eventually, I approached a colleague who shared my nationality to discuss the situation. She explained that my supervisor paid a fixed amount each month based on hours worked, but for the remaining balance, I needed to fill out time sheets and submit them at the reception. This initiated the verification process for my hours and the subsequent transaction for the remainder of my pay.

I was taken aback; no one had informed me about this procedure. I had been left entirely on my own to figure out how to initiate my full payment. This lack of guidance left me feeling both frustrated and somewhat resentful. It wasn't so much the money itself—although important—but the symbolic value it held as a sign of appreciation for my work. Consequently, I felt undervalued, which led to feelings of frustration and resentment toward my supervisor. This incident marked a turning point in my experience with the organization, as I perceived a lack of communication and appreciation that diminished my motivation to work there.

Analysis of the Ninth Autoethnography

A psychological analysis of this autoethnographic account reveals several key issues. First, the central issue that arises is a lack of information regarding the payment process. The protagonist, a course instructor, finds himself struggling with organizational intransparency; he is unaware of the procedures necessary to initiate his payment or even that initiating payment is his responsibility. For the instructor, this experience is not merely a logistical inconvenience but reflects a deeper sense that his needs are not being acknowledged, particularly his need for appreciation. In this case, the delayed or partial payment becomes less an issue of financial necessity and more a symbolic indicator of appreciation or lack thereof.

On the organizational side, the leader's needs appear focused on streamlining the administrative process by shifting responsibility for initiating payments to the employees. This shift reflects an organizational preference for reducing administrative burden across the enterprise. However, as the onus for administrative tasks is transferred to employees, the ability to express appreciation in a meaningful way becomes more challenging.

Thus, the interactional pattern can be described as distant, impersonal, and bureaucratic, demonstrated through the use of time sheets that must be completed to initiate payment. The system of communication in this context is highly administrative, with emphasis placed on documenting the instructor's hours rather than fostering a supportive or appreciative relationship. Although the instructor may ultimately resolve the immediate issue of receiving timely payments by adapting to this process, a secondary conflict remains unresolved: the need for symbolic acknowledgment. While economic concerns are addressed by following the established payment

Table 6.9 Analysis scheme for not getting paid regularly

Problem/ Issue	Personal need (follower's needs)	Social needs (organizational needs)	Interactional patterns	Tool-/ Sign-systems	Solution	Feelings
Not getting paid regularly due to a lack of information	appreciation	Smooth administrative processing of the payment	A-personal, distanced	Absence of signs, then discovery of adm. Signs, bureaucratic signs	Follower needs to adapt to the adm. Processing of his payment sheets	Anger, frustration, Lack of appreciation

procedure, the instructor's emotional responses—anger, frustration, sadness, and feelings of unappreciation—persist, casting doubt on the organization's leadership style as a whole. In essence, meeting the requirement for timely payment does not address the instructor's deeper need for recognition and appreciation.

This situation reveals a disconnect between the organization's assumption of what needs must be met (payment) and the instructor's more pressing, albeit unmet, emotional needs. Thus, we observe a divide between the practical need (payment) and the instructor's fundamental need for appreciation, which remains unfulfilled but could be easily addressed through a simple act of communication or acknowledgment by the leader.

It is also essential to examine the sign system employed in this context. The instructor encounters an absence of guiding cues regarding payment, contrasting sharply with the guidance provided for structuring his classes and accessing instructional materials. This lack of support leaves him struggling to make sense of the complex payment process independently. Once he does uncover the system, he interprets it as impersonal and bureaucratic, leading him to feel underappreciated and distanced from his supervisor. In other words, the combination of absent guidance, administrative procedures, and bureaucratic requirements forms a distinctive "sign field" that the instructor interprets as conveying a lack of appreciation.

This analysis is visually represented in Table 6.9, which summarizes key findings from the autoethnographic report, while Fig. 6.39 illustrates the sign field of de-appreciation as experienced and conceptualized by the instructor.

Field-Theoretical Interpretation of the Ninth Autoethnography

Examining the follower's experiential unit (see Fig. 6.40) through a field-theoretical lens, we observe that he aims to "locomote" toward his goal field—namely, receiving fair and timely payment. However, his progress is refracted by a complex interplay of needs. First, there is the fundamental need for economic stability; within a capitalist context, the follower requires timely payment to secure his livelihood and

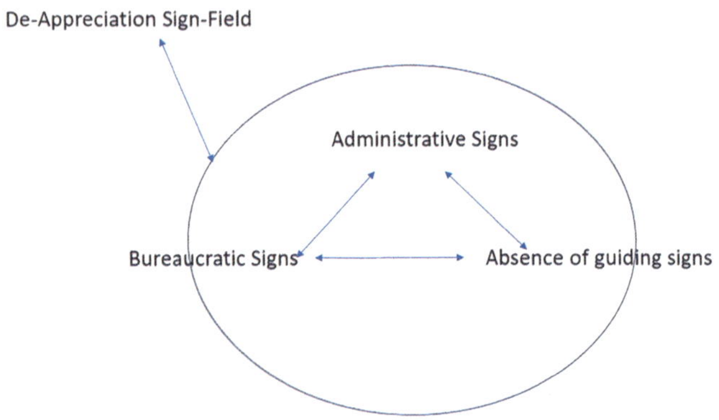

Fig. 6.39 De-appreciation sign field as experienced by the follower within the conflict of not getting paid regularly

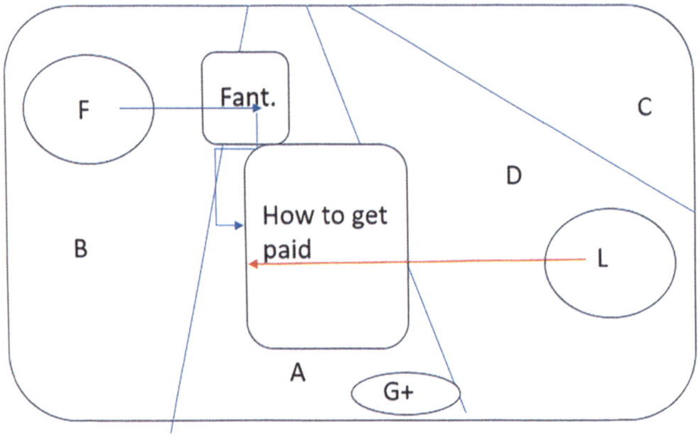

Fig. 6.40 Experiential unit (life-space) follower when wanting to get paid rightfully

meet financial obligations. This is an acquired, yet essential, need to maintain economic viability.

In addition, the follower's desire to reach the goal field is shaped by an expectation that timely payment symbolizes appreciation and respect for his work. Receiving payment on time, for him, is not only a transactional requirement but also an acknowledgment of his contributions and a form of recognition from his leader. This aspect highlights an emotional and symbolic layer to his needs, where he anticipates that his supervisor will support him through the payment process as part of a larger framework of professional validation and acknowledgment.

Thus, the follower's intentions in this field are clearly defined: he expects not only to be paid but also to receive implicit appreciation through that process, with the leader acting as a facilitator. These anticipated outcomes underscore the dual nature of his goal field—combining practical economic needs with deeper psychological needs for appreciation and support.

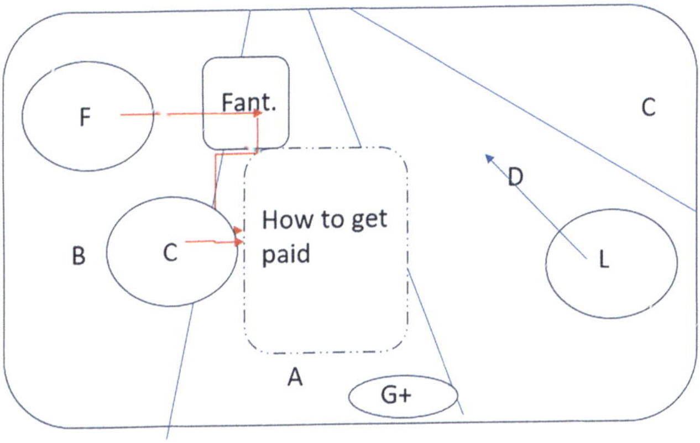

Fig. 6.41 Experiential unit (life-space) leader within the conflict of knowing how to get paid rightfully

In analyzing the leader's life-space (see Fig. 6.41), we observe that the leader assumes the follower will independently discover the enterprise's payment process. This belief reflects the leader's perception that the barrier to receiving payment is permeable, assuming that either the follower will uncover the process on his own or that another person will inform him of the necessary procedures. Consequently, the leader perceives no need to intervene or provide direct guidance in this area, believing the follower will reach the goal field (timely payment) without his assistance.

This perspective allows the leader to focus on his own pressing concerns within his immediate zone, interpreting the situation as one that does not require him to move into the follower's life-space. The leader therefore feels justified in redirecting his attention toward other priorities, viewing the follower's challenge as one that can be resolved independently. This interpretation reveals a divergence in the perceived needs and responsibilities between the leader and the follower, highlighting an implicit gap in understanding and communication.

Sociological Analysis of Leader-Follower Dynamics

The sociological analysis (see Fig. 6.42) highlights a distinct distancing pattern between the leader and the follower, which contradicts the follower's expectations of support. The follower anticipated that the leader would provide guidance to help him navigate the payment process barrier. However, this barrier proves impermeable from the follower's perspective, as he is unable to independently find a way around it or reach his goal of receiving rightful and timely payment. This lack of assistance prevents the follower from approaching his desired goal field.

Meanwhile, the leader operates in a separate zone and remains unaware of the follower's struggles or the impact of this barrier on the follower's experience.

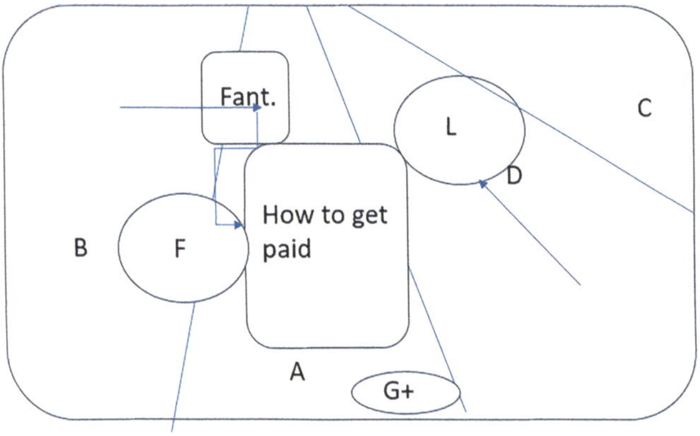

Fig. 6.42 Sociological analysis of the action field within the conflict of not getting paid rightfully

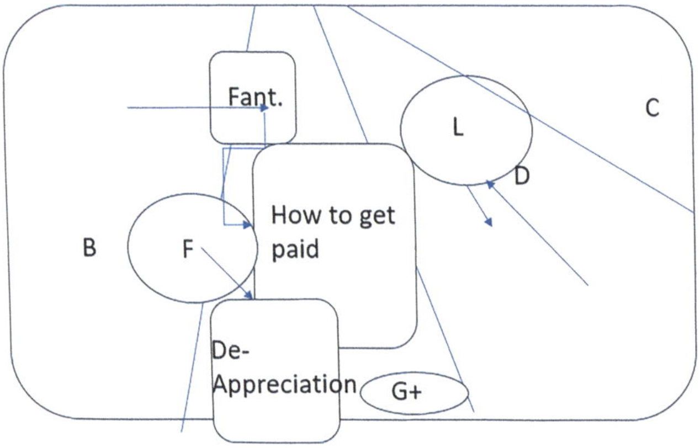

Fig. 6.43 Experiential unit (life-space) of the follower having built up a secondary-order barrier within the primary conflict of not getting paid rightfully

Lacking insight into the follower's difficulties, the leader fails to perceive the need for intervention or cooperative action. As a result, the follower's inability to overcome the primary barrier of the payment process creates a secondary, symbolic barrier, tied to a perceived lack of leadership. This new experiential unit signifies not just procedural difficulty but also a deeper sense of isolation and devaluation, intensifying the follower's frustration.

In effect, the follower must contend with both the initial obstacle—obtaining information about payment—and a secondary, more emotionally charged barrier, stemming from the leader's perceived neglect. The lack of adequate communication channels or tools to resolve the issue escalates into this secondary symbolic conflict, characterized by feelings of unappreciation (see Fig. 6.43). Consequently, the follower's life-space becomes negatively affected by this interconnected, multi-layered conflict.

This analysis shows that the primary conflict of navigating the payment process merges with a secondary conflict over unaddressed emotional needs, creating a polyvalent conflict. The follower's experience is thus complicated by the absence of supportive intervention from the leader, as well as by the accumulating impact of unfulfilled expectations. Without effective means to circumvent either conflict, the follower becomes caught in a cycle of frustration, with no clear path to resolve either the practical or symbolic issues at play.

In continuing our sociological analysis, it becomes evident that the follower, seeking clarification, approaches a colleague to better understand his situation. From this interaction, he receives guidance to collect and complete timesheets, which will allow him to initiate the payment process. This insight effectively resolves the primary conflict concerning how to secure his pay. However, while this procedural issue is addressed, the second-order barrier—rooted in feelings of isolation and a lack of appreciation—persists within the follower's life-space.

This analysis highlights how, despite overcoming the initial barrier, the underlying symbolic conflict remains unaddressed. The follower continues to feel unsupported and undervalued, reflecting a critical gap in leadership communication and engagement. From a field-theoretical perspective, this scenario provides insight into a negative critical incident in leadership, emphasizing the enduring impact of unmet emotional needs in organizational contexts.

We can summarize our findings with the following equation, which complements the previously developed equations:

$$-L(f) = \mathrm{Abs}(CVS)) * B_1(F) \rightarrow B_2(F) \neq g +$$
$$-L(f) = \mathrm{Abs}(CVS) * B_1(F) + \mathrm{Abs}(CVS) * B_2(F) \neq g + (\mathrm{Abs} = \mathrm{Absence})$$

Regarding our equation, we can articulate the following points: A lack of effective leadership is characterized by the absence of an adequate circumvention strategy concerning the life-space and action field of the follower. This deficiency in guidance—manifested through the lack of necessary tools and signs—gives rise to the emergence of a secondary barrier, which also requires circumvention. When this support is not provided, it further obstructs the follower's goal pursuit, rendering it significantly more challenging or even impossible.

Crucially, our equation facilitates the analysis of scenarios in which a leader recognizes a primary conflict and provides assistance to the follower in navigating the issue, believing that this will enable the follower to move freely toward the goal field. However, this assumption may not hold true, as illustrated by our equation. The failure to address the initial barrier results in the emergence of a secondary barrier that also necessitates a concrete circumvention strategy. Without this support, the follower may remain unable to reach the goal field, even though the leader may be convinced that he has fulfilled his role in helping the follower.

In such circumstances, the leader may be aware of the primary barrier but may overlook the interconnected secondary barrier that continues to exert pressure within the follower's life-space. This oversight highlights the complexity of leadership dynamics and the necessity for leaders to recognize and address both primary and secondary barriers in order to effectively support their followers in achieving their goals.

Tenth Autoethnography: How to Proceed with Two Talented Boys

Despite the previous negative example, it is important to highlight a positive incident that occurred between my leader and me. During my first trimester of teaching, I experienced considerable confusion regarding the skill levels of the children in my classes. In my hometown, I was accustomed to working with more advanced players. However, upon moving to this new club in a different country and town, I was surprised by the varying levels of proficiency exhibited by the students. While some had received prior training, others were complete beginners. This diverse skill composition made my role more complex, as I often found myself managing a group that included amateurs of all levels. Back home, the groups were more homogeneous, which greatly facilitated my teaching efforts. Additionally, I noticed that the students in this new environment progressed more slowly than I had anticipated. I was accustomed to training players and teaching the basic set of tennis skills within a short time frame. Yet, I found myself in classes where some participants were not yet able to play independently.

Fortunately, I had one class where two students demonstrated significant progress, showcasing a strong motivation and passion for the sport. Unfortunately, another girl in the group did not align with the overall skill level; she was less talented and lacked the same level of motivation. After a few months, she chose to drop out of the class. It was at this point that I approached my boss, in collaboration with my clients, to propose the idea of continuing to instruct the two talented participants in a private lesson format, rather than in a group setting. I reached out to him via WhatsApp, providing the necessary background information. I explained that both students were highly talented, had made remarkable progress, and required a more focused approach that rendered them ineligible for group training.

Fortunately, my boss agreed to my suggestion and converted the lesson into a private one. I understand that he earns a similar amount (between 90% to 100%) of the normal group price for these lessons, indicating that his agreement was likely a personal favor to me. I expressed my gratitude for his support, and I was thrilled that my students would now have a more suitable environment for learning and improvement.

Several months have passed since my request, and I am pleased to report that my students, who are now six years old, can play well with each other and even engage in matches against one another. They are eager to compete, consistently pushing themselves to their limits and beyond. More importantly, despite their progress, they find joy in being on the court. This enjoyment is significant to me, as I believe tennis is not merely about hitting a ball; it encompasses much more than that.

Analyzing the Tenth Autoethnography

From a psychological perspective, the situation described by the protagonist can be analyzed in terms of how to effectively structure a specific class. The follower reflects on previous experiences where the composition of the class was inadequate due to the presence of students with varying skill levels. This diversity in skill level negatively impacted the follower's ability to teach effectively, which conflicts with his personal objectives. The protagonist emphasizes a desire for his pupils to learn the sport quickly and improve their skills based on their passion and talent. Thus, the follower seeks to implement a talent-specific approach in his classes. However, this method may not align with the broader needs of the enterprise and, consequently, the leader's goals. It is important to note that a heterogeneous group may better serve the leader's interests by accommodating the high demands of clients and their children, who are eager to learn tennis. While converting a group lesson to a private format may not directly result in a loss of revenue for the leader, it does limit the opportunity to include new students who might fit into the group, thereby necessitating their redirection to other classes. Therefore, while the follower's needs do not outright oppose those of the leader, they present challenges in achieving long-term harmony between the two.

Focusing on the interactional dynamics, it becomes evident that there is a distanced and somewhat remote interaction between the leader and the follower. The leader has not personally observed the follower's teaching methods but instead trusts the follower's account without verifying it through direct experience. The autoethnography reveals that the leader responds to the follower via text message and agrees to his request without soliciting additional information. This suggests that the follower has effectively communicated the situation to the leader, prompting the leader to approve the follower's proposal. In this instance, the leader appears to embrace the follower's leadership by internalizing the follower's request and directing it to the reception for administrative processing.

The follower constructs a sign field that reflects the needs of both himself and his clients. He communicates to the leader that some of his students are talented, motivated, and passionate about tennis. Additionally, the follower ensures that the clients are willing to pay for a lesson consisting solely of the two students, which is crucial for the administrative feasibility of the two-pupil class.

Moreover, the follower articulates a desire for a more professional training approach, moving away from the typical teaching style employed in other classes. This construction leads to a unique sign field characterized by interconnected elements such as talent, smooth administrative processes, and personal motivation. Collectively, these signs form a cohesive framework that can be identified as personal structuring.

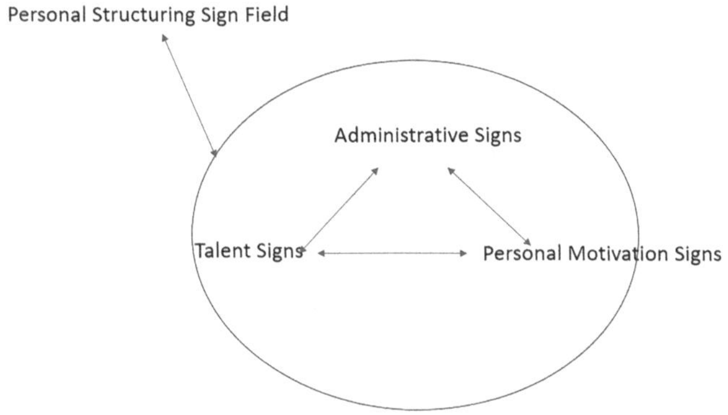

Fig. 6.44 Personal structuring sign field as sign system employed by the follower which becomes interiorized fully by the leader

Table 6.10 Analysis scheme for how to proceed with two talented pupils

Problem/ Issue	Personal need (follower's needs)	Social needs (organizational needs)	Interactional patterns	Tool-/ Sign-systems	Solution	Feelings
How to proceed with two talented pupils so that they can even more improve	Give Quality Training for young talented pupils	All clients need to find their place in the respective groups	Remote, distanced, via messenger	Sign field becomes constructed by the follower based on administrative signs, talent signs and personal motivation signs	Leader interiorized follower's sign field without major co-construction and leads him how the follower wants to be led.	Positive feelings and emotions

In Fig. 6.44, I have depicted the relevant sign field that the leader internalizes to initiate the administrative process, thereby ensuring the establishment of the follower's two-pupil class. This represents a complete internalization of the sign field, initially created by the follower. In essence, the follower effectively guides the leader, facilitating the progression toward his desired outcome. A summary of this analysis is provided in Table 6.10.

Field-Theoretical Interpretation of the Tenth Autoethnography

In a field-theoretical analysis of the autoethnography, we can examine the experiential unit of the follower (see Fig. 6.45). The follower is presented with a unique situation: he possesses a circumvention strategy that he believes could effectively

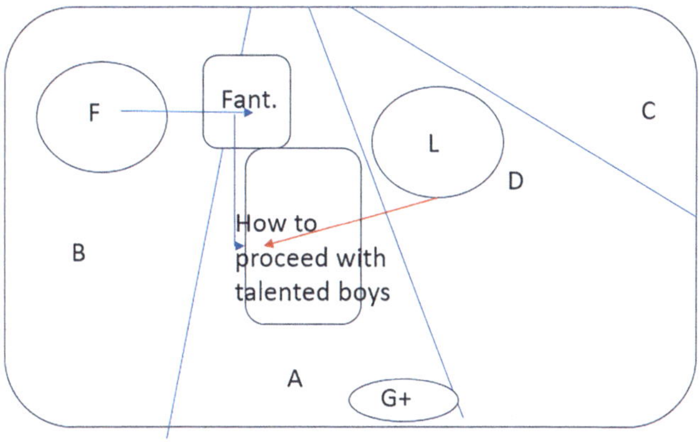

Fig. 6.45 Experiential unit (life-space) of the follower based on the question how to proceed with young talented boys

address the challenges he faces, but he requires approval from his leader to implement it. This scenario highlights the follower's recognition of his own skills and knowledge as sufficient to navigate the barriers he encounters. However, as an employee, he must seek his leader's validation, which introduces a potential for objection or modification to his proposed strategy.

Consequently, while the follower perceives the barrier as permeable based on his competencies, he must pause before executing his circumvention strategy, as he must consider his leader's perspective. In this context, the follower proactively invites the leader into his life-space by reaching out through a private message. In this virtual interaction, the follower constructs a compelling sign field, drawing upon his experiences with his young and talented clients, for whom he passionately advocates. This communication serves not only to inform the leader but also to illustrate the potential benefits of approving the follower's strategy, thereby fostering a collaborative environment that aligns the needs of both the follower and the organization.

Now, when we shift our focus to the experiential unit of the leader, an intriguing dynamic emerges (see Fig. 6.46). Upon being consulted by the follower, the leader gains insight into the follower's life-space, mediated through the signs the follower communicates. This interaction creates a sense of closeness, allowing the leader to approach the follower's zone—not through direct sensory experience, but rather through a cognitive and emotional understanding of the situation. As a result, the leader develops greater psychological proximity to the challenges the follower faces and chooses to place his trust in the follower's request.

In this context, the leader does not merely acknowledge the barrier confronting the follower; he also endorses the proposed circumvention strategy. Consequently, the leader not only gains insight into the complexities of the follower's experiences but also comprehends the follower's approach to overcoming his challenges. The

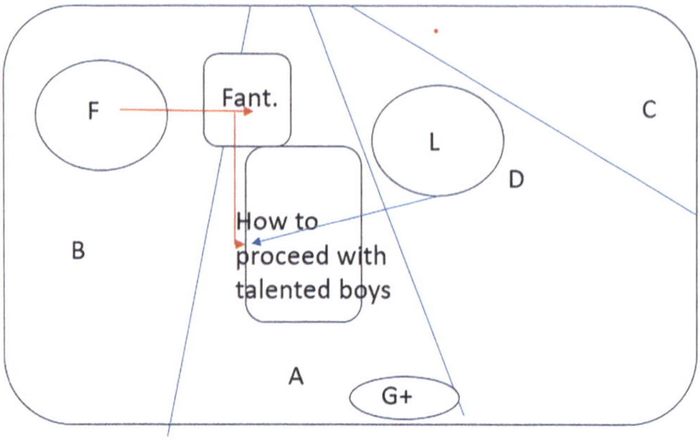

Fig. 6.46 Experiential unit (life-space) of the follower based on the question how to proceed with young talented boys

leader agrees to facilitate the implementation of this circumvention strategy from an administrative standpoint.

While we previously asserted that the leader fully interiorizes the sign field constructed by the follower, this observation holds true to a significant extent. However, it is important to note that the leader is also engaged in a process of semiotic co-construction of the administrative signs within the broader sign field. This involves sending requests to the reception that finalize the follower's demands and integrating those into the organizational IT system. Therefore, even in scenarios where a leader appears to completely interiorize a given sign field, there remains a vital space for semiotic co-construction that enhances collaboration and clarity within the organizational framework.

The sociological analysis (see Fig. 6.47) vividly illustrates how the leader and the follower connect in a virtual space through their messaging interaction. This communication allows the leader to consider the possibility of granting the follower his request while ensuring that his own reputation is upheld—specifically, the delivery of quality training. Consequently, both the leader and the follower come to an agreement regarding the permeability of the boundary and the general circumvention strategy to be employed in order to progress toward the goal field.

With this newfound understanding of the follower's life-space, the leader is now able to shift his focus to other areas where pressing issues may arise, while the follower can concentrate not only on initiating the action plan but also on executing it effectively. I choose not to depict the actualized life-space of the leader and the follower—unlike previous analyses of critical incidents—because such visualizations would not provide additional insights into the events described in the autoethnography. The key psychological mechanisms involved have already been articulated, rendering any further visualization redundant for the readership.

To capture the essence of the autoethnography, we can articulate the following equation: Leadership is a function of the follower's ability to construct a specific

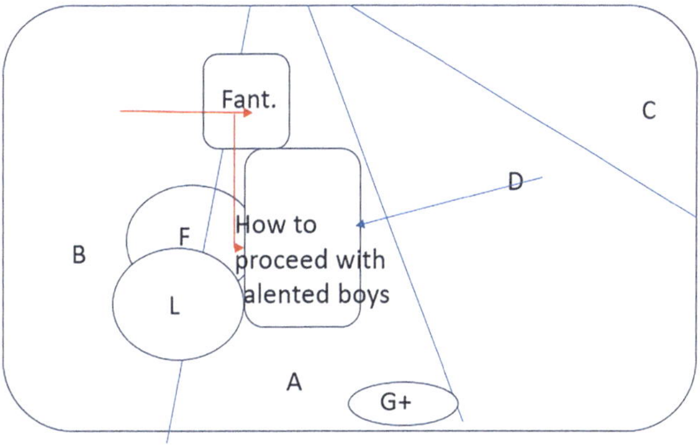

Fig. 6.47 Sociological analysis of the leader and the follower coming together for the structuring of one's class with young talented boys

sign field that can be fully interiorized by the leader, provided it aligns with the leader's primary organizational needs. This suggests that leadership is enriched and diversified through the active engagement of followership. However, it is crucial to recognize that this followership must be understood as an active process, relying on the construction of transparent sign fields that can be easily comprehended and internalized by the leader. Therefore, leadership emerges as a function of active followership.

$$\begin{aligned}&\mathrm{L}(\mathrm{f})=\mathrm{Folsh}^{*}\mathrm{Sign}-\mathrm{Field}(\mathrm{NF},\mathrm{Nl})=\mathrm{g}+(\text{where L}=\text{leadership},\\&\text{Folsh}=\text{followership},\text{N}=\text{Needs},\text{F}=\text{follower},\text{f}=\text{function},\\&\text{l}=\text{leader}) \text{ Active means here that the follower invites the leader}\\&\text{to glimpse into his life}-\text{space and understand his need structure}\\&\text{while linking his needs to the needs of the leader. Only then,}\\&\text{the interiorization of the follower's } \textit{sign} \text{ field might come into being,}\\&\text{successfully.}\end{aligned}$$

Eleventh Autoethnography: How to Deal with One's Absences

Having worked for over three months in the organization, I believed I had gained a fair understanding of the underlying climate and administrative processes in my leader's organization. However, I was soon proven wrong. As Christmas approached, I prepared to leave for Germany to spend time with my family and had planned my vacation accordingly. Back in October, during my first month of work, I had followed the procedure laid out by my boss's head secretary, who instructed me to report my absence in the IT system, assuring me that the reception staff would manage my request. After successfully submitting my absence for October without issue, I felt confident that I had done everything correctly when I reported my absence for Christmas in the system two months before my departure.

Upon arriving back home, however, I fell ill and had to spend a week in bed. On the second day of my illness, I received a sudden phone call from my boss, who asked where I was, as my clients were waiting for me on the court. I was taken aback by his call and explained that I was in Germany and had already reported my absence. There must have been a misunderstanding, I insisted. He agreed but then asked me to send him a screenshot showing that I had informed the reception about my vacation plans. Confused, I reiterated that I had reported my absence through the system. At that point, he clarified that I should have contacted the reception via the instructor/reception chat. It became clear that he viewed this as my mistake. Lacking the energy to argue due to my illness, I apologized and ended the call.

Once I recovered, I reflected on the situation and realized that something was amiss with my leader's approach. No one had informed me that I needed to write to the reception desk regarding my absences. I later discovered that there were specific vacation sheets I was required to fill out to officially report my absence, which further surprised me. The lack of clear communication and transparency regarding the processes left me feeling frustrated, especially considering I had never received a proper induction phase when I joined the organization.

Analyzing the Eleventh Autoethnography

From a psychological perspective, the situation reveals several key issues surrounding the reporting of absences that lack clear guidelines. It appears that while there are various mechanisms through which an employee can report their absence, an official procedure is notably absent. This raises significant transparency concerns regarding vacation planning within the organization.

For the employee, based on previous experiences, the process for reporting absences seemed straightforward; however, this understanding did not align with the expectations of the boss or the reception staff. The absence of clear communication about the appropriate procedure for vacation planning and reporting created a situation ripe for misunderstanding. The organization requires transparency and timely information about employee absences to effectively manage scheduling and ensure that classes are appropriately covered. Conversely, employees also need clear guidelines to facilitate their vacation planning.

The protagonist's feelings of frustration, particularly when blamed for the misunderstanding, highlight a critical gap in communication. Both the personal needs of the employee and the organizational needs converge on a shared requirement for clarity and guidance. Unfortunately, the misunderstanding arose from insufficient prior communication among the leader, the follower, and the reception regarding the proper process for reporting absences. The employee received conflicting information, which ultimately led to his misstep.

The communication dynamics reveal a distant and ineffective exchange about the reporting of absences, largely shaped by the instructions the employee received initially. The follower adhered to the circumvention strategy as outlined by the head secretary, internalizing a sign system regarding absence reporting that failed to account for the organization's requirements.

The repercussions of this incident are considerable. Firstly, the follower experiences negative emotions stemming from being blamed by his boss for the situation. Secondly, the organization suffers reputationally due to the disruption in scheduling, as classes were delayed because of the misunderstanding. Overall, both the follower and the leader face frustration, as the leader is now tasked with managing the fallout of a preventable issue. The summary of this analysis is encapsulated in Table 6.11.

Field-Theoretical Interpretation of the Eleventh Autoethnography

If we focus on the field-theoretical analysis, we become aware of the following. The follower (Fig. 6.48) has fully internalized a given circumvention strategy as suggested by the reception (R = reception). Based on this interiorized circumvention strategy, the follower perceives the barrier (how to report one's absences) as fully permeable and experiences the possibility of locomoting to the respective goal field. The leader does not appear to be important within the pressing zones of the follower; he is perceived as operating in his respective zone and not being significant when solving the issue of reporting one's absences. Hence, we see that the follower trusts fully in the advice given by the reception staff.

If we focus on the experiential unit of the leader (Fig. 6.49), we encounter a different perspective. Here, the leader perceives the follower as stopping and pausing in front of the barrier while consulting or checking in with him. In other words, the leader expects the follower to apply a different circumvention strategy when addressing the barrier and neutralizing it. Thus, the leader desires to be consulted regarding the reporting of absences, as evidenced by his suggestion that the follower should post his absence via a messaging and group function of which he is part. Consequently, before the follower attempts to navigate through the barrier, the leader requires the follower to adopt a specific circumvention strategy, rather than any general approach, as dictated by him.

When we examine the sociological analysis (Fig. 6.50), we encounter a rather complex picture of the situation at hand. The follower navigates to his respective goal field based on the premise that he perceives the barrier as essentially permeable. He circumvents the barrier using a prescribed circumvention strategy and finds himself on vacation. Conversely, the leader approaches the barrier to verify whether the follower has applied a specific circumvention strategy, which, from the leader's perspective, has not occurred. As a result, the leader questions why the follower has

Table 6.11 Analysis scheme for reporting one's absences

Problem/ Issue	Personal need (follower's needs)	Social needs (organizational needs)	Interaction patterns	Tool-/Sign-systems	Solution	Feelings
How to report one's absences	Having planned and unproblematic vacation	Cancel and re-schedule classes	Remote, distanced based on an IT system or WhatsApp Group Chat	Interiorization of reception sign field that is not in accordance with the leader's sign field	Application of Reception Sign Field = Conflict. Afterwards: Adjustment based on Leader's Sign Field	Employee Blamed. Negative Emotions

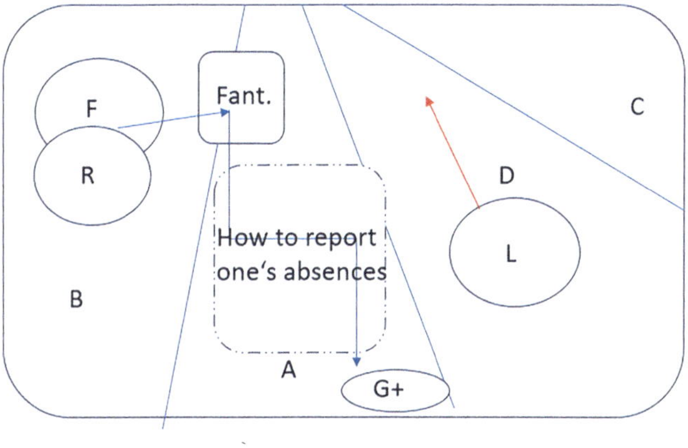

Fig. 6.48 Experiential unit (life-space) of the follower while wanting to report one's absences

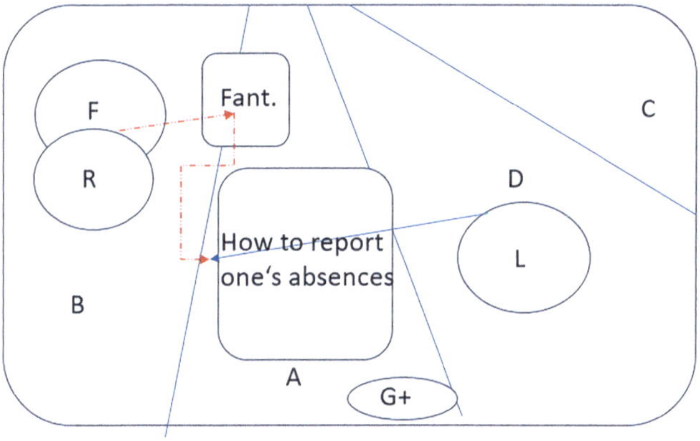

Fig. 6.49 Experiential unit (life-space) leader wanting the follower to report his absence in a specific manner

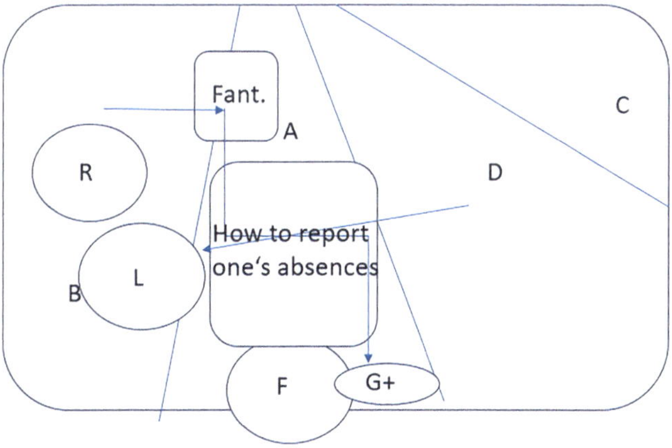

Fig. 6.50 Sociological analysis of the action field within the conflict of how to report one's absences

moved past the barrier without utilizing his designated circumvention strategy. In other words, the barrier is not permeable for the leader, while it is for the follower. The leader wonders why the follower proceeded to his goal field without considering the barrier, whereas the follower believes he did account for it based on the advice from the reception staff.

I refrain from depicting the actualized life spaces of the leader and the follower, as their positions are clear without further visualization. Both the leader and the follower realize they find themselves in different zones, despite the need to be in the same zone, applying a transparent circumvention strategy that is consistently utilized for vacation requests. In this context, the leader asks the follower to provide proof that he communicated his absence to the reception via the group chat; however, the follower demonstrates that this is not what he did, as he was instructed differently. Consequently, the follower comes to internalize the circumvention strategy required by the leader, but this realization only occurs after the conflict or misunderstanding has arisen. Following the conflict or misunderstanding, the leader seizes the opportunity to realign the follower's circumvention strategy with what he believes should be employed.

This elaboration leads us to formulate a new equation that encapsulates our field-theoretical interpretation of autoethnography. We can conclude that a lack of effective leadership arose from the follower's use of a circumvention strategy that did not align with the needs of the leader or the organization, despite adequately addressing the needs of the follower. This misalignment occurred because there was no prior dialogue between the leader and the follower regarding the appropriate strategy for reporting absences.

$$-L(f) = -(DIA) * N(F), N(1) \neq (CVS) * N(F), N(1) \neq g+$$
$$= -L(f) = CVS^{*} N(F) \neq N(1)$$

Twelfth Autoethnography: Preference for Outdoor Play

This autoethnographic reflection describes a significant incident with my supervisor that underscored a discrepancy between my working environment preferences and the available facilities. During early spring, I arrived at the club ahead of schedule, a common occurrence that allows me to read and prepare mentally before starting work. Shortly after, my supervisor arrived, initiating a brief conversation with me, where we covered casual topics such as the weather, clients, and my academic studies.

During this conversation, my supervisor informed me that the outdoor courts were now available for use and suggested that I could conduct my sessions outside if I preferred. Previously unaware of this option, I readily agreed. The club's indoor courts are housed in an inflatable air hall, which, due to its greenhouse effect, can reach temperatures up to 25 degrees Celsius on warm days. Such conditions can be uncomfortable and poorly ventilated, creating an unappealing environment for extended physical activity. In prior instances, I had experienced severe headaches after teaching in this hot, enclosed space.

Thus, my supervisor's suggestion was particularly welcome, as I prefer the outdoor setting due to the fresh air and connection to nature it provides, which are important aspects of my personal well-being. Before concluding our conversation, my supervisor stated that he would coordinate with the reception to confirm which specific outdoor court I could use. I thanked him and resumed my reading.

It is important to note that my supervisor was already aware of my preference for outdoor sessions. I had previously raised concerns with him about the indoor court conditions, and he acknowledged these challenges. This incident illustrates a moment where my needs aligned with my supervisor's flexibility in accommodating them, demonstrating a valuable, albeit informal, responsiveness to staff well-being that positively impacted my work experience.

Psychological Analysis of the Twelfth Autoethnography

From a psychological perspective, this scenario highlights a complex interplay of personal needs, organizational needs, and sign construction between the follower (course instructor) and the leader. The protagonist expresses discomfort and health issues when required to play inside the air hall, where temperatures can become excessively high. This concern underscores two needs: a practical one to avoid adverse physical effects in hot indoor conditions and a personal or "spiritual" need to feel connected to nature by playing outside. In this case, the personal preferences of the follower align with organizational capabilities, as the outdoor courts have recently opened and benefit from regular use to maintain quality. Thus, while the personal and organizational needs are not identical, they complement each other and demonstrate a mutually beneficial relationship.

The interaction between the leader and the follower is characterized by an informal and supportive tone, taking place prior to the follower's scheduled classes. The follower had previously expressed concerns about the uncomfortable indoor temperature, which the leader remembers and addresses by informing him that the outdoor courts are now available. This communication process illustrates the follower's construction of a "sign field," comprised of remarks about the pleasant weather and complaints about the hot indoor conditions. In response, the leader co-constructs this sign field by integrating his own perspective on the situation, which includes both knowledge about the available courts and an understanding of the follower's expressed preferences.

Initially, the follower lacks information about the outdoor court availability. However, upon learning this through conversation with his leader, he recognizes an opportunity to align his work environment with his preferences. The leader's co-construction of the sign field allows the follower to "interiorize" or adopt this newly shared understanding and consider it for his own benefit. As a result, the follower is

Table 6.12 Analysis scheme for unified teaching autoethnography

Problem/ Issue	Personal need (follower's needs)	Social needs (organizational needs)	Interaction patterns	Tool-/ Sign-systems	Solution	Feelings
Not wanting to play in the air all when the temperatures exceed 25 degrees inside	Preferring to play outside, feeling connected to nature	Courts need to be played upon	Informal, personal	Sign field based on problems and preferences (initially from the follower)	Co-construction of the sign field based on the leader's additional knowledge	Feelings of closure

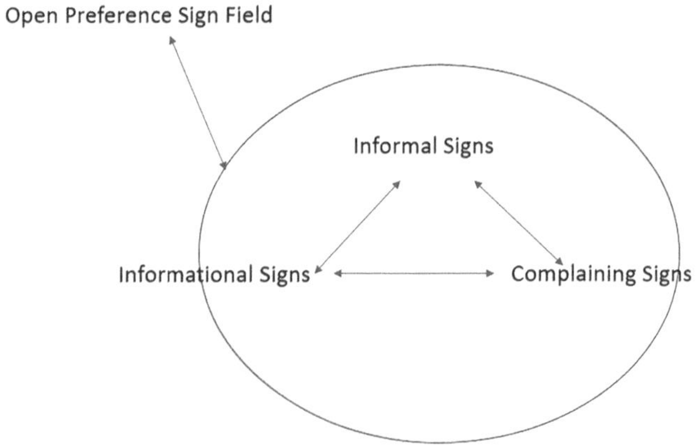

Fig. 6.51 Open preference sign field as constructed by the leader

able to shift his focus back to his reading with a sense of closure, having resolved the question of where to conduct his classes.

In Table 6.12 the analysis outlines the various elements of this interaction, and Fig. 6.51 illustrates the interconnected sign field initially constructed by the follower and subsequently co-constructed by the leader. This co-constructed sign field does not function through additive methods, where the leader simply "adds" signs to the follower's understanding. Rather, the leader shapes both the individual parts and their relationships, resulting in a unified whole that enhances the quality and interrelationships of these parts. The informal and informational elements offered by the follower are thus reformulated within the leader's broader perspective, transforming the sign field and reinforcing a collaborative solution. In Fig. 6.52, we see this co-constructed sign field, interiorized by the follower and applied to fulfill both personal and organizational purposes. This co-construction showcases the holistic nature of the sign process, where each element dynamically influences the collective understanding.

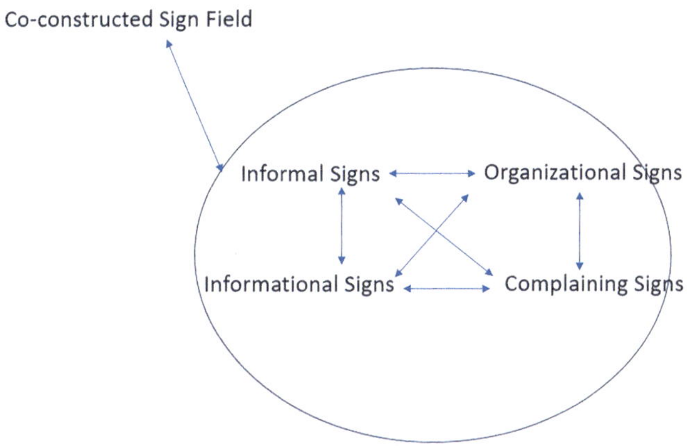

Fig. 6.52 Co-constructed sign field as suggested by the leader based on organizational signs

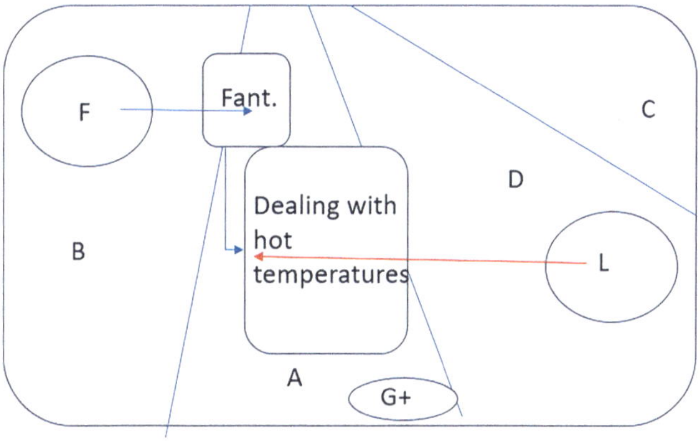

Fig. 6.53 Experiential unit of the follower when perceiving the barrier of dealing with hot temperatures in the air hall

Field-Theoretical Interpretation of the Twelfth Autoethnography

From a field-theoretical perspective (see Fig. 6.53), the follower perceives a significant barrier—namely, how to manage the uncomfortable high temperatures inside the air hall. This barrier restricts the follower's ability to move freely toward his goal of effectively conducting tennis classes. Previously, the follower attempted to disregard the uncomfortable temperatures and proceed with his classes, though this approach led to some health issues. This experience emphasized the need to reconsider his strategy for circumventing the barrier.

In this context, the follower anticipates some assistance from the leader, even if he does not fully know what form it might take. He hopes the leader will move closer to understand his pressing needs and view the barrier from his perspective.

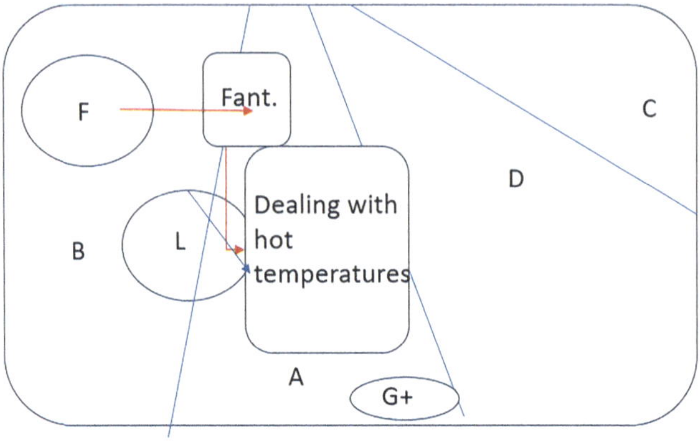

Fig. 6.54 Experiential unit of the leader when perceiving the barrier of dealing with hot temperatures in the air hall

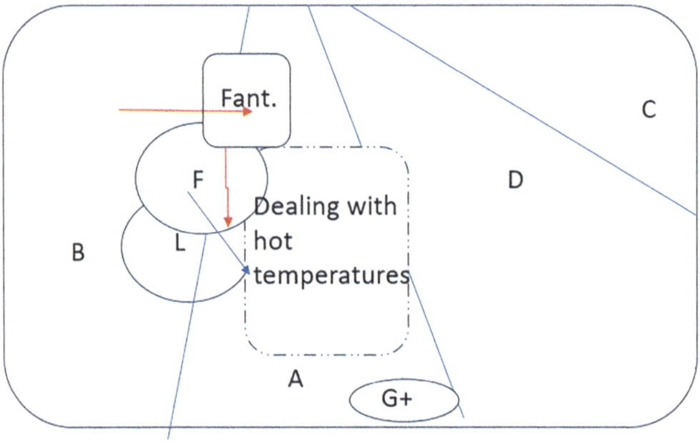

Fig. 6.55 Sociological analysis of the action field of the leader and the follower when wanting to deal with hot temperatures

The follower invites the leader's engagement by initiating small talk, as noted in the autoethnography.

When examining the life-space of the leader (see Fig. 6.54), a different perspective emerges. The leader perceives himself as already positioned close to the follower and the barrier, implying that he understands the follower's perspective on the issue. However, the leader extends beyond this mere observation, anticipating that the follower may encounter difficulties in managing the barrier. In this context, the leader prefers that the follower move toward him, seeking guidance or support in addressing the problem.

In the sociological analysis (*see* Fig. 6.55), both the leader and the follower are situated within the same zone, collaboratively negotiating a strategy to address or circumvent the barrier. The follower initiates this sign construction by expressing

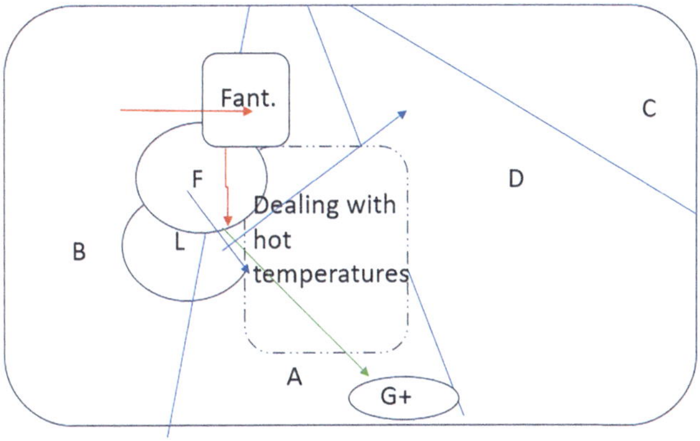

Fig. 6.56 Actualized life-space of the follower when dealing with hot temperatures in the air hall

his discomfort with playing indoors when temperatures exceed 25 degrees. Initially, he introduces the topic informally, discussing the weather without directly mentioning the issue of giving tennis classes. As the conversation progresses, he connects the pleasant outdoor conditions to his discomfort with the indoor environment, articulating his preference to play outside. This connection effectively constructs the sign field, which the leader then co-constructs by adding his own knowledge about the availability of open courts and the option to switch locations. Together, they establish a circumvention strategy that allows the follower to perceive the barrier as permeable, enabling him to achieve his goal while aligning with the organization's needs.

The analysis underscores how the leader and the follower, through small talk, find themselves on the same border between personal and organizational zones. The informal exchange naturally evolves into organizational dialogue, culminating in a mutually beneficial strategy. This sociological dynamic illustrates that informal communication can serve as a bridge to organizational discussions and the co-construction of practical solutions. Consequently, the follower feels prepared to move toward his goal, perceiving the conversation as complete, and expecting the leader to return to his own zone, thereby actualizing his life-space (*see* Fig. 6.56).

I'd like to refrain from further depicting the actualized life-space of the leader and the next sociological analysis, as this type of visualization has already been sufficiently addressed in previous sections. Instead, I will summarize our analysis and interpretation with an equation, as we have done for earlier critical incidents.

In this case, we can formulate the following: Leadership is a function of active followership, wherein an open sign field is constructed based on the follower's needs. This sign field is then co-constructed by the leader, integrating his own pressing needs, which leads to the joint negotiation of a circumvention strategy. This strategy helps the follower to reach his goal field, which is also aligned with the leader's experiential unit and organizational objectives.

$L(f) = Folsh^{*}SignField(NF,Nl) = CVS^{*}N(F), N(l) = g +$ (where leadership is initiated by active followership relying on an open *sign* field related to the follower's needs that can become co – constructed by the leader regarding his pressing needs which results in the negotiation of a joint circumvention strategy mirroring both follower and leader needs.

Longitudinal Interpretation of the Autoethnographic Leadership Patterns

When studying the critical incidents from a longitudinal perspective (see Table 6.13), we can identify additional psychological mechanisms at play. An interesting observation occurs at the transition between the third and fourth critical incidents, where the follower appears to have gained more confidence in approaching his leader for guidance (e.g., stimulation, inspiration). In the fourth critical incident, the follower takes a more proactive approach by requesting a concrete exercise to address a particular issue he faces during his class. This marks a shift, as the follower not only asks for guidance but actively engages in a dialogue with the leader.

In this interaction, the leader suggests a circumvention strategy for the issue at hand, but the follower adapts this strategy to suit his own needs and objectives. Specifically, the follower deviates from the leader's suggestion by applying a similar exercise focused on the backhand. This small adaptation signals a notable shift in the follower's role, which is more active and engaged compared to earlier critical incidents. Initially, the follower's role seemed more passive, as they mostly took on recommendations or imperatives suggested by the leader, or failed to understand the leader due to significant psychological and sociological differences between them.

In subsequent critical incidents, this more active role of the follower is further evident. For example, in a later incident, the follower is presented with a challenging exercise involving structuring a class for young, talented children—an area where he lacks experience. Here, the follower enters into a dialogue with the leader (who is also the father of the client) to negotiate how to structure the class. The leader sets boundaries for what can be done, but it is left to the follower to decide how to fill in these boundaries and which exercises to use. This indicates that not only does the follower perceive his role as more active, but the leader also sees the follower's role as more autonomous. However, this autonomy does not mean complete freedom; rather, it operates within specific limits set by the leader at the outset of their conversation.

Once the follower experiences the benefits of the dialogical approach to leadership, the relationship between the leader and the follower seems to undergo a shift. The follower becomes accustomed to the idea that leadership can be co-constructed through dialogue, which makes him more likely to seek and expect a certain type of leadership guidance. This dynamic is particularly evident in the sixth critical

Table 6.13 Summary of the autoethnographic leadership vignettes and their field-theoretical analysis

Number of autoethnography	Issue	Leadership equation
First job experience		
1	Instructor (follower) Insecurity not addressed by the leader	$-L(f) = l(R) \neq F(R)$ Non-emergence of leadership is a function of the leader reality unequal to the follower reality
2	How to react to de-appreciation by customers—leader provides support	$L(f) = CVS^{*}N(F) \rightarrow g+$ Leadership is a function of providing a circumvention strategy to one's follower—depending on his needs—in order for the follower to locomote more autonomously toward his goal field (g+)
3	Cancellation of a class and leader does not give any rationale for that	$-L(f) = l(R) \neq F(R) = CVS(l) * B(f)$ Lack of Leadership comes into being by the unequalness of the leader's and the follower's psychological and sociological reality which makes the leader suggest circumvention strategies unequal to the quality of the follower's perceived and real barrier.
4	How to teach a client a specific stroke he has difficulties with—getting inspiration by one's boss	$L(f) = N(F), N(l) = CVS^{*}N(F), N(l) \rightarrow g+$ We can argue that leadership becomes a function of the negotiation of a circumvention strategy that mirrors the needs of the follower as well as the needs of the organization (leader's needs).
Second job experience		
5	How to structure a class with young talented kids—leader provides some scaffolding	$L(f) = N(l), F(N) = CVS^{*}Dia\ N(F), N(l) = g+$ Here, we can argue that leadership becomes a function of the negotiation of a circumvention strategy that mirrors the needs of the follower as well as the needs of the organization. This circumvention strategy only comes into being in and through dialogue which helps the follower to make the barrier permeable in order to locomote to the goal field
6	How to prepare one's class in a gymnasium? Leader does not provide any help.	$IST_f(f) = D(EIL)-D(WIL)$ where the distance is proportional to the tension felt within the follower's system (ISTf = Intra-systemic tension follower, D = Distance, EIL = Expected Intentions Leader, WIL (Wished Intentions Leader) Here, we can say that intra-systemic tension within the follower is a function of the distance for the wished and expected intentions for the leader as experienced by the follower:

(continued)

Table 6.13 (continued)

Number of autoethnography	Issue	Leadership equation
7	Course instructor is appealed to actualize his instruction style	$-L(f) = (B1) * N(l)$, $N(F) * Cons(B2) * N(l) = B(1) * Cons\ B(2) * N(l)^2, N(F)$ which shows a pre-domination of leader needs in contrast to follower needs (where the failure of leadership is a function of a jointly agreed barrier depending on the needs of the follower and the needs of the leader while the leader constructs a second-order barrier based on his needs regardless of the needs of the follower in relation to the second-order barrier.
8	Switching tennis courts in a short period of time while the leader provides some assistance in solving the issue	$L(f) = Fol(CoSign) * N(F), N(l) = CVS(F, l) * Bar(F)$ Leadership needs as a pre-requisite active followership that only comes into being when the follower allows the leader to co-construct a given sign field based on the needs of the leader and the follower. This co-construction can lead into a jointly negotiated circumvention strategy that can be autonomously applied to neutralizing a given barrier.
Third job experience		
9	Not get paid regularly—leader does not communicate how to initiate the pay process	$L(f) = Abs(CVS)) * B_1(F) \rightarrow B_2(F) \neq g+$ $-L(f) = Abs(CVS) * B_1(F) + Abs(CVS) * B_2(F) \neq g+$ A lack of leadership is described by the absence of an adequate circumvention strategy regarding the life-space and action field of the respective follower. This absence of guidance (tools and signs) translates into the emergence of a secondary barrier that also demands circumvention – which when it is not provided – hinders additionally the goal pursued of the respective follower
10	How to proceed with classes with two young talented boys	$L(f) = Folsh^*Sign - Field(NF, Nl) = g+$ Leadership becomes a function of the follower constructing a given sign field that can be interiorized fully by the respective leader when it does not contradict his major organizational needs. Hence, leadership becomes diversified and filled with life based on followership.
11	How to report one's absences	$-L(f) = -(DIA) * N(F), N(l) \neq (CVS) * N(F), N(l) \neq g+$ $= -L(f) = CVS^* N(F) \neq N(l)$ lack of leadership came into being due to the application of a circumvention strategy by the follower that does not mirror the needs of the leader or the organization despite the circumvention strategy doing justice to the needs of the follower. Yet, the application of a non-adaptive circumvention strategy came into being because there was no prior dialogue between the leader and the follower about which strategy to apply for reporting one's absences.

(continued)

Table 6.13 (continued)

Number of autoethnography	Issue	Leadership equation
12	Not being able to play in the air hall if temperatures exceed 25 degrees	L (f) = Folsh*SignField(NF, NI) = CVS*N(F), N(l) = g+ Leadership is a function of active followership by means of constructing an open sign field based on one's needs while the sign field becomes co-constructed by the respective leader and his pressing needs resulting in the joint negotiation of a given circumvention strategy that helps the follower to attain his goal field that is also attractive for the leader and his experiential unit.

incident, when the follower expresses frustration about the leader's absence and the inability to solve a problem on his own. In this case, the absence of guidance is interpreted as destructive rather than as an opportunity for autonomous decision-making, as was the case in earlier incidents. The follower views the lack of guidance on a complex task as an act of ignorance, leading to a negative interpretation of the leader's role in this particular situation. This shift in perception illustrates that the follower's expectations for leadership are evolving, particularly in relation to the nature and timing of guidance provided by the leader.

From a longitudinal perspective, a second thematic breakthrough emerges in the seventh autoethnography. At this point, the follower has already built a solid reputation in teaching tennis classes. In other words, the follower has found his own teaching style, one that has been consolidated through positive feedback from his clients. As a result, the follower has developed specific abilities and skills that enable him to work autonomously toward the organization's general goal—providing reliable classes to clients. However, a conflict arises when the leader attempts to change the follower's teaching style. The leader, seeking to unify the teaching approach and address some customer complaints, wants to impose his own technique on the follower and demands that the follower comply with it. Unfortunately, the leader does not offer the follower an opportunity to co-construct or adapt this unified teaching style from his own perspective. Essentially, the leader disregards the follower's existing skills and abilities and attempts to superimpose his teaching method.

This creates a barrier for the follower. Not only must he deal with the previous barrier (the discomfort of playing inside in the heat), but he must now confront a secondary barrier—one created by the leader's interference with his teaching style. The follower experiences this interference as a challenge to his core competencies. For the first time in the critical incidents, we observe that the follower blocks the internalization of the circumvention strategy proposed by the leader. Although the follower listens to the leader and acknowledges what he suggests, he actively resists applying it, as doing so would contradict his system of goals and methods. This blockage raises a crucial question for leadership—why did the follower reject the interiorization of the leader's proposed strategy? In this case, the follower's rejection stems from the leader's disregard for the follower's past achievements, which would result in the follower teaching in a way that he is not convinced of, leading to a sense of estrangement from his own approach.

A third thematic breakthrough occurs in the tenth autoethnography, marking a significant shift in the way the leader and the follower interact. At this point, the follower begins to demonstrate clear signs of active followership. He starts to construct a sign field based on his own initiatives, one that is important for leadership. The follower actively outlines how he wants to be led by the leader, constructing a sign field that mirrors the needs of the leader. This anticipatory approach makes it more likely that the leader will internalize the follower's suggested circumvention strategy, as it already aligns with the leader's pressing needs.

In the tenth autoethnography, the follower's ability to anticipate the leader's needs enables him to construct a sign field that works as a strategy to overcome a barrier. The leader, recognizing that the sign field already incorporates his own needs, accepts the circumvention strategy without requiring further negotiation. This demonstrates that the follower has developed an awareness of the leader's dynamic needs, allowing him to adjust the circumvention strategy based on those needs. Active followership, in this case, is not the result of heightened self-awareness or bravery alone, but rather stems from the follower's ability to anticipate the leader's needs, allowing him to adapt the strategy for both his own and the leader's purposes.

This interactional pattern is further validated in the eleventh autoethnography, where a misunderstanding occurs due to the follower's application of a circumvention strategy that reflects only his own needs. In this instance, the leader misses the opportunity to construct or co-construct a sign field for the procedure in case of absences, leaving the follower to figure it out alone. The follower has become accustomed to the dialogical interaction between himself and the leader, but he assumes that there is no issue in reporting absences, as he perceives no need for further dialogue. Thus, the follower operates under the assumption that the established procedure is clear, leading to a misunderstanding. This can be described as the dialogical taken-for-grantedness stage, where the leader and the follower have established clear interactional patterns that do not require constant renegotiation. In this stage, dialogue is only necessary when a problem or misunderstanding arises, and both parties can anticipate each other's needs without the need for explicit discussion.

This ongoing process reflects the evolving relationship between the leader and the follower, where both anticipate each other's needs and adapt their actions accordingly. However, as demonstrated in the eleventh autoethnography, when this mutual anticipation is disrupted or unaddressed, it leads to misunderstandings, illustrating the importance of ongoing dialogue in maintaining effective leadership and followership dynamics.

While we are not clearly confronted with a fourth thematic breakthrough, we observe some significant precursors for such a step. Here, we become aware that the follower does not consider his circumvention strategy to be the same as the leader's circumvention strategy (or vice versa); instead, the follower relies on constructing a more open sign field. As such, the follower focuses openly on the issue at hand, concentrating on the bare information as well as his interpretation, while allowing the leader to appropriate this interpretation and co-construct it by his own means.

Concretely, we see that the follower argues that the temperatures are too hot inside the air hall and asks whether there are any opportunities to change the air circulation in the hall. Here, the follower focuses simply on his interpretation of the event (too hot), while leaving space for the leader to check on that and intervene based on his own knowledge and needs. This almost fourth step seeks to break free from the dialogical taken-for-grantedness, meaning that the leader and the follower refrain from assuming they see and interpret an event from the same point of view. On the contrary, by redirecting one's efforts solely to the personal interpretation, the follower (or the leader) leaves room for the generalized social other to interpret it from their own perspective, thereby circumventing the dialogical taken-for-grantedness between both actors.

When we summarize our analysis from a longitudinal perspective, we are presented with the following picture.

(A) The follower passively accepts circumvention strategies and imperatives suggested by the leader, or the leader and the follower think and act independently of each other.
(B) Circumvention strategies for overcoming barriers are negotiated between the leader and the follower. However, the leader remains primarily the impulse generator for the given circumvention strategies or leader-follower imperatives.
(C) The follower has built up some generalized working patterns that contribute to a personal reputation. The follower now asks for the open re-negotiation of circumvention strategies and leader-follower imperatives, seeking autonomy and aiming to initiate circumvention strategies independently. Resistance emerges against excessive leader domination, with the follower expecting to co-construct the circumvention strategies.
(D) Dialogical taken-for-grantedness arises, where the leader and the follower perceive that circumvention strategies have already been dialogically negotiated and adjusted to each other's needs, though this may not have actually taken place. A need emerges for the re-negotiation of certain concepts to fulfill both the leader and the follower needs.
(E) The leader and the follower construct open sign fields, focusing on their own experiences, without assuming the social other relates to an event in the same way. As such, they leave space for the other to appropriate the sign field based on their own system of purposes. Leader-follower interactions may proceed in a way that avoids fixing the social other within a foreign interpretational pattern.

With our longitudinal analysis, we have illuminated the development of leadership and followership interpretations, showing how the follower not only becomes braver in approaching the leader but also more open and transparent, allowing the leader to gain insight into the follower's need hierarchy. This openness enables the leader to adjust the circumvention strategy to include the follower's important needs in the coping mechanisms. Similarly, the follower shares his pressing needs openly, allowing the leader to take them into account when co-constructing a given sign or tool system.

To what extent this longitudinal picture is generalizable beyond the present autoethnographies remains an interesting question. However, I believe that there is some external validity to our longitudinal understanding of cultural leadership. Any relationship where leadership plays a crucial role often starts with one party feeling intimidated or dominated by the other, who holds specific powers or gatekeeping functions. Dialogue helps adjust to each other, establishing common ground. Yet, dialogue can become too much taken for granted, leading to a situation where both the leader and the follower get stuck in rigid interpretations of the other's needs, culminating in the experience that such knowledge and transparency become almost impossible to achieve.

This insight underscores the need for both the leader and the follower to construct their sign fields openly (pleromatic), so that the other is more likely to appropriate them. The final step appears to be an ideal version of leader-follower interactions, wherein both the leader and the follower can include the social other in an open and transparent manner. The positive psychological consequences of such an open and transparent understanding of leader-follower interactions have been shown throughout the autoethnographies.

Besides the longitudinal interpretation of the events, we also gain an understanding of the power of needs from the perspective of both the leader and the follower. It remains important to emphasize that, in the successful critical incidents, the leader and the follower do not perceive themselves as separate but as interrelated. Potential circumvention strategies are constructed openly, allowing the social other to contribute to the strategy in their own way. In Table 6.13, the distinct autoethnographies are summarized with their field-theoretical interpretation allowing the reader to understand the longitudinal trends we inferred based on the analysis. Hence, Table 6.13 does not solely serve as a summary for the different vignettes but it also allows to assess how leadership developed over the course of the critical incidents.

Chapter 7
Digesting Field-Theoretical Findings Personally: Between a Letter to One's Future Self and a Policy Brief

Personal Reflection on the Results: Imperatives for the Future Self

The following letter is an important exercise in reflecting on the findings from a first-person perspective. Writing a letter to one's future self allows the author to distill the essence of the autoethnographic study and apply its insights. This approach not only supports alternative validity criteria in qualitative leadership research (e.g., trustworthiness and authenticity) but also helps the author psychologically process the findings. Research has shown that such exercises can mitigate negative emotions arising from challenges encountered in daily life (Chishima et al., 2021; Wetzler & Feltner, 2021). A similar strategy was employed here to provide the author with a framework for interpreting findings constructively and at a healthy distance.

Dear Future Self

We have worked on the concept of leadership for quite some time, and you can be proud of your accomplishments. We have gathered valuable data and made sense of it productively. I am writing this letter to prepare you for future challenges and resistance—whether as a tennis instructor or beyond. Applying scientific insights into one's personal and professional life is often difficult, a complexity that has characterized applied science for centuries. You, my dear future self, are no exception.

Some ideas presented here will sound familiar since we've worked together on leadership extensively. However, as time passes, the central premises of our data and theory might fade from memory. This letter is a reminder for times when you

E. Freiherr von Fircks, *Studying Leadership from a Microgenetic Perspective*, Methodologies in Developmental Sciences,
https://doi.org/10.1007/978-3-031-90214-7_7

feel inadequately treated or stuck in conflict. Let it inspire you to manage conflicts involving your leader or colleagues effectively.

Leaders hold a certain degree of power and often suggest strategies for conflict resolution. While this is a normal part of the leader-follower relationship, you must remain cautious. Leaders' proposed strategies may primarily serve their needs while neglecting yours. Early in your relationship with a leader, it might be necessary to internalize their suggestions as you acclimate to the job's demands. However, avoid remaining confined to this pattern or passively submitting to all forms of leadership guidance.

Our research demonstrates that effective leadership involves more than submission to a leader's guidance. You must consider your own needs and psychological processes. You bear responsibility for advocating for yourself. If you feel unseen or if a conflict resolution strategy does not align with your goals, openly renegotiate the strategy with your leader. Dialogue is crucial. Circumvention strategies are not set in stone—they can and should be adapted to reflect your person and your needs. Be prepared for resistance; leaders may not initially embrace re-negotiation. This is normal. Remember that leader-follower relationships require ongoing adjustment and that this process is dynamic and never fully complete.

You have built a strong reputation. People approach you because they value how you treat them, whether they are colleagues or clients. Appreciate this hard-earned respect—it was not easily achieved. This reputation enhances your position in interactions with your leader, providing you with power to negotiate solutions that align with your needs. If a conflict arises, resist surrendering or become frustrated. You are not "just an employee"; you are much more.

However, even with a strong position, you must remain mindful that this strength does not entitle you to elevate yourself above others. Effective conflict resolution requires considering the needs of your leader and colleagues. A successful solution is not one that benefits you alone but one that fosters collective growth within the organization. Keep in mind that solutions are more widely accepted when they address the needs of multiple stakeholders, enabling them to find balance in their personal and professional lives. People will appreciate this collaborative approach.

When proposing strategies, avoid presenting rigid, pre-determined solutions. Instead, leave room for others to contribute their perspectives. This inclusivity fosters collaboration, which not only helps address job-related challenges but also promotes a sense of coherence and connection in the workplace. If a conflict arises and risks becoming chronic, the following guidelines can help:

(A) Do not passively submit to your leader's circumvention strategies. Take pride in the work patterns you've developed.
(B) Actively negotiate and re-negotiate strategies from your perspective.
(C) Prioritize your needs and evaluate how potential solutions fulfill them.
(D) Recognize that you are part of a larger network—consider the perspectives of your leader and colleagues to foster workplace coherence.

If re-negotiation efforts fail or your leader resists, do not shy away from transparent dialogue. Dialogue can have a transformative and healing impact that should not be underestimated.

For now, this is all I want to share with you. Remember that research can be applied in countless ways and can serve you well if handled thoughtfully.

Warm regards, En.

Policy Brief: Deducing Social Action from One's Qualitative Research Report

This policy brief is written for both employees and management, presenting the results of the current manuscript in a way that is accessible to a lay-oriented audience. The brief aims to recommend actionable steps based on the study's findings, drawing from modern interpretations of action research as advocated by Lewin (Arnautu & Dagenais, 2021; Masset et al., 2013). A significant aspect of this research is not only the creation of the policy brief but also the submission of it to employees to evaluate their reactions to the empirical findings.

Unfortunately, we were unable to present the policy brief to management as initially planned. In collaboration with employees, it was decided that presenting it to management might worsen the leadership dynamic, as management could perceive it as employees expressing unauthorized opinions. Therefore, rather than simply recommending specific actions based on the findings, we aimed to gather feedback from employees to see if our ethnographic study had missed any key insights.

Additionally, this action-oriented research meets the criteria for educative and catalytic authenticity, a vital validity criterion in qualitative research (Klenke, 2008a, 2008b). After presenting the policy brief, we will discuss the employees' reactions.

Leadership In Vivo: Lessons Learned from an Ethnographic Case Study

Leadership continues to be a central topic in academia, but much of the academic discussion often fails to reflect the lived experiences of individuals or translate academic insights into actionable knowledge. This gap is especially notable in leadership research (Klenke, 2008a, 2008b). In other words, there is a disconnect between how leadership research is communicated and how it is experienced by those from whom data are collected and analyzed. As a result, leadership research is often not disseminated effectively to the public, preventing people from utilizing the insights to improve real-world leadership practices (Cardiff et al., 2018). This study challenges that narrative by making research findings tangible for a variety of stakeholders.

In this case, leadership is explored through the lens of a specific case study, with a pragmatic approach to discussing its findings.

The Importance of the Project

Leadership is a sensitive topic, involving power dynamics that should not be underestimated. Employees may fear addressing problems with certain leadership styles due to the potential negative consequences. However, addressing poor leadership is critical, as ineffective leadership can cost an organization significantly, through factors such as deviant workplace behavior and reduced employee commitment, leading to higher turnover rates (Lawrence, 2010). While recent research has focused on the negative aspects of leadership (Conger, 1990), many studies fail to consider context-specific knowledge in leadership case studies, especially within the applied field of leadership research (Klenke, 2008a).

This research adopts a different approach, originating from a concrete case study. The goal was to understand how colleagues interact and lead each other, as well as how management and employees interact over a specific timeframe. Previous studies have emphasized the benefits of case studies in developing context-sensitive insights in qualitative leadership research (Klenke, 2008c), which are essential for facilitating meaning-making within an organization. A dynamic understanding of leadership may be necessary to establish ongoing dialogue between leaders and employees, where adjustments can be negotiated (von Fircks, 2021).

While the current research has not yet investigated the benefits and potential limitations of this dynamic approach, questions about how leadership can be negotiated, how both leaders' and followers' needs can be met, and how chronic conflicts can be resolved are crucial. Such questions deserve further attention from researchers and practitioners aiming to foster a balanced and effective leadership model in the workplace.

Research Approach

To address these questions, an ethnographic research design was employed, focusing on the interactional patterns between bakery employees and management. The study involved observing, documenting, and interpreting leadership patterns from a psychological perspective. The researcher immersed himself in the work environment, observing leadership dynamics during employees' shifts. Interviews were conducted with employees to clarify conflicts and gather additional background information, with data collected over five months. Each month, an ethnographic vignette was written based on the observations.

The research aimed to understand not only how conflicts were resolved but also how employees and management collaborated to develop strategies for tackling issues. A qualitative research approach was adopted to explore dynamic meaning-making patterns essential to leadership. The research was prompted by complaints about poor leadership, which were identified through social media.

Ethnographic data were collected using the Critical Incident Technique (Flanagan, 1954), categorizing leadership patterns into predefined categories (e.g., interactional patterns, problem-solving strategies, needs of followers and management, emotions, etc.). This data was analyzed field-theoretically, following the approach suggested by social psychologist Kurt Lewin (1982).

Results: Ethnographic Findings About Leadership

Within Leadership Patterns

A within-leadership style emerged among the bakery staff, developed step-by-step in response to the work-related demands they faced. Employees created strategies collaboratively to address these challenges, which enabled them to handle their job-related tasks autonomously and situationally. As a result, they felt a sense of mastery and experienced positive emotions in the workplace. For example, employees adjusted the way they filled bread rolls according to customer preferences. However, management did not take advantage of the employees' expertise, imposing strategies for filling bread rolls without consulting the staff. This approach led employees to feel that management's leadership style was disconnected from the actual challenges they faced.

Outside Leadership Patterns

Management, driven by economic interests, prioritized the profitability of the enterprise. While this is a legitimate concern, the problem arose when management failed to align their economic priorities with the specific needs of the employees. This led to a mismatch between the leadership patterns of employees and management, resulting in an antagonism between the two. For example, management imposed a universal bread roll filling plan that led to significant food waste.

Missing Personal Interaction Between Management and Employees

The study also revealed a lack of personal interaction between management and staff. For instance, management introduced a new product without informing the staff, leaving them unable to answer customer questions about the product. Despite attempts by employees to reach out to management for more information, management did not provide the necessary details. As a result, staff had to develop their own solution, undermining their respect for management. This led to a general negative view of management's leadership, which affected employees' anticipation of future leadership actions.

Key Findings

The staff had already developed creative and effective strategies to address issues autonomously. However, management, driven by different needs, attempted to impose their own leadership strategies, leading to a breakdown in cooperation. Rather than working together, management and staff "led across" each other. They were unable to develop joint strategies that addressed both management's and employees' needs.

Implications and Recommendations

1. Acknowledging Inside Leadership Patterns: The leadership strategies developed by the staff demonstrate creative and effective ways of dealing with conflicts autonomously. Management should recognize and consolidate these strategies, which may help foster employee commitment by empowering staff to take leadership roles. This would also contribute to both personal growth and organizational success.
2. Co-constructing Leadership Strategies: Management should recognize the importance of their own economic needs while also valuing the strategies developed by employees. It is crucial for management to avoid dismissing the staff's strategies, as doing so could undermine employee morale and foster feelings of patronization.
3. Fostering Adjusted Cooperation: Both management and staff must engage in ongoing dialogue to develop a joint leadership strategy that meets both parties' needs. Overcoming the antagonism between internal and external leadership patterns requires constant negotiation and collaboration. Management should be more engaged with staff, abandoning remote communication channels in favor

of more direct, hands-on involvement. This approach can help integrate both perspectives into a shared leadership framework.

Interview with the Participant Based on the Policy Brief

When asked about her perception of the policy brief and her thoughts on it, the major participant, Elisa, responded as follows:

> I like the policy brief a lot, and it accurately addresses the issues we experience in the workplace. Especially the key findings hit the nail on the head from my perspective. I appreciate that an 'everyday situation' is being examined psychologically because I believe many people are not aware of the dynamics (and the potential to improve them in a simple way).

Analyzing this quote, it is evident that Elisa is highly satisfied with the report. She feels that the research reflects her experiences at the workplace, which is crucial as it fosters positive emotions such as gratitude and appreciation toward the researcher. What stands out is that Elisa references the dynamics of leadership without formal training in the cultural-psychological theory of leadership. This shows that she grasped the essence of what the policy brief aimed to convey—how leadership develops in specific situations. Additionally, Elisa not only acknowledges the current state but also sees the potential for improvement, highlighting the transformative possibilities of the research. She believes the report has the capacity to stimulate change and bring about constructive leadership patterns, an important aspect of educational and catalytic authenticity. Following up on the question of whether Elisa feels understood, she responded:

> I feel very understood. And I wish that management would put in as much effort to illuminate and reflect on the common working relationship.

This response reveals Elisa's desire for a more active and constructive role from management. She calls for a more engaged, face-to-face relationship between management and employees, rather than maintaining a distant, impersonal approach. Elisa is urging management to take responsibility for investigating the workplace dynamics and addressing the issues that are central to the employees' experiences. The reception of this feedback emphasizes that Elisa wants management to actively engage with employees' perspectives, particularly regarding the nature of their relationship. This connects to the broader issue highlighted in the ethnographic vignettes of maintaining a more intimate and involved management approach. When asked if she thought the policy brief adequately described the situation in the bakery or if there were missing elements, Elisa responded:

> The problems were captured very well. Additionally, I believe it's important to understand and mention that ultimately, employees aim to feel competent, self-effective, and appreciated. Every employee has needs that they hope to satisfy within the context of their work. Perhaps this point could be incorporated as well.

Elisa emphasizes the significance of personal needs—competence, self-efficacy, and appreciation—that employees seek to fulfill in the workplace. She suggests that management should actively consider these needs and develop a deeper understanding of what motivates employees. Elisa's feedback indicates her desire for management to build more personal relationships with workers, showing interest in their lives outside of work. By addressing these personal dynamics, Elisa believes management could foster a more engaged, motivated workforce. This adds to the notion of personality, which was partially discussed in the policy brief but could be explored further in future iterations.

Without using the term fantasms, Elisa is keenly aware that employees are motivated by private needs, and she urges management to adopt a mindset that seeks to understand those needs. This reflects a gap in current research, and future studies could benefit from incorporating a more personalized understanding of leadership dynamics. When asked how she thought management would respond to the policy brief, Elisa said:

> To be honest, I would be really curious about what management would respond to that. The lack of communication often leads to the feeling that different goals are incompatible. Ultimately, both parties (inside and out) aim to deliver a good product to a satisfied customer. The team understands, of course, that economic aspects are most important to management. But does management also understand the goals and wishes of the team? The team is often made to feel less intelligent, and people who don't feel appreciated don't do good work. Wouldn't it therefore also be a higher goal to have satisfied employees? Because satisfied employees do satisfactory work. Satisfactory work brings profit. I often feel that management doesn't realize how important not only the products and revenue are but also the relationship within the work context.

This quote highlights the ongoing tension between management and staff, particularly regarding their different goals. Elisa acknowledges the importance of profitability to management but questions whether management fully appreciates the needs and perspectives of the employees. She suggests that satisfaction among employees should be considered a higher goal, as it leads to better work, which ultimately benefits the company. Elisa's feedback shows a desire to bridge the gap between inside (employee) and outside (management) leadership patterns, aiming for a more unified, collaborative approach to leadership. She proposes that joint higher-order goals could help resolve this divide, fostering mutual understanding and cooperation. Lastly, when asked if she believed this type of research was beneficial, Elisa responded:

> I believe this type of research is essential. Especially the point that the researcher enters the action field seems to me to be a point that has been much too neglected in research so far. One must be at the scene of the action to understand the action. And I believe that this type of research can have great added value because it uncovers concrete problems and offers solutions. Solutions that can have moral added value for both parties in this case. I also believe that management would view this type of research positively because it is not about 'right or wrong', but rather about examining the dynamics psychologically. Thus, the problems in the company/leadership style are placed in a psychological context, which may lead to proposed solutions being more accepted and the importance of reflecting on such dynamics becoming more visible.

Elisa emphasizes the importance of visibility in leadership dynamics, pointing out that the research helps both management and employees better understand one another. She believes that by addressing issues from a psychological perspective, rather than focusing on blame, the research fosters a more constructive approach. Elisa envisions this type of research as a tool for opening up communication and dialogue between management and employees. By making these dynamics visible, the research can help both parties understand the underlying issues and work together to find solutions. This aligns with the purpose of action research, which aims to bring about positive change by fostering a deeper understanding of the problem and promoting collaborative problem-solving.

The Effects of the Policy Brief and Possible Actualizations

Summarizing the key takeaways from confronting Elisa with the policy brief, we can deduce the following:

(A) Elisa does not simply feel understood in her perspective (inside leadership pattern) but also acknowledged and seen. This acknowledgment triggers positive affects, such as gratitude and appreciation toward the research. The policy brief validates Elisa's perspective, strengthening her position within the bakery.

(B) Elisa brings up the notion of personality, highlighting the importance of employees feeling competent, self-effective, and appreciated. She notes that these personal needs should be integrated into the cultural-psychological model of leadership. This feedback suggests that future research could be enriched by a deeper exploration of personality and the role of individual needs in shaping leadership dynamics.

(C) The policy brief has prompted Elisa to think about strategies for overcoming the divide between inside<>outside leadership patterns, particularly by developing joint higher-order goals. This highlights a potential area for the policy brief to improve by including practical solutions for fostering cooperation between management and employees.

(D) The policy brief helps participants, like Elisa, develop a more objective perspective on workplace issues, allowing them to approach challenges without focusing on blame. This objectivity helps reduce the emotional intensity of workplace conflicts and fosters a more constructive, solution-oriented mindset.

References

Arnautu, D., & Dagenais, C. (2021). Use and effectiveness of policy briefs as a knowledge transfer tool: A scoping review. *Humanities and Social Sciences Communications, 8*(1), 1–14.

Cardiff, S., McCormack, B., & McCance, T. (2018). Person-centred leadership: A relational approach to leadership derived through action research. *Journal of Clinical Nursing, 27*(15–16), 3056–3069.

Chishima, Y., Huai-Ching Liu, I. T., & Wilson, A. E. (2021). Temporal distancing during the COVID-19 pandemic: Letter writing with future self can mitigate negative affect. *Applied Psychology: Health and Well-Being, 13*(2), 406–418.
Conger, J. A. (1990). The dark side of leadership. *Organizational Dynamics, 19*(2), 44–55.
Fircks, E. V. (2021). Cultural resources for leadership: When a banana is more than a banana. *Human Arenas*, 1–18.
Flanagan, J. C. (1954). The critical incident technique. *Psychological Bulletin, 51*(4), 327.
Klenke, K. (2008a). Qualitative research as paradigm. In K. Klenke (Ed.), *Qualitative research in the study of leadership* (pp. 3–29). Emerald.
Klenke, K. (2008b). Qualitative research as paradigm. In K. Klenke (Ed.), *Qualitative research as a method* (pp. 31–55). Emerald.
Klenke, K. (2008c). Case studies in leadership research. In K. Klenke (Ed.), *Qualitative research as a method* (pp. 57–84). Emerald.
Lawrence, P. R. (2010). *Driven to lead: Good, bad, and misguided leadership* (Vol. 168). Wiley.
Lewin, K. (1982). Formalisierung und Forschritt in der Psychologie. In C. F. Graumann (Ed.), *Kurt Lewin Werkausgabe: Feldtheorie* (Vol. 4, pp. 41–73). Klett-Cotta.
Masset, E., Gaarder, M., Beynon, P., & Chapoy, C. (2013). What is the impact of a policy brief? Results of an experiment in research dissemination. *Journal of Development Effectiveness, 5*(1), 50–63.
Wetzler, E. L., & Feltner, D. T. (2021). A proflective writing assignment in advanced general psychology for leaders: Letter to the future self. In *Teaching and learning the west point way* (pp. 72–77). Routledge.

Chapter 8
Lessons Learnt from Autoethnographic and Ethnographic Methodology in the Qualitative Study of Leadership

The present manuscript had multiple objectives. Drawing on Klenke (2008a, 2008b), we aimed to develop a middle-range theory of leadership grounded in the foundational premises of Cultural Psychology (von Fircks, 2024a, 2024b). Acknowledging the existence of various traditions and research strands within Cultural Psychology, the initial chapters of this manuscript sought to theoretically synthesize Lewin's Field Theory, Boesch's Symbolic Action Theory, and Vygotsky's Cultural-Historical Theory. We then aimed to test whether this theoretical framework could be applied empirically, defining a methodological approach to study leadership in vivo. To do so, we analyzed autoethnographic and ethnographic data, interpreting the findings through the lens of our theoretical background. These findings were then utilized to create a personal reflection and a policy brief, which was shared with one of the participants, inviting her to reflect on our interpretation. Now, we turn to a broader discussion of the theoretical and empirical findings.

Beyond the Big-Hero Myth in Leadership Research: The Crucial Role of Social Imagined Dialogue

At the outset of this manuscript, we were motivated to develop a social, interpretative, and dialogical theory of leadership that contrasts with the dominant "big-hero" myth (Chap. 1), which still prevails as an overarching paradigm in much of the leadership literature. Our empirical findings challenge this hero-centric view, revealing a more complex operationalization of leadership. Leadership, as our research demonstrates, is a multifaceted field involving multiple agents, and it is not limited to the roles of leader and follower.

In our ethnographic study, several vignettes highlighted the importance of taking into account the generalized role of others—specifically, the role of the customer, as

E. Freiherr von Fircks, *Studying Leadership from a Microgenetic Perspective*, Methodologies in Developmental Sciences,
https://doi.org/10.1007/978-3-031-90214-7_8

interpreted by the follower. In some cases, the customer played a central role in shaping the leadership dynamic. Thus, leadership involves more than just the personal needs of the leader and the follower; it also encompasses the generalized needs of the imagined "social other," such as the customer. This insight presents a more complex, field-theoretical situation that extends beyond the theoretical considerations laid out in the early chapters of this manuscript (Chap. 2). It underscores that leadership is a far more intricate process than we initially assumed.

This complexity has significant implications for applied leadership studies. For instance, leaders and employees may project generalized needs onto others, such as customers, which could conflict with the actual needs of the agents involved. Simply because a leader or follower believes that a customer has a specific need does not mean that this perceived need is, in fact, the most pressing concern for the customer. In this scenario, an imagined dialogue is occurring that may not align with the actual dialogue between the agents involved. This raises critical questions for leadership studies, such as: What does happen when imagined and actual dialogues diverge? How is the imagined dialogue adjusted in response to real interactions between agents?

This leads to a dynamic tension between what *is* and what *could be*—a tension that is negotiated among several agents and is subject to adjustment through their concrete actions. Future research could explore these tensions, particularly how anticipated discrepancies between imagined and real dialogues affect leadership dynamics, and how leaders and followers navigate such tensions.

In leadership practice, it may be essential to recognize where imagined and real dialogues diverge before these discrepancies lead to conflict or misunderstandings. By doing so, we can better understand how the roles of agents—such as leaders, followers, and customers—are constructed and adjusted within specific field-theoretical situations. As a result, we propose a revision to our initial model of leadership with the following premise:

1. Leadership, when understood from a field-theoretical perspective, must account for the tension between imagined and real dialogues among multiple agents, including generalized or imagined agents. This understanding can help researchers and practitioners anticipate potential misunderstandings between leaders, followers, and other central figures, such as customers, whose roles and needs are often perceived differently. By recognizing where these imagined and real dialogues might diverge or fail to materialize, leadership practices can be better attuned to addressing the dynamic interactions and expectations among all parties involved.

Leadership Needs to Be Defined by Actions Taken in the Work Context

Second, we need to revisit the role of the leader from the perspective introduced in the initial chapters. There, we hypothesized that leadership is not fully described as merely providing or negotiating circumvention strategies that help followers overcome barriers and move closer to their goal fields. We also posited that leadership involves helping followers become aware of the underlying fantasms—the unconscious motivations driving their actions within the action field (Chap. 2). Additionally, we suggested that leaders play a crucial role in monitoring what happens when followers fail to circumvent barriers, especially when they are left alone to deal with unsuccessful attempts at neutralizing obstacles. This perspective, implicitly influenced by psychotherapeutic readings of E.E. Boesch (1975), assumes a deeper engagement between leaders and followers.

However, our empirical findings did not confirm this idealized view. In both the autoethnographic and ethnographic studies, leaders did not intervene to assist followers in becoming aware of their deeper motivations, nor did they monitor the psychological or physical effects of failing to overcome barriers. While this notion of leadership remains theoretically appealing, it did not manifest in the empirical data gathered from the real-world settings we studied.

What we did observe, however, was the significant role of co-constructing circumvention strategies between leaders and followers in successful critical incidents. In these instances, both parties approached each other with openness, presenting potential strategies for overcoming barriers, while allowing the other to appropriate and adapt the strategy according to their own needs and perspectives. This process of mutual co-construction, rather than a top-down directive approach, emerged as central to the successful negotiation of obstacles. Importantly, the roles of leader and follower were not fixed; they interacted on an equal footing, with both contributing to the development of effective circumvention strategies.

Thus, leadership needs to be understood from a dynamic perspective. In our empirical studies, leaders initiated cooperation by suggesting circumvention strategies and inviting followers to co-construct these strategies based on their individual needs and perspectives. This dynamic, co-constructive approach to leadership aligns with contemporary understandings of leadership as a shared, collaborative process (Tsuchimoto, 2024). Leadership, therefore, is not tied to formal roles (such as the business owner or manager), but is defined by specific tasks where cooperation and adaptation are necessary.

While we did not find evidence of leaders helping followers to be conscious of their underlying motivations or monitor the psychological effects of failure, we did demonstrate the power of co-constructing circumvention strategies. These strategies united the different needs of leaders and followers into joint semiotic resources (von Fircks, 2023). This highlights that leadership is not only dynamic in the sense that personal and ecological factors shift over time, but also in the sense that the roles of leader and follower are fluid and interchangeable. In summary, we were able to show the following:

2. The dynamics of leadership can be characterized by the fluidity and flexibility of roles between leaders and followers, with these roles potentially alternating depending on the situation. However, this alternation is not arbitrary; it emerges through specific psychological mechanisms. For instance, the leader typically initiates cooperation by presenting a strategy or approach to address a particular challenge. The follower, in turn, engages in the co-construction of this initiative, adapting it based on their own needs and perspective. Thus, leadership is not predetermined by fixed categories such as ownership, hierarchy, or seniority, but rather by the social actions undertaken within a particular context. Leadership is defined by the capacity to initiate and facilitate cooperation and the reciprocal involvement of others in shaping that process, highlighting the importance of adaptive and situational leadership practices.

Why Leadership Needs to be Studied Genetically: Working with the Hyper-Generalization of Leadership Patterns over Time

Leadership should be studied genetically, meaning that its development and evolution over time should be analyzed to better understand how leadership patterns emerge, stabilize, and change. In our research, we observed how leadership patterns—both successful and unsuccessful—can hyper-generalize over time, becoming ingrained in the perceptions of employees and shaping their interactions with management—a classical microgenetic perspective.

When leadership is dynamic, allowing for the co-construction of strategies to overcome challenges (or "circumvention strategies"), it fosters cooperation and mutual respect between leaders and followers. However, in instances where management denied this co-construction and imposed strategies without considering the follower's perspective, employees experienced this as an intrusion into their psychological reality. The degree to which a follower interprets this as an intrusion depends on their life space and individual experience. For example, in the early months of a new job, young professionals might welcome strong guidance, especially when they are uncertain about how to interpret or navigate certain situations. This is a time when employees rely more heavily on leadership to provide structure and meaning.

However, as employees gain experience and develop their own methods of overcoming barriers, they begin to value autonomy and self-reliance. At this stage, if leadership continues to impose strategies without recognizing the follower's existing competencies and successful circumvention strategies, the follower may perceive this as a denial of their experience and expertise. This denial often results in negative interpretations of leadership, and employees may begin to hyper-generalize these experiences, seeing management not as supporters but as opponents.

Our ethnographic and autoethnographic findings highlight the damaging effects of this hyper-generalization. When employees perceive management as adversaries, it fosters resentment and distrust, which can significantly impair the relationship between management and staff, as well as the overall functioning of the organization.

To counter the negative interpretations that arise from hyper-generalized destructive leadership patterns, future research needs to focus on identifying interventions that can alter these perceptions. One key area of investigation should explore how management can initiate actions that respect the psychological realities of their employees, incorporating employees' existing strategies and fostering a sense of shared problem-solving. This approach not only validates the experiences of employees but also facilitates the emergence of more positive, constructive leadership patterns.

Moreover, research should examine how management can prevent or neutralize second-order barriers. Second-order barriers arise when unresolved conflicts or leadership failures create new challenges, compounding existing issues for employees. For instance, when management does not adequately address an initial conflict or barrier, it can lead to a second layer of problems, further complicating the work environment.

Future studies should focus on identifying the mechanisms that allow for the neutralization of first-order and second-order barriers within the life space of employees. Research should explore how leadership interventions can reframe negative leadership perceptions and promote more productive interactions between management and staff. Key questions include how management can facilitate the co-construction of solutions that reflect the needs and competencies of their employees, and how they can transform destructive leadership patterns into more collaborative and supportive ones.

By studying leadership genetically, we can better understand how these patterns evolve and learn how to prevent the hyper-generalization of negative leadership experiences. This approach allows for a more nuanced understanding of leadership, which takes into account the dynamic interplay between management and employees over time, as well as the psychological realities that impact how leadership actions are interpreted.

3. The guidance of followers, and the degree to which it is provided, must be tailored to their psychological realities and their most pressing needs. For instance, it is inappropriate to assume that full guidance is inherently maladaptive, as new employees or followers might require more intensive support early in their tenure. However, as their experience grows, the guidance should evolve accordingly. If leadership fails to adjust its level of guidance in response to the developing needs of the follower, it risks being perceived negatively, potentially leading to a destructive interpretation of leadership. This lack of adaptation can give rise to second-order barriers—additional conflicts and challenges within the

followers' life spaces and action fields—which complicate leadership even further.

Sign-Systems and Their Power to Alter the Quality of a Barrier

A key aspect that requires further discussion is the role of sign systems as circumvention strategies within the life space and action field of both followers and leaders. Our study has demonstrated that these sign systems serve as powerful semiotic resources (Gillespie & Zittoun, 2013), but what makes them particularly effective is their ability to not only neutralize barriers but to transform them, making the barriers permeable. This transformation allowed individuals to navigate toward their goal fields more effectively.

But how exactly does this permeability arise? When a particular circumvention strategy—using a specific sign system—is applied, the barrier itself undergoes a transformation. Instead of requiring the follower to change fundamentally, the barrier is altered in a way that makes it more digestible for the individual's existing skills and abilities. This process aligns with a microgenetic perspective (Wagoner, 2009), suggesting that the effectiveness of semiotic resources comes from their capacity to adapt the environment to the person, rather than forcing the person to adapt to the environment.

This insight reveals a significant mechanism in adaptive problem solving: by applying a circumvention strategy, the person transforms the quality of the barrier, making it psychologically more manageable. This has profound implications for leadership, which, from a cultural-psychological perspective, could involve shifting the environment in such a way that followers find it more aligned with their inner motivations and competencies (Ghazi & von Fircks, 2024). Leadership, therefore, may not necessarily involve constant training or the development of new skills, but rather facilitating conditions that allow employees to leverage their pre-existing abilities.

This finding has particular relevance for the enterprises involved in this study. Leadership in these contexts involves trusting the creative abilities and problem-solving skills that employees already possess. In many cases, only a minor adjustment in the situation's ecological factors may be required to empower employees to overcome barriers using their own competencies. This approach aligns with a person-centered leadership model, where the emphasis is on believing in the individual's capacity to interpret and alter the situation by their own means.

Nevertheless, as has been frequently critiqued in the literature, we still lack a thorough understanding of the psychological mechanisms that determine when a person feels confident enough to harness their creative potential (May, 1994). Our research provides some insights into these mechanisms, suggesting that leadership plays a role in helping followers reshape the situation to better align with their pressing needs. Future studies should aim to deepen this understanding by examining the specific sign systems that facilitate this permeability shift, investigating whether similar strategies appear across different professional fields and how they function within various contexts.

This expanded understanding of sign systems requires us to consider whether the patterns we observed in the present study are field-specific or whether more generalizable strategies exist across different industries. However, it is not sufficient to merely categorize these systems; future research should maintain a genetic focus, exploring what sign systems do to barriers within the life spaces of followers and leaders, and how they alter the dynamics of the field-theoretical situation.

This broader perspective also extends our initial understanding of leadership from the introductory chapters, where the permeability of barriers was not yet thematized. Conducting inquiries across different professional fields will allow us to investigate whether similar sign systems emerge in different contexts, and whether leadership's role in facilitating these shifts can be generalized. In this way, we can develop a more comprehensive understanding of leadership as a dynamic, semiotic process that enables followers to navigate their environments more effectively.

4. Sign systems serve as powerful semiotic resources that enable both leaders and followers to alter the permeability of barriers within their respective action fields. In this process, leaders and followers modify the ecological determinants of a given situation, allowing individuals to effectively address barriers using their existing abilities and skills. However, further research is necessary to determine whether there are more generalizable sign systems applicable across various challenges in multiple job fields, or if these sign systems remain context-sensitive, as suggested in this research program. Additionally, there is a need to explore similarities between our cultural-psychological understanding of leadership and competing theories of person-centered leadership.

The Importance of Dialogical Negotiation of Circumvention Strategies

In the context of the longitudinal study of leadership, it is essential to investigate how leadership patterns develop over time. Focusing on the findings from the autoethnographic study, we observe that certain circumvention strategies have been negotiated between leaders and followers. This indicates that an agreement has been reached between staff and management on how to address specific issues. However, both management and staff have perceived these circumvention strategies as static, a perspective that becomes evident throughout the autoethnographic vignettes. Once negotiated, these strategies were understood by both agents as fixed in time.

This static viewpoint is problematic because the challenges and issues faced by management and staff are continually evolving, necessitating a re-adjustment of the negotiated leadership patterns. This need for re-adjustment was often overlooked by leaders and followers, particularly in the later examples from the autoethnographic study. Such an understanding appears to have permeated the psychological realities of both staff and management, captured in the notion that, "*Now that we have negotiated how to proceed and what to do with the barrier, we are set for the next challenges*." However, this static perspective does not align with the psychological realities of leaders and followers, whose consistency lies in its inconsistency. Both agents are continually required to actualize their positions in response to new environmental challenges.

Consequently, it is vital to consider the ongoing re-negotiation of circumvention strategies. Unfortunately, the current data do not provide insights into how this continuous re-negotiation may occur or which psychological mechanisms might trigger the actualization of jointly negotiated circumvention strategies. Therefore, there is a pressing need to understand the practical implications of our leadership study and how we might facilitate the emergence of open and transparent re-negotiation concerning previously debated circumvention strategies.

For instance, we might consider what frameworks could be established to support these psychological processes. One possibility could involve leaders and followers meeting monthly or bi-monthly to discuss problems and challenges encountered in their daily work. In these discussions, the focus should not solely be on the problems themselves, but also on how these issues were previously addressed and where difficulties arose as the situations evolved over time.

To simplify, leaders and followers should explore strategies to institutionalize—and thereby habituate—dialogue that regulates the re-negotiation of circumvention strategies. Based on our findings, leaders and followers require a transparent forum where they can candidly discuss both previous and new leadership patterns regarding pressing issues. These forums must address the internal and external tensions associated with leadership. Rather than ignoring or suppressing this tension, it should be leveraged for the benefit of the entire organization. Such tensions must be afforded space, as they indicate pressing needs that remain unsatisfied or are yet to be addressed.

This brings us to the next crucial point: we must reconsider our perceptions of conflicts and tensions, refraining from interpreting them as inherently negative. Conversely, if the framework within which tension and conflict are situated is appropriate, they can be fertile grounds for the adaptive reorganization of leadership. A review of the data from the ethnographic and autoethnographic vignettes reveals that attitudes toward conflicts and tensions were largely implicit, failing to emerge into the conceptual and verbal realms of leaders and followers. However, addressing this issue is crucial, as it may encourage leaders and followers to engage with the underlying pressing needs of both parties.

5. The dialogical negotiation of joint circumvention strategies between leaders and followers is a fundamental component of a cultural-psychological theory of leadership. However, both scientists and practitioners must exercise caution in interpreting this dialogical negotiation as it unfolds. Specifically, these circumvention strategies must be re-negotiated at critical junctures. Leaders and

followers need to initiate a process of actualizing the circumvention strategy to ensure its alignment with the evolving ecological determinants within the respective job field. Future research should elucidate how this ongoing re-negotiation of leadership patterns can be successfully achieved, potentially through the establishment of monthly leader-follower forums in which these issues are openly discussed.

The Dangers of Interpretivism

An additional point worthy of discussion regarding the autoethnographic and ethnographic findings pertains to the aspect of our theory we designated as interpretative. It is essential to recognize how leaders and followers interpret their mutually interrelated actions. Both parties are in urgent need of understanding not only what the social other did but also the significance of a specific action. In other words, leaders and followers continuously engage in sense-making of their interactions—a critical interpretative endeavor that should not be underestimated. However, we must exercise caution when labeling our theory as interpretative.

Not all issues related to leadership are governed solely by specific interpretations, whether these are positively or negatively connotated. Consequently, we should refrain from overemphasizing the notion of interpretation, as doing so may lead us to overlook the underlying actions that are being interpreted. In line with cultural psychologists such as Boesch (2021), it is important to recognize that interpretation cannot be separated from the respective action.

For instance, a leader who seeks to assist a follower in circumventing a potential barrier may be perceived as intrusive or patronizing by that follower. This scenario illustrates an incongruity between the action and its underlying interpretation, highlighting a divergence in how the action was intended versus how it was interpreted by the follower. Another example arises when a follower desires support, while the leader aims to provide autonomy. Here, the leader's initial action of allowing space for autonomy may be interpreted negatively by the follower, possibly as a passive leadership style that fails to address the follower's actual needs.

If issues cannot be resolved effectively, psychological researchers and practitioners should be cautious in attributing the problem solely to misinterpretation. This perspective risks underestimating the complexities involved in the situations encountered in the ethnographic and autoethnographic vignettes. When employees struggle to understand the intended meaning behind specific leadership behaviors—such as a proposed circumvention strategy—it is insufficient for practitioners to merely encourage followers to reassess the meaning through specific exercises (Prilleltensky, 1997). Instead, leaders must also be prompted to consider how they can transform their initial actions to facilitate the follower's comprehension of the intended leadership approach.

To advance our research, we must address both ends of the leader-follower equation. This necessitates that both leaders and followers engage in transforming their interactions and openly discuss (dialogize) the meanings of their respective interactions (signifier and signified) on an ongoing basis. In summary, we can articulate this point as follows:

6. We must avoid succumbing to a simplistic interpretivism that some schools of Cultural Psychology advocate (Bruner, 2009). Such an approach is insufficient for the applied study of leadership, as demonstrated in the various ethnographic and autoethnographic vignettes. Therefore, our primary focus should be on examining the interaction between action and meaning that unfolds between leaders and followers. Issues must be addressed from an applied perspective, wherein actions are modified to facilitate the follower's comprehension of the intended meaning. Additionally, it is crucial to stimulate the followers to reconsider how they interpret the leader's intended actions.

The Power of Autoethnography and Its Potential for Assessing Hyper-Generalized Fantasms

The empirical findings of this manuscript underscore the power of autoethnography in assessing interrelated fantasms, which we refer to as hyper-generalized fantasms. Through the autoethnographic vignettes, we gained an in-depth understanding of the personal world of the follower, revealing the hyper-generalized motivational patterns that catalyzed their actions (or locomotions). This insight allowed us to comprehend the reasons behind the follower's specific patterns of conduct, as the hyper-generalized fantasm consistently impacted the narrative emerging from the follower's experiences.

In many organizational studies, exploring the underlying fantasms of employees can be a challenging endeavor, both theoretically and methodologically. This difficulty often arises because enterprises may prioritize task completion over understanding the motivations of their workforce, or because the methods employed—such as correlational studies—fail to provide a nuanced view of employees' personal worlds. Quantitative studies typically do not allow for an in-depth exploration of meaning-making patterns that may evolve over time.

For instance, we demonstrated that the first author was deeply invested in facilitating the growth of his talented children, driven by a desire to catalyze their development in tennis despite facing resistance from his organization. The hyper-generalized fantasm empowered the follower to organize their psychological and physiological resources to navigate towards their goal field while circumventing emerging barriers throughout this process. The follower's resilience in the face of organizational challenges exemplifies the potency of hyper-generalized fantasms in shaping inner and outer patterns of conduct (e.g., reflection, perception, and planning) over extended periods.

These findings have significant implications for the study of leadership and beyond: What occurs when a follower is unable to circumvent a barrier? As illustrated in this manuscript's empirical section, this inability may stem from the absence of a negotiated circumvention strategy with their leader or from the follower's lack of skills to effectively implement the necessary strategy. In some instances, however, a follower may possess sufficient circumvention strategies and a supportive leader but still lack motivation to act. This lack of motivation can arise when the follower's predominant fantasms are not relevant to the specific action at hand.

For example, a follower may desire a salary increase but be unwilling to provide evidence of their ability to attract new customers as a basis for their request. Instead, they might argue that their contribution lies in enhancing team coordination, motivated by hyper-generalized social fantasms. This example illustrates that failing to circumvent a barrier can stem from multiple factors—beyond mere deficiencies in knowledge or skills or unsuccessful negotiations with leadership. Often, the follower may simply lack the motivation to engage in specific actions because these actions do not align with their hyper-generalized fantasms, which organize their inner and outer conduct.

Therefore, leaders must explore the reasons behind a follower's inability to circumvent a barrier. They should differentiate between scenarios of inability and unwillingness, as the required interventions will vary accordingly. Leaders might benefit from employing the autoethnographic method to gain insight into the interrelated network of fantasms impacting their followers while also elucidating how individuals process social situations amidst various field forces. Consequently, autoethnographic vignettes can serve as valuable tools for psychologists interested in the dynamics of social relationships, but they may also serve as a starting point for leaders to genuinely understand their followers—an essential prerequisite for effective leadership.

7. Autoethnographies serve as a powerful tool for assessing hyper-generalized fantasms and, consequently, the underlying motivations and non-motivations to circumvent barriers. With this understanding, leaders can utilize autoethnographic vignettes as an intervention tool to better comprehend their followers. This insight is essential for fostering motivation and facilitating discussions on how and why to overcome barriers. In other words, autoethnography should not merely be viewed as a research instrument; it has the potential to be integrated into a broader intervention framework that can be developed in future research programs.

References

Boesch, E. E. (1975). *Zwischen Angst und Triumph: Über das Ich und seine Bestätigungen*. Huber.
Boesch, E. E. (2021). *Musik, Sprache und die Sehnsucht nach dem Paradies*. Psychosozial-Verlag.
Bruner, J. S. (2009). *Actual minds, possible worlds*. Harvard University Press.

Fircks, E. (2024a). Towards a theoretical understanding of culture and leadership [Manuscript submitted for publication]. In E. von Fircks (Ed.), *Culture and leadership: From approximation towards symbiosis*. IAP.

Fircks, E. (2024b). Between Lewin and Vygotsky: Understanding leader-follower interactions through a cultural psychological lens [Manuscript submitted for publication]. In E. von Fircks (Ed.), *Culture and leadership: From approximation towards symbiosis*. IAP.

Ghazi, A., & von Fircks, E. (2024). From an emotional autoethnography towards a theory of Symbolic Action Leading (SAL) [Manuscript submitted for publication]. In E. von Fircks (Ed.), *Culture and leadership: From approximation towards symbiosis*. IAP.

Gillespie, A., & Zittoun, T. (2013). Meaning making in motion: Bodies and minds moving through institutional and semiotic structures. *Culture & Psychology, 19*(4), 518–532.

Klenke, K. (2008a). Qualitative research as paradigm. In K. Klenke (Ed.), *Qualitative research in the study of leadership* (pp. 3–29). Emerald.

Klenke, K. (2008b). Qualitative research as paradigm. In K. Klenke (Ed.), *Qualitative research as a method* (pp. 31–55). Emerald.

May, R. (1994). *The courage to create*. WW Norton.

Prilleltensky, I. (1997). Values, assumptions, and practices: Assessing the moral implications of psychological discourse and action. *American Psychologist, 52*(5), 517.

Tsuchimoto, T. (2024). Transductive leadership: Rupture and transition of a beginning teacher in a Japanese school abroad [Manuscript submitted for publication]. In E. von Fircks (Ed.), *Culture and leadership: From approximation towards symbiosis*. IAP.

von Fircks, E. F. (2023). Cultural resources for leadership: When a banana is more than a banana. *Human Arenas, 6*(3), 444–461.

Wagoner, B. (2009). The experimental methodology of constructive microgenesis. In J. Valsiner, N. Chaudhary, M. C. D. P. Lyra, & P. C. M. Molenaar (Eds.), *Dynamic process methodology in the social and developmental sciences* (pp. 99–121). Springer.

Chapter 9
Pitfalls and Future Research Directions of Cultural-Psychological Leadership

Methodological Issues with Autoethnographies

A key limitation lies in the autoethnographic research design. Autoethnographic vignettes, as acknowledged in previous research, are inherently susceptible to bias (Butz & Besio, 2009; Méndez, 2013; Tolich, 2010). In this study, the Critical Incident Technique was used to sample successful and unsuccessful examples of leadership, based on the author's recollection of leadership experiences in three distinct enterprises. However, this process may have introduced bias, as the selection of vignettes could have been influenced by the theoretical framework presented in the introductory chapters. It is possible that only those vignettes aligning with the general cultural-psychological theory of leadership were reported. This is a well-recognized critique of autoethnography (Ellis et al., 2010), permeating the broader literature on qualitative research methods.

In acknowledging the inherent subjectivity of autoethnography, we sought to mitigate bias by developing autoethnographic protocols. These protocols guided the selection of significant data from the autoethnographic pool, providing a more systematic approach to the analysis without compromising the creative and reflective nature of autoethnography, which is a central aspect of the method (Ellis et al., 2010). Our systematization, grounded in cultural-psychological theory, focused on protocolling data related to needs, interactions, sign- and tool-systems, solutions, and emotions. This approach enabled us to transparently convey how we handled the data and distinguish between descriptive and analytical aspects of the phenomenon from a cultural-psychological perspective. As a result, the reader is better equipped to assess whether our analysis meets the standards of scientific rigor (Stern, 1911).

This approach also allowed us to account for contradictory data. For example, we included cases where no sign-system was applied to a particular challenge. Within our analysis, the absence of a sign-system was itself interpreted as a meaningful

E. Freiherr von Fircks, *Studying Leadership from a Microgenetic Perspective*, Methodologies in Developmental Sciences,
https://doi.org/10.1007/978-3-031-90214-7_9

sign (Ohnuki-Tierney, 1994). In this context, the lack of a sign-system indicated that employees felt abandoned by management, resulting in a leadership vacuum. This ability to interpret seemingly contradictory results strengthens the trustworthiness of our qualitative research, adhering to the alternative validity criteria discussed in Chap. 4.

Moreover, separating description from analysis via the autoethnographic protocols enables future researchers to reinterpret our vignettes through alternative theoretical lenses, such as existential or psychoanalytic frameworks. For instance, the insecurities described in the first autoethnography could be analyzed from an existential-humanistic perspective (von Fircks, 2020). One might argue that the follower's anxiety, rooted in insecurities about structuring the class and meeting job demands, reflects a common theme in existential psychology, where anxiety is seen as a potentially positive force (Schneider & Krug, 2010). Had the leader engaged in dialogue with the follower about this anxiety, it could have been reframed as a sign of personal growth, demonstrating areas for improvement and fostering a more constructive relationship with anxiety. However, such a leadership intervention did not occur, suggesting the leader's approach diverged from existential-humanistic principles of leadership.

This example underscores that our data can be analyzed within competing theoretical frameworks, which further bolsters the trustworthiness of our findings by allowing for multiple interpretations—a key criterion in qualitative research. The central role of dialogue—either in our cultural-psychological or in the existential-humanistic interpretation—bolsters the relevance of interpersonal coordination of meaning-making systems.

The Notion of Authenticity and Some Limitations

In addition to trustworthiness, we must also address the notion of *authenticity*, which we identified as a second key validity criterion for our qualitative inquiry into leadership. A potential critique of this research is that it may have been too narrowly focused from the outset. Critics might argue that we developed a theory and then sought either to confirm or disconfirm it through the empirical component of the study. This approach could be seen as overly restrictive, especially in comparison to other qualitative methods, such as grounded theory, where the data itself serves as the foundation for developing theoretical implications.

While we acknowledge this critique, we counter it with several key points. First, as Klenke (2008a, 2008b) notes, qualitative research in leadership encompasses a wide range of theoretical positions. There is no inherent issue in approaching a study with a pre-defined theory, nor in using a theory-free approach like grounded theory. Both approaches are valid within the broader spectrum of qualitative leadership research (Klenke, 2008c, 2008d).

It is important to emphasize, however, that we did not use our theory in a positivist sense—meaning we were not simply seeking to confirm or disprove our cultural-psychological theory of leadership. Instead, we remained open to revising and re-actualizing the theory based on the empirical findings (see Chap. 7). This openness is a key aspect of ontological authenticity in qualitative research, where theoretical frameworks evolve through interaction with the data.

For example, while our initial theoretical model proposed that a leader should help employees become aware of their underlying fantasms and assist them in monitoring the psychological and physical effects of failing to circumvent barriers, the empirical findings did not fully support these functions as central to the leader's role. These theoretical constructs, outlined in earlier chapters as an idealized vision of leadership, did not emerge as significant in the ethnographic and autoethnographic vignettes. Further analysis suggested that psychotherapeutic theories might have impacted our original conceptualization of leadership, limiting its alignment with an ecological theory of leadership. As a result, we revised our initial model, eliminating certain leadership functions that were not substantiated by the data.

This process of theory revision, prompted by empirical findings, illustrates a crucial aspect of ontological authenticity. Our study did not rigidly adhere to a predefined theory but rather evolved in response to the lived experiences of leaders and followers captured in the ethnographic and autoethnographic data. One significant revision concerns the co-construction of circumvention strategies between leader and follower. The empirical findings revealed that, rather than the leader alone facilitating circumvention, the barrier itself could be transformed in collaboration with the follower. This transformation alters the nature of the barrier, making it permeable to the follower's skills and abilities. This insight extends the genetic potential of our study, advancing the theoretical model that we initially proposed.

In summary, the empirical findings allowed us to refine our cultural-psychological theory of leadership, highlighting mechanisms that were either absent from or added to the original theoretical model. This iterative process underscores the importance of authenticity in qualitative research, ensuring that theoretical models remain dynamic and responsive to real-world data.

The Notion of Applied Implications

Critics may question the practical implications of our ethnographic and autoethnographic vignettes, wondering how the findings translate into concrete outcomes both theoretically and practically. Addressing this critique from an applied perspective, we argue that the empirical findings led directly to actionable recommendations. For example, based on the ethnographic findings, we developed a policy brief that articulated the divide between internal and external perspectives on leadership. This brief was written in accessible language, ensuring that both employees and management could engage with and act upon the insights it presented.

To validate the practical relevance of our findings, we interviewed a follower from the bakery setting, asking whether the recommended actions aligned with her experience and needs. The interview confirmed that the recommendations resonated with her, empowering her to co-construct leadership alongside management. The follower's sense of being heard and understood was itself a critical outcome, reinforcing her ability to challenge rigid leadership patterns. This process enabled her to actively negotiate leadership rather than passively accept managerial directives, highlighting the applied potential of our research.[1]

This empowerment—helping an individual actualize their position within an organizational setting—is a key practical implication. By enabling the follower to assert her needs and take action accordingly, our research demonstrates that it can stimulate both internal and external change. Through the dialogical negotiation of the policy brief, we also identified areas for revising our cultural-psychological theory of leadership, such as incorporating personality into the framework. In this way, the research not only generated practical outcomes but also informed theoretical refinements.

In terms of validity, this process aligns with the criteria of authenticity, specifically educative and strategic authenticity, as discussed in the methodology chapter. The findings from the autoethnographic study further support this criterion. For instance, the letter written to the future self of the study's author offered concrete actions for navigating future leadership conflicts. This letter emphasized the importance of recognizing and asserting one's own co-constructive role in leadership, encouraging the future self to actively shape leadership dynamics rather than passively accept management-imposed patterns.

This perspective challenges traditional leadership theories that often portray leadership and followership as static roles. Instead, our findings suggest that leadership is a dynamic process of action—specifically, the construction and co-construction of strategies to address challenges in one's action field. Leadership, as we define it, is not simply a role but emerges from actions taken to navigate specific barriers. This expanded definition of leadership exemplifies the ontological authenticity of our study, reflecting how our empirical findings have enriched the theoretical model.

In conclusion, not only have we demonstrated the practical implications of our research, but we have also fulfilled key qualitative validity criteria, such as trustworthiness and authenticity, ensuring that our findings hold relevance both in theory and in practice.

Beyond the European and American Context of Leadership

Some parts of this manuscript were reviewed by *the Global South Network in Cultural Psychology*, hosted by Pina Marsico. In recent years, this network has significantly advanced cultural psychology by focusing on field-theoretical and

[1] It comes not unsurprising that the follower decided two quit her job two months after the study took place as management did not listen to staff or incorporate their perspectives. In fact, the whole staff quit.

action-oriented approaches, leading to substantial publications in Cultural Psychology (Pérez & Marsico, 2021). The Brazilian researcher Livia Simao, for instance, has made notable contributions to Symbolic Action Theory, applying and expanding Cultural Psychology (Simão, 2001)—something that the theory's founding figure, E.E. Boesch, advocated, as his own theoretical and methodological developments were rooted in his experience in Thailand.

The reviewers have raised an important critique regarding the *Eurocentric* orientation of the manuscript, noting that it lacks a clear emphasis on how its theory and methodology might be adapted for local or indigenous research contexts and how it could support leadership practices in the *Global South*. This critique holds particular importance for Small Act Psychology, a field rooted in the work of Lewin, Boesch, and Vygotsky, and it warrants further exploration. While I do not claim expertise in *Global South Cultural Psychology*, there are some relevant considerations. Although Field Theory, Symbolic Action Theory, and Cultural-Historical Theory emerged from European and Russian scholarship, they have indeed been applied beyond European and American contexts. Examples include Luria's study in the Kazakh region (Luria, 1976), Lewin's Russian collaborators, such as Zeigarnik, and Boesch's development of Cultural Psychology based on his work in Thailand. Furthermore, Lewin's application of field theory to cultural studies—such as his comparisons of American and German life spaces—demonstrates an embedded cultural sensitivity derived from the historical background of these theories.

However, the cultural sensitivity inherent in Field Theory and Symbolic Action Theory goes beyond historical context. These models prioritize the experiential unit of the individual (von Fircks, 2022). Within each experiential unit, the objective environment is psychologically appropriated based on the constitution and emergence of personal needs (Lewin, 1982). Additionally, subjective appropriation is shaped by field-theoretical determinants—social, economic, and material factors—such as other people who impact one's life space and the resources one has or lacks. Field Theory does not assume that needs are identical across a group; rather, it emphasizes analyzing the unique life space of each individual and understanding how actions emerge from the interaction of personal and socio-material forces. This approach requires an in-depth exploration of the person as a qualitative whole within their cultural-historical situation, involving specific semiotic resources, such as signs and tools.

Thus, Field Theory also serves as an idiographic method, illustrating how a person's cultured life emerges and is impacted by various forces. Yet it goes beyond individual cases, encompassing the imperative of change by asking how actions can be transformed—a process that necessarily depends on the interaction between field forces and personal forces. While this manuscript applies and develops Small Act Psychology primarily within a European context, it is essential to recognize that Field Theory is centered on the experiential unit of each person, assessed by mapping the distinct field forces that shape the emergence and fulfillment of needs. These factors inevitably vary across contexts—whether among different European settings or in Latin American contexts, for example.

The critique suggests that to broaden the scope of this work, we must apply the theoretical and methodological framework to other cultural contexts to assess whether adjustments to the theory and methodology are required. This approach aligns with the goal of expanding Field Theory through diverse perspectives, addressing the fact that Field Theory, despite its inherent cultural sensitivity, has primarily been applied in North American contexts (notably in Iowa). By expanding Field Theory's application, we can fully explore its cultural-sensitive utility and further refine its adaptability.

Power Relations: A Necessary Addition?

An additional consideration worth addressing is the role of power relations. Reviewers have questioned how this issue integrates with the field-theoretical framework elaborated in the manuscript. From a field-theoretical perspective, power relations can be understood as follows: A leader who holds a certain degree of power can channel the actions of a follower by introducing specific barriers and resistances along the follower's path toward goal fulfillment. By inserting a barrier into the follower's life-space, the leader can increase the complexity of the field-theoretical situation, thereby directing the follower to take specific paths to attain their goals. Through such mechanisms, the leader can enforce the internalization of specific circumvention strategies by narrowing the range of field-theoretical options available for achieving a goal.

In field-theoretical terms, power may be defined as the capacity to either facilitate or complicate a follower's goal attainment by removing or introducing particular barriers, including second-order barriers, as discussed in the manuscript's empirical chapters. This conceptualization offers a critical advancement in the present work, lending cross-validity as it enables the appropriation and definition of related concepts within this framework. However, power is not solely vested in the leader, as demonstrated in the empirical work. The follower may resist the internalization of a given circumvention strategy or the leader's imposed path to goal attainment. That is, the follower retains the ability to resist, exit the field, or renegotiate the circumvention strategy with the leader.

Since a defining characteristic of leadership is the delegation of tasks (Janet, 1929, 1930), a leader must rely on followers to execute specific actions. Without this, the leadership situation loses coherence, compelling the leader to seek new followers who must be trained. The follower's psychological engagement—through negotiating a circumvention strategy—thus becomes essential for fostering the commitment necessary to advance the enterprise's broader objectives. If a follower can effectively demonstrate to the leader that the co-construction of circumvention strategies, as well as related signs and tools, aligns with these wider goals, they signal the need for cooperation. For this co-construction to be feasible, the follower must possess the skills and abilities to advocate for the negotiation of circumvention strategies.

In contrast, the leader does not necessarily need to justify their circumvention strategy, as they can simply introduce it into the work environment to observe its outcomes. The follower's power to influence, however, emerges through more complex mechanisms. To increase the likelihood of successful co-construction, the follower must, for example, demonstrate that allowing such a collaborative approach may prevent further barriers that could impede timely goal achievement. Therefore, while the follower's power is often implicit, it can become explicit through dialogue with the leader.

These considerations imply further practical applications. A need arises for *meta-leadership* in which followers are trained in effectively negotiating and renegotiating circumvention strategies. By fostering followers' skills and abilities in this area, power distribution within the field-theoretical framework could become more balanced.

The Issue of Generalizability

One of the most pressing critiques that must be addressed is the issue of generalizability. In the introductory chapters, we argued that our cultural-psychological theory of leadership is inherently context-sensitive, and we continue to uphold that view. However, based on the empirical findings of this study, we aim to expand our understanding of generalizability. We have established that the empirical findings, as discussed earlier, are situational and bound by context. This has allowed us to reflect on the practical implications of the study and develop targeted recommendations through mechanisms such as the policy brief, which specifically addresses the particular needs of the organization and its members.

Nevertheless, I contend that our theory and methodology hold relevance beyond the specific empirical cases we examined. This is supported by the fact that we successfully applied our cultural-psychological theory and methodology to both autoethnographic and ethnographic vignettes, validating and refining the theory through two distinct but inter-related studies. This demonstrates that the theoretical framework can be flexibly applied to different methodological approaches, suggesting a broader utility.

However, caution must be exercised in interpreting this validation. We are not referring to the controversial concept of replication, which is often viewed as a positivist illusion (von Fircks, 2024). Instead, we focus on how a scientific framework can be adapted to understand, analyze, interpret, and intervene in different empirical contexts. Importantly, our studies did not demonstrate a simple convergence of findings. For example, we did not observe the same sign systems being used across both the autoethnographic and ethnographic vignettes. Instead, what emerged was the identification of a field-theoretical situation—a type of situation that applies across contexts (Lewin, 1982), requiring individuals to respond similarly, whether in work or other life situations.

What we have contributed, beyond the existing literature on field theory (Lewin et al., 1939), is the insight into the co-construction of circumvention strategies between leader and follower. A key finding is that these jointly negotiated strategies can transform barriers, making them more permeable and enabling the follower to move toward their goal. This genetic perspective highlights how leadership emerges through the dynamic interaction between leader and follower. Using a longitudinal approach, we explored both successful and failed according to the Critical Incident Technique. This approach allowed us to demonstrate the benefits of jointly co-constructed semiotic resources, such as sign systems, and to analyze the consequences when such co-construction does not occur, leading to outcomes like the hyper-generalization of an external leadership perspective that disregards the followers' experiences.

These findings suggest the presence of potential universals in leader-follower interactions, though they are mediated by specific ecological and personal factors. Table 9.1 summarizes these potential universals, which, rather than contradicting

Table 9.1 Potential universals framing leader-follower interactions beyond the present empirical findings

	Leader-follower interactions	Implications
Potential Universals within a cultural-psychological theory of leadership	Leadership is more than a role. Leadership comes into being by taking specific actions such as the initiation of tackling a barrier with a suggested circumvention strategy.	Researchers and practitioners need to focus on actions and interactions between leaders and followers.
	Leadership needs to acknowledge the power of construction and co-construction (negotiation and co-negotiation) of sign systems that work as circumvention strategies.	Researchers and practitioners need to study leader-follower interactions as they unfold—genetic imperative of leadership studies.
	Leadership needs to take into account how barriers are transformed by given circumvention strategies and study their permeability over a sequence of time.	Researchers and practitioners are appealed to study how the qualities (e.g. barriers) that are part and parcel of the life-spaces become altered by the respective persons.
	The motivation to face a barrier and to circumvent it becomes refracted through fantasms (personal needs) and denotes an important psychological force of a given leader or follower. Denying the co-construction of leadership, denies equally the experiential unit of a given person and its underlying motivation to possibly circumvent the barrier.	Researchers and practitioners need to study the inter-relatedness between experience, motivation, construction of leadership, hindrances, and issues.

the context-sensitivity of our cultural-psychological theory, exist in a productive tension with it. To illustrate this, consider two examples from the table. First, while the specific suggestion and negotiation of sign systems vary according to personal and situational determinants, the importance of semiotic resources in circumventing barriers appears to be universal across the vignettes. Second, while personal motivation plays a critical role in overcoming barriers, the substance and degree of that motivation differ from person to person. For example, one individual might seek to bypass the barrier quickly to avoid tension, while another might prefer a more measured approach to ensure accuracy.

These examples illustrate that personal motivation acts as a catalyst for action within the leader-follower dynamic, but the way individuals interpret and respond to barriers and goals varies widely. Future research that applies the cultural-psychological lens to leadership should investigate these potential universals in greater depth, examining leader-follower interactions across a broader range of professional contexts.

References

Butz, D., & Besio, K. (2009). Autoethnography. *Geography Compass, 3*(5), 1660–1674.

Ellis, C., Adams, T. E., & Bochner, A. P. (2010). Autoethnografie. *Handbuch qualitative forschung in der psychologie*, 345–357.

Janet, P. (1929). *L'évolution psychologique de la personnalité* (Tome 1). Cahine.

Janet, P. (1930). *L'évolution psychologique de la personnalité* (Tome 2). Cahine.

Klenke, K. (2008a). Case studies in leadership research. In K. Klenke (Ed.), *Qualitative research in the study of leadership* (pp. 57–84). Emerald.

Klenke, K. (2008b). Grounded theory, ethnography and historiometry. In K. Klenke (Ed.), *Qualitative research in the study of leadership* (pp. 185–213). Emerald.

Klenke, K. (2008c). Qualitative research as paradigm. In K. Klenke (Ed.), *Qualitative research in the study of leadership* (pp. 3–29). Emerald.

Klenke, K. (2008d). Qualitative research as a method. In K. Klenke (Ed.), *Qualitative research in the study of leadership* (pp. 31–55). Emerald.

Lewin, K. (1982). Formalisierung und Forschritt in der Psychologie. In C. F. Graumann (Ed.), *Kurt Lewin Werkausgabe: Feldtheorie* (Vol. 4, pp. 41–73). Klett-Cotta.

Lewin, K., Lippitt, R., & White, R. K. (1939). Patterns of aggressive behavior in experimentally created "social climates". *The Journal of Social Psychology, 10*(2), 269–299. https://doi.org/10.1080/00224545.1939.9713366

Luria, A. R. (1976). *Cognitive development: Its cultural and social foundations*. Harvard University Press.

Méndez, M. (2013). Autoethnography as a research method: Advantages, limitations and criticisms. *Colombian Applied Linguistics Journal, 15*(2), 279–287.

Ohnuki-Tierney, E. (1994). The power of absence: Zero signifiers and their transgressions. *L'Homme*, 59–76.

Pérez, C., & Marsico, G. (2021). Return to the ancestral land: The semiotic map of the Mapuche people. *Culture & Psychology, 27*(2), 258–269. https://doi.org/10.1177/1354067X20984359

Schneider, K. J., & Krug, O. T. (2010). *Existential-humanistic therapy* (pp. x–164). American Psychological Association.

Simão, L. M. (2001). Boesch's symbolic action theory in interaction. *Culture & Psychology, 7*(4), 485–493. https://doi.org/10.1177/1354067X0174006

Stern, W. (1911). *Die differentielle Psychologie in ihren methodischen Grundlagen*. J.A. Barth.
Tolich, M. (2010). A critique of current practice: Ten foundational guidelines for autoethnographers. *Qualitative Health Research, 20*(12), 1599–1610.
von Fircks, E. F. (2020). Existential humanistic leadership (EHL) as a dialogical process: Equality of the non-equality in organizations. *Integrative Psychological and Behavioral Science, 54*(4), 719–741.
von Fircks, E. (2022). Setting the seeds for a normative expansion of Lewinian field theory for cultural-psychological practitioners. *Human Arenas*, 1–21. https://doi.org/10.1007/s42087-022-00307-5
von Fircks, E. (2024). Advocating a valid cultural Alltagspsychologie. *Trends in Psychology, 32*(1), 231–250.

Chapter 10
Toward an Actualized Cultural-Psychological Theory of Leadership

Cultural Psychology of Leadership Dynamics (CPLD)

We began this manuscript with the goal of developing a cultural-psychological theory for the qualitative scientific inquiry of leadership, aiming to propose a middle-range theory that provides a dynamic and developmental (genetic) perspective for understanding leader-follower interactions. To achieve this, we synthesized the theories of Lewin, Boesch, and Vygotsky, resulting in a general model of leadership from a cultural-psychological standpoint. Utilizing a qualitative empirical protocol, we established a flexible methodology that investigated leadership through autoethnographic and ethnographic vignettes. Specifically, we examined how leadership emerged within each vignette and whether longitudinal trends could be observed over the course of the analysis.

Our methodology was designed to examine the ethnographic and autoethnographic vignettes both from a within-case and cross-case perspective, focusing on differences in how leadership was applied and evolved over time. In adherence to the methodological imperative of separating description from analysis, we explored how conflicts and challenges manifest as barriers in an individual's life-space, and how these barriers can be circumvented through the co-negotiation of sign systems.

Two major findings emerged in the results section of this study. First, we identified an ideal pattern within the positive critical incidents sampled in the autoethnographic and ethnographic vignettes. In these cases, the construction and co-construction of sign systems between leader and follower were central to neutralizing barriers and altering their permeability. This co-construction process allowed both the leader and the follower to address their underlying needs, which motivated them to co-create the sign system. Through this negotiation, both parties imprinted their pressing needs and life-spaces onto the circumvention strategy,

E. Freiherr von Fircks, *Studying Leadership from a Microgenetic Perspective*, Methodologies in Developmental Sciences,
https://doi.org/10.1007/978-3-031-90214-7_10

enabling shifts in the environment and within themselves that aligned with their goals.

Second, this ideal pattern only emerged after the follower had gained some job-related experience. In the early stages of the autoethnographic vignettes, the follower sought less co-construction and relied more on the leader's suggestions. However, as the followers developed within the leader-follower relationship and accumulated more job-related experience, they demanded a more active role in co-constructing the sign system. The negative critical incidents in the study revolved around scenarios where the follower had already developed a strong, autonomous perspective based on their prior job experience, yet their potential for action was not acknowledged by the leader. When the follower's perspective was disregarded, collaboration broke down, and followers often felt patronized. This resulted in a hyper-generalization of negative leadership experiences, which in turn impacted their expectations of future interactions.

Consequently, we argue for a dynamic redefinition of leadership within our cultural-psychological theory, viewing leadership not as a static role but as a set of specific actions that involve the suggestion, construction, and potential co-construction of sign- and tool systems. Our findings illustrate that leadership and followership roles are fluid, alternating based on who takes action at a particular point in time.

In satisfying the alternative validity criteria outlined in qualitative leadership research, we followed Klenke's recommendation to include and reflect upon these criteria rigorously, as this remains rare in the general domain of qualitative leadership studies.

In this section, we discussed the concept of *trustworthiness*, adhering to the principle of separating description, analysis, and interpretation in our ethnographic and autoethnographic vignettes. We also explored an alternative analytical and interpretive approach to leader-follower interactions—an existential-humanistic exegesis, as applied in the discussion chapter of this manuscript. In line with the notion of trustworthiness, we also examined how to ensure that we adhered to the principle of *authenticity*. We clarified our theoretical notion of cultural-psychological leadership based on the empirical findings of the study, leading to the rejection of specific leadership actions that were not observed in any of the vignettes (e.g., helping the follower become aware of underlying fantasms). Importantly, we complemented the clarification of ontological authenticity with the concepts of *educative* and *strategic* authenticity.

To demonstrate this, we wrote a policy brief based on the ethnographic study, inviting the key participant to reflect on how the policy brief might impact her future actions. Similarly, for the autoethnographic study, we developed an exercise (a letter to the future self), allowing the participant to consult the findings when desired, especially in times of conflict. This was essential to contextualize the results and make them applicable for anticipating future situations, whether for the autoethnographic participant or for individuals in similar circumstances.

This analysis naturally led us into the discussion of one of the most significant issues in the present study—*generalizability*. Rather than claiming to have found a universal circumvention strategy applicable to all ethnographic and autoethnographic cases, we argued against this possibility, as our aim was to develop a context-sensitive approach to leadership. What we found instead was an interesting pattern—not a repetition of a single circumvention strategy, but the importance of constructing, negotiating, and sometimes failing to negotiate circumvention strategies in response to pressing underlying needs. We illustrated how a barrier can be transformed through cooperative activity, making it more manageable for the follower. In this way, the barrier becomes personally digestible, facilitating its neutralization.

Here, we may have tapped into a fundamental cleavage in scientific inquiry: the tension between *universals* and *particulars*. The universal element we identified is the necessity of negotiating circumvention strategies, while the particulars are the personal and situational needs at play within the life-space of the leader and/or follower. We cautiously suggested that there may be potential universals emerging from this study, while explicitly refraining from presenting them as definitive solutions to leadership research.

Finally, we developed within this manuscript a promising new applied field within Cultural Psychology, which is still rare in the discipline's history: *Cultural Psychology of Leadership Dynamics* (CPLD). This study represents a first, modest attempt at laying the systematic foundations for this emerging field—a field that, given the findings and theoretical developments, seems timely and necessary for further exploration.

Appendices

Appendix A: Interview Transcript Policy Brief

Was denkst du über diesen Policy Brief?

Wie fühlt er sich für dich an?

Mir gefällt der policy Brief gut und er trifft die Problematik, welche wir am Arbeitsplatz erleben sehr genau. Vor allem die key findings treffen aus meiner Sicht den Nagel auf den Kopf. Mir gefällt es, dass eine „alltägliche Situation" psychologisch beleuchtet wird, denn ich denke viele Menschen, sind sich den Dynamiken (und dem Potential die Dynamiken auf simple Weise zu verbessern) gar nicht bewusst.

Fühlst du dich verstanden?

Ich fühle mich sehr verstanden. Und ich wünschte, dass Management würde sich so viel Mühe geben, das gemeinsame Arbeitsverhältnis so zu beleuchten und zu reflektieren.

Trifft er den Kern eurer Probleme am Arbeitsplatz? Wenn ja, welcher? Wenn nein, welche Punkte wurden im Policy Brief nicht berücksichtigt?

Die Probleme wurden sehr gut erfasst. Ich finde, darüber hinaus ist es wichtig zu verstehen und zu erwähnen, dass es im Endeffekt Mitarbeitern darum geht sich kompetent, selbstwirksam und wertgeschätzt zu fühlen. Jeder Arbeitnehmer hat Bedürfnisse, die er hofft auch innerhalb des Arbeitskontextes befriedigen zu können. Vielleicht könnte dieser Punkt noch mit einfließen.

Wie denkst du, dass management darauf reagieren würde?

Ehrlich gesagt, wäre ich total gespannt, was das Management darauf antworten würde. Die fehlende Kommunikation bringt mit sich, dass man oft das Gefühl hat, dass unterschiedliche Ziele nicht miteinander vereinbar wären. Im Endeffekt geht es doch beiden Partein (inside and out) darum, ein gutes Produkt an einen zufriedenen Kunden zu bringen. Das Team versteht selbstverständlich, dass die ökonomischen Aspekte dem Management am wichtigsten sind. Doch versteht das Management

E. Freiherr von Fircks, *Studying Leadership from a Microgenetic Perspective*, Methodologies in Developmental Sciences,
https://doi.org/10.1007/978-3-031-90214-7

auch die Ziele und Wünsche des Teams? Dem Team wird oft das Gefühl vermittelt weniger schlau zu sein und Menschen, die sich nicht wertgeschätzt fühlen, leisten auch keine gute Arbeit. Wäre es nicht demnach auch ein übergeordnetes Ziel, zufriedene Mitarbeiter zu haben? Denn zufriedene Mitarbeiter leisten zufriedenstellende Arbeit. Zufriedenstellende Arbeit bringt Profit. Ich habe oft das Gefühl, das Management realisiert nicht, wie WICHTIG nicht nur die Produkte und der Umsatz ist, sondern auch das Beziehungsverhältnis innerhalb des Arbeitskontextes.

Glaubst du, dass diese Art von Forschung hilfreich ist?

Ich glaube diese Art von Forschung ist essenziell. Gerade der Punkt, dass der Researcher sich in das Action field begibt, scheint mir ein Punkt zu sein, der in der Forschung bislang viel zu sehr vernachlässigt wird. Man muss am Ort des Geschehens sein, um das Geschehen zu verstehen. Und ich glaube, dass diese Art von Forschung einen großen Mehrwehrt haben kann, da es konkrete Probleme aufdeckt und Lösungen bietet. Lösungen, die für beide Parteien in diesem Fall sittlichen Mehrwehrt haben können. Auch glaube ich, dass das Management positiv auf so eine Art Forschung blicken würde, da es nicht um „Recht oder Unrecht haben" geht, sondern psychologisch die Dynamiken untersucht werden. Somit werden die Probleme im Unternehmen/der Führungsstil in einen psychologischen Kontext gestellt, wodurch Lösungsvorschläge möglicherweise auf mehr Akzeptanz stößt und die Wichtigkeit der Reflexion solcher Dynamiken sichtbarer werden.

Appendix B: Autoethnographic and Ethnographic Analysis Scheme

Problem/ Issue	Personal need (follower's needs)	Social needs (organizational needs)	Interactional patterns	Tool-/ Sign-systems	Solution	Feelings
–	–	–	–	–	–	–
–	–	–	–	–	–	–
–	–	–	–	–	–	–
–	–	–	–	–	–	–
–	–	–	–	–	–	–
–	–	–	–	–	–	–
–	–	–	–	–	–	–

Index

E. Freiherr von Fircks, *Studying Leadership from a Microgenetic Perspective*, Methodologies in Developmental Sciences,
https://doi.org/10.1007/978-3-031-90214-7

The manufacturer's authorised representative in the EU is Springer Nature Customer Service Centre GmbH, Europaplatz 3, 69115 Heidelberg, Germany. If you have any concerns regarding our products, please contact ProductSafety@springernature.com

Printed and bound by CPI Group (UK) Ltd, Croydon, CR0 4YY
01/10/2026
02225949-0006